In this concluding volume of his trilogy on social theory, W. G. Runciman applies to the case of twentieth-century English society the methodology (distinguishing reportage, explanation, description and evaluation) and theory of the preceding two volumes. Volume III shows how England's capitalist mode of production, liberal mode of persuasion, and democratic mode of coercion evolved in the aftermath of World War I from what they had been since the 1880s, but did not, in turn, evolve significantly further following World War II. The explanation rests on an analysis of the selective pressures favouring some economic, ideological and political practices over others in an increasingly complex environment which policy-makers could neither predict nor control. This explanation is supported by a graphic account of the changes themselves and of how they were experienced by the different segments of English society.

A treatise on social theory

VOLUME THREE

A treatise on social theory

VOLUME III: APPLIED SOCIAL THEORY

W. G. Runciman, FBA

FELLOW OF TRINITY COLLEGE, CAMBRIDGE

CAMBRIDGE
UNIVERSITY PRESS

PUBLISHED BY THE PRESS SYNDICATE OF THE UNIVERSITY OF CAMBRIDGE
The Pitt Building, Trumpington Street, Cambridge

CAMBRIDGE UNIVERSITY PRESS
The Edinburgh Building, Cambridge CB2 2RU, United Kingdom
40 West 20th Street, New York, NY 10011–4211, USA
10 Stamford Road, Oakleigh, Melbourne 3166, Australia

First published 1997

Printed in the United Kingdom at the University Press, Cambridge

Typeset in 10 on 13 point Ehrhardt by Computape (Pickering) Ltd, North Yorkshire

A catalogue record for this book is available from the British Library

ISBN 0 521 24960 0 hardback
ISBN 0 521 58801 4 paperback

CE

A treatise on social theory

VOLUME III

Applied social theory

Contents

Preface

This concluding volume of a trilogy on social theory is not a social history of twentieth-century England, let alone of Britain. Nor is it a sociology of it, if by that is meant a comprehensive account of its structure and culture. It is no more – but also no less – than an application to twentieth-century English society of the substantive social theory advanced in volume II in accordance with the methodology advanced in volume I. It does not, therefore, narrate even in outline the salient events of the period; it does not offer an assessment of the country's economic performance or diagnosis of its relative decline; it does not trace the careers of individual politicians, intellectuals, entrepreneurs, trade-union leaders, grass-roots activists, or anyone else; it has nothing to say about the progress of science or literature or art; and it barely mentions the technological discoveries by which the daily lives of English people have been transformed over the period which it covers. Its concerns are first, to report in outline the modes of production, persuasion, and coercion of English society over the years in question; second, to explain why they have evolved (or not) as they have in response to the selective pressures which have acted on the practices defining their constituent roles; third, to describe what the resultant changes (or the lack of them) were, broadly speaking, like for representative role-incumbents in different systacts[1] and milieux who experienced them; and finally, to assess their impact in terms of the benefit (or otherwise) which they have brought to the persons affected by them by standards generally recognized by those persons themselves and the policy-makers seeking to benefit them.

By now, however, I am inevitably conscious of what I would rewrite if I could in volumes I and II. Although I have no doubts about the value of the

---

[1] This – the one neologism in the whole treatise – is the term introduced in volume II to stand for clusters of roles similarly located in a three-dimensional social space whose axes correspond to the three forms of power: the economic (hence, mode of production), the ideological (hence, mode of persuasion), and the political (hence, mode of coercion). The need for it arises because no existing sociological term, least of all 'class', is at the same time specific in assigning the designated roles an ordinal ranking relative to other such clusters and neutral between the dimensions in which they are ranked.

fourfold distinction between reportage, explanation, description, and evaluation expounded in volume I, I recognize that it is by no means as exhaustive as I may have made it appear. Sociologists can and do have many things to say whose illocutionary force cannot be neatly accommodated within it, if at all. They may be refining statistical methods, categorizing social relationships, ruminating about the human condition, championing the oppressed, rewriting the history of sociology, undermining the reputations of rival sociologists, prophesying the future of the world, or even, to quote from the deconstruction by Clifford Geertz (1988, p. 48) of Lévi-Strauss's *Tristes Tropiques*, 'neither picturing lives nor evoking them, neither interpreting them nor explaining them, but rather arranging and rearranging the material the lives have somehow left behind into formal systems of correspondences'. Nor is it as if this volume has been, or could possibly be, so written that chapter 2 consists entirely of accurately reported sociological facts, chapter 3 entirely of validated explanatory hypotheses, chapter 4 entirely of authenticated descriptions of what 'their' lives have been like for 'them', and chapter 5 entirely of coherent evaluations of England's modes of production, persuasion, and coercion in accordance with 'their' standards. But I now feel more strongly, if anything, than I did that sociologists (and, for that matter, anthropologists and historians) need to do all that they can, and therefore more than they usually do, to make clear to their readers just what kinds of questions about human behaviour they see themselves as answering and just what kinds of conclusions they are therefore trying to persuade their readers to share. Readers of this volume who have not read volume I will, I hope, be able nevertheless to grasp how important to my argument is the difference between reporting what has happened in twentieth-century England, explaining why it has happened, and describing what it has been like for the different groups or categories of English people to whom it has happened – and thus how wide the discrepancy can be between understanding the subjective experience of belonging to a society in a particular role and understanding how that society functions and why it has evolved as it has.

At the same time, I am aware that since volume I was written the notion that there are such things as sociological facts whose explanation can be intersubjectively established has, as it periodically does, become the target of a fresh wave of sceptical and relativist attacks. But 'post-modernism', ironically and therefore appropriately, exemplifies one of the central themes of volume I. If objectivity is unattainable, the doctrines of 'post-modernism' can carry no more conviction than those which it claims to subvert. It does not follow that literary and philosophical reflection about the human condition is without meaning or purpose of its own: 'To acknowledge the genius of Darwin is not to devalue the genius of Nietzsche, or vice versa' (Runciman 1993, p. 22). But it does follow that 'post-modernist' discourse is incommensurable with, and therefore irrelevant to, the discourse in which this volume is written – a discourse in which claims of fact are to be rejected not because they are meaningless but because they are demonstrably false, hypotheses of cause and effect to be rejected not because they are arbitrary but because they cannot stand up to invalidation in the face of the evidence, and descriptions of other people's experience to be rejected not because they are ineluctably self-referential but because they fail the test of authenticity in the terms of those whose experience they purport to convey.

The inadequacies of volume II, as I now see them, are of a very different kind. The one of which I was first made aware is the weakness of its proffered typology of human societies, which is too rudimentary for even the limited function which I claimed for it (Wickham 1991). But if, on the other hand, there is a weakness in its exposition of the theory of social selection, it does not lie in any fatal flaw which has since been pointed out to me in the basic propositions of the theory. I could, as I now realize, have set out more systematically the implications of the idea that social evolution is analogous but not reducible to natural selection, and I could have done more to anticipate the responses of fellow-sociologists still disposed to dismiss it out of hand without any attempt to test those implications against the evidence of the historical and ethnographic record. But I also failed to take proper account of the contributions of other disciplines to our understanding of the evolution of social behaviour patterns in human societies. As seems so often to happen in the history of ideas, I was unaware while writing volume II how many other people were, in different ways, seeking also to work out the implications for the study of human social behaviour of Darwin's insight that evolution comes about, and can only come about, through a process of what he called 'descent with modification'. Now, we have an increasingly clear understanding of what natural selection can and cannot explain directly about human behaviour, and of the analogous process by which cultural differences are transmitted between adjacent or successive human populations.[2] We also know much more than we

---

[2] There is as yet no agreed term for the objects of cultural selection as there is for the genes which natural selection selects and the practices which social selection selects. But the distinction between the three is unambiguous. Genes are transmitted through biological inheritance from one organism to another. Cultural 'traits' or 'memes' (if that is the word which catches on for units or bundles of information affecting phenotype) are transmitted through imitation or learning from the mind (or brain) of one person to that of another. Practices, which are units of *reciprocal* action, are transmitted through relations of domination or cooperation from one to another pair or larger group of roles. See further my 'Introduction' to the proceedings of the Royal Society/British Academy joint discussion meeting held in 1995 on the evolution of social behaviour patterns in primates and man (Runciman 1996b); and for a sense of how far the conventional wisdoms of the 'Standard Social Science Model' have been undermined by recent

did about the ecological and demographic influences which caused the emergence of the distinguishing features of human societies as such. And we can say not only that the evolution of human societies from one distinctive kind to another is a 'Darwinian' process in a sense equally different from what 'Historical Materialists' on the one hand and 'Social Darwinists' on the other have taken it to be, but also that we are no longer, thanks to recent advances in evolutionary and cognitive psychology and the study of artificial intelligence, quite as far as we were from the 'much more nearly adequate understanding of human psychology' whose lack I lamented in the penultimate paragraph of volume II. Sociology is still a long way from achievements comparable to those which in biology have taken Darwin's fundamental contribution forward to a comprehensive theory accounting for both the sources of diversity and the constraints on it which determine the evolution of species. But the ambition does not look quite as unrealistic now as it did when I started writing volume II.

In this volume, I have made no attempt to go back over the ground which was covered in volumes I and II. Their deficiencies, however much I should like to put them right, do not, in my view, significantly weaken the conclusions of this third and final volume about the modes of production, persuasion, and coercion of twentieth-century England. Where those conclusions need to be modified, as no doubt they do, it will be because I have neglected or mishandled some of the relevant evidence, as no doubt I have. The amount of relevant evidence is in any case far more than a single researcher could hope to master, and the secondary literature is growing all the time. As in volume II, I have supplied references where it seems to me that readers are likely to want to ask one or more of the questions 'who did you get that from?', 'what makes you so sure?', and 'where can I go for a little more detail than you have chosen to give?'. But I have not thought it necessary to cite every source which I have consulted, and the list of references covers only a selection of the secondary works on which I have drawn. No more than in volume II could I trace, even if I wanted to, the serendipitous route which has led me to one rather than another part of what a comprehensive bibliography would contain.

I have also, not without hesitation, drawn at some points on my own experience as a participant-observer in what is, after all, my own society. I am well aware of the risks in so doing. But a government census, an anthropological monograph, a sample survey, a contemporary diary, or an independently commissioned research report are not intrinsically more reliable[3] than a

---

research, see Tooby and Cosmides (1992). Readers unfamiliar with the notion of *cultural* selection are recommended to start with Boyd and Richerson (1985).

[3] Readers of volume I may recall that according to the 1951 census there were in the United Kingdom in that year 2 clergymen, 4 solicitors, 4 doctors, 1 accountant, 10 opticians, 23 chiropodists, and 34 qualified accountants all under sixteen years of age (Marsh 1958, p. 163 n.1).

recollection of events, processes, or states of affairs witnessed at first hand. Although, as I said in the preface to volume I, it is for my readers and not for me to judge whether I am a better sociologist because I am also a practising capitalist, it remains the case that as a practising capitalist I have both observed and taken part in aspects of the functioning of twentieth-century English society about which I could not have found out as much as I have in any other way. As I have remarked elsewhere (Runciman 1989, p. 14), talking to some of my fellow-sociologists about the workings of capitalism makes me feel as if I were a Trobriand Islander who had wandered into a seminar of Malinowski's. Conversely, talking to some of my fellow-capitalists makes me feel as if I were a mole from an alien culture not yet detected by MI5. But either way, the methodological point is the same one. Where I have mishandled evidence derived from my own participant observation, I deserve to be criticized by criteria no different from where I have mishandled evidence derived from the observations of someone else. This holds equally where, or if, my own moral or political values might be thought to be involved. For reasons set out in full in volume I, this point ought not to need to be argued here at all. Just because many sociologists, whether deliberately or not, allow their explanatory or descriptive conclusions to be influenced by their moral or political attitudes, it doesn't follow either that they couldn't do otherwise or that other sociologists need do so too; and in any case, any claim to have detected a bias of this kind entails a claim that it can be discounted accordingly. It is true that a book such as this one is inescapably personal. No other sociologist who had undertaken the same task would carry it out in the same way, least of all in chapter 4 where it is fundamental, as I argued in volume I, to the distinction between explanation and description that descriptions remain discretionary even after all the evidence is in. But although it does so happen that the picture of English society which the evidence dictates is not what would exemplify my personal ideals, no sentence in this volume would need to be differently written if it were otherwise.

The publication of this volume, which was already behind my original timetable, has been further delayed by my appointment as Chairman of the Royal Commission on Criminal Justice in England and Wales which sat between 1991 and 1993. This further delay has, however, had two advantages. It has significantly increased my knowledge of the workings of a set of institutions central to the mode of coercion of English society; and it has enabled me to draw on recent publications which lend support to my account of the period which this volume covers. For reasons which I touch on at the conclusion of chapter 2, I suspect that 1990 may turn out, like 1880, to be a year which will be used by future historians and sociologists to mark the end, or at least the beginning of the end, of one sub-type of capitalist liberal democracy and thus the beginning of English society's evolution into another. But whether or not this turns out to be so, it has at any rate been helpful to see the years of so-called 'Thatcherism' in retrospect and to be reinforced in the conviction that, as I thought at the time, the systemic (as opposed to merely attitudinal) changes attributed to it by both its enemies and its friends were much exaggerated, just as were the changes attributed by both its enemies and its friends to the Attlee government of 1945–51.

My particular thanks are due to David Lockwood, Ross McKibbin, and Pat Thane, who read the whole of this volume in draft and whose comments and suggestions have been of very great value. Where I have failed to follow their advice (and I sometimes have), the responsibility is entirely mine. I should have liked also to be able to thank by name the many friends and colleagues with whom I have discussed the topics covered by this volume during the years of its composition. But I have not kept any systematic record, and I can only hope that if they read the volume they may here and there recognize traces of their influence. My thanks are due also to Hilary Edwards for long and patient application to it of her word-processing skills. As throughout the whole project since I first conceived it thirty years ago, it would be impossible to exaggerate the debt which I owe to my wife for her support. And I must once again repeat my thanks to the Council of my College for successive renewals of the Senior Research Fellowship without which the project could not have been realized.

Trinity College, Cambridge   W. G. R.
May, 1996

CHAPTER ONE

Introduction: the case of twentieth-century England

THE UNIQUENESS OF THE CASE

§1. In the theory of social selection, no one society is privileged for study any more than any one species in the theory of natural selection. All societies have their distinctive modes and sub-types of production, persuasion, and coercion. When they evolve (as they all do, sooner or later) out of one into another, it is because the practices defining the earlier one have been displaced by mutant practices which confer greater competitive advantage on the roles which carry them in their changed ecological, demographic, and institutional environment. But later societies are not on that account more deserving of attention than earlier, or Western than Eastern, or the stronger than the weaker, or the more technologically advanced than the less – or vice versa. The evolution of societies, like the evolution of species, is a story with a beginning but not an end: it points no moral, vindicates no religious or political doctrine, and entitles no one group or category of human beings to regard themselves as the norm to which others are the backward or deviant exceptions.

Yet England does have a special place in the annals of social evolution, partly because it is the society where the technical innovations and concomitant mutations of practices amounting to the 'Industrial Revolution' occurred and partly because the changes of structure and culture which followed it were, to many people's surprise both then and since, as limited as they were. There was no comprehensive transformation of the mode of production, no categorical repudiation of the mode of persuasion, no revolutionary subversion of the mode of coercion. To be sure, the lives of countless men and women were radically altered by it, often (earlier on) for what they felt to be the worse and often (later on) for what they felt to be the better. Mutant economic, ideological, and political practices were replicated and diffused while existing ones declined or disappeared; the nature of work and its relation to patterns of residence and kinship were transformed; urban life ceased to be the exception and became overwhelmingly the rule; regional differences in manners and mores began to be merged within a national culture; and the technological changes which industrialization made possible steadily improved both public amenities and the furnishings of the home. But to the sociologist concerned to explain, describe, and evaluate changes (or their absence) in England's modes of production, persuasion, and coercion, the continuities are at least as striking as the differences.

There was nothing inevitable about these continuities. As always in social evolution, there are hypothetical might-have-beens by which the central institutions of English society could have been changed out of recognition, whether from without or within. But they weren't. In 1800, the mode of production had rested on a commercialized network of bankers, merchants, shopkeepers, artisans, and small manufacturers with agriculture largely depen-dent on capitalist tenant farming; the mode of persuasion had rested on a hierarchy of inherited status and patronage symbolically legitimated by a quasi-hereditary monarchy and a Church which was both formally and informally allied to the institutions of government; and the mode of coercion had rested on an oligarchy answerable to a small and venal electorate, staffed by a minimal bureaucracy, and reliant on a scattered local gentry commanding a half-trained militia. By 1900, the franchise had been progressively widened and the first representatives of the working-class interest had been elected to Parliament; the hierarchy of place and patronage had begun to give way to an ideology of professionalism, formally equal opportunity, and at least notionally vocational education; and the economy had in many sectors and regions (although by no means all) become a factory-based industrial system[1] in which the owners of the means of production hired for wages the labour of a proletariat in the modern sense of that term. Both during the course of this evolution, as later, there were many observers and participants who predicted, and in some cases actively worked for, either an authoritarian or a socialist alternative. But the practices defining the roles constitutive of English society remained obstinately capitalist, liberal, and democratic, both before and after the transition from a sub-type of capitalist liberal democracy which lasted from about 1880 to the First World War to the sub-type which evolved thereafter. When or how this transition might have come about without the First World War we have no way of knowing; what we do know, and what therefore dictates the agenda of this volume, is that between 1915 and 1922 it did. What is more, it came about despite the frequent assertions of commentators on both Left and Right that

---

[1] 'Factory-based' is not to be taken literally. Mines, docks, and shipyards exemplified equally well the new mode of production and concomitant pattern of social relations (Benson 1989, p. 40). Cf. F. M. L. Thompson (1988, p. 31): 'Industrialization, even considered in the restrictive and potentially misleading sense as something that happened simply to manufacturing industry rather than to all sectors of the economy, was far from being a one-way procession into the factory.'

nothing significant had changed – to the Left, because capitalism was (alas!) still visibly unreformed, and to the Right, because 'normalcy', as it came to be called, had (thank goodness!) been restored.

Within this mode, English society's differences from other capitalist liberal democracies became, as the century progressed, more marked, not less. Far from being the paradigm for those societies which followed it down the evolutionary road to 'modernization', British institutions came to look increasingly distinctive and even anomalous when contrasted with those of France or Germany or the United States or Sweden or Australia or Switzerland or Japan. To Marx and Engels it had seemed that the dialectic of social change unfolding itself in England before their eyes must be repeated in due course elsewhere: as Marx had said to his German readers in his preface to volume I of *Capital*, *'de te fabula narratur'*. But this was mistaken twice over. Not only were the circumstances of England's transition to industrialism unique, but it widened rather than constrained the range of evolutionary alternatives open to societies which industrialized after it. What is more, the selective pressures which had transformed England's mode of production in the first place continued to influence its structure and culture long after the process of industrialization was complete. As I pointed out in the various references to England in volume II, the peculiarity of its institutions can be traced all the way back through the commercialization of the economy, the defeat of monarchical absolutism, and the formation of a homogeneous but open aristocracy to before the Norman Conquest, when an increasingly active land market, relatively high rates of social mobility, and control of the means of coercion by local magnates loyal to a patrimonial monarchy foreshadowed much of what was later to evolve in more or less permanent form. The particular mutations of economic, ideological, and political practices which were necessary to bring all this about can, for the purposes of the present volume, be taken as given. But once England had escaped invasion or defeat in any but a colonial war, and the might-have-beens of internal subversion or anarchy had failed to eventuate, this state of affairs itself imposed lasting constraints on its subsequent evolution from one to another mode of production, persuasion, and coercion alike.

Admittedly, the force of these constraints can be overstated. But observers of all persuasions have commented time and again on the conservatism of England's central institutions; and as soon as explanation of the actual course of the society's evolution shades over into description of what it was like for those who experienced it, myths of continuity have to be treated as if they were true. The 'Englishness' invoked by English people in explanation and description (and, very often, evaluation) of their own roles and institutions may not deserve to be taken too seriously by sociologists who well know how little substance there is to self-created images of national character and how much of what passes for English tradition is of altogether more recent invention than most English people suppose (Hobsbawm and Ranger, 1983; Porter, 1992). But they cannot ignore the fact that English people hold the views about their own society which they do; and they must acknowledge that these views are not only fundamental to the description of what it is like to be one of 'them' but may also explain a part, even if not the most important part, of their reciprocal behaviour as incumbents of the different roles and thereby members of the different systacts of which English society is composed.[2]

'Englishness', indeed, is itself one of the reasons for which this volume deals, as its title makes clear, only with English and not with the whole of British society in the twentieth century. In part, the restriction is due to the difficulty of doing adequate justice to the very different local structure and culture of parts of Scotland, Wales, and Ireland, the roles of whose inhabitants, citizens as they may be of a 'United Kingdom', have had hardly less tenuous a connection with its central institutions than did the roles of their grandparents. But it is also because the distinctive characteristics of these regions are largely irrelevant to the modes of production, persuasion, and coercion of an English society whose dominance of them in all three dimensions was, by 1900, indisputable. This is not to deny that what has happened in the peripheries has had a significant influence on what has happened at the centre: events in Clydeside, Belfast, and the valleys of South Wales have been more important to the history of twentieth-century England than events in Humberside, Exeter, or the Vale of Evesham. But for all the impact of Ireland, in particular, on English politics, neither the fission of the Irish Republic nor the continuing attachment of the counties of Ulster to the Crown made any fundamental difference to the modes of production, persuasion, and coercion of English society as they evolved after the First World War. Nor did the intermittent upsurges of either Welsh or Scottish nationalism. I do not underestimate the importance of the careers of thousands of men and women from those regions in roles which were an integral part of twentieth-century English society. But those careers are themselves a testimony to the peripheral nature of the structure and culture they had left behind them. Lloyd George, Ramsay MacDonald, Aneurin Bevan, and Neil Kinnock performed their roles in England's Parliament, just as Welsh, Scottish, and Irish regiments fought in England's wars, and Welsh, Scottish, and Irish authors contributed to English literature. Whatever value-judgements you may choose to make about the rights and wrongs of England's 'internal colonialism', as it is sometimes called,

---

[2] It may, however, be worth my repeating from chapter 1 of volume II that societal boundaries can be 'both fluid and tenuous, and many roles and institutions either overlap or transcend them': for English examples, think only of Basil Hume, the Cardinal Archbishop of Westminster, at one end of the spectrum and Kim Philby, the Soviet agent, at the other.

and whatever the self-regarding illusions which English people may nourish about it, it is a culture and a structure dominated by English institutions with which the sociologist (as opposed to the anthropologist or the historian) of twentieth-century Britain must be concerned.

§2. Both the distinctiveness of England's history and the sense which English people had of it were, by 1900, a familiar theme, however differently they might be interpreted by rival observers with different presuppositions and purposes in mind. Nor was there anything very remarkable in the manifestations of complacent insularity and strident patriotism which can be documented in all systacts and milieux in late-Victorian and Edwardian England. However much Engels might proclaim himself, when writing to Plekhanov in May of 1894, 'driven to despair by these English workers with their sense of imaginary national superiority', he can hardly have been surprised by it. Engels did not live long enough to share the dismay of both socialist and liberal observers at the enthusiasm with which workers and their families in East London celebrated Mafeking night. But whatever the reservations of a minority of intellectuals, the consciousness that England had won all its major wars except one, had made itself the 'workshop of the world', had preserved its freedom from 'despotism', and had diffused its influence throughout an empire out of all proportion to its apparent strength could not fail to generate a sense of collective self-esteem transcending divisions of region, religion, and class.

Indeed, it could hardly be questioned that it *had* been a remarkable history. Romanticized as it has been both by the nostalgic sociologists and historians of the Right for the better and by the utopian sociologists and historians of the Left for the worse, there cannot fail to be agreement among observers of all theoretical schools about the fact of Britain's brief era of global hegemony. Well before the end of the late-Victorian and Edwardian period, there was no lack of informed opinion to warn that this hegemony was under threat. The industrial might of the United States, the efficiency of German scientific and technical education, the mounting intensity of competition in overseas markets for British goods, and the economic costs as well as the strategic risks of a far-flung and loose-knit empire were all themes increasingly commonplace in public debate; and the Boer War, whatever may have been its short-term effect in rallying popular patriotism, exposed not only the vulnerability of the nation's army but also the inadequacy of the physical condition of an alarming proportion of the potential recruits to it. But these were anxieties which arose as a function of earlier success. If relative decline was in prospect, it was decline from a position reached after a long evolution which had established an institutional tradition all the more deeply entrenched because it appeared to have served England so well in inter-societal competition. This was recognized and even welcomed not only by complacent apologists but also by observers who could not possibly be accused of wishing to maintain the modes of production, persuasion, and coercion unchanged. Orwell, writing in the darkest days of the Second World War, caught this sense of uniqueness very well: 'The whole conception of the militarised continental state, with its secret police, its censored literature and its conscript labour is utterly different from that of the loose maritime democracy, with its slums and unemployment, its strikes and party politics' (1941, pp. 121–2). It is a remark which could just as well have been made, and with the very same overtones, half a century earlier or, for that matter, half a century later.

Orwell can be, and has been, accused of demystifying other people's descriptions of England only to misdescribe it in his own way in turn (Williams 1958, p. 283; Gloversmith 1980, pp. 109–23). Nor do any of his readers need guidance from literary critics to be aware that he is sometimes more revealing about his own attitudes and beliefs than about those of the people whom he describes. But there could be no disputing that England was a society where a certain minimum of formal liberties had long been recognized. To speak in these terms is not to impute any special good sense to its statesmen or any special taste for reasoned argument to its people. The notion that 'moderation' was merely a fortunate consequence of the fact that England had fought its civil war and solved the problem of its peasantry a long time ago (Moore 1966, chapter 1) had long been a commonplace of history teaching in English schools. There had indeed been a time when Englishmen tortured and killed one another for their beliefs, forcibly deprived one another of the means of subsistence, waged war on one another on English soil, and denied one another freedom of movement as well as of expression (Plumb 1967, chapter 1). But by 1900, all that was long since over and done with – was it not?

'Whiggish' narratives of a progressive evolution towards economic prosperity, ideological consensus, and political freedom were not without their effective critics, then and since. But even those most concerned to deny that England's evolution was in any way a matter for self-congratulation did not dispute that English society remained, whether for better or for worse, capitalist, liberal, and democratic. Perhaps the distinctive features of its structure and culture might have permitted either an authoritarian or a socialist mode of the distribution of power to evolve in some distinctively English form. Granted (it might be said) that an evolution to Fascism was as implausible as an evolution to Communism, was it not possible to envisage a sort of 'gentlemanly' authoritarianism in which a 'national' government would seek genuinely to incorporate the representatives of organized labour into the workings of the state and to exercise social control with a minimum of recourse to paramilitary auxiliaries? Or, alternatively, was it not possible to envisage the evolution of a socialism 'with a human face' in which central control of the means of production would be exercised with a minimum of bureaucratic centralism, and ideological dissent be tolerated up to the limits compatible with the proletarian party's 'leading role'? But such speculations are academic in a double sense. First, they presuppose that these distinctively English sub-types could somehow overcome the constraints and contradictions which, on the evidence summarized in volume II, confront all authoritarian and socialist societies. Second, they have to counter the objection that even in their 'English' forms the programmes of the carriers, or would-be carriers, of either authoritarian or socialist practices never commanded the support of more than a small minority even of the members of those systacts whose interests would, at least in theory, have been advanced had they come to power.

The relative lack of support for the Communist Party of Great Britain (CPGB) between the Bolshevik Revolution of 1917 and the collapse of the Soviet Union in 1989 calls for comment not only because of its presumptive appeal to the sense of relative deprivation of unemployed and low-paid wage-earners but also because of the events which might have been supposed to work to its advantage. The apparent success of the Soviet five-year plans, the failure of the Labour governments of the 1920s to deal with unemployment, the difficulties faced by workers in the strongly unionized but steadily declining staple industries, and the rise of Fascism in Germany and Italy might all have been expected to encourage the belief that only a workers' seizure of power from the faltering hands of the ruling class could bring about the transformation of capitalism. A number of contingent influences can be cited in explanation, of which the determination of established trade-union leaders and officials to resist being overtaken from the Left is one, systematic infiltration, surveillance, and intimidation by the police another,[3] the subservience of the CPGB to Moscow a third, and the British worker's dislike of being preached at by anybody a fourth. But in any event, how would a takeover of the British Labour movement by a committed socialist faction have come about? Where in the institutional environment were the selective pressures favouring the mutant practices of which the roles making up that faction were the carriers? It is sometimes suggested that if war had not broken out in 1914, the widespread industrial unrest of the time could have been welded under syndicalist rather than communist inspiration and leadership into a revolutionary movement directed to the overthrow of the capitalist state. But the overwhelming majority of the strikers themselves, however militantly disposed towards both their

---

[3] Not that its effectiveness should be overestimated: I cannot resist citing from Pelling (1958, pp. 28–9) the episode in 1924 when two plain-clothes officers were found hiding under the stage of the theatre where the Party Executive was about to meet: the two were promptly handed over to the nearest uniformed constable who, not realizing who they were, took them in charge.

employers and those of their union officials whom they held to be too willing to settle with them, were not concerned at all with attacking the state;[4] and in any case, the syndicalists faced the inescapable contradiction that they could not weld their followers into a disciplined force capable of wresting control of the means of coercion from the governing élite without the adoption of practices which would violate the very principles from which their appeal to the rank and file derived.

If, therefore, neither the syndicalist nor the communist Left could pose a serious threat to England's capitalist, liberal, and democratic mode of the distribution of power (and still less the middle-class intellectuals of the Independent Labour Party (ILP)), what of the authoritarians on the Right? They, after all, had some active sympathizers within the governing élite, and were well placed by both doctrine and practice to recruit and train the paramilitary auxiliaries who might be strong enough for a coup which would put a government of their choosing in control of the state. In the General Strike of 1926, middle-class men turned out in force to do working-class men's jobs. But the far-Right 'volunteer' was as little of a threat to the established modes of production, persuasion, and coercion as the far-Left 'agitator'.[5] It is likely that many members of the police were more sympathetic to Mosley's blackshirts than to the demonstrators who marched and protested against them. But the Public Order Act of 1936 was deployed against the blackshirts as and when the Home Office thought it expedient to do so, and their ranks were infiltrated by informers just as effectively as were those of the Communists. Similarly, although there were Conservatives both in and outside of Parliament who would have welcomed a single-party state, a restructuring of industry imposed from above, and the radical curtailment of trade-union power, few if any were disposed to take part in paramilitary defiance of the traditions of peaceful protest, constitutional debate, and respect for the formal liberties of the individual citizen. Whatever the hopes of right-wing admirers of Mussolini or the fears of left-wing theoreticians for whom Fascism was the natural form into which capitalism was being driven in self-defence, Fascism in Britain was a failure.

There were, admittedly, sub-sets of roles among which the practices and doctrines of extremist factions began to spread. Fascism did appeal to a

---

[4] G. D. H. Cole's retrospective comment was that 'If a new temper was abroad, and the moderate leaders found their control of the movement seriously threatened, this did not imply a wholesale conversion of the British working class to revolutionary doctrines' (1927, p. 71).

[5] The two roles are placed in quotation marks as illuminating examples of the way in which the vernacular terminology reflects the dominant ideology. The 'volunteer' is by implication a patriotic citizen moved to action in defence of the national interest; the 'agitator' is by implication a trouble-maker whose disruptive activities have therefore to be countered by the 'volunteer'.

number of middle- and lower-middle-class ex-servicemen or non-unionized or unemployed workers from traditionally Conservative Northern constituencies (Webber 1986, p. 44) whose ideological predispositions could be channelled into a simultaneous hostility to working-class Communists on the one hand and Jewish financiers on the other. Communism had an equally evident appeal for wage-workers in homogeneous working-class communities with established traditions of militancy – the 'little Moscows' as they were designated by the press, partly to the pride and partly to the embarrassment of their inhabitants.[6] But it was hardly as if they felt a sense of relative deprivation, whether regional or sectoral, sufficiently intense to mobilize militant Welshmen and Scotsmen, or militant coalminers and transport workers, for a guerilla war, or even a sustained campaign of civil disobedience, against the state. These loyalties undoubtedly furthered a disposition to industrial militancy at local level, and commentators then and since have noticed that where immigrants were concentrated within particular regions or communities outbreaks of industrial unrest were likely to be more difficult either to settle or to control. But again, this only serves further to illustrate the domination, economic, ideological, and political alike, of English society over its non-English peripheries. What is more, the ablest leaders from peripheral communities and regions always had open to them the opportunity of individual upward mobility into England's central institutions. Lloyd George and Ramsay MacDonald apart, James Maxton and the other 'Clydesiders' of the inter-war period were perhaps the most celebrated (Middlemas, 1965); but they are by no means the only ones. This mobility was important not for its scale, which was always small, but for its effects. Here as elsewhere, it served the double function of voicing the sense of relative deprivation of the underprivileged and at the same time depriving them of leaders who, had they remained in their roles, might have become the carriers of more militant practices and doctrines rather than less. This process has been as much deplored by observers on the Left as it has been welcomed (not always explicitly) by observers on the Right. But whichever the view to which your evaluative presuppositions may incline you, it is a well-attested sociological fact about the structure and culture of twentieth-century (and earlier) England.

§3. Relative stability in the modes of production, persuasion, and coercion has not ruled out events and changes in the lives of English men and women as significant by any measure as those which took place over the course of earlier centuries than the twentieth. Two world wars of unprecedented scale and

---

[6] Macintyre (1980, p. 16) found that 'Paradoxically, when some of the residents of Mardy were interviewed in their old age, a sense of pride about Mardy's radical identity was expressed by the less political informants, while leading Communists were apt to dwell on its disadvantages.'

duration brought not only death and bereavement to some but hitherto undreamt of opportunities and rewards to others. The twists and turns of both domestic and international politics signalled triumph or disaster for life-histories no less dramatic than those of Disraeli or Palmerston or Pitt. Great fortunes were as spectacularly made, and sometimes lost, as they had ever been. Clashes between opposing ideologies affected those embroiled in them just as deeply as had any of the religious conflicts of the previous era. Employers and employees contested their rival claims with as much at stake for both as had their predecessors in the high noon of nineteenth-century industrialization. And however much the academic observer may be impressed, with hindsight, by the mismatch between the attitudes and beliefs of con-temporaries and the reality of the processes of social selection actually at work, their written or spoken words reflect strongly felt subjective experiences which are more often than not being authentically described in their own contem-porary terms.

But subjective experiences can never provide the explanation of why the structure and culture of English society in the twentieth century have changed both as much and as little as they have. There is a fundamental and persistent disjunction between description of what the changes in it have been like for 'them' and explanation of why the practices defining its pervasive roles and central institutions so changed as to require it to be assigned to a different sub-type of the capitalist-liberal-democratic mode in the years between the after-math of the First World War and the time of writing from the year of Queen Victoria's death. At the turn of the century, English society was in the middle of what I shall continue to call its 'late-Victorian and Edwardian' evolutionary stage. After the First World War, it became capitalist, liberal, and democratic in a qualitatively different sense which, however it should be labelled, and however it was seen by the people who lived through it, made the institutions of the pre-war era irrecoverable even for those who were most determined to restore them and most reluctant to accept that the world, and England's place in it, would not be the same again.

But then what (it might be asked) about the Second World War? Did that war not bring about further changes which mark off the 1950s and 1960s from the 1920s and 1930s as much as they are marked off from the period between 1880 and 1914? Is there not an enormous difference between the experience of a demobilized wage-earner who, after 1918, went through a short-lived boom and a wave of strikes only then to be faced with the prospect of a wage-cut or the loss of his job, and that of one who, after 1945, returned to a period of full employment and, despite a continuance of rationing and shortages, a much higher level of collective provision for his and his dependants' welfare than he would have thought possible a generation before? And wasn't there, more generally, an unarguable difference in the national mood, however described, between the 1940s and 1950s and the inter-war years? But these questions only reinforce the point that life-histories and the subjective experiences that go with them are a very misleading guide to the underlying mutations of practices and consequent emergence of novel roles which are the necessary and sufficient conditions of an evolution from one to another sub-type of a given mode of production, persuasion, and coercion. The changes which took place in, or in the aftermath of, the Second World War did undoubtedly make England a better place to live in for many of its citizens. But those changes were in no sense fundamental to its modes of production, persuasion, and coercion, and they can in any case be traced back to selective pressures which antedated the outbreak of war. English society did undergo an evolution from one to another sub-type of capitalist liberal democracy between 1915 and 1922, despite all the contemporary rhetoric about 'normalcy'. But after 1945, it did not, despite all the contemporary rhetoric about a 'social revolution'. However the changes which followed the Second World War are to be explained, described, or evaluated, they cannot be reported as an evolution out of one into another sub-type, let alone mode, of the distribution of power.

1945 serves also as a warning against seeing in the to-and-fro of party-political conflict evidence of change in (let alone of) the modes of production, persuasion, or coercion. The General Election of 1945 was, admittedly, more bitterly contested than many, and the replacement of the Liberals by the Labour Party as the principal parliamentary opposition to the Conservatives in the aftermath of the First World War was of fundamental significance to it. But the alternation of members of different parties in governmental roles took place within a set of central institutions which none of the incumbents of the dominant roles sought to overturn or would have succeeded in overturning if they had. The displacement of the Liberals after 1919 had the tacit connivance of the Conservatives,[7] and in the following decades, it was a Conservative government which placed broadcasting and the electricity supply under public control just as it was a Labour government which was willing to invoke emergency powers in the face of a transport strike. More ironically still, the policy which helped to lose the Conservative Party the elections of both 1906 and 1923 – tariff reform – was to become, under other labels, the policy of the Labour Party in opposition to the free-trade policy of the Conservative Party

---

[7] At least in part because 'It enabled the second rank of Conservative ministers to overturn their leaders and then use Labour to corner the leaders they had overturned' (Cowling 1971, p. 479). But 'high politics', so called, cannot explain why the modes of production, persuasion, and coercion evolved as they did: what it explains is how successive incumbents of governmental roles accommodated (or failed to accommodate) to changes which they could sometimes promote or retard but never predict, let alone control.

after 1979, when the Thatcher government, for all its pronouncements implying the contrary, was continuing to spend much the same proportion of the national income as its predecessors. The economic interests of British wage-earners might or might not be better served by tariff barriers and import substitution than by decontrolled markets and active international trade. But the conviction of Joseph Chamberlain and his supporters in the late-Victorian and Edwardian period that 'Free Trade was good for the foreigner but was bad for the English workman' (Semmel 1960, p. 180), and the related conviction that the influence of the City of London should be curbed in favour of the interests of British manufacturers, came to be directly echoed by Labour politicians and trade unionists in the 1980s. It is true that the visions inspired by these convictions could less easily be reconciled than the convictions themselves. Chamberlainite tariff reformers who had dreamed of a society of sturdy yeomen and patriotic labourers sustained in secure employment by the fruits of empire and ruled by a government dedicated to the elimination of class conflict could hardly share a platform with anti-Thatcherite little-Englanders dreaming of a neutralist Britain ruled by a government committed to rigorous import and exchange controls and the subsidy of domestic production at the direction of the representatives of the organized working class. But the parallel is there, all the same.

What is more, it is striking not only how far both the Labour and the Conservative parties remained committed to a capitalist, liberal, and democratic mode of the distribution of power but how little, even within that mode, they moved in the direction of a sub-type which might seem more appropriate to their respective history and doctrines. Granted, it might be said, that those on the leftward fringe of the Labour Party who aimed at a transition to a socialist mode stood as little chance of success as those on the rightward fringe of the Conservative Party who aimed at a transition to an authoritarian one, might not Labour have succeeded in bringing about an evolution to what might be labelled a 'Swedish' sub-type of capitalist liberal democracy, or the Conservatives an evolution to what might be labelled a 'Japanese' one?[8] But for reasons to which I shall briefly return at the end of chapter 3, it didn't happen. The constraints acting on the central institutions of English society channelled the careers of even those politicians most determined to bring about major systemic changes into directions as contradictory in retrospect as they had been improbable in prospect. It is not, as I have already said, the concern of this volume to narrate them. But they are a testimony at the same time to the persistence and intensity of party-political conflict and to the greater impor-

---

[8] A brief account of these from the perspective of the theory of social selection is given in volume II: see particularly pp. 260–2 on Sweden and pp. 416–27 on Japan.

tance of the selective pressures which, whether or not the policy-makers were aware of it, determined the competitive advantage conferred by their defining practices on the roles constitutive of the society's modes of production, persuasion, and coercion.

Before, however, any explanation (let alone description or evaluation) is advanced, it needs to be more fully expounded than I have done so far what it means to say that twentieth-century English society has remained, despite all the changes which followed the First World War and its immediate aftermath, 'capitalist', 'liberal', and 'democratic'. These are all sociological terms of the kind which, as I argued in volume I, have to be construed as functioning according to the presuppositions and purposes of the author who deploys them. This does not, as I also argued, prevent them from being used as terms of reportage which can be transposed *salva veritate* between alternative explanatory, descriptive, or evaluative theories. But the evolution from one to another sub-type of capitalist liberal democracy cannot be reported as such to the satisfaction of rival observers until it has been spelt out in exactly what sense the practices defining the roles which constitute the mode of production are indeed 'capitalist', those defining the roles which constitute the mode of persuasion 'liberal', and those defining the roles which constitute the mode of coercion 'democratic'. In what follows, I assume without further argument that power is of three and only three analytically distinct but empirically interrelated kinds – the economic, the ideological, and the political; that any society's constituent roles are, therefore, located as vectors in a three-dimensional social space; and that, as I put it in the opening section of volume II, 'the study of societies is the study of people in roles, and the study of people in roles is the study of the institutional distribution of power'. But that makes it all the more important to immunize the rest of this volume against objections of the form of 'That's not what *I* mean when I talk about capitalism, liberalism, and democracy.'

A CAPITALIST MODE OF PRODUCTION

§4. Terms like 'capitalism' can be defined partly, at least, by their opposites. But in 1900, 'socialism' meant even more things to more different people than 'capitalism' did. To its detractors, it meant a subversive doctrine of Continental origin which, with an inconsistency not always perceived, was at the same time dismissed as irrelevant and denounced as dangerous. But to other observers, it meant a vision of a world organized not for domination but for cooperation in which the fruits of labour would be shared for use, not profit. To yet others, it meant a scientific philosophy of history according to whose laws the present mode of production was destined to collapse through its own internal contradictions. To others again, it meant the assumption by the state of responsibility for the health, housing, and education of its citizens. And to some, it meant simply a new-found disposition on the part of unionized workers to usurp the traditional right of the owners of the means of production to manage their own affairs as they might decide. But under none of these definitions could the central institutions of English society be labelled 'socialist' in more than the most preliminary and questionable sense. There *were* thoroughgoing socialists to be found of any and all these kinds in a variety of roles both intellectual and practical, including municipal government. But they were a minority, and an almost powerless one. Observers of different theoretical schools might apply the label 'capitalist' to the practices and roles which constituted the late-Victorian and Edwardian mode of production in somewhat different senses from one another. But only under a highly eccentric definition could it possibly be reported as anything else.

During and after the First World War, as the power attaching to the roles of government ministers and officials on one side and of trade-union leaders and shop stewards on the other increased at the expense, and under the eyes, of the proprietors and controllers of the means of production, the cry of 'socialism' came to seem more plausible; and when, in the aftermath of the Second World War, a self-styled socialist government with an unassailable majority in the House of Commons proceeded to take the mines, the railways, and the Bank of England into public control, the cry was no longer confined to die-hard Tories or catch-penny publicists. But in whatever sense the government of 1945–51 might be labelled 'socialist' by its opponents, it was not 'socialist' in either the sense meant by those of its supporters for whom any compromise with the institutions of capitalism was treachery, or the sense used in this treatise, according to which collective ownership of the means of production is directly administered by a single ruling party whose legitimacy rests on its ideological commitment to the interests of the working class. The 'Big Five' – Attlee, Bevin, Dalton, Morrison, and Cripps – were all as committed as each other to the use of the power attaching to their and their officials' roles to correct the failings and curb the excesses of the capitalist mode of production and to provide universal welfare services at the taxpayer's expense. But they had no intention of abolishing the market in labour and commodities, or expropriating all private owners of property, or denying the right of employees to negotiate the terms of their employment directly with their employers. To Attlee, whatever he might sometimes have said in the 1930s, a 'full Socialist programme' was neither practicable nor even desirable in principle (K. Harris 1982, p. 326); and it was no more so to Wilson in 1964, or to Callaghan in 1979, or to Kinnock in 1992.

Whatever the slogans to which either Labour or Conservative candidates might appeal in soliciting the favour of the electorate, their ministerial roles, if and when they came to occupy and perform them, functioned only to regulate, not to undermine, the capitalist mode of production. The intervention in the economy practised by National or Conservative governments fell as far short of an authoritarian mode of production as that practised by Labour governments fell short of a socialist one. It is not just that they all remained committed to the practices and institutions of a democratic mode of coercion and therewith the prospective surrender of the power to impose a command economy from the hands of one party to those of another. No twentieth-century British government assumed direct control of the means of production except on a selective and strictly temporary basis. Even in wartime, the powers exercised by British governments were less than those exercised by either authoritarian or socialist governments in peacetime; and they were explicitly seen to be, and presented to Parliament and the public as being, emergency powers which would lapse when peace returned.

In any case, it was not as if the transfer of part of the means of production from private to public ownership transformed the operation of the industries where it was put into effect. On the contrary, they continued to be run by much the same people in much the same way. Hopes that labour relations would automatically be improved – how, once the mines belonged to the people, could the miners strike against themselves? – were as quickly dispelled as fears of workers' control by the back door.[9] In the year after nationalization, there were more unofficial strikes in the mines than there had been in the year before it; in the railways, the unions complained that nothing had changed; and in iron and steel, the unions said that they did not want nationalization at all. For some observers, both on the Left and on the Right, nationalization was 'socialistic' by definition. But even if the fact is ignored that it was the Conservative Party which had earlier nationalized not only broadcasting and electricity supply but also the airways, what difference had been made to the relations between employer and employee? What mutant practices had modified their respective roles? Trade-union appointees might be given seats on nationalized industry boards in the name of worker participation, but there was no suggestion that this would mean the end of collective bargaining, or of free mobility of labour, or of the right to strike any more than that it would lead to the replacement of directors by party cadres or workers' soviets. The difference was only that from the directors' point of view they were dealing with a single

---

[9] Cf. Dennis *et al.* (1956, p. 76): 'Nationalization, a long-standing aim of the miners, has been achieved. The prestige of the miner in the working class is higher than it has ever been, and the miner knows this. Does all this mean that the miner has experienced a basic change in his status and role in society, a change which goes with a transformation of the relation between the miner and his work? In fact no such basic change has occurred.'

shareholder whose priorities might differ in some ways from those which a constellation of private investors would be likely to have.[10] The government of the day could nationalize (or privatize) whatever of the means of production it might decide. But in the English context, for all the heat which the question generated in party-political debate, that carried no implication whatever that the mode of production had evolved from a capitalist to a socialist one (or back again).

§5. It is, however, true to say that the British Labour movement had, from its earliest days, viewed the capitalist system as its enemy; and if to be an opponent of *laissez-faire* is to be socialist, then not only the Labour Party in its 1918 constitution but the trade unions also were, in that sense, socialist. But behind the rhetoric of displacing the pursuit of private profit and the anarchy of unplanned production with a new economic order, there lay an attachment to practices which depended for their continuing replication on the institutional environment of a formally free market. It was not just that the advancement of workers' interests required a tactical accommodation with the forces of capital – that, as Citrine rhetorically put it to the Trades Union Congress (TUC) of 1928, 'We cannot await the advent of the breakdown of capitalism before we start marching towards control' (*Report*, p. 413). It was that central direction of the economy, even if exercised for the benefit of the working class, would deprive the unions of the functions which they had been brought into being to perform.

It is doubtful how many union members or officials recognized this. No doubt the Communists did. But the Communists explicitly envisaged a mutation of practices on the Leninist model which would turn their roles into those of state-employed bureaucrats whose task it would be to convey the decisions of the ruling party and its planners to the rank and file of union members. Bevin realized it too, which was one of the reasons for his implacable opposition to the infiltration of Communists into either the trade unions or the Labour Party. When, in 1940, he was brought into the Cabinet by Churchill to take charge of labour, his concern was not to take powers of direction (they were, in effect, thrust into his hand, and virtually never used), but to ensure

---

[10] Moreover, this could work either way so far as negotiations over pay and conditions were concerned. It might be supposed that nationalized industries would be more indulgent to their workforces whereas privatized ones would be more concerned to raise productivity per head – i.e. in Marxist terminology, to heighten the rate of exploitation (cf. O'Connell Davidson 1993 on the water industry). But a nationalized industry could (and did in both coal and steel) resist a national strike more resolutely than a privatized one could have afforded to, whereas the most notoriously featherbedded workforce in the whole period covered by this volume were the printers in the privately owned newspaper industry prior to the purchase of *The Times* by Rupert Murdoch.

that trade-union rights would be preserved to be reexercised after the war was over. But the dilemma was not one which Bevan, for example, seems ever to have formulated explicitly, any more than did his middle-class intellectual allies. Their impatience with the 'gradualism' of the unions and their repudiation of anything which hinted at compromise with the system they sought to replace concealed from them the strength of the selective pressures which favoured the practices defining the roles of trade-union leaders answerable to their members on the one side and of controllers of the means of production answerable to their shareholders – whether private or public – on the other.

At the core of that relationship was the set of practices which constituted the institution of collective bargaining – a term which had first been used by Beatrice Webb (then Potter) in 1891. The practice of negotiation between employers and employees over terms and conditions was as old as the roles of capitalist and wage-labourer themselves. But its mutation is a classic illustration of evolution through competitive selection in which the advantages conferred on its carriers were only partially recognized at the time. Some employers supported collective bargaining, as did some trade unionists, in the hope that it would weaken the influence of extremists among the rank and file. Some employers opposed it as conceding to union leaders an unacceptable entitlement to interfere in managers' right to manage. Some trade unionists opposed it as curtailing the ability of skilled craftsmen to exploit their privileged position in direct negotiation with individual employers. But in the late-Victorian and Edwardian period, as industry continued to expand and the complexity of both organization and technique to accelerate, the pressure for more systematic definition and regulation of the relations between employers and employees in such industries as mining, textiles, construction, rail transport, and heavy engineering became increasingly inescapable. Many of the agreements made were improvised and provisional, and many collapsed under circumstances which the original parties to them had not foreseen. But in the late-Victorian and Edwardian environment, what was the alternative? Governments had no incentive to interfere directly; employers could no longer go it alone as they once had; and union officials had no more effective means of improving the wages and conditions of their members or, no less important, keeping the threat of non-union labour at bay.

There were, as is only to be expected, large differences between one industry and the next, and there continued to be large areas of the economy where unionism did not penetrate at all, both in service industry and in small-scale manufacturing. Even by 1911, less than a quarter of the male, and barely a sixteenth of the female, workforce was unionized; and only about a third of all employees were covered by either district or national agreements. But these were employees in industries whose importance to the economy as a whole was not in doubt, and it was in them that, for all the rhetoric of intransigent employers and militant unionists, collective bargaining came to assume an increasingly routinized form. The most aggressive of all the employers during the late-Victorian and Edwardian period were those who had established the Engineering Employers' Federation (EEF) in 1896 and in the following year imposed a selective lockout which resulted in the almost total defeat of the Amalgamated Society of Engineers. But even the EEF was not seeking to put an end to collective bargaining over wages and conditions: the issues which mattered to its members were entry, apprenticeship, and craft controls. Similarly, the most aggressive unionists – on paper, at least – were the leaders of the transport workers, railwaymen, and mineworkers who came together to form the 'Triple Alliance' which might, in the view of some observers, have initiated a nationwide general strike in 1914 but for the outbreak of war. But the proceedings of the Joint Executive Committees of April and July of that year lend no support to that view. The intention seems, on the contrary, to have been to synchronize the timing of the expiry of existing collective agreements and by the threat of joint action compel the government to intervene in the unions' favour as it had done in the railway and transport strikes of 1911 and the mining dispute of 1912 (Phillips 1971, pp. 63–5). Collective bargaining, with or without intervention by government, had become the established institution within which the claims of organized labour were negotiated from one round to the next.

In all this, the function of the state – that is, of the practices defining the roles of ministers and officials – was, until the First World War, largely passive. From 1896, the Board of Trade was charged with the enforcement of the Conciliation (Trades Disputes) Act of that year, and after 1906 its officials intervened with increasing frequency and vigour in almost all large-scale industrial disputes and many smaller ones. But this intervention was persistently tempered by the realization that both unions and employers had to be cajoled rather than coerced into accepting their roles as legitimate. The arbitrators on whom the Board depended had no legal sanctions with which to enforce their decisions. The power attaching to their roles rested purely on their presenting themselves as expert and impartial between the two sides in any given dispute. They were as ready to put pressure on intransigent employers as on unrealistic union leaders in securing a settlement which could be accepted by both parties without loss of face. But the criterion by which they were guided was the state of the market, not the raising or even the maintenance of wage-workers' living standards. They not merely ignored but refused even to countenance demands by labour negotiators for a 'socialistic minimum' or a 'living wage' (Davidson 1978, pp. 586–7).

Syndicalist opposition did, admittedly, threaten both to cut across traditional divisions of sector and craft and to undermine the 'collaborationism' of the existing union leadership. But despite major differences between the pre-1914 and post-1918 system of industrial relations, the effect both before and after the First World War was an adaptation of the capitalist mode of production to incorporate the threat. Prior to 1914, collective bargaining was extended as a means of containing syndicalist militancy, and existing procedures were renegotiated where this would diminish the risk of escalation of local disputes. Between the wars, when shop-steward militancy was particularly active in the aircraft industry and certain sections of transport, its association with the Communist Party ensured the hostility of the trade-union leaders. After the Second World War, when mounting doubts about the state of industrial relations law led to the establishment of the Royal Commission of 1965, successive governments addressed themselves to curbing the ability of local militants to call 'unofficial' strikes, whether, as under Wilson, directly or, as under Thatcher, by legislating to 'return the unions to their members'. Each time, union leaders fought to keep the principle of collective bargaining intact while at the same time holding back from constitutional confrontation. Citrine's successors at the TUC, however ready to stage protests against the government of the day or to support individual unions in their disputes with employers, remained as committed as he to preserving the autonomy of individual union leaders within a system which depended as little as possible on legal sanctions.

Relations between both unionized and non-unionized wage-workers and their employers, therefore, remained governed by negotiations over pay and conditions freely entered into within an open labour market in which agreements were voluntarily adhered to (or not) in the absence of direct enforcement by the state. Indeed, even those trade unionists most opposed to the existing structure of collective bargaining sought to alter it only in favour of alternative negotiations, whether at plant or, on the contrary, cross-sectional level, whose purpose remained the sale of workers' labour-power to their employers on the best terms they could secure. No doubt these negotiations were conducted, after the First World War, within a political environment which constrained it within limits unacceptable to even the most far-sighted employers of 1914. No doubt too, many more trade unionists than the minority of would-be revolutionary socialists remained strongly opposed to what they saw as the loss of autonomy, uncertainty of employment, lack of dignity, and inadequacy of reward imposed on them by the capitalist mode of production. But capitalist it has remained, and their attempts to mitigate its effects, however much more apparently successful than those of their late-Victorian and Edwardian predecessors, have done nothing to alter the fundamental nature of the practices and thereby roles by which it is defined.

§6. There remains the possible objection that even if the practices constitutive of free collective bargaining have been replicated intact, the extent and degree of 'corporatist' collaboration at a higher level during and since the First World War has been such as to distort the workings of the market beyond the point at which the term 'capitalism' can properly be applied. But 'corporatism', if by that is meant a coalition between representatives of government and representatives of non-governmental interest-groups whereby the interest-groups receive specified benefits in return for their acceptance of specified government policies,[11] is not a new, non-capitalist mode of production. It is true that for polemicists of the Right, it is a term used to signal the danger that tripartite cooperation between government, employers, and unions will be a step on the road to a socialist mode in which acquiescence in the demands of labour will be forced on the employers at the expense of the free play of market forces, while for polemicists of the Left, it is a term which signals the danger that tripartite cooperation will lead to the surrender of trade-union rights to an authoritarian mode in which proclamation of the national interest will be a cover for a surreptitious evolution to Fascism. But once these pre-emptive implications are discarded, 'corporatist' practices need not amount, and have not amounted, to more than intermittent cooperation between the three in their own interests within the same set of central institutions. By comparison with the late-Victorian and Edwardian period, the period since the First World War is unarguably distinguished by a greater involvement by the state in the affairs of capital and labour alike. But any new 'corporatist arrangements' have still rested on voluntary cooperation between the incumbents of the roles constitutive of the three. All have remained free to back away at any point; and it only needs one of them to do so for any allegedly incipient evolution out of a capitalist into either an authoritarian or a socialist mode of production to be halted then and there.

This has not prevented the trade unions from seeking to enlist ministers on their side in their dealings with employers. Even in the late-Victorian and Edwardian period, union leaders had come to recognize that they needed the state to protect what they had won. But their recourse to it has consistently been in the cause of their own autonomy. As Halévy put it, 'Were the unions opposed to State intervention in any shape or form? Certainly not. Perhaps the principal functions of the great cotton and coal unions was to see that the Factory Acts were fully carried out in workshops and mines. But, if we insist on regarding the Factory Acts as a beginning of Socialism, we must admit that contemporary labour leaders were entirely unaware of it' (1961, p. 213). The

---

[11] This way of putting it is adapted from the definition of 'corporatist arrangements' given by Crouch and Dore (1990, p. 3).

same can equally be said of the various subsequent interventions by ministers on the unions' behalf and their successive attempts to enlist the unions' support in return for such interventions. Thus, the Trade Disputes Act of 1906 was not, although sometimes so represented, a charter for an all-out offensive against the employers, but only a safeguard for free collective bargaining (K. D. Brown 1982, p. 131). Nor were the Mond–Turner talks of 1928 between 'moderate' unionists and 'progressive' employers the step down the path to a radical change in the relations between the two which some commentators have seen them as being: the union leaders envisaged any scheme for industrial 'reorganization' as being negotiated between themselves and the appropriate trade association within the existing institution of collective bargaining (Phillips 1987, p. 194). Later still, when both Conservative and Labour Governments of the 1970s offered to concede participation in the making of economic and fiscal policy in return for some form of wage restraint, the union leaders were again prepared only to agree terms which did not compromise collective bargaining. Nor could they do otherwise, since even if they had wished to, they were only too well aware that they could not carry their members with them.

The employers, on their side, remained no less wary of cooperation with the state even in the face of enhanced trade–union power. The minority who would willingly have participated in a 'national' economic strategy which would involve abrogation of strikes could exercise no serious influence either on their fellow-employers or on government. Part of this wariness sprang from a reluctance to countenance interference in the workings of the market. But part of it sprang from a pragmatic apprehension that industrial relations might be worsened rather than improved if the state sought to influence them directly. There is no more striking expression of this than the 'startling' statement (Sked and Cook 1984, p. 287) of the then Director-General of the Confederation of British Industries (CBI) during the General Election campaign of 1974 that the Industrial Relations Act of 1971 had 'sullied every relationship at every level between unions and employers and ought to be repealed rather than amended'. But it will have sounded rather less startling in the ears of any employer whose recollections went back two generations to the controversies over 'dilution' – that is, the use of women and unskilled men to do the work of craftsmen – in the munitions factories of Clydeside during the First World War. The employers, far from welcoming the attack on craft controls, had then 'regarded it as the Ministry's job, not theirs, to impose dilution. They were not prepared to pull Lloyd George's chestnuts out of the fire, and find themselves with strikes on their hands which could be avoided if dilution were quietly ignored' (McLean 1974, pp. 216–17).

Nor, on the side of the state, did either ministers or officials become any more anxious for their roles to be widened to include direct responsibility for a command economy. Admittedly, it was not only in the two world wars that they took measures which involved intervention in the workings of the market: investment incentives, regional development grants, and interest-rate and exchange-rate management are no less cases in point than manpower planning or food rationing, to say nothing of the steady rise in the output of parliamentary bills in the fields of tax, company, and employment law alike. But these interventions were not such as to alter the mode of production. They did not involve representatives of either capital or labour in decisions taken over the heads of their members to the detriment of their traditional rights to manage on the one side and bargain over pay and conditions on the other. Although Attlee's government did retain many wartime controls for the first few years of peace, he had no intention of 'planning' the economy beyond the sense in which Keynesian income and expenditure budgets were 'plans', or the siting of new towns and preservation of green belts were 'town and country planning'.[12] Physical controls were replaced by budgetary demand management; and in any case, their retention would have required trade-union agreement to a wages policy and direction of labour, which was out of the question (Brooke 1991). 'Planning' did become something of a vogue word in the 1930s, and again in the 1960s. But it meant little more than what, in the language of Lloyd George's Ministry of Reconstruction, had been called 'enquiry, research and reflection', or what any management consultant would recommend to the head of any large organization – careful sifting of information, conscious decision on priorities, and consistent execution of the decisions taken. Adaptive responses to the increasing complexity of economic institutions must not be equated with an evolution out of a capitalist mode of production into something else.

A LIBERAL MODE OF PERSUASION

§7. Objections similar to those which can be urged against the application of the label 'capitalist' to the mode of production of mid-twentieth-century England might be urged against the application of the label 'liberal' to its mode of persuasion. But even those observers for whom the ideology of liberalism was exposed, in and after the First World War, as what they regarded as a

---

[12] Cairncross (1985, p. 303) describes the views of Attlee's ministers of the planning process as 'nebulous but exalted'. The *Financial Times* (4.11.46) talked of 'a veneer of planning gospel over a vast deal of higgledy-piggledy departmental practice' (quoted by R. S. Barker 1986, p. 28). Tomlinson (1995, p. 91) quotes James Meade when head of the Economic Section of the Treasury in 1947 on the contrast with France, where planning operated 'outside the normal administrative machinery'.

sham were bound to agree that liberalism is what it remained an ideology of. It is undeniable that Prime Ministers since Lloyd George have used their role to manipulate, and sometimes deliberately to mislead, public opinion. It is also undeniable that the BBC, once in being, was far more partisan in its deployment of the means of persuasion than the rhetoric of impartiality implies, and that books, films, plays, and television programmes have often been banned or altered by ministerial decision. But however valid Beatrice Webb's complaint (in her diary for 4 January 1932) that 'the BBC has been collared by the defenders of capitalist enterprise',[13] the difference between the exclusion of views regarded as a threat to the liberties which the state is there to uphold, and the routine distortion of reported facts for the purpose of discrediting any section of the community which opposes government policy, is the very difference to which the ideology of liberalism appeals. A liberal mode of persuasion is not defined by a lack of censorship in any form, but by the difference between the censorship of what is claimed (however unconvincingly) to be so libellous, seditious, or obscene as to be unacceptable to public opinion and a censorship which proscribes as heretical all views not directly in accordance with the doctrines and purposes of the incumbents of governmental roles. The freedom from 'despotism' on which, as I remarked in section 2, the English had long prided themselves was, among other things, a degree of freedom of opinion which they believed to be denied to the subjects of less fortunate regimes where the heavy hands of the policeman and the priest kept from being printed and circulated opinions of any unwelcome kind whatever.

At the same time, a liberal mode of persuasion implies that the means of it are bound to be more readily accessible to the incumbents of higher-ranking than lower-ranking roles. What is more, their opinions, or the opinions of the publicists whom they hire, are likely to favour the institutions of the status quo. But again, the contrast is between a society in which there is a market in opinion to which access is formally free, and one in which there is not – whether because, as in an authoritarian mode of persuasion, the market is controlled by the state or, as in a socialist mode, the market has been abolished. In twentieth-century England, there has been relatively little formal restriction on the freedom of any person, association, or corporation to circulate views critical and even, up to a point, subversive of the government of the day if they can acquire the means of doing so. Any observer disposed to question this needs only to consult the files of the many newspapers, pamphlets, and periodicals which testify to it. How far these have been at a disadvantage in competing with the pro-capitalist press for readers among the systacts whose

---

[13] M. Cole (1956, p. 297). Cf. the entry for 15 July 1919, where she says of Lloyd George that 'It will be the capitalist press which will enable him to keep his hold on a chaotic democracy at the mercy of suggestion' (M. Cole 1952, p. 165).

interests they purport to advance is a question which can only be settled case by case. The overwhelming right-wing bias in the mass-circulation press suggests that they have. But it is possible that, for example, the *Daily Herald*, commercially unsuccessful as it was,[14] did more to further the opinions which inspired its founders than can be said of the *Daily Express*: for all the power attributed to Beaverbrook by Labour and Conservative commentators alike, the particular cause for the promotion of which the *Express* had initially been bought[15] gained little or nothing from its backing.

The alternative ideologies which had already found enthusiastic expression in the late-Victorian and Edwardian period included not only those of the Marxist Left but those of the Hegelian Right. But, as many commentators have remarked, they elicited curiously little response from the educated public. The conception of the state as the 'higher good' – or as Bertrand Russell was to caricature it, Hegel's conception of freedom as 'freedom to obey the police' – never overturned, and hardly even modified, the entrenched individualist creed. The foundations on which that individualism rested may, as its opponents did not fail to argue, have been mythical. But even if, as American observers were apt to remark, there was much self-deception in this,[16] individual liberty was nonetheless the value to which appeal could most effectively be made in public debate. Lip-service continued to be paid to it no less by Labour than by Conservative Party spokesmen,[17] even when seeking to challenge the unwelcome conclusions, as they saw them, to which nineteenth-century doctrines of *laissez-faire* had led. All continue to agree not only that

---

[14] No less, and perhaps more, influential in promoting the ideology of the Left was the 'fragile network' of local Labour papers (D. Hopkins 1985, p. 124).

[15] Beaverbrook (1963, pp. 16–17): 'I had undertaken the arduous duty and dangerous financial obligation of rescuing the bankrupt *Daily Express* for the sole and only purpose of promoting Empire solidarity and the political future of Bonar Law. For, as I firmly believed, he was destined to give us of the Empire movement the prize we sought – Empire Free Trade.'

[16] Margaret Halsey, wife of a visiting professor at the University of Exeter in 1937, is an authentic representative of the American view of the 'relentless subservience of the lower classes' (1938, p. 149).

[17] Witness, for example, the preamble to the Labour Party's Kinnock/Hattersley 'Statement of Principles' of 1988: 'The true purpose of Socialism, and therefore the true aim of the Labour Party, is the creation of a genuinely free society, in which the fundamental objective of government is the protection and extension of individual liberty.' Is there a conscious echo here of the Webbs' *Constitution for the Socialist Commonwealth of Great Britain* of 1920 where the freedom that the Commonwealth was to maximize was likewise an 'individual' one? Or even of Crosland's Fabian Society pamphlet of 1960 (*Can Labour Win?*), which among the 'basic Socialist values' listed 'A belief, not merely in Parliamentary democracy, but in the rights and liberty of the individual as against the state, the police, private or public bureaucracy, and organised intolerance of any kind' (p. 1)? The Labour Party's 'Statement of Aims', which declared that the party stood for the 'freedom of the individual against the glorification of the state', likewise showed it as remaining 'true to its *laissez-faire* liberal individualism' (Currie 1979, p. 185).

Englishmen – and, as the movement for women's rights gains strength, Englishwomen too – are and should be free to subscribe to whatever political creed they choose, but also that all are as fully entitled as one another to use whatever of the means of persuasion they can lawfully command to bring their fellow-citizens round to their point of view.

§8. This self-image of a society of freedom-loving individualists does, however, invite further objection along Mrs Halsey's lines. England, as successive domestic and foreign observers have also pointed out, is a society riddled by 'class' – the term being here used not in the academic sense of inequalities in the power attaching to different roles deriving from their relation to the means of production, but in the vernacular sense of differences in the way English people can be seen to behave towards each other on account of life-style, education, inherited rank, and conventionally defined prestige. How, therefore, can the dominant ideology reconcile its commitment to the value of individual freedom with a simultaneous acceptance of criteria which rank these free individuals in an institutional hierarchy of deference? How can the myth of 'liberalism' carry conviction in the mouths of a dominant status-group which continued, after both world wars, to send its children to exclusive fee-paying schools, to fill almost all the higher-ranked roles within the professions and the Civil Service, to defer as readily to ascribed as to achieved systactic location, and to distinguish itself not merely by its manners and mores but even by its 'superior' pronunciation of the English language itself?

One possible answer is to say simply that the reconciliation is and always has been hypocritical. But there is more to the dominant ideology than this; and of all the documents which might be cited in which a reconciliation is explicitly attempted, none known to me is more revealing than a speech made by Palmerston at the prizegiving of the South London Industrial Exhibition in April, 1865, in which he said:[18]

> the constitution under which we have the good fortune to live . . . opens to every man having talents, energy, perseverance, and good conduct any honours and distinctions which his turn of mind and attainments may qualify him to aspire to . . . the medals distributed to-day have inscribed on them the names of a great number of men who, starting from very small beginnings, attained, by their talents, their industry, their perseverance, and their good conduct, the very highest positions of social merit and distinction . . . Look at all the great men who have figured in public life. Look at your Army, your Navy, your Law, your Church, your statesmen. You will find in every one of these careers men who have risen to the highest points, who have either themselves started from the smallest beginnings, or whose fathers began with nothing but their talents, their

[18] The report of it is quoted in full from the *Illustrated London News* of 8 April 1865 by Best (1971, pp. 234–6).

industry, and their energy to aid them . . . I may be told that the examples I have
cited of men who attained great wealth or distinguished positions are few, while
the competitors are many, and that to the bulk of those who struggle to arrive at
such goals the effort must be hopeless. I would ask whether many of you have
not gone on a fine bright day, in the beginning of summer, to that great seat of
amusement, Epsom racecourse, and seen horses run for that celebrated race, the
Derby? Three or four hundred horses entered for the race, but only one won the
prize. All the rest failed to obtain the object of their ambition. But those luckless
horses that did not win the Derby won other races. If they were good for
anything they all won something. And thus the training, the industry, the pains,
and the expense of those who had fitted them for the competition in which they
were to take part were eventually repaid.

What this speech so frankly reveals is an explicit recognition of wide
inequalities of power and low rates of long-distance upward mobility in the
same breath as an unblushing complacency about the fact that such mobility
should be possible at all. The horse-racing metaphor is also characteristically
English. But the crucial point is that social mobility is assumed to be not
merely possible but admirable. There is no suggestion that those who rise into
roles to which there attaches high prestige will not be accorded recognition by
the other members of the status-group of which they thereby become a part.
That status-group was, admittedly, dominated in Palmerston's time by a
hereditary aristocracy, but one whose members neither refused to admit new
entrants into its ranks nor disdained to occupy 'bourgeois' occupational roles
themselves. Distinctions of prestige were still drawn by those reluctant to
admit 'new' money to social intercourse on the same footing of equality with
'old'. But it was already a proverbial saying of long standing that 'gentility is
but ancient riches'. Here, the critical practice is status-group exogamy; and by
the late-Victorian and Edwardian period, the families of ancient lineage had
shed any lingering inhibitions about the marriage of their sons to the daughters
of the unaristocratic rich. For all the complacency of Palmerston's speech, the
institutional difference which it emphasizes is a real one – the difference, that
is, between a society in which mobility in the ideological dimension of power is
legitimate, and those truly castelike societies in which mobility is only possible
for people who can 'pass' by concealing their origins.

It is, perhaps, more questionable whether this legitimacy was so readily
accorded to those of 'non-British' origin. But however formidable the obstacles
they might encounter, the dominant ideology did not dispute the legitimacy of
their surmounting them if they could. The obvious test is elevation to the
peerage, which by the end of the nineteenth century had already been achieved
by a handful of Jews, colonials, and second-generation foreigners. Palmerston
might have been startled to be told that by the second half of the twentieth
century women as well as men, and persons with black skins as well as white

ones, would be sitting on the benches of the House of Lords. But he would have had to acknowledge it as no more than a natural extension of the principle he had himself proclaimed – an evolution (not that he would have put it that way) from one sub-type to another of the liberal mode of persuasion. Such promotion into the status élite for a fortunate few did not rule out xenophobia, discrimination, and prejudice (to which I shall return in section 10 of chapter 2). But although the public ideology of successive governments might be belied by the private behaviour of many of the population at large (and some of themselves), it was never officially surrendered to it.

It might still be objected, from a different angle, that the skilled working class as it had evolved by the aftermath of the First World War was composed of trade unionists whose ideology was very different from that of the self-improving mid-Victorian artisans to whom Palmerston's speech was addressed. But that has not been reflected in any marked unwillingness on the part of trade unionists and Labour politicians themselves to accept the titles bestowed by the conventional honours system. To those on the far Left, as might be expected, the system was anathema: Citrine, who accepted a knighthood in 1935, was subjected to what he himself regarded as a 'vicious attack' by Bevan's wife, Jenny Lee (Citrine 1964, p. 314). But Jenny Lee was to accept a life peerage in 1970; and Anne Godwin of the Women Clerks and Secretaries, who moved a resolution at the 1935 annual meeting of the TUC criticizing (by implication) Citrine and Arthur Pugh of the Metalworkers for accepting knighthoods from a Conservative government, was to accept a DBE from a Conservative government in 1962. Even David Kirkwood, one of the original 'Clydesiders', accepted a peerage on his retirement from the House of Commons in 1951. There had been no opposition when three trade-union leaders accepted knighthoods from the Labour government in 1931; and in 1935, both Pugh and Citrine were congratulated by numerous union members whose pleasure at the official recognition of their services echoed their own.[19] Whatever the reservations of the minority for whom this was a symptom of 'collaborationism' with a system they were seeking to abolish, it can hardly be disputed that the majority of the Labour movement applauded the explicit legitimation of the kind of long-range individual mobility denoted by such autobiographical titles as Burns's *From Workshop to War Cabinet* or Hodge's *From Workman's Cottage to Windsor Castle*.

If there was anywhere where more nearly insurmountable barriers to individual mobility were to be observed, it was in the educational system. Not only did the overwhelming majority of working-class children complete their

---

[19] Pugh, in his union's journal *Man and Metal*, recorded his 'keen appreciation for the large number of messages of congratulations . . . received from members, branches and branch officers' (V. L. Allen 1957, p. 357).

formal education several years younger than their middle-class contemporaries, but the further difference between state and private education was that, in the words of one historian, 'The children of the masses went to free day schools until the age of 14; the children of the privileged went to expensive boarding schools until 13. The dividing line between them was as hard as that between Hindu castes. No child ever crossed it' (A. J. P. Taylor 1965, p. 171). Yet there was no inconsistency with the liberal ideology of formal equality of opportunity: any child whose parents, guardians, or benefactors were able to afford the fees was eligible for private schooling, however remote such an aspiration might be in families whose priority was, on the contrary, that children should leave school as early as possible in order to start earning. And at the level of 'higher' education, the Palmerstonian principle was put clearly into practice. The number of full-time university students was, until well after the Second World War, very small – no more than some 30,000 even in 1931 – and the number of them who had been born into working-class families was an almost imperceptible proportion of the working class as a whole. But they were there, and they thereby gained entry to a status-group to which they could assimilate on equal terms and within which success was accorded recognition independently of systactic origin. There was no suggestion on the part of either its defenders or its would-be reformers that there existed 'parity of esteem', as it came to be called, between the different sectors and levels of the educational system. But then a liberal mode of persuasion does not require that there should.

§9. It might still be argued against all this that the liberal ideology, powerful as it had remained in the late-Victorian and Edwardian period, was so effectively smothered by the collectivist doctrines invoked by both Left and Right after the First World War to legitimate the extension of the power of the state that the evolution is, after all, not just of sub-type but of mode. But it is not as if the ideology of individualism and 'bourgeois' freedom, whatever concessions its advocates may have made under pressure from either authoritarian or socialist doctrines, ever came near to surrendering to them. However far from a 'Gladstonian' ideal-type the invocations of the concept of freedom by mid-twentieth-century politicians, it could not be claimed that collectivism as defined in either an authoritarian or a socialist mode became the dominant ideology instead.

To insist on this is not to underestimate the strength of the traditional ideology of the Labour movement – the ideology, that is, of fraternal collaboration between manual workers and their middle-class allies as well as commitment to the ideal of a society based on mutual self-help instead of competition for private profit. But as we have just seen, collaboration within the Labour movement was directed above all to the preservation and extension of free collective bargaining; and this has meant the freedom of individual unions to pursue their own interests as they see them irrespective of conflicts either with other unions or with Labour governments whose appeals to loyalty are apt to fall on studiously deaf ears as soon as collective bargaining rights are thought to be at stake. The fate of the Wilson government's White Paper of 1969, *In Place of Strife*, affords the most dramatic illustration, but it is by no means the only one. It is not that the rhetoric of brotherhood is spurious. On the contrary, it has often been put successfully to the test in confrontation with governments or employers, and sometimes both. But voluntarism has always been at the heart of the demands made by trade-union leaders on their supporters and opponents alike. Dictatorial as they can on occasions be in their dealings with their own members, the ideology to which they appeal has still been one of voluntary cooperation in pursuit of legitimate sectional aims.

It is symptomatic of this ideology that during the late-Victorian and Edwardian period, when collectivism was first being actively propagated in not only Fabian but Marxian forms, the writings of Marx should have found so little response among working-class readers and those of Robert Blatchford, by contrast, so much. Blatchford, the self-taught ex-NCO whose *Merrie England* sold three-quarters of a million copies within a year of its publication in 1893, is sometimes dismissed as an eccentric jingo who, as he said of himself, was a Briton first and a Socialist second (1937, p. 199) and whose outspoken militarism in and after the Boer War lost him much of his erstwhile support. But there was more to his Socialism than cycling clubs, good fellowship, and nostalgia for the pre-industrial past. *Merrie England* explicitly disavows the violent expropriation of private property, but it no less explicitly advocates collective ownership of the means of production, to be achieved by a 'Democratic Parliament with a Socialistic public behind it'. Unrealistic as this might sound both to Marxist or Syndicalist militants on one flank and to Liberal or Conservative defenders of the existing order on the other, it captures the mood of the British Labour movement much more closely than the goal of a 'revolutionary dictatorship of the proletariat' to which H. M. Hyndman and his Social Democratic Federation sought, with remarkably little success, to convert it.[20] Unlike the Webbs, few if any of the trade-union members who voted (which not all of them did) for the Labour Party were drawn towards the Soviet brand of collectivism which the Webbs, in their old age, came to hail as a 'new civilization'. The conviction that British Socialism, whatever institutional changes it might require, would remain peaceable,

---

[20] To G. D. H. Cole, for example, writing in *The Guildsman* in July of 1920, 'Certainly there could hardly be a less inspiring programme than dictatorship of the proletariat' (quoted by Carpenter 1973, p. 97).

tolerant, and democratic testifies all the more to the strength of the dominant ideology of liberalism if it is held, as by its opponents on both flanks, to be an illusion.

The nostalgic anti-industrialism which runs through the Socialism of Blatchford and William Morris had its adherents too at the opposite end of the spectrum among Conservatives who were the ideological heirs of the 'Tory Radicals' who had campaigned throughout the 1830s and 1840s against the factory system and the New Poor Law. But this qualified paternalism, like the qualified collectivism of the trade unions, was anti-liberal in a very particular sense. To both, the intervention of the state was necessary because only the state could temper the harmful side-effects of capitalist industrialization on the works whose exploitation it involved. It can therefore be said uncontroversially enough that 'Like Socialist Democracy, Tory Democracy legitimizes a massive concentration of political power' and that Tory Democrats, like Socialist Democrats, 'accept a broad and continuous, indeed a Collectivist, intervention by government in society and especially in economic affairs' (Beer 1965, p. 91). But both are prepared to concede this power to the state only because individual citizens will thereby be protected against the threat to their freedom to lead their lives as they would otherwise choose which is posed by unbridled market forces and the concentration of power in the hands of an economic, rather than a political, élite. Taken to its extreme, 'Tory Democracy' shades over into an authoritarianism in which all decisions are taken by the governors on behalf of the governed and the relation of elector to representative becomes that of client to patron. Similarly 'Socialist Democracy', taken to its extreme, shades over into a collectivism in which decisions taken in the name of the proletariat are imposed on its members without the possibility of consultation or protest. But it was only by a tiny minority that either *was* taken to its extreme. The overwhelming majority of English men and women who were concerned with such matters at all were seeking to modify the dominant liberal mode of persuasion, not to replace it.

A DEMOCRATIC MODE OF COERCION

§10. The definitional problem is in one respect still more obtrusive in the remaining dimension of social structure, since the idea of a 'democratic' mode of coercion may seem to be being stretched too far if it covers both nineteenth-century governments elected on a limited franchise whose diminutive standing army and rudimentary police were almost haphazardly brought to bear on their fellow-citizens and governments with not only the legitimation of universal suffrage but also the much greater powers of surveillance and control enjoyed by prime ministers since Lloyd George. But yet again, we are dealing with a change of sub-type, not of mode. It is true that, before as well as after the First World War, the distribution of the means of coercion in favour of the roles of agents of the state was massively unequal. The implication of the term 'democratic' is no more than that to a qualitatively greater degree than in either a socialist or an authoritarian mode, the use of force against groups or categories of citizens seeking to alter the distribution of power by extra-legal means depends on 'public opinion' – by which is meant that the government needs to secure sufficiently widespread support, or at least acquiescence, among the electorate on whose votes its tenure of office depends. After the First World War, governments had more power than ever before over the ordinary citizen, and, as always, much more power over the propertyless and stigmatized than over the rich and prestigious. But at the same time, they had to be more careful in some ways than before about how they used it.

Descriptively, there is no more vivid and illuminating evidence for the flavour of these considerations than the report of the discussion among Lloyd George's Cabinet on 2 February 1919 given in the diaries of its Assistant Secretary, Tom Jones (Middlemas 1969, I, pp. 99–103). It seems that Lloyd George himself did not, at least on that occasion, take seriously the threat of imminent revolution. Indeed, Jones reports him as doing 'a lot of unsuspected leg-pulling' in the belief that the Home Office had been 'got at' by the War Office with the aim of increasing the number of army recruits. But behind the leg-pulling, and despite Bonar Law's repeated and apparently serious refer-ences to the stockbrokers of England as 'a loyal and fighting class', both the preparations envisaged in the discussion and, for that matter, the fact of its being held at all, license the inference that Lloyd George would not have hesitated to deploy the means of coercion against 'extremists' had the occasion arisen which called for it. Beatrice Webb, in *her* diary, reports him as saying of the miners on 22 February, 'We shall beat them – we control the food' (M. Cole 1952, p. 147). Not only did he have a more formidable apparatus of coercion at his disposal than his late-Victorian and Edwardian predecessors had had, but he was personally uninhibited about the use of Special Branch information and private funds to supplement recourse to the means of coercion with manipulation of the means of persuasion. This, to the extent that it was done without reference to Parliament, could fairly be said not to be 'demo-cratic' at all. But its success, as he well recognized, depended on the acceptability to public opinion of his use of the power of the state no less than on his capacity to call on it.

The occasion when the means of coercion were most visibly deployed was in January 1919, when no less than 12,000 troops, backed up by 6 tanks, were called in to keep order in Glasgow in the aftermath of the disturbances which resulted from a baton charge by the police against a crowd of strikers and unemployed. But nobody was killed – as, by contrast, they were later that year in Cardiff, where a riot directed not against employers or the government but against black merchant seamen caused three deaths – and no serious challenge to the government was mounted either inside Parliament or outside it. Successive prime ministers were faced with difficult tactical choices as to when and how to deploy the means of coercion rather than persuasion. Baldwin gave way to the mineworkers in 1925 only to stand firm against them in 1926, just as Thatcher gave way to them in 1982 only to stand firm against them in 1984. But for all the concern periodically voiced by ministers and senior civil servants about the capacity of the army and police to maintain public order against widespread subversion or unrest, no government ever lost the tacit support of the majority of public opinion when it chose to bring the means of coercion to bear.

To say that this meant that the rule of law was never challenged would be blatant misreportage. Not only militant trade unionists or extra-parliamentary pressure groups but governments and their agents ignored or evaded the democratic 'will of Parliament' when they thought it in their interests to do so. Nor did legislation interpreted as 'anti-union' ever carry legitimacy in the eyes of even the most moderate of trade-union leaders. But it was, nevertheless, in Parliament and the courts, rather than on the picket line and the streets, that the respective claims of governments, employers, trade unions, and pressure groups continued to be decided. The roles through which the competition for political power was acted out remained those of the magistrate, the advocate, the tribunal chairman, the backbench MP, the trade-union official, and the political lobbyist, not the vigilante, the paramilitary gang-leader, or the industrial saboteur. The overwhelming response of those who disputed the legitimacy of a piece of legislation, or of a decision in the courts interpreting and reflecting that legislation, was to get it changed, whether by inducing the government which had passed it to repeal or amend it or by changing that government for another which would. The fact that the methods adopted for the purpose sometimes involved a breach of what was, at least for the moment, the law is not an argument against the 'democratic' nature of the institutions concerned. Indeed, some such breaches can even be claimed as evidence in favour of it. In the words of the authors of a detailed study of the effects of the Heath government's ill-fated Industrial Relations Act of 1971, 'Arguably the response to the IR Act, far from challenging democratic theory, actually gave evidence of its continued validity' (Weekes *et al.* 1975, p. 231).

§11. The means of coercion, accordingly, however much more formidable after the First World War than before it, were deployed (or not) in much the same way whatever the political party in power. It was not just Ramsay

MacDonald among Labour politicians who was prepared, when in office, to use force against strikers whose actions were held to amount to a threat to the legitimacy of the state itself: even Bevan was ready to do so in 1948 against dockworkers who were attempting to overturn the wage freeze imposed by Stafford Cripps (K. O. Morgan 1984, p. 58; J. Campbell 1987, p. 191). Nor, as I have already remarked, were Conservative governments any readier than Labour governments to tolerate violence on the streets organized by a faction on the Right: the offer of Fascist assistance in the General Strike was categorically refused (Griffiths 1980, p. 88).

To be sure, it would be misleading to speak of competition for power in English society as being 'democratically' settled if that were taken to imply that conflicts of interest are resolved exclusively by debate. The practices through which disagreement was most strongly expressed were the demonstration and the strike. But the strike – that is, the co-ordinated, voluntary withdrawal of labour from employers, whether private or public – is one of the legal and customary rights central to the capitalist-liberal-democratic mode; and, as I have emphasized already, it was never exercised for the revolutionary purposes for which Syndicalists and Marxists hoped in vain. In 1919 the threat of 'Direct Action' may have helped to restrain the government from further military intervention in Soviet Russia (although the unions are generally held by then to have been pushing at an open door), and in 1982 a 'Day of Action' was called by the TUC to protest against the industrial relations policies of the government (although it was generally regarded as an embarrassing failure). But all-out confrontation with the state was never in question. Armed workers taking to the barricades in order to force the government of the day to surrender power to a British Lenin remained as implausible a scenario as the House of Commons being intimidated into voting emergency powers to a British Hitler by brown-shirted mobs chanting 'Give us the Bill or fire and murder'. In the English institutional environment, 'Direct Action' was a threat which depended for its effectiveness on remaining one. It could only fail if the bluff was called; and in 1919 Lloyd George called it. Robert Smillie, the President of the Miners Federation, recalled later that although 'truculently determined not to be talked over by the seductive and eloquent Welshman', they 'were beaten and we knew we were' from the moment that Lloyd George asked them directly if they had weighed the consequences of succeeding in bringing about the government's defeat and thereby precipitating a constitutional crisis.[21]

Sporadic violence was never wholly absent during industrial disputes or, for that matter, General Elections, when 'rowdyism', as the newspapers of the

---

[21] The source for this often-quoted story is Bevan (1952, pp. 21–2).

inter-war period called it, was quite often a feature of political meetings. But it was never in any sense pervasive, and still less did it ever become central to the functioning of the electoral system. Public opinion was normally brought to bear on the government of the day by swings of the vote – supplemented, after the Second World War, by opinion polls based on statistical sampling of the electorate. How far the government might respond varied from case to case. In 1922, adverse by-election results drew concessions from Lloyd George's Cabinet on proposed reductions in public expenditure on education. In 1944, Churchill's Cabinet virtually ignored by-election results which, with hindsight, could be seen to anticipate Labour's victory in the General Election called the following year. But the vote, supplemented on occasion by the petition, the march, or the withdrawal of labour (or threat of it) remained the recognized method of protest.

If there is any single episode which exemplifies this aspect of the democratic mode of coercion in operation, it is the nationwide protest which followed the introduction in 1935 of 'a new kind of centralized Poor Law' (Davison 1938, p. 41), in which the scales of unemployment relief were to be regulated by a newly created Unemployment Assistance Board rather than locally by Public Assistance Committees whose discretion had, in the government's view, been widely abused. The government had assumed, in the absence of firm evidence, that most recipients would be awarded small increases and that only in the areas where discretion had been over-generously exercised would the new rates involve reduction. In the event, however, it became apparent that nearly half of all those affected would have their benefits reduced. Protest was immediate and, by English standards, spectacular. In Sheffield alone, 10,000 people marched on the town hall where scuffles broke out. Back-bench Conservative as well as Labour MPs joined with Church leaders and local councillors in pressing the government to annul the reductions. There were scenes in the public galleries of the House of Commons which Lansbury, speaking as Leader of the Opposition, said he could not without hypocrisy deplore (Runciman 1966, p. 79). In South Wales, where the unexpected success of almost wholly spontaneous demonstrations encouraged similar responses elsewhere (Miller 1979, p. 336), over 300,000 people are estimated to have taken to the streets. The government backed down almost at once. The increases were allowed to stand, and the reductions annulled. No changes were made until the following year, and they were then significantly more generously interpreted than had been envisaged in 1935.

Within this mode of coercion, the function performed by the courts was generally viewed, both by those who approved and by those who wished it otherwise, to be conservative in the sense of tending, other things equal, to hand down decisions favouring English institutions as they stood. Indeed, it could hardly be otherwise in a system where the tradition of the common law required the judiciary to have regard primarily to precedent. In a society whose mode of production had long rested on private ownership of the means of production, this could only mean a categorical commitment to the sanctity of property, and to this extent the much-vaunted independence of the judiciary could be argued to be compromised from the start. But however much more powerful the post-1918 than the pre-1914 state, there have been numerous judicial decisions where the English courts have shown themselves unwilling to interpret the existing statutes in the way that the government of the day might be expected to favour in the absence of a clear-cut expression of the will of Parliament. There is no more a disposition to defer to the will of the state as it might be interpreted in an authoritarian mode than to seek to further the interest of the people as it might be interpreted in a socialist one. So far as the English courts are concerned, it is in Parliament that sovereignty continues to reside, and the extent to which previous Acts of Parliament and decisions of the courts interpreting them do or do not accord with either the opinions of a majority of the population on the one hand or the wishes of ministers and officials on the other is not a matter to which the judiciary need have any more regard than they choose.

§12. In the mode of coercion of twentieth-century English society, the army has played – except in Ireland – only an occasional part; and events in Ireland had, as I have said already, little or no impact on the modes of production, persuasion, or coercion in England (or Scotland or Wales). It is true that in section 10 we have just seen the army out in force, tanks included, in the streets of Glasgow in 1919; and in the rail strike of the same year, 23,000 troops were deployed on protection duties with a further 30,000 held in reserve (Jeffery 1981, p. 279). In the General Strike of 1926, armoured cars escorted food wagons from the London docks and two companies of tanks were deployed to guard Whitehall. But the troops never used their weapons, and the military authorities were anxious that if possible they never should. The maintenance of law and order remained the task of the police, and the principal concern of those responsible for their deployment was not whether they might either need to call on military help or have it thrust on them by the government of the day, but how responsibility should be allocated and co-ordinated between regional and metropolitan forces. The policeman's role did become 'militarized' in the sense that the shield-bearing ranks of specially trained riot control squads deployed against striking miners in 1984 are a far cry from the late-Victorian and Edwardian 'bobby' with his overcoat and truncheon. But even if the Home Secretary's role can be said to have evolved by then into that of Minister of Police, the institutional function of the police remained the same. The exercise of that function involved, as it was bound to do, the use of force, and it was by no means always in response to violence on the other side. Just as the police in Glasgow in 1919 had launched the baton charge which created the disturbance, so did the police in Yorkshire in 1984 sometimes charge striking miners who had not always stoned them first.[22] But the full-scale deployment of military force (as was happening in Ireland in 1919 and in Northern Ireland in 1984) would have been another matter entirely.

So far as concerned English society, the army remained, even after the mass mobilization of the First World War, a separate corporation in the technical sense, with its own distinctive structure and culture but with little or no influence of any kind on the mode of the distribution of power. This was in part the result of its traditional function in governing the Empire. Regular soldiers lived large parts of their careers overseas, and their wives and children with them, and when they returned home on retirement or discharge they tended to feel detached and even alienated from the institutions of domestic English life. But it was also the result of a long and pervasive anti-military tradition. Within individual families, sons might follow fathers into military roles in accordance with inherited rank. But even if, by the late-Victorian and Edwardian period, imperialist sentiment was generating 'unprecedently adulatory attitudes' towards the professional soldiery (Anderson 1971, p. 46), it could not be said that a military career was popular in the country at large. Kipling's poem 'Tommy' well conveys the disdain with which the 'brutal and licentious soldiery' were regarded except at those times when England was directly engaged in war: 'For it's Tommy this an' Tommy that and "Chuck him out, the brute!", But it's "Saviour of 'is country" when the guns begin to shoot.'

The paradox is that this anti-militarism was combined with a ready and even fervent patriotism. This, perhaps, is only to be expected in a society whose location in the inter-societal rank-order was due to naval rather than military power and to the pursuit of territorial influence in the interests of trade rather than territorial absorption by conquest. But it was a consequence also of a domestic history in which a standing army had long been viewed with distrust as an instrument of oppression of the people by the state. The result was not only that the regular army was treated as a race apart, but that even the most vociferous patriots, such as the spokesmen of the Edwardian National Service

---

[22] Geary (1985, pp. 146–7) sees the 1980s as 'a reversion to an earlier and more violent pattern', but believes that the distinctive features of the miners' strike of 1984 will not be repeated. Townshend (1993, p. 201), on the other hand, questions 'whether the stresses of modern political violence have exhausted the flexibility which has always been the chief virtue of the unwritten constitution'. But Townshend's warning only has point because a democratic mode of coercion is still in place.

League, acknowledged that 'conscription could never be established except by near-universal consent' (Summers 1976, p. 114). Popular militarism, if such it could be called, found its outlet in the volunteer (or, as it became after 1907, 'Territorial'), not the regular, army.[23] When, therefore, the regular army was swollen with unprecedented numbers of new recruits in both world wars, the influx was regarded by both sides as temporary. The regular army retained its own hierarchy of ranks, together with its own ritual practices and corporate values. In wartime, promotion could be rapid, and officers were recruited from well outside the status-groups normally drawn on in peacetime. But tradition reasserted itself quickly enough when hostilities were over: even after the Second World War, during the prolongation of conscription (or 'National Service', as it was called), the regiments of the Household Brigade would take potential young officers only from schools and families considered traditionally suitable. Long-range upward mobility was always possible, just as Palmerston had maintained: Field-Marshal Sir William Robertson rose from the ranks to be Chief of the Imperial General Staff from 1915 to 1918. But it was very rare. The barrier between the sergeants' and the officers' mess was as castelike as that between the state 'primary' and the private 'preparatory' school.

Moreover, the army's lack of corporate power was compounded by the higher prestige traditionally enjoyed by the navy. This was not simply a matter of social esteem. It extended also to the proportion of available resources allocated by Parliament to the army as opposed to the navy (and, after the First World War, the Royal Air Force). This was as true of the years before the Second World War, when annual expenditure on the army was less than a quarter of what was spent on the navy, as of the years after the Boer War, when a ratio of 3:2 in the navy's favour had been accepted as normal even by the advocates of conscription. The navy was the primary arm of defence, and no more was expected of the army than that it should be capable of garrisoning the colonies and – perhaps – despatching a small but well-trained expeditionary force for a limited conflict on the continent of Europe. Ireland is the admitted exception. But the 50,000 troops stationed there in 1919, like the 20,000 stationed in Northern Ireland after 1969, were performing a colonial rather than a domestic function.

The British armed services, therefore, have remained, even after the experience of 'total' war, institutionally autonomous in a way that they would not be in a socialist mode of coercion, and under parliamentary control in a way that they would not be in an authoritarian one. It is true to say that England's mode of coercion is 'democratic' in what is, once again, the

---

[23] The Boy Scout movement, too, had its paramilitary side; but that was one reason (another being the cost of the uniform) why working-class boys, particularly in the North, were under-represented in it (Springhall 1971).

'bourgeois' sense of the term. Except where matters of military policy are a General Election issue, decisions about it are settled behind closed doors by the incumbents of a very small number of connected roles who are almost all drawn from a common systactic origin and share a common sub-culture. By comparison, therefore, with the direct democracy of the 'citizen' mode as discussed in volume II, where in the extreme case incumbents of political roles could be chosen by lot and unpopular generals could find themselves voted out of office and into exile at any time, the system is hardly 'democratic' at all. But the roles to which there attaches access to the means of coercion are institutionally subordinate to those of the members of the government of the day, and the government of the day, however little it involves the public in its decisions, has been voted into office by electors for whom there has been, and sooner or later will be again, a choice of rival parties for whose candidates to cast their votes. No evaluative presupposition underlies the definition: whether a 'democratic' mode of coercion in this sense is better than a socialist or authoritarian mode or than the direct democracy of 'citizen' societies is, as always, up to you. But it serves to restate once more the question to be addressed in the following chapters – the question, that is, why twentieth-century English society, having evolved between 1915 and 1922 from one to another sub-type of capitalist liberal democracy, did not then evolve out of a capitalist-liberal-democratic into either a socialist or an authoritarian or any other new mode or even sub-type of the distribution of power.

THE 'VICTORIAN' LEGACY

§13. To take 1901 as a starting-point, and thereby to summarize the immediately preceding history of English institutions as a bequest from a 'Victorian' past, is, as I have already implied, to use the incidental fact of the Queen's death for a purpose to which it can have no serious sociological relevance.[24] But it does so happen, all the same, that the turn of the century coincides with events which aptly symbolize the evolution of England's central institutions out of their mid-Victorian into their late-Victorian and Edwardian sub-type of capitalist liberal democracy, including not only the formation of the Labour Representation Committee but, for example, the petition for the vote signed by

---

[24] Cf. Cecil (1964, p. 170): 'the Muse of History is not so considerate to her servants as to arrange that the successive phases of England's development should coincide exactly with the successive reigns of her sovereigns. The so-called "Victorian" age ended some time before the death of Queen Victoria; the so-called "Edwardian" period started about 1880 and went on till 1914.' Likewise G. M. Young in the Introduction to the second edition of *Portrait of an Age*: 'I see now that I should have carried my book to 1914, and treated late Victorian and Edwardian England as the *ancien régime* of the England in which I was writing' (1953, p. vi).

10,000 Lancashire women cotton operatives in 1901 (H. A. Turner 1962, p. 185), or Rosebery's 'much-noticed London speech' in the summer of the same year linking support of the empire with social reform, including old age pensions and housing (Briggs 1964, p. 53). By the beginning of Victoria's reign, England had evolved out of its 'Georgian' commercial-aristocratic-oligarchic mode into a recognizably capitalist-liberal-democratic one. But by the end of it, it had no less unmistakably evolved into a very different sub-type; and it had done so in not one but two distinguishable stages. Early-Victorian society is still a transitional sub-type in which the legitimacy of industrial capitalism as a mode of production is by no means unquestioned and a mode of coercion resting on universal suffrage virtually unthinkable. Mid-Victorian society, aptly labelled 'the age of equipoise' (Burn 1964), is one in which capital and labour have come to terms within a restricted franchise and an ideology of individualism and self-help. Late-Victorian and Edwardian society is one in which both capital and labour are organized in new forms under the ideology of something now visibly more intrusive than a 'night-watchman' state. So summary an account is, inevitably, an oversimplification: government did on occasion intervene in the economy even during the 'early-Victorian' period; the ideology of individualism was not unchallenged in the 'mid-Victorian' period; and the 'late-Victorian and Edwardian' period, for all that it brought independent working-class representation in Parliament, turned out to retain enough of a still recognizable mid-Victorian ideology for the Liberal Party to triumph at the polls in 1906 on what was, for all the emphasis on welfare reform, still a recognizably traditional anti-Conservative programme of peace and free trade. But on any theory, the changes which took place between the death of William IV and the death of Edward VII were both too protracted and too complex to be reported in terms of a single uniform 'Victorian' stage in the evolution of English society.

During the two transitions, the mutant practices of most immediate relevance to the mode of the distribution of power were those which defined the changing roles of the politically and ideologically dominant owners of the means of production on the one hand and the unenfranchised and under-educated vendors of their labour on the other. The early-Victorian working class, to the limited extent that it was a self-conscious systact united by awareness of a common interest, was more artisan than proletarian and more Jacobin than Socialist. The period which culminated in the final Chartist demonstration in 1848 is one whose interpretation continues to be debated among historians. But by 1851, when working-class families from the Midlands were coming by excursion trains organized by Thomas Cook to the Crystal Palace for the 'shilling days' at the Great Exhibition, observers of all persuasions were voicing a sense that English society was moving into a period of greater economic affluence, ideological harmony, and political order. Parliament was becoming, however hesitantly, the arbiter between contending systactic interests rather than simply the servant of the roles to which economic, ideological, and coercive power traditionally attached. Real wages were beginning to move upwards; hours of work were beginning to come down; and the working conditions of women and children, from whose labour much of the national product continued to be derived, were beginning at least marginally to improve.

Yet this new institutional equilibrium, stable as it might appear, did not remain unchanged for long. Selective pressures were at work which were undermining the role of the respectable artisan at the same time as furthering the interests of the unskilled. Organizational and technological changes were compelling employers to modify their relations with one another as well as with their employees. The growing need for administrative and clerical workers was creating a burgeoning lower-middle class in the service of both commerce and government. Leisure, and the various uses to which a higher proportion of the occupied workforce were now in a position to put it, was favouring new practices and the roles defined by them at the same time as enlarging the scope of existing ones. The Church of England was beginning to lose its traditional power to define the terms of moral and political debate. The functions of local as well as national government were continuing to expand. Extension of the franchise was becoming more and more obviously inescapable. The balance between industry and agriculture was tilting further and further towards industry. The choice of a date to mark the transition to 'late-Victorian and Edwardian' society is bound to be arguable. But in the economic dimension, 1880 was the year after which 'world economic forces compelled manufacturers, if they were to remain competitive, to press ahead with rationalization and speed up' (Meacham 1977, p. 139);[25] in the ideological dimension, it was the year that the 'New Journalism' was ushered in by George Newnes's *Tit-Bits* 'to catch the new popularly educated classes' (Thomson 1950, p. 176); and in the political dimension it was the year of a General Election 'which may, with some justification, be regarded as the first modern election' (Pugh 1982, p. 1).[26] By the mid-1880s, at the very latest, no observer could question that both the structure and the culture of English society were qualitatively different from a generation before.

This evolution of the central institutions of the late-Victorian and Edwardian out of the mid-Victorian sub-type of capitalist liberal democracy offers a telling

[25] It is worth noting too that the term 'unemployed' first gains currency in the early 1880s. The mid-Victorian term for unemployment had been 'casual distress' (Hennock 1976, p. 77).

[26] Equally symbolic of the change from the mid-Victorian sub-type of the mode of coercion was the creation of the role of Director of Public Prosecutions in 1879.

reminder, if one is needed, that the emergence by way of mutant or recombinant practices of novel roles and consequent changes in the systactic structure is a two-sided process. Workmen had been combining against their employers for many generations before the legislation of 1875. But that legislation, although enacted by a Conservative government, enhanced the status of trade unions and increased the power attaching to the roles of their officials in a way which increasingly favoured the new set of practices through which the vendors of their labour bargained with the employers to whom it was being sold. The Employers and Workmen Act which replaced the previous Master and Servant Act, together with the Conspiracy and Protection of Property Act which removed collective action in furtherance of a trade dispute from the scope of the law of criminal conspiracy, implied a change in the distribution of power which no employer could ignore. All that employers could do – and from the 1880s onwards did – was to respond to the increasing strength of organized labour by an increasing associational solidarity of their own: by 1914, the number of employers' organizations had risen to 1,487 (Garside and Gospel 1982, p. 104). They might not be seeking to destroy the unions, but they had no choice but to resist them as best they could. Both sides, accordingly, found themselves moving steadily towards the late-Victorian and Edwardian system of collective bargaining for which ministers and officials, for their part, found themselves holding the ring.

The working-class child who entered his or her first adult role at the turn of the century thereby entered a very different institutional environment from a generation before. Urban industrial workers were now more and more likely to be the children of urban industrial workers and more and more likely to remain urban industrial workers for the rest of their lives. If they were skilled men in regular work, their wages were now high enough to generate some modest surplus beyond what was needed to feed, clothe, and house themselves and their families. But any accumulation of capital was still virtually impossible, and that surplus, even if not all spent on recreation, or drink, or tobacco, or the small luxuries of a decorated front parlour or a Sunday suit of clothes, was always vulnerable to sickness or accident or a downturn in trade. As I remarked in section 6, even in 1911 only a small minority of men and a tiny minority of women were trade-union members, and even in the upsurge of 'new' unionism in the late 1880s there had been only $1\frac{1}{2}$ million trade unionists, at most, out of a workforce some eight times that number. But the norms of the now established working-class culture were, while still personally individualist, collectively defensive to a perceptibly greater degree. When unemployment was low, trade profitable, and employers therefore susceptible to pressure, groups of workers could and did successfully combine to withhold their labour in pursuit of better pay; and if they felt threatened by wage-cuts (or falling real

wages), or dilution of their skills, or withdrawal of their accustomed perqui-
sites, their combinations, whether successful or not, might take a militant and
even violent form. Yet this was far from being the relative deprivation of an
organized proletariat consciously seeking the overthrow of industrial capitalism. The aims of the overwhelming majority of industrial workers were the
protection of their earnings and their jobs, some small but sustained improvement in their conditions, and savings sufficient (with perhaps the help of a club
or friendly society) to avoid destitution in old age.

At the same time, however, as the late-Victorian and Edwardian working
class developed some greater degree of common systactic consciousness, it
began to be incorporated, ideologically as well as politically, into the institutions
of the dominant élite. The Education Act of 1870, which effectively ensured
that all children up to the age of thirteen attended *a* school,[27] is from this
perspective no less significant than the trade-union legislation of 1875. It had
not merely the immediate effect of dragging some hundreds of thousands of
street urchins into the classroom but also the longer-term effect of bringing a
small but important number of trade unionists, and also of women, onto local
school boards, Poor Law boards, and rural and borough councils. It could
hardly be called a revolution. But it is a revealing symptom of the way in which
the representatives of organized labour were being accorded the measure of
both social prestige and political influence which followed from their admission
to other and hitherto middle-class roles. No less remarkable than the incumbency of national political roles by 'working men' in the late-Victorian and
Edwardian period is their acceptance in local politics. If we look beyond the
1884 Reform Act and the Local Government Act of 1888 to 1910, we find 77
members of the National Union of Boot and Shoe Operatives occupying no
less than 85 official roles – 5 magistrates, 2 aldermen, 13 town councillors, 27
urban district councillors, 1 county councillor, 10 rural district councillors, 20
poor law guardians, 1 school board member, 2 borough auditors, 3 co-opted
members of education committees and 1 Board of Trade commissioner.[28] It

---

[27] Strictly, it was not until the novel role of attendance officer had become established and local
school boards had taken up the powers now entrusted to them that attendance can accurately be
reported as compulsory. But 1870 also marks a tiny but symptomatic mutation of practice at the
opposite end of the educational scale: it was the last year in which, at Oxford, undergraduates of
noble birth wore golden tassels ('tufts') on their caps. And it is the year which saw the first
conference of the National Union of Teachers.

[28] Fox (1983, p. 267), drawing on his own history of the Boot and Shoe Operatives published in
1958. John Burns, in the 1912 franchise debate, reminded his listeners that 'over a thousand
Members of Parliament, Aldermen, Councillors, Magistrates and Privy Councillors are men
who have either been artisans or labourers in their early days' (Hansard 5th Ser. H. C. Deb. 40
c.2119).

might be objected that incumbents like these of roles like these were unrepresentative of the working class as a whole: not only were they a tiny minority of it, but the rank and file were far less disposed to accommodate to the system than the reformist leaders of the old craft unions. But their representativeness or otherwise is not what matters in the evolution of the society's modes of production, persuasion, and coercion; what matters is the mutation of practices whereby, in the late-Victorian and Edwardian period, working-class people began to be actively welcomed into the institutions of the state.

The institutional environment as it had by then evolved was not one within which the relations between roles and systacts looked to any contemporary observer likely to remain exactly as they were. None expected either the structure or the culture of English society to reproduce itself unchanged in the generation after theirs; and some predicted that its central institutions would prove fatally incapable of adapting to the pressures which would be imposed on them. But it was, as we can see more clearly than they, much more probable than not that the mode of the distribution of power would remain, even if in a modified form, capitalist, liberal, and democratic. In this sense, and to this extent, Disraeli's often-quoted remark to Hyndman can stand as an epigraph for the 'Victorian' legacy as a whole: 'It is a very difficult country to move, Mr. Hyndman, a very difficult country indeed.'

§14. Can it then be said of English society as bequeathed by Queen Victoria to Edward VII in 1901 that it was not merely capitalist, liberal, and democratic but 'bourgeois' *tout court*? It had long been so in the sense that despite its continued preservation of a monarchy, England was not and never had been an absolutist monarchy but an oligarchy in which a powerful commercial systact coexisted on equal, or near-equal, terms with a landed aristocracy. But if that is all that the term denotes, there is little purpose in invoking it. Its value here lies rather in conveying the sense of what it felt like, in the descriptive overtones of domesticity, respectability, an almost religious concern for the sanctity of private property, a self-conscious repudiation of extremes in either thought or conduct, a commitment to formal liberty combined with a horror of 'licence', an insistent celebration of the virtues of honesty and diligence, and an unabashed acceptance of the image of England as a 'nation of shopkeepers'.

It was not as if English society as a whole could authentically be described as 'middle-class'. It was, rather, that 'bourgeois' practices and attitudes pervaded, albeit in different forms, almost every systact and milieu. Queen Victoria herself, however far out of sympathy with the changing circumstances of her people, was almost quintessentially bourgeois in her deportment and attitudes,[29] as were the trade unionists who drove Engels, writing to Sorge in December of 1889, to complain that 'The most repulsive thing here is the bourgeois "respectability" bred into the bones of the workers.' Of course there were exceptions, ranging from die-hard peers to *fin-de-siècle* bohemians to militant socialists to 'lumpen'-proletarians of a defiantly unrespectable kind. But they were exceptions within a culture to which the term bourgeois attaches almost, as it were, of its own accord.

This applies not least to late-Victorian and Edwardian England's particular version of 'bourgeois' democracy – a democracy in which all women and well over a third of men were still denied the vote. It was a democracy for the freeholder, the ratepayer, and the settled, not the casual, working man: not only recipients of poor relief, domestic tenants, and sons living with their parents were excluded but also electors qualifying under the household franchise who had not been in possession for twelve months before registering. It was intended only to represent men of some property and (if possible) some education to go with it. Its constituency boundaries favoured the Conservative interest, especially in the strongholds of 'villa Toryism'. It offered little or no electoral foothold for the carriers of the practices of socialism unless this were defined in such a way as would have been as acceptable to John Stuart Mill as to Keir Hardie. It is true that the founders of the ILP in 1893 saw the achievement of socialism as their ultimate goal, that committed socialists were active in both municipal and trade-union politics, that the writings of Blatchford, William Morris, and the Webbs had done much to make socialism intellectually respectable on ethical as well as 'scientific' grounds, and that a group of rebels against Hyndman's leadership of the Social Democratic Federation formed a breakaway Socialist Labour Party in 1903. But no thoroughgoing socialist faction ever acquired sufficient power within either the industrial or the political wing of the Labour movement to deflect it away from the constitutional pursuit of the sectional interests of its members. The function of the roles of the Labour members of the House of Commons was to further the interests of labour – which meant organized labour – by bringing parliamentary pressure to bear, just as the function of trade-union officials was to secure what advantages they could for their members within the now established institution of collective bargaining (and to confirm their own incumbency of their roles in the process). The

---

[29] Witness her obstinate refusal to wear her crown and robes at her own Golden Jubilee, as well as her conventional domesticity, her obsessive dependence on the memory of the Prince Consort, and her exclusion from her court until 1887 of even the innocent party to a divorce. It has been well said that life at Balmoral (where chess might be played on Sunday, but not cards) was more like life at Broadstairs than either was like life at Versailles. Cf. Henry Adams: 'The taste of Louis Philippe was *bourgeois* beyond any taste except that of Queen Victoria' (1946, p. 195).

legitimacy of 'bourgeois' democracy was as effectively conceded by the one as the legitimacy of 'bourgeois' property rights by the other. Nor were either of them likely to be under any illusions about securing sufficient working-class support either to vote a committed anti-parliamentary Socialist into the House of Commons[30] or to mount an effective strike directed to political rather than industrial ends.

It would, nonetheless, be a serious inaccuracy to report the roles of the manual workers of 1900 as defined by a common set of practices and related norms and values shared with the clerks, salesmen, shopkeepers, technicians, schoolteachers, managers, and small proprietors of the late-Victorian and Edwardian middle class. But the late-Victorian and Edwardian working-class culture was a sub-culture, not a counter-culture. The music hall, the brass band, the public bar, and the association football match were divided by a gulf as wide as it was deep from the 'legitimate' stage, the classical concert, the hotel lounge, and the tennis club. Both, however, involved a commitment to forms of sociability as carefully ritualized and reliably conformist as each other. Middle-class reformers who vainly sought to cajole or harangue the working classes into habits of thrift, temperance, and 'useful hobbies' consistently failed to recognize not only that the material circumstances of working-class life could not fail to give rise to an outlook radically different from their own but also that, for example, the possession of a bar in working men's clubs was of itself an important and valued symbol of independence from aristocratic or ecclesiastical interference (Stedman Jones 1983, p. 198 n.44). Yet within that other institutional catchment area, ideological ranking of roles was no less clearly discernible. The difference between the two can (as I pointed out in section 14 of the opening chapter of volume I) be viewed in a very different light, depending on what your own evaluative presuppositions may happen to be. From one perfectly coherent standpoint, it was not merely foolish but wrong for middle-class observers to assume that working-class people ought, ostensibly for their own sake, to be converted to middle-class practices. But any account, whether explanatory, descriptive, or evaluative in purpose, has to begin by recognizing as a matter of straightforward reportage how large a difference it was.

This said, the practices defining the roles of the English working classes at

---

[30] Victor Grayson, narrowly elected for Colne Valley in a three-way by-election in 1907 as the ILP candidate in defiance of the Labour Party, is an exception of a kind. But his subsequent career and disappearance is as much a symbol of the long-term ineffectiveness of anti-parliamentary Socialism as of the short-term appeal of eloquent advocacy on behalf of the underprivileged in its name. He was pushed into third place in the General Election of January 1910; and some commentators on the Left in any case interpreted the 1907 result as a victory for Labour rather than Socialism (Pelling 1968, p. 144).

the turn of the century can still, albeit in their different way, be labelled 'bourgeois' too.[31] By this I mean not that manual workers and their families were secretly aspiring to be absorbed into the middle class, but that their own way of life rested no less firmly on a commitment to the central institution of private property and a tacit acceptance of the dominant ideology of individualism. The fact that certain forms of collective organization and the attitudes which went with them were imposed on many of them by the division and specialization of labour did not mean that their domestic lives were governed by other than the desire to preserve what they could of individual amenities and opportunities for their families and themselves. The fluctuations and uncertainties of working-class incomes made 'thrift' on the middle-class model unattractive as well as unrealistic for all except the minority of artisans whose steady earnings enabled them to think in terms of home-ownership, an account with a Trustee Savings Bank, and perhaps even a private annuity. For many more late-Victorian and Edwardian wage-earners, faced as they were with a continuing struggle to cover immediate outgoings and a constant risk of interruptions in income, it was not the savings bank but the pawnshop – supplemented, where possible, by credit from the local tradesman – around which the weekly budget revolved. But the household possessions whose apparently irresponsible purchase, pawn, and repurchase was so often criticized by middle-class observers were symbols not simply of conspicuous consumption but also of a version of thrift. Sunday clothes, which I have instanced already as a near-standard item of purchase for families where a small surplus of revenue over outgoings was achieved, might have to be pledged on a Monday morning in order to pay the rent. But, regular as the recourse to the pawnshop might be, it was, except in times where the entire community was in particular hardship, a matter of shame. However widespread the practice, loss of prestige was involved, and secrecy was, so far as possible, sought.[32] It is a nice anthropological question how much more social esteem might be gained by the wearing of Sunday clothes than might be lost by being seen to have to pawn them. But whatever the answer, if this is not, in a descriptively authentic use of the term, a 'bourgeois' norm, it is hard to know what is.

The same holds equally of the near-universal custom of saving to avoid a pauper's funeral, on which the comments of Charles Booth at the turn of the

---

[31] Notably in the friendly societies, by which 'Individualistic middle-class values such as sobriety, self-help, and thrift were appropriated, redefined, and deployed in collective contexts' (Cordery 1995, p. 41).

[32] Johnson (1983b, p. 155) quotes the testimony of a pawnbroker's assistant to the Select Committee of 1870 to the effect that 'the person who visits the pawnbroker has a great degree of shame, and does not want to be seen'. Hence the discreetly placed entrances, the false names often given, and the ambivalent jokes.

century are echoed in near-identical terms a generation later by the Pilgrim Trust researchers whose study of *Men Without Work* was published in 1938. Here too, no doubt, there was an element of conspicuous consumption in the display of the coffin in the (normally unused) front parlour, the 'splash' on food and drink, and the cost of the carriage drawn by horses in plumes. Nor was the cost of burial insurance, with its built-in overheads and penalty for default, justifiable by middle-class standards of 'rational' budgeting.[33] But it is unarguable testimony to the hold of the ideology of independence and respectability and the stigma attached by it to a pauper's burial. 'Rattle his bones Over the stones, He's only a pauper Whom nobody owns.' Whatever the resentment and hostility which the Victorian Poor Law had aroused (and which numbers of middle-class commentators had shared), the criterion of status which it implied was in this way tacitly acknowledged by the overwhelming majority of working-class people.

Exceptions there were, as I have conceded already. But they were exceptions peripheral to the culture of the central institutions of English society. The Highland crofter might be as impervious to that culture as the Irish navvy, and its catchment area might fall equally far short of the middle-class rebel as of the working-class vagrant. But these were deviants from a set of norms of private property and individual self-esteem not only strongly entrenched but widely spread. The different sub-cultural forms which it took might vary by region, ethnicity, and gender as well as by class. But socialist ideas of collective ownership were as alien to it on one side as authoritarian ideas of collective discipline on the other. Engels was right. Late-Victorian and Edwardian England *was* a 'bourgeois' society, like it or not as you please.

§15. But if the culture of late-Victorian and Edwardian English society was unequivocally 'bourgeois', what can be said of its systactic structure? It was the outcome of selective pressures both endogenous and exogenous which had, as we have seen, changed it almost out of recognition in all three dimensions from what it had been at the time of the First Reform Bill and the early debates over the factory system. Almost, but not quite. A boy or girl born in commercial-aristocratic-oligarchic Georgian England who had lived through the loss of the American colonies, the emergence and repression of English Jacobinism, the long wars against Napoleon's France, and the struggle of organized labour and its allies for the repeal of the Combination Acts, would no doubt have been astonished to be confronted by such novel roles as the Lib.-Lab. miners' MP, the female trade unionist, the Board of Trade conciliator or, come to that, the

---

[33] As could be, and frequently was, also said of working-class gambling. But in the face of the occasional splendid windfall and the interest and excitement generated even without it, what credibility had middle-class admonishment got (McKibbin 1990, chapter 4)?

professional football player and the fish-and-chip shop proprietor. But such a person would recognize at once the high prestige of the landed aristocracy, the affluence of the mercantile and professional classes, the arduous working conditions of the miners, dockworkers, seamen, quarriers, and agricultural labourers, the ubiquity of resident domestic servants in the houses of even the modestly rich, and the teeming presence in certain parts of London, above all, of the poor 'who are always with us'.

If, as I argued in volume II, the most useful approach to the structure of any but very small and simple societies is to divide them initially into four broadly distinguishable systacts, then it is sensible to begin by characterizing first, the élite; second, the administrative or 'service' class; third, the general body of wage-workers without either access to or control of the means of production or marketable professional skills; and fourth, the un- or under-employed 'casual' labourers, the semi- or more than semi-criminals and the destitute. As always, the distinction needs to be qualified by the further distinction between the economic, ideological, and coercive forms of power and therefore dimensions of the society's structure. But it will serve well enough as a starting-point for the comparisons to follow, and it can be allowed, except where there is evidence to show otherwise, to presuppose that at the turn of the century the majority of English women should be accorded 'secondary' rank in accordance with the role of their husband or other male household head.[34]

By then, the landed aristocracy and the newer class of urban financial and industrial capitalists had more or less fused into what was coming to be called a single 'plutocracy'. The old conflict between the agricultural and mercantile interests was largely a thing of the past; the roles of landowner and urban capitalist were coming increasingly to be occupied by the same incumbents; and the different sources of the wealth of the richest few families were less and less relevant to their common life-styles, mores, and outlook. This systact, comprising less than 1 per cent of the total population, was not only a dominant class but a status-group acknowledged as standing second only to the royal family itself in the hierarchy of deference, some of whose members still enjoyed much indirect political influence (and a few still occupied ministerial roles in the government of the day, whether Conservative or Liberal).

[34] This is not to deny the importance of the changes which differentiated the position of middle-class women from what it had been in the mid-Victorian period, including not only the Married Women's Property Acts but the establishment of women's organizations and involvement of women in canvassing in parliamentary elections by both the major political parties (Hollis 1987, p. 55). The campaign against the Contagious Diseases Acts 'shattered the convention that it was dangerous and improper for a woman to speak in public, even upon such subjects as venereal disease and the vaginal inspection of prostitutes' (J. Harris 1993, p. 24). By the 1890s, perhaps as many as half a million women were 'continually and semi-professionally' involved in voluntary activities (Thane 1988, p. 190).

Below this élite, there were some 10 per cent to 15 per cent of households the roles of whose members belonged to a 'middle class' which was, however, expanding all the time as the number of clerical, administrative, and professional roles which needed to be filled continued to increase (and, in a small but increasing number of cases, to be open to women as well as men). These households were almost all employers of at least one resident domestic servant. But the poorest of them, where the household head was a junior clerk, or shop assistant, or small proprietor, were distinguished from the better-off 'working' class by the gentility of their life-style and the relative security of their employment rather than by any marked difference in income; and the richest of them, whose male heads were the barristers, stockbrokers, joint-stock company directors, high-feed doctors or surgeons, and a handful of senior civil servants, were distinguishable as both a class and a status-group from the lower-ranked professionals, farmers, managers, shopkeepers, administrators, engineers, teachers, journalists, officials, and clergy.

The 'working' class, to which over three-quarters of households belonged, was also far from homogeneous. There were the artisans, the semi-skilled operatives, and the unskilled labourers. But even the artisan owning the tools of his trade was vulnerable to the cycles of boom and recession; 'skill' was becoming less a matter of abilities which could only be inculcated through training and experience than of restrictions on entry into relatively better-paid or more specialized or autonomous forms of manual labour; and many men moved up this hierarchy and down it again over the course of their working lives.[35] It is true that many 'skilled' workers were well aware of the differences in life-style between themselves and the less respectable, and that many of them, including the leaders and officials of the old craft unions, were politically conservative as well. But any talk of them as an 'aristocracy of labour' has to be carefully qualified (Harrison and Zeitlin 1985). In the first place, they were by no means always more securely employed or more consistently highly paid than many of the less 'skilled'; in the second, they were far from exclusive in their social contacts with, and their attitudes towards, those alongside whom they worked (Penn 1984, Part III); and in the third, they could just as well be found on the side of radical as of conservative political factions. Although there might be individual late-Victorian and Edwardian trade unionists for whom the pre-emptive implications of the term 'aristocracy' were descriptively apt, there was no clearly identifiable systact to which it can be applied as such.

[35] Lady Bell (1907, p. 109) noticed how many ironworkers employed in her husband's works in Middlesbrough ended their working lives doing labourer's jobs for perhaps half of what they had been able to earn in their prime; and the same was true on the railways for drivers and footplatemen whose health began to fail or whose eyesight was no longer adequate (F. McKenna 1976, p. 32).

Among the poorest households, there were likewise significant distinctions to be drawn. Indeed, the difference between the respectable and unrespectable was fundamental here, since the roles which implied an honest day's work if only it was available were categorically different from roles whose incumbents had no intention of doing anything of the kind. The observer who penetrated the alleys, courts, and rookeries of the slums of the major cities would find them inhabited on the one hand by itinerant casual labourers, odd-job men, rag-pickers, street vendors, washerwomen, and part-time domestic outworkers (together with a sprinkling of failed or disgraced attorneys, shopkeepers, clerks, or clerics who had seen better days), and on the other hand by house-breakers, 'mobsmen', pickpockets, fences, brothel-keepers, professional beggars, and fugitives from justice. In neither case can they be credited with a systactic consciousness out of which they might act cooperatively in pursuit of a perceived common interest. But they constituted a cluster of roles located very near to the lowest point on the axes of economic, ideological, and political power alike. The professional criminal might, to be sure, enjoy at least momentarily a considerable affluence, the esteem of his peers, and the service of followers ready to use violence on his behalf. But there was no organized gangsterism of a kind which could have created a mafia-like corporation with its own internal hierarchy and its part-cooperative, part-antagonistic relations with the government and the police. The total number of the underclass[36] in the late-Victorian and Edwardian period cannot be accurately calculated; but to talk of a 'submerged tenth' is probably as good a guess as any.

Both within and between the four broad systactic categories, there was a certain amount of individual social mobility, both inter- and intra-generational. But much of it was lateral rather than vertical. The member of a landed family who joined the Indian Civil Service, the manufacturer's son who opted for a professional rather than a business career, the otherwise home-bound daughter of a clerk or salesman who became a nurse or stenographer, and the agricultural labourer who moved into building or factory work did not thereby cross a systactic boundary. There were a few spectacular cases of long-distance upward mobility; there was a good deal of intra-generational mobility both ways, and inter-generational mobility upwards, across the boundary between the top of the 'working' and the bottom of the 'middle' class; there were

---

[36] The term is one only to be used if very clearly free of evaluative overtones and particularly any implication that its members must be in it through their own fault (Gallie and Marsh 1993, p. 28). In this volume, it denotes those roles whose incumbents are both excluded from the formal labour market and without private means of support: it thus includes those whose only employment, if any, is informal but not those whose formal employment is interrupted even by lengthy and/or successive periods out of work. The 'long-term' unemployed of the 1980s, as of the 1930s, are 'not so much stable members of an underclass as unstable members of the working class' (Buck 1992, p. 19).

women in all systacts who rose by marrying men of higher rank than their fathers; and there were 'skidders' who through indolence, mismanagement, or ill luck fell as far and as fast as others were rising. But the great majority of English men and women reaching adulthood at the turn of the century were destined to spend the rest of their lives in their systact of origin.

In that sense, the society of late-Victorian and Edwardian England can accurately be reported as 'stratified'. But its constituent systacts cannot strictly be called strata, if a stratum is defined (as in section 6 of chapter 1 in volume II) as consisting of roles which are both self-reproducing and consistently ranked across the three dimensions of social structure. Careers like those of F. E. Smith in the Conservative and John Burns in the Liberal Party, however unusual, are still testimony to the permeability of the élite; and however useful the contacts and connections available to those who could display the 'old school tie', they were not a guarantee against *déclassement*. Nor did attainment of higher rank in any one of the three dimensions of social structure lead automatically to equivalent rank in the other two. This was, accordingly, a structure in which the incumbents of roles at all systactic levels might experience a distinct sense of relative deprivation either individually or collectively or both. On the one hand, mobility was sufficiently possible, and sufficiently visibly possible, to encourage the ambitious member of a lower-ranked systact to rise out of it rather than with it. But on the other, it was sufficiently rare to reinforce the attitudes of those who held that the remedy for the inequalities of power which they perceived around them was a collective diminution of the social distance separating one systact from the next.

§16. There remains one final aspect of the 'Victorian' legacy which I have thus far touched on only in passing, but which is relevant to the general theme of this volume as well as to the particular concerns of chapter 5. 1901 was also the year of the publication of Benjamin Seebohm Rowntree's *Poverty, a Study of Town Life*. It was not the first systematic study of the condition of the urban poor, about which public concern mounted steadily during the 1880s; the first volume of Charles Booth's monumental *Life and Labour of the People in London* had been published in 1889 and the seventeenth and last was to appear in 1903. But Rowntree's study of York was to be the more influential. Its most widely quoted paragraph, in which he expounds his 'poverty line' of 21s 8d per week for a family of five, merits reproduction in full:

> A family living upon the scale allowed for in this estimate must never spend a penny on railway fare or omnibus. They must never go into the country unless they walk. They must never purchase a half-penny newspaper or spend a penny to buy a ticket for a popular concert. They must write no letters to absent children, for they cannot afford to pay the postage. They must never contribute

anything to their church or chapel, or give any help to a neighbour which costs them money. They cannot save, nor can they join a sick club or Trade Union, because they cannot pay the necessary subscriptions. The children must have no pocket money for dolls, marbles or sweets. The father must smoke no tobacco and must drink no beer. The mother must never buy any pretty clothes for herself or for her children, the character of the family wardrobe as for the family diet being governed by the regulation, 'Nothing must be bought but that which is absolutely necessary for the maintenance of physical health, and what must be bought must be of the plainest description.' Should a child fall ill, it must be attended by the parish doctor: should it die, it must be buried by the parish. Finally, the wage earner must never be absent from his work for a single day.
(pp. 133-4)

This was the condition in which Rowntree claimed that a not insignificant minority of working-class families in York were living; and one of his reasons for choosing York, apart from his own connection with it, had been that Booth's study had been restricted to the East End of London where it was well known that a long-standing 'problem of poverty' existed. Moreover, Rowntree's findings appeared less vulnerable to criticism than Booth's because of his choice of a measure which, being based on physical efficiency, could therefore be presented as 'scientific'.[37] The 'poverty line', and the associated concept of 'primary' as opposed to 'secondary' poverty, did still generate considerable controversy, not all of it from readers disposed to resist the conclusions which Rowntree had drawn. But it placed the burden of the argument on those who wished to maintain that poverty was attributable solely to the improvidence of the poor rather than to the inadequacy of wages relative to the inescapable costs of maintaining a family; and it carried the obvious implication – as acceptable to 'New Liberals' as it was unacceptable to most if not all of the members of the Charity Organization Society – that the solution must lie in the hands of the state.[38]

This was not, in one sense, a novel conclusion. It was, after all, the problem of dealing with the 'able-bodied' poor which had led to the substitution of the New Poor Law for the old system of parochial relief – a substitution avowedly

---

[37] Not that it really was: minimum dietary needs *could* have been met with perhaps half the expenditure on food which Rowntree allowed (Johnson 1988, p. 31). Nor was his estimate of the extent of poverty in York related as it should have been to accurate information about family incomes (Hennock 1991, p. 194).

[38] The difference between the late-Victorian and Edwardian period and the decades after the First World War is strikingly illustrated by the fact that 'As late as 1911, the gross annual receipts of registered charities exceeded public expenditure on the poor law – a figure that takes no account of unregistered charities nor of such bastions of voluntarism as friendly societies, trade unions and other forms of institutional self-help' (J. Harris 1990, p. 68). Seen from the voluntarists' point of view, the period from 1880 to 1914 'witnessed the emergence of issues and ideas which, while presenting opportunities for a continuing role for voluntary social endeavour of various kinds, also presented a challenge to that endeavour' (Finlayson 1994, p. 198).

engineered in the cause of free employment at market wages for those who would seek it and subsistence in the workhouse for those who would not. But between the early-Victorian and the late-Victorian and Edwardian periods, the question had been stood on its head: 'where earlier it had been assumed that the deserving poor were deserving because they were not a social problem and therefore did not require the assistance of society, now it was assumed that the deserving poor were a social problem requiring assistance precisely because they were deserving' (Himmelfarb 1984, pp. 530–1). The Liberal government's Old Age Pensions Act of 1908 and National Insurance Act of 1911 were carefully limited in scope,[39] and they carried an implicit (or, for the pensioners, explicit) justification by desert rather than need; but at the same time, they opened the way to a recognition that those who could not, despite their own best efforts, maintain themselves and their dependants through periods of unemployment and sickness into old age were entitled as of right to look to the state for help. The antecedents of these measures were complex, and their longer-term consequences unpredicted and unplanned. So far as a motivational explanation is concerned, they were inspired as much by the example of Germany and the need to outflank the Left as by a recognition of the logical merits of the philanthropic case. But as always in social evolution, it is not the origin of a mutation of practices which counts, but its subsequent function. A principle had been accepted and a precedent set which thereafter differentiated the 'new' Liberalism from the 'old'; and after the First World War it was the 'new' which came to dominate social policy despite the fact that some of the most influential carriers of its doctrines and practices operated outside of the Liberal Party itself. So familiar has this principle become that it is not always easy to recall how controversial as well as how limited it was in the late-Victorian and Edwardian period. That the state had some obligation to the destitute might, if as loosely phrased as this, be a proposition acceptable to all but the most extreme 'Social Darwinists'. But ought not insurance against sickness to be a matter of private arrangement rather than collective provision? Is there not a duty for individuals and families to set aside what they need for their maintenance in old age? And when the state, in the Education (Provision of Meals) Act 1906, goes so far as to start feeding school children, is this not – as Dicey, for one, quite explicitly argued – licensing parental irresponsibility out of the public purse? In the event, these questions remained, as I have phrased them, rhetorical. But the implied concern that the improvident should not benefit from their improvidence at the taxpayer's expense was a serious one. The Webbs' 'enforced minimum' of civilized life would, as they

---

[39] The Rowntrees themselves had established a company pension scheme in 1906 which much more closely anticipated the practices which were later to be regarded as normal (Briggs 1961, pp. 100–2).

themselves recognized, involve a higher level of personal taxation than otherwise; it could not simply be assumed that an adequate surplus for the purpose would be generated out of a continuous expansion of trade. Was there not, then, a risk not merely that improvidence would be rewarded undeservedly but also that the institution of private property would itself come under threat?

Such fears were to prove groundless, however. In the years after the First World War, the concept of the 'minimum' did, it is true, broaden to include not merely a pension in old age and 'uncovenanted' unemployment benefit, but a decent house or flat to live in, an adequate standard of medical care, and a proper education of some kind for every child. But the egalitarian implications were extremely modest, and the sanctity of private property remained untouched. Not even the Webbs envisaged that those who had accumulated significant wealth, or inherited it from those who had, should be deprived of it in order that the minimum should be raised *per capita* by whatever the mechanism of expropriation might allow. Nor did they ever envisage that the needy, however deserving, should themselves control the allocation of the resources redistributed to them. Fabian Socialism, just as much as either 'New' Liberalism or 'Birmingham' Toryism, viewed the aim of social policy as the doing of good to the underprivileged as the doers might choose to define it, not as it might be defined by those to whom it was being done. Taxation did in due course rise to heights which even the Webbs would, before the First World War, have regarded as punitive, and the break with the assumptions of the 'old', mid-Victorian, Liberalism did, indeed, turn out to be irreversible after it. But whatever the hopes and fears of the supporters or opponents of what replaced it, the mutant practices incorporated in the inter-war legislation and consummated in the legislation of 1946 to 1948 were at least as far from the ideology of egalitarian socialism as they were from that of Gladstone and Samuel Smiles. Yet again, we are dealing with symptoms of a different sub-type, but not mode, of the distribution of power.

CONCLUSION

§17. This, then, is the starting-point from which the changes (or lack of them) in the capitalist mode of production, liberal mode of persuasion, and democratic mode of coercion of twentieth-century English society will first be reported and then explained, described, and evaluated. The terms in which its evolution out of the late-Victorian and Edwardian sub-type of the capitalist-liberal-democratic mode is reported are theory-neutral (but not, of course, presuppositionless) in the sense expounded in volume I. Chapter 2 of this volume, in other words, is based on empirical observations which are in principle verifiable by reference to the recording angel's archives without in any way pre-empting the explanation of why this and not some other evolution took place or the description of what it was like for those English people who lived through it – let alone the answer to the question whether it turned out to be a good thing or a bad thing from the viewpoint of those people themselves. But they have at the same time been chosen for reportage with a preconceived purpose. They are not what would necessarily be reported by a visitor from outer space (whatever that might imply) or even by a trained sociologist from a different culture. The observer whom they presuppose is exclusively interested in the distribution of the means of production, persuasion, and coercion among the roles by whose itemization English society at the beginning and end of the period in question is defined, and in the movement of roles and their incumbents in the three separate dimensions of structure which correspond to the economic, ideological, and political forms of power.

CHAPTER TWO

The case reported

THE PATTERN OF ROLES

§1. Once given that twentieth-century English society, like any other, is to be reported in terms of the itemization of its constituent roles, observers of all theoretical schools should be able to agree in broad terms on what these roles and their defining practices actually are at any given time. They will, no doubt, disagree about why they have changed (or not) as they have, what the changes have been like for their representative incumbents, and whether the evolution of a different pattern of roles would have been better or worse from the incumbents' own (or anyone else's) point of view. Nor will they agree about the precise amount of economic, ideological, or coercive power attaching to any particular role, or about the precise delineation of the boundary between one systact and another, or about the precise date at which the evolution from one to another mode or sub-type of production, persuasion, or coercion can be said to have taken place. But the evidence for the assertion that English society as it had been since approximately 1880 evolved during the First World War and its aftermath into an unmistakably different sub-type of the capitalist mode of production, liberal mode of persuasion, and democratic mode of coercion is there for all to see.

This is not to deny that the itemization of roles may involve methodological difficulties of the kind discussed at length in volume I. But the more intractable of them have little application to the kind of evidence which it is the purpose of this chapter to report. Some statistics may be unreliable, some informants untruthful, some behaviour ambiguous or contradictory, and some aspects of the performance of some roles inaccessible to observation. But most English people have a clear idea of what they do, institutionally speaking, and few of them will deliberately misreport it. Some will, of course: criminals are unlikely to represent themselves as such to the census enumerators, rich businessmen usually understate (but sometimes overstate) their income and wealth, people of high as well as low ascriptive status are quite capable of deliberately disowning it, and politicians and civil servants are equally capable of exaggerating or downplaying the power attaching to their roles. But the hypothetical observer whom I introduced in the concluding section of chapter 1 will find on the whole that the vernacular terms for the roles defining English society are straightforward enough, and that their incumbents know broadly speaking where they stand within the overall structure of English society.

It may be objected, and fairly so, that although most people can assign an appropriate systactic location to their roles, they tend to be very ill-informed about the defining practices and relative location of roles at all distant from their own. Only those directly involved in the central institutions of English society, together with a handful of academics and journalists, have a detailed knowledge of their workings, and even they may be mistaken or prejudiced (or both) about their recent history and present condition. And when the attitudes of English people to what they see as their 'class' are systematically explored by academic sociologists, they often turn out to be not merely imprecise but apparently contradictory. But none of this prevents rival observers who set themselves to it from identifying and reporting the practices which define the roles which English people occupy and perform. People are, as I insisted in volume I, privileged observers both of what they themselves do and of what it is like for them to do it, even though they are not privileged observers of why they do it, or of what other people do, except in so far as their own roles are defined by their responses to others' behaviour towards themselves.

Only when it comes to dividing the society's constituent roles into separate systacts is there a pre-emptive implication of a theoretical kind. But although no reference to 'élite' or 'middle-class' or 'underclass' roles can be theory-neutral in the sense expounded in volume I, it is still possible to introduce terms of this kind into a report of the society's modes of production, persuasion and coercion in such a way as to permit transposition *salva veritate* into whatever terms a rival observer from a different theoretical school may prefer. A statement that, say, '6 per cent of households are in the underclass' is potentially controversial, even if used without any evaluative overtones, in a way that '6 per cent of the population are aged between 60 and 64' is not. But provided that 'underclass' has been, as it can be, operationally defined in a way that rival observers can modify as they choose (D. Smith 1992), no explanation, description, or evaluation has been pre-empted thereby; and the test of its usefulness, as of the terms 'capitalist', 'liberal', and 'democratic' themselves, lies in the explanations, descriptions, or evaluations to which it leads.

§2. Let me start, accordingly, from some straightforward sociological statistics. In 1901, the population of England and Wales had reached some 32.5 million people – an increase of more than 80 per cent over the previous fifty years.

There were more women than men, as there had been ever since records were kept and despite an excess of male over female births in every year since 1871. Within the categories of those of working age (taken as the 12.134 million men and 13.19 million women aged ten and above), under 10 per cent of the men and under 0.5 per cent of the women were engaged in agriculture, and of employed women, 42 per cent were in domestic service. Although it was not until after the First World War that more than half the population lived in cities of over 50,000 inhabitants, already by 1901 77 per cent could be classified as urban rather than rural, and already the population of Greater London was more than 6.5 million. The occupational tables of the 1901 census disclose not merely the extent to which agriculture had given way to industry but also the extent to which service and professional roles were expanding in parallel with roles in manufacturing industry.[1] The definition of 'manual' as opposed to 'non-manual' work cannot be taken as given;[2] it is, as we shall see, less a matter of the nature of the task than of the conditions that go with it. But even if maximum allowance is made for doubtful or borderline roles, there has been a steady and incontestable decline since the turn of the century in the size of the category of 'manual' workers in relation to the total occupied population. In 1901, three-quarters of the total employed workforce of 13.7 million were manual workers. But by the 1990s, less than half of English people in employment were in manual occupations, even though for men the proportion was still more than half as against something like a third for women.[3] The decline in the absolute size of the manual workforce in the decades after the First World War was particularly dramatic in certain sectors of industry, such as coal, textiles, and shipbuilding. It resumed afresh after the Second World War, and was not compensated by an equivalent growth in the expanding sectors such as electricity, chemicals, and non-ferrous metals. Instead, there was a continuation of the long shift away from manufacturing and towards service industry which was to take the proportion of the male workforce engaged in manufacturing down below 30 per cent in the 1990s; and this was accompanied by both a late trend towards intermittent or part-time employment (particularly of women) and a late increase in self-employment which, following a fall from about one in fifteen before the First World War to one in thirty in the 1960s, accelerated sufficiently in the 1970s and 1980s to bring the proportion of self-employed within the total occupied population up to one in

---

[1] In terms of national income rather than the distribution of occupational roles, already by the turn of the century over half was derived from the service sector (Supple 1977, p. 11).

[2] Particularly some of the work of the kind more often done by women (Heath and Britten 1984, p. 477).

[3] An analysis of the economically active population derived from the 1981 census yielded 45 per cent of 'manual' workers once the 4.2 per cent classified as 'supervisors and foremen' had been excluded (Heath and McDonald 1987, p. 364 n.1).

eight, of whom roughly four out of five were men.[4] At the same time, there has from 1921 onwards been a steep and steady decline in participation rates for men of sixty-five and over (Johnson 1994).

The 'new middle class' which has come into being since the late-Victorian and Edwardian period consists partly of occupational roles created by new technology and the services generated by it: there could hardly, for example, be any airline pilots, television producers or computer programmers in the census of 1901. But from the First World War onwards there has also been a steady expansion in the number of roles needing to be filled in the traditional professions and the ancillary clerical services associated with them; and both central and local government have continued to require more and more of these. Some roles in both manufacturing and service industry, although convention- ally defined as 'non-manual', are of so routine and subordinate a kind, and offer so little premium on experience or prospect of a career, that they ought therefore to be assigned to the unskilled working rather than the lower-middle class. Moreover, there is always some intra-generational mobility, across whatever dividing line is drawn, much of it by women who will not be long- term members of the labour force and ought for that reason to be assigned 'secondary' rank in accordance with the location of their husbands' or household heads' occupational roles.[5] But no sociologist will dispute that the working class, as conventionally defined, has shrunk since the late-Victorian and Edwardian period from some four-fifths of the adult population to less than a half of it.

The number of occupational roles open to women had, as I have already remarked, begun to increase before the turn of the century, and by the census of 1911 there were in England and Wales nearly 500 'lady' doctors, over 50,000 women employed by central or local government, and over 150,000 female clerks in industry or commerce.[6] But it was only during the First World War that the number who entered the non-domestic workforce increased on any

---

[4] Movement out of temporary self-employment into employment (or, for some, unemployment) has always been frequent, but its precise extent is under-researched. The British Household Panel Survey of 1990–2 found that over 16 per cent of self-employed men and 33 per cent of self-employed women had changed their employment status by the time of the second interview and that of both these over half became employees (Buck *et al.* 1994, p. 180).

[5] Later in the century, this assumption was to be vigorously debated in an extensive academic literature (see e.g. Roberts and Marshall 1995 and the references there listed). From within the theory of social selection, however, the answer to the question whether the individual or the family (or household) is the unit of class (or more broadly systact) composition is that it is neither. *Roles* are what systacts consist of, and individuals can occupy and perform more than one role at a time: the relative importance of the practices defining one rather than another is then a question for empirical research.

[6] Some guesswork is needed in the analysis of the figures. Zimmeck (1986, p. 154) estimates that 166,000 out of a total of 843,000 clerks were women, most of whom were employed in typing, sorting, telephones, or telegraphy, or checking accounts in commercial (not legal or banking) firms, the Civil Service, or local government.

substantial scale and only after it that all formal restrictions on women entering the professions were removed and women became legally entitled to dispose of property on the same terms as men; and it was only in and after the Second World War that the proportion of married women in employment, which had been roughly a tenth in 1911,[7] rose to over a half. By the 1950s, the combination of full employment and the availability of labour-saving devices for the home helped increasing numbers of working-class wives to take jobs which augmented their household earnings sufficiently for the labour-saving devices to be purchased (often on 'hire purchase', as it was called). At the same time, moreover, these devices helped the better-off middle-class households to replace the resident domestic servants on whom they had depended hitherto. Before the First World War, as many as one household in five had had at least one resident domestic servant. But thereafter, the role begins steadily to disappear. Already in 1923, a non-departmental committee set up by the Ministry of Labour reported that the shortage of servants was not (as often alleged by would-be employers) due to the payment of unemployment benefit for women suitable for such work, but to the unattractiveness of the wages, hours, and conditions offered. Despite this, the absolute number (1.3 million women and 78 thousand men) was still fractionally higher in 1931 than 1911, which was not then surprising in view of the lack of alternative employment during the worst of the inter-war depression.[8] It was only in and after the Second World War that the better-off middle-class households had to do without them. But between the censuses of 1931 and 1951, the percentage of women employed as resident domestic servants more than halved. By the 1960s, the 'daily help' (and sometimes the *au pair*) had replaced the 'maid' altogether; and by the census of 1971, the resident domestic servant of either sex was an anachronism confined to the households of the very rich.

Whatever the worries voiced by observers of different political persuasions about the failure of the British economy to generate as much income per head as it should, there has been throughout the century a steady rise in it. This has not prevented the continuing reproduction of a distribution of income and wealth with – to use the standard statistical measure of inequality – a high Gini coefficient and also a long Pareto tail. But the degree of inequality began to diminish in and after the First World War,[9] and as home-ownership and

---

[7] With substantial regional variations, from 44 per cent in Blackburn down to less than 3 per cent in Co. Durham (Beveridge 1932, p. 76). For 1921, the figures are virtually unchanged: 43 per cent in Blackburn and 2 per cent in Co. Durham.

[8] Again, there are marked regional variations, with higher proportions of women in domestic service in spa towns and holiday resorts and lower proportions in cities like Birmingham which offered a range of alternative industries (P. Taylor 1979, p. 123).

[9] Accurate estimation is fraught with difficulty (see e.g. Atkinson 1975, chapter 7), but the trend is clear – on Atkinson's calculation, the top 5 per cent of the population aged twenty-five and over

membership of pension schemes spread increasingly widely, it diminished further still.[10] Before the First World War, the working classes had been paying more in taxes than they received in social services (Clark 1937, p. 141). After it, they received more than they had paid for, and the proportion of national income spent on the social services roughly doubled. Then and since, there has been continuing debate between left-wing and right-wing observers over whether the level of expenditure is too high or too low. But the change was unmistakable. However vehement the attacks of 'dry' politicians of the 1980s, like 'anti-waste' politicians of the 1920s, on the level of welfare expenditure, even ten years of 'Thatcherite' government could make only a marginal difference to the 'Leviathan' (*Economist* 3.2.90): behind the rhetoric of 'tax-cutting' was only a shift from more progressive and direct to more regressive and indirect taxation. Any observer tempted to conclude that a reversion to the late-Victorian and Edwardian mode of production was taking place needed only to be reminded that Keir Hardie's suggestion that unearned incomes should be taxed at 1s 6d in the pound with an additional super-tax rising from $\frac{1}{2}$ per cent to $7\frac{1}{2}$ per cent 'seemed utterly ludicrous to the majority of informed opinion' (Emy 1972, p. 118), and that many late-Victorian and Edwardian trade unionists believed that working people should avoid dependence on the state for welfare benefits and work instead to receive better wages and conditions from their employers (Thane 1984, p. 885).

In the mode of persuasion, the change which took place in and after the First World War has inevitably to be reported in anecdotal rather than statistical terms. But the anecdotal evidence licenses a clear semi-deductive inference to a decline in the deference institutionally accorded by the incumbents of working-class roles to their 'betters'. Whatever the ideological contrast which an American observer like Mrs Halsey might be disposed to draw between the continuing 'subservience' which she found in Exeter by comparison with American manners and mores, English and American observers were agreed in seeing a difference between the manners and mores of late-Victorian and Edwardian England and those of 1915 onwards. There were, as could readily be predicted, marked regional differences. The change was most visible in the bigger cities where the high wages paid in the burgeoning munitions industry led to an immediate improvement in working-class life-styles – including the sometimes (but not always) apocryphal tales of purchases of fur coats and pianos – and least visible in country towns where,

---

owned 81 per cent of total personal wealth in 1924, but this had dropped to 55 per cent by 1968, while the share of the top 1 per cent had halved from 60 per cent to 30 per cent.

[10] A study drawing on the Financial Research Survey conducted by National Opinion Polls for 1991/92 found that when both state and private pensions are included, the percentage of total wealth held by the richest 10 per cent of the population was 36 per cent (Banks *et al.*, 1994).

as one new arrival in Banbury shortly after the war later described it, it was still 'pure *Cranford*' (Stacey 1960, pp. 10–11). But Robert Roberts's reminiscences of Salford, for example, document the sense of change not only in regard to the reluctance of working-class men to defer to their traditional superiors, and labourers to artisans, but also in regard to the new independence from their husbands experienced by working-class wives (1971, p. 161). Perhaps the most striking anecdote in the contemporary literature is that told by an American journalist who reported 'an old Oxford friend' lamenting after the war that when he entered a crowded bus a working-class man would no longer touch his cap to him and give him his seat (Gleason 1920, p. 250). Without access to the recording angel's archives, there is no way of knowing either how often such behaviour by working-class men actually occurred before the war or how widely its non-occurrence was actually lamented by middle-class men after it. But Gleason's comment that 'The workers are beginning to use a manner of jaunty equality in dealing with those passengers who travel through life on a first-class ticket' catches the contemporary sense of the change very well.

This change coincided with the extension of the franchise which, as we have seen, had before 1918 been open only to more or less settled, propertied, and respectable working men. Moreover, franchise reform coincided also with a marked increase in trade-union membership and activity, and a more vigorous Labour Party organization, which together made the Labour movement into a political force of a qualitatively different kind from what it had been before the war. It is true that not every newly enfranchised elector exercised his or her right to vote and that those that did often confounded the expectations of contemporary observers about their choice of party. But for the sociologist's purpose, as opposed to the political historian's, the pattern of voting is of interest not because of the changes of government which it did or didn't produce but because it shows the working class as such now participating in the central institution of 'bourgeois' democracy. However much they may differ in their interpretations of the consequences, observers of all theoretical schools will once again not dispute the fact.

§3. At the same time, there is (to quote directly from section 3 of chapter 3 in volume II) 'a subjective aspect to all this, since institutional instability is, among other things, a function of the extent to which particular incumbents of subordinate roles are disposed to a sense of relative deprivation sufficiently intense that they seek either to modify the practices which define their roles or to escape from them altogether'. Evidence for the existence of the kind of systactic consciousness which may find expression in collective action is not easy to assemble or straightforward to report, and when it is found it may turn out to be of little or no explanatory value. Sample surveys, no less than memoirs or anecdotes or quasi-anthropological enquiries in the manner of 'Mass Observation', yield impressions of popular opinion which can all too readily be misunderstood in the primary sense. Moreover, even unquestionably authentic descriptions of subjective experiences and feelings given by representative members of different systacts may bear little relation to the behaviour which they evince as the practices defining their roles mutate or recombine in a changing environment which neither they nor, for that matter, the contemporary sociologist observing them can yet fully understand (in the secondary, explanatory sense). Yet such evidence as there is points strongly to an awareness of persistent systactic differences among the overwhelming majority of English people. Dissatisfaction with the existing structure and culture of English society has throughout the century been common enough. But it is difficult to find more than fleeting and limited traces of what could possibly be called a revolutionary mentality – 'revolutionary' implying, in accordance with section 15 of chapter 4 in volume II, an explicit intention to alter both the existing structure and the existing culture together.[11]

There were always, despite this, observers on the Left ready to interpret any reported upsurge in the expression of working-class discontent as evidence that the British proletariat had arrived at a revolutionary class-consciousness *für sich*, just as there were always observers on the Right ready to draw from the same evidence the conclusion that the country was becoming 'ungovernable'. But for reasons to be analysed in chapter 3, both were as mistaken as each other. In the immediate aftermath of the First World War, Lloyd George had reason to take seriously the threat posed by particular groups of workers, including not least the police, whose concerted withdrawal of their labour might jeopardize the maintenance of law and order as well as of the day-to-day functioning of the economy. Furthermore, there were many observers ready to point out that the workers, as Rowntree put it in the revised edition of *Poverty*, 'claim as a right a better maintenance than they would once have begged as a privilege' (1922, p. xv). But there is no evidence to support the view that disenchantment with the policies of the Coalition, intense as it undoubtedly was, ever amounted to a serious intention on the part of more than a handful of would-be Leninists to overturn it by other than constitutional means.

---

[11] Cf. Marshall *et al.* (1988, p. 187): 'in so far as it is possible to generalize on the basis of our investigation, we should say that the "class consciousness" of the majority of people in our sample is characterized by its complexity, ambivalence, and occasional contradictions. It does not reflect a rigorously consistent interpretation of the world with an underlying rationale rooted in perceived class interest alone.'

After the onset of persistently high levels of unemployment, there were likewise hopes (on the Left) and fears (on the Right) of increasingly large and well-coordinated demonstrations by, or on behalf of, the unemployed. Wal Hannington, the Communist founder of the National Unemployed Workers Movement (NUWM), looked to former shop stewards, now unemployed, who combined the experience of workshop organization with a 'socialist under-standing' (Hannington 1936, p. 15), and there were employers and members of the security forces very ready to agree with him. But the NUWM was by Hannington's own admission a failure (p. 323). Throughout the inter-war depression, observers of all persuasions were struck by the absence of militancy; and as I pointed out in section 12 of chapter 1, the one notable outbreak of it was a response not to unemployment as such but to perceived reductions in expected benefit. As Priestley reported of a couple he visited in Blackburn, 'Lots worse off than them. They all say that' (1934, p. 281). Wight Bakke, who came from the United States to study the workings of unemployment insurance, found in Greenwich that 'the talk of revolution is conspicuous by its absence' (1933, p. 60); and the Pilgrim Trust investigators found that 'The Durham miner who has been out of work for five years has not a perpetual sense of grievance, but rather . . . a determination to make the best of things' (1938, p. 75). Half a century later, when unemployment had risen back to similar or even higher levels, Bagguley (1991, p. 140) found in Brighton that the radical Unemployed Workers Union which developed out of a TUC centre relied on a hard core of activists never numbering more than around thirty or forty and often fewer than this. The low level of militant discontent may or may not be explicable by the provision of unemployment benefit on a level sufficient in at least some cases to function as a disincentive to return to work. But there is no dispute among rival observers that the level was low.

After the Second World War, the roles which most obviously carried a revolutionary potential were those of the members of the Labour Party or the Communist Party itself who saw the Labour government of 1945–51, and subsequently those of 1964–70 and 1974–9, as having betrayed the Socialist cause. But the militants never represented the views of the majority of the working class, let alone of the non-Conservative electorate. The coalition of left-wing intellectuals and trade unionists which dominated the Labour Party conference of 1980 had been visible already at the conference of 1952, when a motion calling for direct industrial action to bring down the Conservative government secured 1.728 million card votes. But the public opinion polls which were by then being systematically conducted showed the unrepresenta-tiveness of the party activists of both Left and Right. Similarly in industrial disputes, even during the upsurge of militancy in the 1970s, there is little evidence which would license an inference to revolutionary class-consciousness in its Marxist sense.[12] The industries in which disputes were most intense and protracted were in any case far from typical of manual employment as a whole. The miners, whose leaders continued to see them as the shock-troops of the labour vanguard, were the least typical of all in their history, their conditions of work, and their close-knit residential-cum-occupational communities; and even they differed markedly in attitudes and behaviour from region to region, with the antagonism between Nottinghamshire and Yorkshire a theme running through from the 1920s to the 1980s and beyond. The motor industry, which acquired a growing reputation for militancy in and after the late 1950s, was less atypical of manufacturing generally. But even within manufacturing, large plants, assembly-line methods, and aggressive trade unions were more the exception than the rule. It is true that the size of manufacturing establishments had increased: whereas out of all workers in manufacturing establishments only about a fifth were in establishments employing more than a thousand in the mid-1930s, this proportion had risen to 31 per cent by 1951. But this growth in the numbers employed in larger establishments took place without a decline in the absolute numbers employed in smaller ones (G. C. Allen 1966, pp. 51–2); and in later decades, as the shift from manufacturing into services continued, so did there begin to be a decline in those sectors of manufacturing where the workplace was concentrated in large, highly unionized plants (Daniel 1990, p. 23).

Nor could it be the case that, as some contemporary observers believed, traditional working-class solidarity was eroded during the 1950s and 1960s, for the simple reason that the alleged degree of solidarity had never existed in actual fact. As I remarked in section 14 of chapter 1, the late-Victorian and Edwardian working class was both individualist and collectivist: a greater willingness to be organized for joint defence of wages, conditions, and work-place control was combined with a continuing attachment to domestic and private interests. An 'instrumental' attitude to work, an awareness of intra-class conflicts of interest, and a sensitivity to differences of status within the same working-class residential community are a consistent theme in the history of the British working class from the period of its formation. Within it, there were always some incumbents of unequivocally proletarian roles who conformed in behaviour and outlook to the ideal type of the 'traditional' worker (Lockwood 1966) just as there were always some 'aristocrats of labour' who shared much of the life-style and attitudes of the self-employed lower-middle class. But, excepting always the miners (and to some extent the dockers and stevedores of

---

[12] Even the miners, who struck in 1972 and again in 1974, 'wanted only wage increases on both occasions. They did not aim to threaten the Government, nor did they blame the institution of Government' (V. L. Allen 1981, p. 320).

the ports of London and Liverpool),[13] they never constituted a cohesive group or category, let alone a systact distinguishable as such. Detailed research into, for example, shipyard workers on Teesside (R. K. Brown *et al.* 1972) disclosed communities which were unarguably proletarian in the sense of a common incumbency of manual occupational roles, but equally unarguably differentiated within themselves to an extent incompatible with the Marxist model of a working class *für sich*.

On the other hand, there is ample evidence for what some sociologists call 'class awareness' as explicitly contrasted with 'class consciousness'. However far short they may be of the detailed knowledge of the facts on which the conclusions of academic sociologists are based, and however different their own terminology from that of the interviewer to whose questions they consent to respond, the overwhelming majority of the members of twentieth-century English society do perceive it as in some sense stratified by economic, ideological, and political power. In particular, the substantial literature on 'self-rated class' discloses a general recognition of a broad distinction between 'middle-class' and 'working-class' practices and roles. Some manual workers, including some 'unskilled' ones, will assign themselves to the 'middle' class (Willmott and Young 1960, p. 115),[14] just as some professionals and managers will assign themselves to the 'working' class – perhaps thereby reflecting an increasing prestige attaching to 'work' (Jacobs and Worcester 1990, pp. 141–3). But these anomalies[15] are not sufficient to undermine the generalization that 'the two-class formulation is much more than an analytical simplification of those who have studied social class. It is a formulation which has a profound hold on the perceptions of class found in British society' (Kahan *et al.* 1966, p. 124). It does not preclude awareness of an élite at the top of the social structure (Moorhouse 1976, p. 488) as well as an underclass at the bottom. But these are seen as small minorities – which, particularly in the case of the élite, they are. The great majority of the members of twentieth-century English society have continued to see themselves and each other as belonging to one or

---

[13] Even in the docks, there underlay the periodic manifestations of solidarity significant conflicts of interest within a workforce which was more differentiated (including between a 'blue' and a 'white' union) than it appeared (University of Liverpool 1954, p. 67). A distinctive occupational sub-culture was still observable after 1967: 'the practices of casualization outlived the casual system itself' (Turnbull 1992, p. 103). But it did not survive the 1980s.

[14] There are also a few manual workers who altogether repudiate 'bourgeois' criteria of occupational prestige (Young and Willmott 1956), as do the 'drop-outs who join the counter-culture' after leaving school (Argyle 1994, p. 213).

[15] If such they are: responses to sample surveys may fail to tap a coherent set of underlying beliefs which only depth interviews can adequately disclose (Lockwood 1992, pp. 340–1). Cf. the comment of Hiller (1975, p. 256) that 'Generally speaking, a very small amount of data from each respondent has served as the basis from which whole complexes of meaning have been inferred.'

other of two broad sets of roles defined by reference partly to manual and non-manual occupations as conventionally defined and partly to the norms and life-styles conventionally associated with these. The extent to which this sense of differentiation is reflected in political attitudes is difficult to establish precisely.[16] But even where it is found (Heath *et al.* 1985, chapter 3), it is palpably not 'revolutionary'.

Our hypothetical observer might well, therefore, conclude that the search for evidence of a collective sense of exclusion from economic, ideological, or political power could more usefully be extended beyond occupational roles and consequential class membership to the attitudes of the same people in their incumbency of roles of other kinds; and of these, the most obvious are ethnicity and gender. In both of them, the issue is consciousness of status rather than, although associated with, consciousness of class.[17] But a strong collective sense of relative deprivation of status can, in some circumstances, provide a context in which mutant practices potentially subversive of the status quo will be more likely to be replicated and diffused, particularly if there is a significant overlap between consciousness of ascriptive status and consciousness of class. Thus already in the 1930s there was pressure for equal pay between men and women in the Civil Service, and once the Second World War had broken out the demand for women's labour triggered an immediate revival of feminism (H. Smith 1981, pp. 654–5). Similarly, the difficulties faced by Afro-Caribbean immigrants in the labour market in the 1960s and thereafter coincided unmistakably with status discrimination based on 'race' (C. Brown 1984, pp. 296–7). The times when ethnicity and gender assumed the importance which they did in political debate were to some degree fortuitous. But whatever the rhetoric, support for movements of or on behalf of both women and ethnic minorities in twentieth-century England has been coalitional rather than systactic. The militancy of the suffragettes in the period just prior to the First World War may, although it is impossible to demonstrate conclusively, have been counter-productive on balance (B. Harrison 1978, pp. 192–3): perhaps

---

[16] It is disputed among political scientists how far 'class awareness' has continued to underlie the choice of party at successive General Elections. But it seems unwarranted to infer from the electoral dominance of the Conservatives in the 1980s that there was any significant change from the time of Labour's victories in the 1960s (Evans 1993, p. 463). Devine (1992, p. 246), who reinterviewed a sample of Luton's 'affluent workers', found that despite their disillusionment with the Labour Party, their 'working class identity was clearly salient in the political domain'.

[17] A not uncommon conceptual confusion may need to be resolved here, given how often the misleading assertion is made that gender and ethnicity are 'distinct dimensions of inequality' (Westergaard 1995, p. 144). Men are indisputably different from women and black people from white ones; but if they are on that account unequal, it is because, in the society of which they are members, they are institutionally accorded more or less power of one or other of the three, and only three, kinds.

more important was the 'successful realization of democratic-suffragist strategy in feminist-labour alliances' (Holton 1986, p. 6). But whatever the causes of its earlier failure and subsequent success, the movement for women's suffrage could not have succeeded at all if it had not brought together as it did both women and their male supporters from different classes, status-groups, and factions. Likewise, whatever the causes of the pattern of ethnic relations as it evolved when immigration from the former colonies reached significant proportions, without the involvement of white middle-class supporters the movement for legislative measures against discrimination could not have succeeded to the extent that it did. To make this point is not to pre-empt the explanation of why the sub-type of capitalist liberal democracy which evolved between 1915 and 1922 remained as stable as it did for as long as it did thereafter. But it does cast doubt on any presupposition either that the mutant practices which social selection turns out to favour will be found at a single location within the social structure or that a collective systactic consciousness will be a guarantee, or even a harbinger, of evolution from one to another mode or sub-type of production, persuasion, or coercion.

ECONOMIC EVOLUTION

§4. The classes into which English society in 1900 could most obviously be divided were, as I summarized it in section 15 of chapter 1, a tiny 'plutocracy', a small middle class of administrative, clerical, and professional roles, a large manual working class, and a 'submerged tenth' of casuals, vagrants, petty criminals, mendicants, and permanently unemployed. But within each of these classes, there were roles with both different employment statuses and different interests in different market conditions and government policies; and there were also differences in the economic power attaching to them sufficient to make it necessary not only to distinguish a 'skilled' from an 'unskilled' working class but also to divide the middle class into three – 'upper', 'middle', and 'lower'. All of these distinctions continued to hold good, but in what were, after the First World War, very different ways. Not only was there a significant shift in the relative sizes of the different classes; in addition, their constituent roles changed in ways which, as we shall see in chapter 3, can be directly traced to endogenous selective pressures on the practices defining them.

There is no better starting-point for the reportage of the late-Victorian and Edwardian class structure than the brief account given by D'Aeth (1910; cf. Descamps 1914, p. 233). His language may now seem dated and his analysis simplistic. But his categorization corresponds to what can accurately be labelled an upper class, an upper-middle, middle-middle, and lower-middle class, a skilled and unskilled working class, and an underclass. D'Aeth, who was probably influenced by Booth, labels his seven classes 'A' to 'G', going from the bottom upwards. But if we reverse his order, his G ('the rich') is the upper class; his F ('professional and administrative class') is the upper-middle class; his E ('smaller business class') is the middle-middle class; his D ('smaller shopkeeper and clerk' class) is the lower-middle class; his C (the 'artisan' class) is the skilled working class; his B ('low-skilled labour') is the unskilled working class; and his A ('loafer' class) is the underclass. Moreover, as his examples make clear, he is well aware that although differences of employment status as well as of income are relevant to the assignation of roles to classes, they do not in themselves determine it. Thus, his class G includes 'a few salaried posts' alongside 'manufacturers' and 'heads of firms'; his class F includes some heads of firms alongside 'administrative posts'; his class E includes 'smaller professionals' alongside businessmen; his class D includes teachers and commercial travellers alongside 'smaller shopkeepers'; and his class B includes 'lowest type of clerk, shop assistant etc'. It hardly needs saying that the class structure of 1990 is different from that of 1910, even apart from the much greater involvement of women in the non-domestic workforce. But it is still a structure of seven classes defined by the economic power, whether in terms of ownership, marketability, or control, which attaches to their constituent roles (Runciman 1990, p. 380). The differences are not such as either to reduce the number to six through the disappearance of the roles constitutive of one of them or to increase it to eight through the emergence of a new set of roles which cannot be assigned to any one of the existing seven. Instead, there have been a number of related changes within the seven-fold structure, all of which date from the aftermath of the First World War.

The first was the change within the upper and middle classes away from proprietorial towards managerial roles. This was not simply a matter of the increasing number of managerial roles in national and local government as well as in commerce and industry which needed to be filled, but also of a shift from roles in which income was 'unearned' to roles in which it was 'earned'. Sons of upper- and upper-middle-class families who, in the late-Victorian and Edwardian period, would have been shareholders in privately owned companies became likelier after the War to be directors or managers in publicly owned ones, and those who would have been partners in professional firms became likelier to be salaried employees. Neither income nor inheritance taxes were raised to such levels as to eliminate altogether the possibility of living on investment income alone, and the interest rates on the government stocks which had been issued to finance the war were attractively high in real as well as nominal terms. But the proportion of roles classified by the Registrar-General as 'employers and proprietors' in the census of 1911 fell steadily in the post-war period, while the proportion classified as 'managers

and administrators' steadily rose;[18] and the new 'salariat' included a much
increased proportion of women who would not, in the late-Victorian and
Edwardian period, have been in paid work at all. Arthur Bowley's estimate
(1931, p. 141) is that the number of salaried men increased by 50 per cent
between 1914 and 1924 and the number of salaried women by 111 per cent.

   The second change was at the level of the lower-middle class. The much
enlarged female salariat was composed principally of clerical workers, whether
in private industry or government service, and the consequent trend was
towards a two-tier clerical workforce of men with long-term prospects of
promotion and women in the more routine jobs who were unlikely to return to
them after marriage (Lockwood 1989, pp. 222–3). At the same time, the 1920s
saw the beginning of a marked expansion in the number of multiple retailers
with their hundreds of regional branches centrally controlled (Bushell 1921,
p. 64 quoted by Benson 1989, p. 25), and therewith in the number of sales
assistants who were no longer the starch-collared young men behind the
counters of the owner-managed shops of the late-Victorian and Edwardian
period but young girls from working-class families who preferred the department store to the factory and both to domestic service. The extent to which
these changes have amounted to a 'proletarianization' of the roles concerned
has been matter of debate between sociologists of rival theoretical schools ever
since. Bowley (1931, p. 143) drew attention to the combined tendency for the
number of routine clerical roles to increase and for women to replace men in
them, and Klingender (1935, pp. 62–4, 95) argued that the mechanization of
office work was irreversibly proletarianizing clerical labour. But many clerical
roles continued to carry an element of discretion in the performance of
assigned tasks, a proximity to authority associating them with the direction of
the enterprise, and a premium on experience which combined to locate them
firmly within the lower-middle class (Bain and Price, 1972), whereas, as I have
remarked already, many other 'non-manual' roles (such as those of security
guards, copy-typists, or shop cashiers) conferred no premium on experience,
offered no prospects of a career, and required no apprenticeship or training of
the kind which would locate them in the skilled working, let alone the lower-
middle, class. When, therefore, the debate over 'proletarianization' was revived
in the 1970s and 1980s in the context of computerization rather than

---

[18] Routh (1965, Table 1) shows a fractional increase (from 6.71% to 6.92%) in the proportion of
employers and proprietors between 1911 and 1921 followed by a fall to 4.97% in 1951; managers
and administrators rose fractionally (from 3.43% to 3.64%) between 1911 and 1921, and
thereafter to 5.53% in 1951. But if professional, managerial, and administrative employees are
added together, they amount to 11.6% in 1951 against 7.4% in 1921, while if 'own account'
professionals, employers, proprietors, managers, and administrators are added together, they
amount to 5.5% in 1951 against 3.5% in 1921. Routh's figures, it should be noted, are for
Scotland as well as England and Wales.

mechanization (Crompton and Jones 1984, chapter 2) and some observers were again readier to find it behind the sales counter than in the office (Marshall *et al.* 1988, pp. 120–1), it could nevertheless be agreed that the lower-middle class of the 1980s was more like that of the 1920s than either was like that of the late-Victorian and Edwardian period.

The third change was at the top of the working class. For D'Aeth, as for other observers of the late-Victorian and Edwardian social structure, the role of 'artisan' was one which placed the skilled craftsmen and foremen on the same level as the lower-level clerks and petty officials. But after the war, the combination of the dilution of old craft skills and the progressive withdrawal of control over production from the shop-floor to the office[19] sharpened the distinction between skilled manual and lower-grade clerical roles: the latest reference known to me to 'the clerk-artisan class' is by the Chairman of the Manchester Corporation Housing Committee in 1929 (quoted by Waites 1987, p. 173). Before 1914, there had, as I have already reported, been a threefold contrast among manual workers between the so-called 'aristocrats of labour', the machine-minding 'operatives', and the casual or seasonal 'labourers' on or below the poverty line. But thereafter, the distinction was between the 'skilled' worker on the one hand and the semi- and unskilled on the other. 'Skill' did not then, any more than now, denote a definable technical aptitude, even though some 'skilled' roles might require a period of formal apprenticeship. But 'skilled' roles can all be distinguished from roles which, even if some minimal training is required for them, can effectively be performed by anyone available for employment. From the viewpoint of employers and potential employees alike (Ashton 1973, p. 116), the difference is between roles which command only a 'going rate' and roles which, although they carry no prospects of a career, still carry a premium in terms of either ownership of tools or equipment, control over some part of the process of production, some element of discretion and responsibility, or marketability of experience in a given 'trade'. The distinction is not always clear-cut: many manufacturing firms continued to have a continuum of grades on which employees might move both up and down. But from the perspective of the observer concerned only with changes in the class structure at the macrosociological level, the social

---

[19] See e.g. Gospel (1987, pp. 177–8): 'In the interwar years, though the number of foremen increased they were on the whole less powerful, more dependent on top management for their authority, and had more to enforce company rules rather than their own.' There of course continued to be supervisory roles carried out on the shop-floor, and Goldthorpe (1980, p. 42) wishes still to distinguish a separate ' "blue-collar" élite' including supervisors of manual work as a separate class for the purpose of analysing social mobility. He himself concedes, however, that their authority is 'subject to close monitoring and control from above' and that they have 'less favourable economic prospects than staff that are more completely integrated into administrative and managerial bureaucracies'.

distance between the roles at the top and the roles at the bottom of the working class diminishes after the First World War to the point that it is no longer plausible to subdivide it, like the middle class, into three, but only into two; and the consequent bracketing of the semi-skilled with the unskilled becomes the conventional form of reportage for employers and sociologists alike.

Finally, there was the change in the composition of the underclass which removed from it the seasonal and casual labourers and placed them firmly in the unskilled working class. A sustained fall in family size and rise in minimum real wages coincided with the permanent extension of unemployment benefit (Bowley and Hogg 1925). There was, and continued to be, an overlap between the roles of the casual or itinerant labourer and those of the beggar, the illegal trader, and the petty thief (Henry 1982). But whereas the stereotype of the underclass of 1910 was a white, male, intermittently employed, unskilled labourer living in a succession of privately rented rooms and perennially in arrears with the rent, by 1990 the stereotype had become a single mother from an ethnic minority living on state benefit in local-authority accommodation (and dependent on 'housing benefit'). The extension of benefits never entirely did away with the practices of scrounging, bartering, pawning, borrowing (and not always repaying), and drawing on the resources of private charity as and where available. Nor did a higher level of minimum wages mean that there did not continue to be groups and categories of unskilled workers who in periods of high unemployment were particularly at risk of long-term exclusion from the labour market. But the roles of which the underclass predominantly consisted (leaving aside the 'criminals', of whom some should be assigned to the lower-middle class in any case) were unmistakably different in the 1920s and thereafter from what they had been when Booth was compiling his *Life and Labour of the People in London*.

Taken together, these changes amount to a clearly discernible evolution of the class structure from one to another sub-type of the capitalist mode of production. But it remains a structure of seven distinguishable classes which shed their old roles and absorbed their new ones with only minor alterations in their relative systactic location. The decline in domestic service, the trend away from proprietorial to managerial roles, the feminization of routine sales and clerical labour, the steady increase in professional and administrative roles in both the private and public sectors, and the simultaneous deskilling of some and reskilling of other jobs within the working class as a whole all took place within a recognizably similar overall pattern. The domestic servants, whose gradual disappearance I reported in section 2, had in any case never belonged in a single class: the £50-a-year-and-all-found cooks and butlers disappeared from among D'Aeth's 'artisans', the housemaids and odd-job men from the unskilled working class, and the casual 'skivvies' from the underclass. The new generation of managers joined the upper-middle, middle-middle, or lower-middle class in accordance with whether they were in 'senior', 'middle', or 'junior' management. The proprietors remained in the upper-middle, middle-middle, or lower-middle class depending on whether they were owners of substantial enterprises, proprietors solely responsible for the direction of their relatively few employees, or self-employed domestic workers working alongside either family members or a very small number of outside wage-workers (Scase and Goffee 1982, pp. 24–6). Among manual workers, the nature of the tasks performed and the methods of recruitment to them changed as first the electrical and chemical industries and then the electronic and computer industries modified the techniques of production and widened the range of goods and services offered in the market. But here too an unmistakable difference between 'skilled' and 'semi-skilled' or 'unskilled' roles and the degree of economic power (or lack of it) attaching to them remained.

§5. These changes in the class structure proceeded in parallel with institutional changes in the organization and management of industrial and commercial firms. The most obvious was the concentration of the means of production in larger units of ownership and control and the corresponding concentration of the power of organized labour in a smaller number of larger trade unions. Our hypothetical observer is now, so to speak, in the world of Imperial Chemical Industries on the one side and the Transport and General Workers Union (T&GWU) on the other. Novel occupational roles came into being which widened the contrast between the old industries and the new; administrative roles proliferated; and educational qualifications became increasingly important as credentials for entry into an increasingly wide range of 'professional' roles.

It might be objected that this summary account understates the extent to which established practices and the roles defined by them continued to replicate themselves unchanged in many sectors, industries, and regions. Just as, in the nineteenth century, the new, factory-based mode of production emerged in an institutional environment of persisting small handicrafts and artisan manufacture, so, in the twentieth, did the practices and roles of 'modern' industry and commerce emerge in an environment in which a large number of small firms continued to account for a substantial proportion of manufacturing output. The progress of mechanization was hesitant and patchy, sub-contracting remained commonplace, and the new techniques of managerial discipline (including the professionalization of 'welfare') were often resisted or bypassed. Not only, for example, did housebuilding remain almost entirely unmechanized, but even coalmining was still a long way from complete mechanization prior to the Second World War (Buxton 1970, p. 482); and only in the 1930s did the British Army start to spend more on petrol than on oats and hay. But, as always in the study of social evolution, it is on the mutant practices which will turn out to confer competitive advantage on their carriers that the observer's attention needs to be concentrated. The pace of change may have been slower and its extent less widespread than many observers (and some later historians) assumed.[20] But there can be no dispute about its direction.

The concentration of the means of production into fewer hands was first evident in the wave of mergers in the 1920s which, together with the concomitant organizational developments within the larger corporations, 'marked the birth of the modern corporate economy in Britain' (Hannah 1983, p. 7). The practices which defined the roles of the new generation of corporate managers were professional in a double sense: they reflected not only the increasing importance of the disciplines of accountancy, law, and personnel relations but also the new ideology of 'scientific' management which was invoked to legitimate them.[21] The so-called 'divorce of ownership and control', which became an increasingly fashionable theme in public discussion from the 1930s onwards, should not be exaggerated. Despite the steady spread of share-ownership from controlling families to unrelated individual or institutional shareholders such as investment trusts and pension funds, it remained true that boards of directors had usually to have regard to 'the wishes and interests of the constellation of leading shareholders' (Scott 1988, p. 452). But more and more firms now sought access to wider sources of finance as well as to new techniques of management. In this sense, and to this extent, the role of capitalist could be said to be no longer what it used to be: the owners and controllers of the means of production were becoming dependent to a degree which their late-Victorian and Edwardian predecessors had never contemplated on the roles both of hired administrators within their organizations and of independent professionals outside them.

On the other side of the divide between capital and labour, the rise in the number of trade-union members from 4.1 million in 1913 to 8.3 million in 1920 and the enhanced influence with government which their leaders had won during the war seemed to many contemporary observers, whether they welcomed it or feared it, to presage a radical change in the distribution of economic power. But the mood was, as we have seen already, short-lived; and

---

[20] Change was also slower in the countryside, as it usually is: the role of 'agribusinessman' appears only after the Second World War (Newby 1979, p. 262).

[21] The same applied in the field of social policy: 'In the history of social policy wars and depressions are accidents, however important their consequences may be. But beneath the surface we can discover processes of growth which are the product of the evolutionary forces at work within social policy itself. Before the first war social reform was a political adventure run by enthusiastic amateurs; in the inter-war years social administration became a science practised by professionals' (Marshall 1965, p. 61).

when the post-war boom had collapsed, the Triple Alliance had been defeated, and the number of union members started to fall back down towards its pre-war level,[22] it seemed rather that labour was back on the defensive once again. Yet to leave the matter there would be to misreport what had changed, institutionally speaking, since 1914. It is true that the proportion of union members out of the potential total, which reached 45 per cent in 1920, was by 1933, at 22.6 per cent, even lower than it had been in 1913 (Price and Bain 1983). But these statistics should not be read as licensing a semi-deductive inference to a weakening of the power of the organized working class relative to what it had been before 1914. Union membership continued to rise and fall in cycles. After it had reached a peak of 55.4 per cent in 1979 it fell to 31 per cent in 1994; yet this is still 8 per cent more than it had been in the middle of the inter-war depression. More to the point, in contrasting the period after the First World War with the period before it, is that union leaders never entirely lost the influence which had accrued to their roles after 1915. That influence, like the size of their membership, rose and fell in cycles. But by the time of the Second World War, the TUC, for all the constraints imposed on it by its affiliated unions, had achieved an internal authority which one historian has called 'awesome' by comparison (R. M. Martin 1980, p. 283). This does not by a long way justify the claim that it had become a 'governing institution' (Middlemas 1979, p. 190): whether the government in power was as friendly to it as Wilson's or as hostile to it as Thatcher's, it still had no more effective sanctions over its members than ministers and officials had over it. But the fact that such a claim can be made at all is testimony of a kind to a qualitative difference from the late-Victorian and Edwardian period.

There is, moreover, another sense in which the economic power of the working class was significantly greater in the 1920s and thereafter than it had been in the late-Victorian and Edwardian period. Before the First World War, working-class families were just beginning to flex their economic muscles, so to speak, in their roles as consumers. But their collective surplus after food, clothing, and housing had been paid for left a very exiguous margin by comparison with the inter-war years when 'grown children' in working-class households (Bowley and Hogg 1925, p. 16) contributed some of their earnings to the household but kept the remainer to spend on themselves. The teenage 'consumer', like the 'affluent' worker, emerged not, as often assumed, in the 1950s but the 1920s (Fowler 1992). Although many of the gains in earnings made during the war were lost soon after it, hours of work stayed lower and

---

[22] A fall which was sharper among manual than non-manual workers: density among manual workers, which was 34.7 per cent in 1921, dropped to 24 per cent by 1931 whereas among non-manual workers, 24.4 per cent of whom were unionized in 1921, 21.2 per cent were still unionized ten years later (Bain and Price 1980).

wage-rates higher than when, in the 1890s, manual workers had been fully exposed to the force of the market and their employers exploited their bargaining advantage to the full. Despite the severity of the recession after 1920, the working week remained relatively short and wage-rates relatively inflexible (A. Booth 1987, p. 520).

To report this is not to understate the level of unemployment and the subordination of those out of work to the authority attaching to the roles of the officials charged with administering unemployment benefit. But for the majority who *were* in work, the rise in real wages in the inter-war period created the opportunity of entry into the roles not only of 'consumer' but, in a small but growing minority of cases, of home-owner. There is, as it happens, no official source for the statistics of home-ownership in the early part of the century (although its steady increase after the Second World War to more than two-thirds[23] at the time of writing is accurately documented). But the best estimate that can be made is that it virtually doubled from perhaps 10 per cent in the working class at the turn of the century to 19 per cent by the outbreak of the Second World War (Swenarton and Taylor 1983, p. 391). This figure conceals marked regional variations between boom towns like Coventry and declining regions like South Wales. What is more, during the worst of the inter-war Depression home-ownership in a declining region could be a liability rather than an asset, since it could prevent the working-class home-owner from emigrating to a region with better prospects of employment (Jennings 1934, pp. 85–6). But however modest the change might seem by comparison with the much greater propensity of teachers, civil servants, or local government officials to buy their homes – three times as much, according to a survey conducted in 1938 by the Civil Service Research Bureau (M. Bowley 1945, p. 177) – it was a notable change from the late-Victorian and Edwardian period. When the provision of rented housing by local authorities is also taken into account, the dependence of working-class families on private rented accommodation, which by 1979 was to have dropped so far as to amount to not much more than 10 per cent of all housing, had declined from an estimated 90 per cent in 1918 to an estimated 71 per cent in 1939 (Benson 1989, Table 8).

This may seem a surprising figure in view of Lloyd George's notorious failure to redeem his supposed promise of 'homes fit for heroes to live in':[24]

---

[23] This is the figure for Great Britain as a whole. Scotland, for historical reasons which would need to be analysed separately, has always had markedly lower rates of owner-occupation, so that England is a society of which it can be said that nearer three-quarters than two-thirds of households are owner-occupiers – albeit with repossessions at the rate of 80,000 a year in 1991 (but falling thereafter).

[24] Not that Lloyd George himself ever used precisely those words, any more than Harold Macmillan ever used precisely the words 'you've never had it so good'. But they might as well have: that is how myths are made.

not only was the total number of houses built with government assistance before the fall of the Coalition in 1922 far below the government's initial hopes, but many of the houses which *were* built went to middle-class rather than working-class occupiers. But the government remained involved in housing policy in a way which had not even been contemplated before 1914. The practices initiated by the Coalition continued to be replicated under both its Labour and its Conservative successors, and the local authorities, for all their recalcitrance in submitting schemes as they were supposed to do under Addison's Act of 1919, continued to be substantial providers of housing for working-class families. With this topic, however, we are led directly to the undisputed fact of the state's increasing involvement in the workings of the economy which would be enough by itself to mark off British capitalism in the 1920s and thereafter from the late-Victorian and Edwardian sub-type of the capitalist mode.

§6. This involvement was not less significant by comparison with the late-Victorian and Edwardian period because it was unforeseen, reluctant, and even furtive (Richard Roberts 1984, p. 96). Indeed, the growth of state intervention between the wars offers a classic illustration of the perennial need to distinguish the rhetoric of individual role-incumbents about their roles from the actual mutations in the practices by which their roles are defined. In the immediate aftermath of the war, the practices and roles of what had seemed to some contemporary observers 'something very like practical Socialism' (J. M. Read, quoted by A. Reid 1985, p. 70) were comprehensively dismantled.[25] But the return to 'Home Rule for Industry' was very far from being as complete as it was proclaimed to be. The Ministry of Labour survived the Geddes Committee's recommendation that it should be abolished; the Treasury, for all that its officials used the enlarged powers now attaching to their roles to curb rather than expand public expenditure, retained a greater dominance over a larger Civil Service than could have been contemplated before 1914;[26] and the powers of surveillance and control over organized labour built up under Lloyd

---

[25] The conclusion of the FBI (Federation of British Industries)'s Committee on Industrial and Commercial Efficiency in December 1917 was that 'One effect of the War has been to cause an almost universal dislike and distrust of State interference, which is always cumbersome, expensive, and irritating' (quoted by J. Turner 1992, p. 379). Cf. Whiteside (1979, p. 513), on the 'bitterness, administrative confusion, and official expense' generated by central direction of industry.

[26] The precise extent of the power now attaching to the Permanent Secretary's role as also 'Head of the Civil Service' is a matter of some controversy among historians; but even on the most cautious view it is safe to say that 'while the customary and statutory authority of the Treasury had not been inflated in any way, its effectiveness had been considerably reinforced' (Roseveare 1969, p. 249). Peden (1983, p. 384) suggests that the Treasury's authority between the wars derived partly from the lack of a fully developed Cabinet Office or Prime Minister's Office.

George were retained by his successors. The Industrial Unrest Committee set up in 1919 in response to the threat of a transport strike in London and subsequently retitled the 'Supply and Transport' Committee was the prototype for the succession of institutionalized means of maintaining essential services which were retained thereafter. After the Second World War, the 'Supply and Transport' organization was effectively recreated by the Attlee government without ever actually being referred to by the 'Industrial Emergencies' Committee which did it (Jeffrey and Hennessy 1983, p. 176).

Intervention in industry, likewise, continued throughout the inter-war period in a manner inconceivable before 1914. Legislation like the Agriculture Act of 1920 or Safeguarding of Industries Act of 1921 could be presented as being compatible with earlier precedents.[27] But the same could hardly be said of the provision in Chamberlain's Local Government Act of 1929 for rate-relieving the railways on condition that they reduced their own freight rates on coal and steel, or the Agricultural Marketing Acts of 1931 and 1933 or the North Atlantic Shipping Act of 1934 or the Cotton Spinning Industry Act of 1936 or the Road Haulage Wages Act or Holidays with Pay Act of 1938; and still less could it be said of the direct involvement of ministers and officials in the aircraft industry after 1935.

More directly visible, and at least as different from the late-Victorian and Edwardian period, was the level of personal taxation. It was not maintained at the peak to which it had been raised during the war. But taxpayers at the top of the income distribution who in 1914 had been paying some 8 per cent of their incomes in tax were in 1930 paying some four times as much; and estate duty, which had horrified Gladstone when it was introduced at a rate of 8 per cent on estates worth over £1 million in 1894, was raised from 15 per cent in 1914 to 40 per cent by 1919 and 60 per cent by 1939. The sense of relative deprivation voiced by members of the upper and upper-middle classes at this degree of confiscation does not need to be taken entirely at face value, any more than do the similar complaints voiced in the aftermath of the Second World War. But there is unmistakable evidence of a qualitative change in the distribution of economic power in the land sales which immediately followed the First World War. In 1914, only 11 per cent of the agricultural land in England and Wales was occupied by its owners. But by 1927, the figure had risen to 36 per cent – a transfer largely concentrated between 1918 and 1923 and probably unequalled in scale and speed since the Norman Conquest (F. M. L. Thompson 1963, pp. 332–3). The overwhelming majority of the purchasers were the sitting tenants, and although they did not benefit

[27] The Safeguarding of Industries Act had originally been devised as a protection against Germany; having been shelved in 1919, it was 'hurriedly dusted off and presented to Parliament as a specific for unemployment' (J. Turner 1984, p. 10).

immediately in financial terms, when, by the 1970s, land values had substantially risen, any farmer with 1,800 acres was a paper millionaire (Rubinstein 1981, p. 244). It is true that greater equality (or diminished inequality) in the distribution of marketable assets does not license an inference to a qualitative change in the class structure, and still less to a significant enrichment of working-class households.[28] But the working classes were never again as relatively poor as they had been in 1914.[29]

Nor was the involvement of ministers and officials in the workings of the market restricted to the sphere of work. Leisure came increasingly under the influence of legislation not merely in the censorship of books, plays and (by now) the cinema but in the control of drinking, gambling, camping, rambling, and physical training (H. Jones 1987, p. 165). Education, too, although it had been increasingly a concern of government in the late-Victorian and Edwardian period, became much more a matter of direct involvement after 1918. The Education Act of 1918 made schooling compulsory up to the age of fourteen; inter-war governments promoted the provision of free or at least means-tested secondary school places for children whose parents could not pay fees; and already by the end of the 1920s, central government 'had an established place in the funding of all higher education' (Sutherland 1990, p. 167). The impact of these changes on the systactic structure was less than some contemporary observers supposed: despite such claims as that there was 'an upthrust of new strata of the population into the secondary schools' (Lowndes 1937, p. 128), secondary schooling remained far more accessible to middle-class than to working-class children,[30] and the Education Act of 1944, although claimed by some observers both then and since as a significant reform, 'created little in the way of innovation or social levelling' (Thom 1986, p. 124). But there could be no dispute that the powers of intervention now attaching to the roles of ministers and officials were significantly greater than they had been at the time of the Education Act of 1902; and these powers functioned in the interests of what would come to be called 'meritocratic' principles to an extent never envisaged before 1914.

Even more significant for the evolution of the mode of production was the

---

[28] Working-class property-ownership, in particular, was apt to be misreported by contemporary commentators: the 'typical working-class family with its £300 in the bank' in the 1930s was a statistical figment (Hilton 1944, p. 72), and even in the 1950s the Oxford Savings Surveys found 12 per cent of 'income units' in debt and a third with no liquid assets at all (Hill 1955, p. 155).

[29] No less relevant than the distribution of cash and marketable assets was the cheapness of labour, and particularly women's labour, to those in a position to pay for it in the late-Victorian and Edwardian period (Perkin 1989, p. 78).

[30] The pressure on working-class children to start earning was compounded, then as later, by their own wish to have their status within the home raised from the role of 'schoolboy' to that of 'worker' (Hargreaves 1967, p. 173).

growing involvement of the state in the economy as an employer. It had two aspects – the steady and simultaneous diffusion of bureaucratic practices and increase in the proportion of workers directly employed by the state. Already between the wars the number of civil servants required to plan, operate, inspect, and advise on the provision of welfare had more or less doubled, and the range of public-sector employment had widened far beyond what it had been in the late-Victorian and Edwardian period. As I remarked in section 5 of chapter 1, this carried no necessary implication of a qualitative change in the relations between employers and employees. But it did carry an immediate implication for the relation of government to organized labour; and it was once again during the First World War that the change occurred. Whatever the explanation for it, there was a sudden and unanticipated readiness on the part of ministers and officials to accept unionization among their own employees after the publication of the first of the Whitley Reports in the summer of 1917. Unions with long-established procedures of collective bargaining were largely indifferent to the Whitley recommendations. But the Civil Service and postal unions responded enthusiastically to them, and the government accepted in principle their application to its own establishments (Clegg 1985, pp. 206–7). From then on, whatever stage might be reached in the cycle of governmental policies from conciliation to confrontation to conciliation of the unions in general, a unionized workforce in the direct employment of the state became an established feature of the economy, and remained so on a scale unthinkable before 1914.

Against this background, the aftermath of the Second World War can be seen still more clearly not to have involved a change in the mode of production comparable to that which took place in the aftermath of the First. The plausibility of attaching a 'Socialist' label to the 1945 government rested partly on its programme of nationalization and partly on its creation of what came to be called the 'welfare state'. But the measures so designated were not so much a radical innovation as a logical extension of an already established consensus about the responsibilities of the state towards its citizens. The critical mutation of practices had occurred as far back as March 1921, when there was conceded to certain categories of the unemployed the right to 'uncovenanted' benefit. However justified, according to whatever your evaluative presuppositions may be, the complaints of left-wing critics throughout the inter-war period about the inadequacy of the benefits provided for the needy and the lack of sympathy with which they were administered, it can nevertheless be claimed that 'The social services in Britain, taken all in all, were the most advanced in the world in 1939' (Addison 1975, p. 33), and that as women, in particular, pressed their local authorities to implement the Maternity and Child Welfare Act of 1918, 'maternal and child welfare services, despite falling very seriously short of any ideal and despite local variations due to differing local conditions as well as differing political priorities, were significantly improved by 1939 compared to 1918' (Thane 1991a, p. 106).[31] The National Health Service itself was the product of an evolution which in narrative terms can be traced back to the Dawson Report of 1920 or even, as regards the future of the Poor Law hospitals, the Maclean Committee of 1918. Consultation and debate continued throughout the inter-war years, and 'Policy development after 1918 involved a gradual erosion of market-related mechanisms and a transition to forms of health care less related to the market' (Webster 1990, p. 150). By 1937, when PEP published a report on the health services which fell short of what was later to be enacted only through its assumption that a free comprehensive service would be too expensive to be practicable – as, indeed, it subsequently turned out to be – it was welcomed no less by the medical profession than by 'middle opinion' (Marwick, 1964). The final form which the National Health Service took, however it actually came about,[32] was no more (if no less) than implementation of the sort of health service foreshadowed in the Coalition Government's White Paper of 1944.

The view that the welfare legislation enacted by the Attlee government is evidence of a significant change in the capitalist mode of production was influentially argued in the official history of social policy (Titmuss 1950), and there were many contemporary observers who believed that the measures taken by the state in and immediately after the war to alleviate the hardship suffered by the population as a whole were a reflection of a transformation of public attitudes in favour of collective and egalitarian solutions. But no such transformation had in fact taken place. The common sense of hardship and unity of purpose engendered by the early years of the war concealed rather than resolved the major differences between the representatives of different corporate and systactic interests about what ought to be done when it was over.[33] If instead the question is asked what mutations of practices actually occurred which constituted a qualitative change in the roles defining English society, the answer is that there were none. No more than claims that a

---

[31] Cf. Eleanor Barton, General Secretary of the Women's Cooperative Guild, in a BBC discussion with Hugh Dalton in 1932: 'yes I'm sure that children's welfare centres and maternity clinics and other social services of that character have been of immense value to working-class mothers' (Beveridge 1932, p. 78).

[32] The political ingenuity of Bevan's nationalization of the municipal and voluntary hospitals lay in upsetting Conservative supporters of the voluntary hospitals and Labour supporters of the municipal hospitals in equal measure while favouring the interests of the hospital doctors whose support for a universal service was essential (J. Campbell 1987, p. 167).

[33] José Harris (1986, p. 238) remarks that 'An historian who surveys the wartime literature on reconstruction is soon struck by the fact that a common language of visionary patriotism and a common sense of national unity continued to mask an immense diversity of values and goals.'

'revolutionary' Conservative administration 'dismantled' the 'welfare state' in the 1980s, during which public expenditure on education, housing, health, and social security remained at just under a quarter of the gross national product, can claims that a 'revolutionary' Labour administration 'created' it in the 1940s be taken as a report of sociological facts which the recording angel would confirm. By the 1950s, when under a Labour administration rationing had been virtually abolished, subsidies cut, income tax reduced, and the 'bonfire of controls' lit, it had become apparent not only that poverty had not been abolished but that the 'welfare state' was benefiting the middle classes at least as much as the working classes. The 1940s, like the 1980s, exemplify not a qualitative change in the relations between the economy and the state but rather the continuing disjunction between the rhetoric of politicians and journalists and the underlying processes of social evolution which only with hindsight can be seen for what they were.

IDEOLOGICAL EVOLUTION

§7. On any theory, the link between the location of roles in the economic and ideological dimensions of the structure of a capitalist-liberal-democratic society will be sufficiently close that there will be no serious inaccuracy if the second is reported initially in terms of the first. But status-groups are not just economic classes viewed in terms of their consequential ideological power. The criteria of status in a society like England are a function of differences in relationship to the means of persuasion as well as of production (and coercion): not all 'respectable' manual workers are 'skilled' any more than all 'gentry' are 'landed' or all 'intellectuals' are 'bourgeois', and there are differences not only of education and life-style but of gender, ethnicity, and even religion by which the incumbents of otherwise similar roles are ranked in social esteem by their fellow-citizens. What is more, it is seldom that the systactic dividing-lines are so clear-cut that individual roles – let alone individual incumbents of multiple roles – can be assigned a precise location in social space. It is not merely that, as I pointed out in section 2, change has to be reported in anecdotal rather than statistical terms, but that the standard indicators of social distance – commensalism, endogamy, and subjectively evaluated manners and mores – are impossible to translate into scores on a scale which rival observers can transpose *salva veritate* from one theory to another.

But despite all this, there is in broad terms a demonstrable evolution from the late-Victorian and Edwardian sub-type of the liberal mode of persuasion to that of the period from the 1920s onwards parallel to that in the capitalist mode of production. Before about 1880, the principal systactic distinctions in the hierarchy of status had been between a hereditary aristocracy, a small 'middle class' of manufacturers and clerisy, and a 'vast residuum' to which, as Matthew Arnold put it in *Culture and Anarchy*, 'we may with great propriety give the name of *Populace*'. But in the 1880s the ideological as well as the economic ascendancy of the aristocracy began to diminish. The acceptance of new, 'plutocratic' wealth in the topmost status-group can be directly inferred from the changing criteria of elevation to the peerage: the proportion of those whose careers had been in the fields of industry and commerce, which had been only 10.4 per cent for the period between 1837 and 1885, rose to 31.1 per cent for the period between 1885 and 1911 (Pumphrey 1959, p. 11). At the same time, the Order of Merit was created, as its name implied, to recognize achieved prestige in science, scholarship, and the arts as well as political or military service to the state. Ideological domination is always to some degree a matter of self-confidence, and during the 1880s a nobility and gentry whose inherited entitlement to deference had been unquestioned began for the first time to feel themselves under threat. Except in Ireland, the threat did not become a reality until after the First World War. But by 1886, the year in which Tennyson's lament for the old social order in 'Locksley Hall' was neatly paralleled in fiction by W. H. Mallock's *The Old Order Changeth* (Cannadine 1990, p. 30), both those who deplored it and those who welcomed it realized that the traditional preeminence of the 'lords of human kind' might be coming to a close. Not much of this, it is true, is conveyed by contemporary accounts of the London 'season' of 1914; it was in 1918 that the then Duke of Marlborough pronounced the old order finally 'doomed'. But the years from 1880 to 1914 are as clearly different in this respect from the period which preceded it as they are from that which followed it.

Yet, as in the mode of production, some continuities are hardly less striking than the differences. Two generations later, for all the lack of resident domestic servants, the relaxation of attitudes and manners symbolic of social deference, and the presence of women in roles previously reserved for men, the monarchy continued to enjoy no less prestige than it had in the mid-Victorian period (when the Queen had been by no means universally popular); the rituals and conventions of the House of Lords were unchanged, despite the curtailment of its powers and the introduction of life as well as hereditary peers; the Archbishop of Canterbury still presided, despite the diminished prestige of the Church of England, over the episcopacy from Lambeth Palace; the 'ancient' universities still outranked the 'provincial', and the regiments of the Household Brigade the regiments of the line; and there remained the same castelike divide between the schooling of the children of the higher-ranking status-groups and of the rest.

Although successive governments voiced increasing concern about educational reform, the public schools were left untouched[34] to provide, in the inter-war years, something like a quarter of all university students and an overwhelming majority of Oxford and Cambridge undergraduates. This preponderance was eroded to some degree after the Second World War. But as we shall see in more detail in section 13, the roles at the top of the more prestigious professions continued to be occupied predominantly by men recruited into their careers by that route. Although aristocratic incumbency of the offices of state became altogether exceptional, entry to the bar, the Church, and the officer ranks of the armed services remained open to the sons of the topmost status-group to an extent out of all proportion to their numbers. There was no lack of criticism from the Left. Maxton, to whom Oxford and Cambridge were 'those centres of snobbery and exclusiveness', would have liked to close them down altogether (McAllister 1935, p. 157); Crosland in the 1950s, like Tawney in the 1920s, denounced the public schools as socially divisive as well as unfair in their exclusion of more talented children of lower-ranking status-groups; in the 1960s, John Vaizey, for whom the public schools were responsible for inculcating into the 'governing classes – and by example, into the rest of us – virtues of "leadership" which have brought the country to the verge of bankruptcy', the solution was that they should be turned into either comprehensive boarding schools or junior colleges (1962, pp. 43, 55);[35] and the Wilson government in due course set up a Royal Commission which reported in 1968 and 1970. But no changes followed. Only the direct-grant schools had government funding withdrawn from them in 1974.

It would, however, be a mistake to report the public schools as the preserve of the topmost status-group together with the new rich aspiring to enter it. With the possible exception of Eton, they never in the twentieth century had a majority of pupils who were sons of the aristocracy and landed gentry, and indeed they traditionally catered not only to the upper-middle class but also to the poorer clergy and the lesser professions (Perkin 1989, p. 259). To the extent, therefore, that a public-school education marks a systactic boundary, the status-group so defined extends some way down the scale of economic class. The most readily detectable indicator is accent ('U' rather than 'non-U')

---

[34] Some sections of the Labour Party, as well as the TUC, were explicitly in favour of their abolition. But the policy of the Labour Party was always that they should be supervised and adapted, but retained (Brooke 1992, p. 131). Crosland (1956, p. 261) professed himself unable to understand why Socialists obsessed with the grammar schools were so indifferent to the 'much more glaring injustice' of the independent ones.

[35] Is it symptomatic of the strength of the institutions which he was then attacking that he ended his career on the Conservative benches of the House of Lords and sent his own children to a public school?

and the most useful vernacular term for the role (although not coined until the 1980s) is 'Sloane Ranger'. The *Official Sloane Ranger Handbook* (Barr and York 1982) may strike some readers as an unusual kind of source to cite in a work of academic sociology, since it is not only humorous in intent but also partly directed to advertising the services offered to the clientele which it depicts. But it contains accurate as well as satirical observations of the life-style and mores of the status-group which it delimits, and that status-group is just as distinctive in its way as is the 'respectable' working class. The correlation (whatever the explanation of it) between a public-school education and a career in the law, the army, the City, certain professions (including, for example, medicine but not dentistry), and land-owning (or estate agency) was as clear in the 1970s and 1980s as it had been in the 1920s and 1930s: the difference was not in what occupational roles had become 'democratized' – music and the stage, for example, having always had a 'classless' ethos and image – but only in what roles had become more recently acceptable, such as accountancy and journalism.

At this point, it might be objected that the superiority of this status-group and the practices defining its members' roles, as of the élite to which its members defer in their turn, is not unanimously recognized even by its own members. There are and have always been articulate dissenters who may be similarly located by ascription in the ideological dimension of the social structure but who explicitly reject the criteria which place them there. Even in the late-Victorian and Edwardian period there had been republicans hostile to the monarchy, radicals dismissive of honours and titles, and bohemians as contemptuous of plutocratic as of aristocratic life-styles. But none of them were carriers of practices capable of subverting the established mode of persuasion in the way that the Nonconformist churches had been able to do against the Church of England in the late-Victorian and Edwardian period, when the dominant ideology had still been ostensibly religious rather than secular. The members of the higher-ranked status-groups might all be aware of a neglect of conventions once more strictly adhered to and a tolerance of conduct once more widely censured as immoral. Some, moreover, might see their own sons and daughters adopting deviant practices and life-styles in explicit repudiation of the conventional criteria of social prestige, whether as drug-takers,[36] anarchists, squatters, drop-outs, 'hippies', or 'travellers'. But the fact remains that the deviants never acquired, and often never even sought to

---

[36] The emergence of the 'drug underworld', and its subsequent demonization in the popular press, can be precisely dated to 28 July 1916 when under Defence of the Realm Regulation 40B possession of cocaine or opium other than by authorized professionals became a criminal offence (Kohn 1992, p. 44).

acquire, the countervailing ideological power which would enable them to replace those criteria with their own.[37]

§8. That, however, is still the view from the top; and as I remarked in section 12 of chapter 2 in volume II, incumbents of higher-ranked roles in all complex societies are apt to draw systactic distinctions which are irrelevant or even meaningless to those further down. To the great majority of the population of twentieth-century England, gradations of social prestige within the 'U-speaking' status-group are of no concern whatever. Even the assimilation of working-class leaders into the conventional honours system was a matter of indifference to all except a handful of gratified colleagues or indignant rivals.[38] To the sociologist concerned to report the evolution of the mode of persuasion over the course of the century, the question to be asked about the working classes is not whether their members changed their view about the criteria of social prestige to which the middle classes subscribed but whether there was an erosion of the dividing-line between 'manual' and 'non-manual' workers and their families from the point of view of differences in ideological rather than, or as well as, economic power.

In the late-Victorian and Edwardian period, there emerged a distinctive urban working-class life-style which, as I remarked in section 15 of chapter 1, acknowledged the value of 'respectability' no less than, but in a very different sense from, that of the middle-class observers who studied it. From the 1880s onwards, middle-class participation in the activities of working-class families away from their place of work effectively ceased. The involvement of the clergy declined almost to vanishing-point; working-men's clubs, once emancipated from aristocratic or middle-class patronage, divided into those which retained a direct party affiliation and those for entertainment only (J. Taylor 1977, p. 56); the seaside holiday resorts which increasing numbers of working-class families could now afford to patronize became segregated as between working-class and middle-class clienteles, with Blackpool as the most celebrated example; and the rise of association football as a mass working-class spectator sport whose players were themselves of working-class origin was aptly symbolized in the defeat of the Old Etonians by Bolton in the Cup Final of 1883. In the aftermath of the First World War, the further change which had occurred was equally aptly symbolized by royal attendance (albeit for the second time) at the Cup Final of 1923.[39]

---

[37] Moreover, 'Most of the lower-working-class sub-cultures displayed a sharp antagonism towards hippie culture. The bohemian life-style was despised as effeminate and weak by both skins and bike boys' (B. Martin 1985, p. 148).

[38] Of a national sample polled in 1990, only 7 per cent expressed themselves in favour of the 'Honours List' as currently constituted (*Financial Times*, 31.1.90).

[39] Cricket, by contrast, remained relatively undemocratic. But it may be worth noting one tiny

Between the wars, a narrowing of social distance and an assimilation of working-class and middle-class life-styles became something of a commonplace – always excepting the homogeneous working-class communities where the old staple industries were concentrated. Carr-Saunders and Caradog Jones, who thought that an 'upper class' was no longer externally distinguishable even in the 1920s (1927, p. 71), were rhetorically asking ten years later: 'Is it not a misreading of the social structure of this country to dwell on class divisions when, in respect of speech, dress and use of leisure, all members of the community are coming to resemble one another?' (1937, p. 67). Orwell commented on the emergence after 1918 of an indeterminate 'class' (i.e. status-group) whose members' position could not be inferred from their clothes, manners, and accent, and went on to argue that 'in tastes, habits, manners and outlook the working and the middle classes are drawing together' (1941, p. 53). Priestley, in his *English Journey*, talked of a 'new post-war England' of by-passes, bungalows, swimming pools, and 'factory girls looking like actresses',[40] an England 'at last without privilege' and 'as near to a classless society as we have got yet' (1934, pp. 401–3). But what these observers neglected to report was not only the distinctiveness of the middle-class and increasingly suburban life-style of newly built, mortgage-financed, semi-detached houses with a telephone, a refrigerator, and a garage for the Austin Seven, but also the extent to which lower-middle-class families remained determined to maintain the social distance between themselves and working-class families: as it was put by a letter-writer to the *Watling Resident* in 1931, 'There is a tendency on the part of certain groups of people to regard themselves as the "aristocracy" of the Estate, because they happen to wear clean collars, pressed trousers and speak with a tolerable air of assurance' (Durant 1939, p. 46 n.1). Ferdynand Zweig, in a study carried out in London immediately after the Second World War, found the difference in mentality, attitude, and behaviour between manual and non-manual workers 'perhaps the most outstanding single fact' brought to light in the course of it (1948, p. 88), and although he modified this conclusion in a later study of manual workers in the 'affluent' 1950s, he nevertheless still reported that despite the breaking-down of 'cleavages between classes in economic terms', cleavages of education and culture were 'stronger and more powerful than ever' (1961, p. 211). Willmott and Young, in their study of Woodford in the late 1950s, reported that 'the nearer the classes are drawn by the objective facts of income, style of life and housing, the more are middle-

mutation of practice analogous in its way to the abolition of 'tufts' at Oxford which I noted in section 14 of chapter 1: after 1922, *The Times* no longer reported amateur, but not professional, cricketers as 'Mr', although it still gave them, but not the professionals, their initials.

[40] Or at any rate *trying* to look like their favourite film star (*New Survey of London Life and Labour* 1934, p. 47).

class people apt to pull them apart by exaggerating the differences subjectively regarded' (1960, p. 122). Later still, Richard Hoggart observed of Farnham in the early 1990s that 'As in all things English, there is a pecking-order among bargain-hunting places. On the whole, middle-class people . . . do not go to jumble sales or to the Chapel Market . . . People from all parts of the town's society visit the Maltings Market but working-class people will not go to the genuine antiques fair' (1994, p. 150); and he commented too on the middle-aged, middle-class women's 'held-on-to-sense of status' which 'affects above all their voices' (p. 178).

In the Second World War, even more than in the First, the involvement of the working class in the war effort was recognized explicitly in official propaganda. Moreover, the ideological reaction of much middle-class as well as working-class opinion against what was seen as the discredited complacency of the traditional élite went so far as to amount to what one historian calls a 'marked redistribution of social esteem which the state helped to promote' (McKibbin 1990, p. 291). Symptomatically, the portrayal of the working class in the media became noticeably less patronising. *Punch* no longer published cartoons whose only point lay in the inherent comicality of working-class people to middle-class readers, like that of 30 January 1932 in which two working-class children were depicted in a fashionable area of London with the girl saying to her small brother 'Come now, Alf – this ain't the Mile End Road. If yer can't walk proper try and look as if yer knowed *how*'; and the cinema of the 1950s and 1960s began in a way that had never happened in the 1930s to combine perceptive social criticism with accurate representation of working-class life-styles (Marwick 1982, p. 138).[41] At the same time, the vocative use of 'Sir' and 'Madam' declined so far as to strike an informed American observer as the symptom of the 'new populism' of the 1970s 'most impressive to the returning foreigner' (Beer 1982, p. 149). But none of this licensed an inference, any more than did working-class 'affluence', to assimilation of working-class and middle-class norms and values, let alone abolition of the systactic dividing-line between 'U-speakers' and the rest. G. D. H. Cole, writing towards the end of his life, saw the change in the 'lower' classes' sense of exclusion from 'equal intercourse' between the inter-war period and the 1950s as 'much less striking' than the change between his youth (in the late-Victorian and Edwardian period) and the inter-war period (1956, p. 42).

Regional differences persisted no less in the ideological than the economic

---

[41] There was, in the 1930s, a left-wing Film Movement, but the films made by these 'amateur and shoestring groups', however useful as sources for left-wing ideology, 'had little significance as contemporary influences upon the beliefs of the general public, being limited in exhibition almost exclusively to the converted, at political meetings and film societies' (Hollins 1981, p. 359).

dimension of the social structure. No one community can be taken to be representative of the changes taking place (or not) across English society. But a study of Banbury (Stacey 1960), for which the fieldwork was carried out in 1948–51, reports both change and continuity in the criteria by which social prestige was assigned, and Banbury was in this respect far from unique. I have quoted already, in section 2, the newcomer who described it shortly after the First World War as 'pure *Cranford*', and there were still, after the Second World War, residents who could recall the vanished practices of touching the cap or curtseying to the squire and his lady. But between 1918 and 1945, the traditional ranking of public-school-educated county and gentry, upper-middle professionals, middle-middle proprietors and managers, and lower-middle branch managers and small proprietors, was disrupted by the intrusion of non-traditional middle-class roles – executive civil servants, grammar-school teachers, and industrial technicians – whose incumbents attached more importance to economic achievement than to ascribed social prestige.[42] Despite this, however, the researchers found that the differences in 'manner of life, attitudes, and beliefs' of upper-class, middle-class, and working-class status-groups were 'so great that any intimacy between members of each is difficult if not impossible' (p. 164). By the time of the restudy (Stacey *et al.* 1975) for which the fieldwork was done in 1966–8, the three middle-class 'sets' – town-dwelling businessmen, country-dwelling professionals and gentry, and town-dwelling intelligentsia – were found to be too loosely ranked to be placed on a vertical scale (p. 118) and manual workers, whether or not they identified with the 'working class' or perceived class conflict as important, showed equally little deference to an aristocratic élite (p. 121). But a distinction between middle-class and working-class status-groups was still clearly discernible between manual and non-manual occupational roles (p. 123).[43]

Within the working class, the distinction between 'rough' and 'respectable' status-groups was thoroughly familiar to late-Victorian and Edwardian observers. But they would all have agreed that 'respectability was a relative term and what might be respectable for some would be shocking to others' (Johnson 1983a, p. 226); and this combination of local variation within a nationally recognizable ideological norm continued after not only the First World War but also after the Second. In broad terms, the indifference to, or defiance of,

---

[42] Cf. Roper Power (1937, p. 405) on the 'more exclusively pecuniary standard of social eligibility' and 'wider class range of social contacts' of inter-war newcomers to Hertford.

[43] Cf. Collison (1960, p. 596) who found in a study of Oxford based on the 1951 census tracts that 'people at the top of the occupational and education hierarchies are sharply differentiated from the remainder in their style of life, insofar, at least, as it is reflected in housing', and that 'In both residential dissimilarity and housing quality . . . the manual workers as a group are set off sharply from the remainder.'

conventional norms on the part of the 'unrespectable' working class persisted in similar contrast to the conformity of the 'respectable'. But the practices which defined the roles of the unrespectable working class became no more nearly pervasive than did those of middle-class drop-outs. Professional criminals, indeed, tended to be not merely patriotic but reactionary in their values and attitudes,[44] and although there were occasional counter-cultural groups or movements whose practices were directed at not merely rejecting but overturning those of the 'respectable'[45] the location of 'unrespectable' roles remained unchanged.

§9. There are, however, other criteria by which deference has been sought, accorded, or denied in twentieth-century English society; and of these, ethnicity and gender have been recognized as the most important by rival observers of all theoretical schools. The definition of 'ethnicity' is not uncontroversial. For the purposes of this chapter, however, it is enough to say that certain groups or categories of members of twentieth-century English society have been consistently denied legitimate status mobility on ascriptive grounds deriving from imputed 'race'. This has not necessarily prevented individual members of such status-groups from achieving upward mobility: as I remarked in section 9 of chapter 1, the dominant liberal ideology has always allowed to Jews, foreigners, colonials, and Blacks the possibility of rising to the top of the hierarchy of status, however slender their chances of doing so. But it is a matter of demonstrable sociological fact that they, like women, have faced not only discrimination but prejudice – that is, not only unfavourable treatment but pejorative stereotyping.

In the late-Victorian and Edwardian period, the two status-groups most explicitly identified as alien were the Irish, who were distinguished as much by religion as by nationality, and the Jews, particularly those of Ashkenazi rather than Sephardi origin who were fleeing from discrimination and, often, outright persecution in Russia and Eastern Europe.[46] Until 1905, when immigration

---

[44] Arthur Harding, as recorded by Samuel (1981), comments several times on the Conservatism of his family as well as many of his associates and (less surprisingly) the publicans of the East End.

[45] For example, the members of the 'Angry Brigade' of the early 1970s whose ideology and life-style was totally ununderstandable in the tertiary, descriptive sense to the police: 'The antagonism and mutual incomprehension was at its worst when the police, mostly working class or lower middle class in origin, who accepted the values that society expected them to uphold, personally confronted a group of people from the same social background, but who had rejected those values utterly' (G. Carr 1975, p. 87). Cf. the 'vehemence' (J. P. Martin 1987, p. 171) of the police reaction to the 'hippie convoys' which converged on Stonehenge at midsummer in 1985 and 1986.

[46] Many were, or hoped to be, on the way to the United States but were compelled to remain in England through lack of funds (Krausz 1971, pp. 25–6).

controls were imposed in the Aliens Act which followed the Royal Commission set up in 1902, it had scarcely been thinkable that foreigners (if not gypsies) should not be free to enter and leave England as they pleased or that they should be issued with visas or permits or required to register with the police. Nor indeed did the Irish, of whom there were already over 600,000 in England and Wales in the mid-Victorian period, ever suffer the same restrictions as would-be immigrants of either Jewish or, as it came to be called, 'New Commonwealth' origin. But after the First World War, the issues raised by immigration became a more, not less, important and contentious item on the agenda of public policy. In the 1930s, when the rise of Nazism in Germany coincided with a detectable increase in anti-semitism in both working-class and middle-class status-groups, it was the admission of 'refujews', as they were colloquially labelled, which generated protest and controversy. In the 1950s and 1960s it was the admission of members of societies which had been colonies or dependencies of Britain. The problem was not entirely new: outbreaks of violence against Blacks had occurred before the First World War, and in 1919 there was the particularly serious one in Cardiff to which I referred in section 12 of chapter 1 and which one latter-day commentator has claimed to have done 'incalculable' harm to race relations in the area (Ramdin 1987, p. 73). But it was only in the 1960s and 1970s that legislation was enacted dealing directly with discrimination and prejudice and that the issue became a national and not merely a local one. By then, many members of the non-white population of England were disposed to label English society as unequivocally 'racist'; and although the term carries too many pre-emptive overtones to be usable for the purpose of reportage, its use does support a semi-deductive inference that there has been a change in the mode of persuasion and the pattern of roles associated with it.

The relevant behaviour, which is well documented in a by now extensive academic literature, ranges all the way from the discreet discrimination practised by clubs and schools through discrimination in the labour and housing markets against applicants presumed 'unsuitable' to organized violence by native-born 'skinheads' against targeted persons or households. As its incidence increased, there was at the same time an increase in governmental action designed to moderate and curtail it, notably the Race Relations Acts of 1965 and 1976. To what extent legislation of this kind can prevent the replication or inhibit the diffusion of the practices against which it is directed is controversial: in the view of many of those affected by discrimination and prejudice, it represents no more than lip-service to a 'liberal' ideal to which, in their experience, few of their fellow-citizens genuinely subscribe, while in the view of some, at least, of those fellow-citizens in dominant status-groups it functions only to exacerbate what it purports to remedy. But however much more antagonistic ethnic relations became, the official ideology remained as liberal as ever.

In this respect, governmental responses to Jewish immigration between the wars were much the same as to Afro-Caribbean and Asian immigration after the Second World War. The restrictions on the number of refugees from Nazi Germany were not explicitly framed to exclude Jews as such, any more than the Aliens Act of 1919 had been. But the authorities were well aware of the extent of anti-semitism and reluctant to exacerbate it, and not only trade unionists[47] but the incumbents of professional roles (notably in medicine) were concerned to protect their positions in the labour market. Although observers then and since have differed about the importance of anti-semitism as a component of the ideology of British Fascism, the practices by which Jews were stereotyped and discriminated against were for a time increasingly overt (particularly in parts of London). But English Jews were too widely differentiated systactically and too well assimilated in their life-style to respond to discrimination and prejudice as a cohesive and visible status-group (E. R. Smith 1989, p. 61). Although anti-semitic practices survived, whether (among the élite and the middle classes) more discreetly or (among the working classes and underclass) less, they were no more than marginally relevant after 1945 to a report of changes in the mode of persuasion and the dominant ideology underlying it.

From the late 1950s, however, the steady increase in immigration from India, Pakistan, and the West Indies brought about what successive governments perceived as a 'race relations problem' of a more intractable kind. Not only did the number of new arrivals arouse fears and resentments among members of the white working class directly affected in the housing and labour markets, but their distinguishability by colour made status-group assimilation correspondingly more difficult than for the Irish or the Jews, not only for themselves but for the next generation of native-born 'Black British'. There began to be formed an increasing number of associations directly concerned to uphold the status and promote the interests of ethnic minorities. This had always been true, although to a lesser extent, of the Jews (while for the Irish, the Catholic Church had performed an analogous function). But associations such as the Racial Action Adjustment Society or the United Coloured Peoples Association were constituted by roles and practices very different from the Jewish Boards of Guardians. They expressed a systactic consciousness directed both to defence of their members against harassment and to the assertion of

---

[47] The advertisements for donations to the Lord Baldwin Fund for Refugees said explicitly that refugees from Germany 'will not be allowed to take the jobs of British workers here or to receive unemployment benefit. The Trade Unions are satisfied about that' (illustration following p. 128 in Kee 1984).

specifically 'black' claims to greater equality of status with the dominant white majority. This common consciousness did not extend across the division between the Asian and West Indian communities (Layton-Henry 1984, p. 177), and attempts by Afro-Caribbean (and some white) propagandists to establish a terminology whereby all non-white members of British society should be designated 'black' found relatively little support within the Asian community where, in any case, individual upward mobility tended to be more actively pursued and self-identification by adherence to Islam more salient (*Economist*, 18.10.89; Modood 1994). But whatever the variations in the pattern of ethnic relations by region, religion, nationality, and systactic origin, there had come about an unmistakable change from the pattern in late-Victorian and Edwardian society.

This trend was not peculiar to the field of ethnic relations. Feminism, which had weakened as a 'socio-political' movement after the achievement of universal adult suffrage (Kent 1988, p. 232),[48] still persisted, as I reported in section 3, through the 1930s and 1940s, and reemerged in strength in the 1960s and 1970s, and protest against discrimination by gender ran to some extent in parallel with protest against discrimination by ethnicity. Similarly, associations and pressure groups formed to represent the interests of tenants or claimants or single parents or disabled people were at least in part expressive of claims to equality of social esteem for their roles and repudiation of stigmatizing stereotypes and terminology. But they too framed their propaganda and organized their campaigns in terms of the dominant liberal mode of persuasion, just as the propagandists and organizers of the trade-union movement had done before them on behalf of manual workers and their families. The difference was not so much in the nature of the ideology in whose name collective upward mobility was demanded as in its less exclusive connection with the division of labour and class structure. There *was* still a connection: the under-representation of women in the more lucrative and prestigious occupational roles was as readily demonstrable as the under-representation of ethnic minorities. But the evidence of both community studies and opinion surveys – fluctuating and ambiguous as these can be – licenses an inference to the significance of ideological criteria of discrimination and prejudice independent of class, of which ethnicity carried the greatest potential for instability within the existing mode of production and coercion as well as persuasion.

Yet again, therefore, we are faced with a change of sub-type but not of mode. To contemporary observers of the late-Victorian and Edwardian mode of persuasion, it would have been as difficult to foresee the establishment of a

---

[48] Or, to report it more precisely, 'Faith in women's ability to revolutionise political life for the benefit of all had been replaced by an anxiety simply to ameliorate the day-to-day problems of the most disadvantaged women' (Holton 1986, p. 152).

Commission for Racial Equality specifically empowered by Parliament to issue codes of practice and carry out formal investigations directed to the promotion of equality of opportunity and improvement of social relations between what they would have called 'racial' groups as to envisage the possibility that 'black consciousness' should become a factor of not negligible importance in national party politics or that 'political correctness' should require the excision of allegedly pejorative references to Blacks from literary texts. It is true that there had existed even before then pressure groups such as the Anti-Slavery Society which were dedicated to raising the social location of specified groups or categories of the underprivileged. But an ideology, however limited, of 'positive discrimination' and an articulate ethnic counter-culture explicitly laying claim to parity with the indigenous myth of 'English' homogeneity (Saifullah Khan 1987, p. 228) marks yet another evolutionary stage beyond the unreconstructed individualistic ideology of Palmerston and the 'age of equipoise'. To what extent this modification of a still dominant liberalism should be seen, morally speaking, as progress is, as always, up to you. But there is an unmistakable change between the period from 1880 to 1914 and the period after the First World War.

POLITICAL EVOLUTION

§10. The extension of the franchise in 1918 could be said to amount by itself to an evolution from one to another sub-type of the democratic mode of coercion: 'Social and political change caused primarily by war and electoral reform transformed the contours of party debate' (Jarvis 1996, p. 64). But as I remarked in section 2, it was not as if the enlarged electorate then used it to move the British state out of the democratic into a socialist or authoritarian or any other novel mode. The extension of the franchise, together with revision of constituency boundaries, may or may not have been decisive in the replacement of the Liberals by Labour as the principal party of opposition to the Conservatives. This is likely to remain a matter of controversy among historians, since there is no possible way of finding out what would have happened if either the franchise had been extended without the war or if the Liberals had not split in the course of it. All that can be reported without risk of contradiction is that in the event, the war left Labour in a better position than the Liberals to exploit it (Pugh 1982, p. 181). But the arguments of this volume are not affected one way or the other by the validity of the competing hypotheses invoked to explain the Liberal 'downfall' (T. Wilson 1968). Quite apart from the difficulty in interpreting the act of voting itself, which raises many of the methodological problems of 'primary' understanding discussed in chapter 2 of volume I, the outcome of successive General Elections is peripheral to the interests of our hypothetical observer concerned only with changes (or the lack of them) in the modes of production, persuasion, and coercion. What matters is the nature of the concomitant mutation or diffusion of political practices which amounted to a change from one sub-type of the democratic mode of coercion to another.

It is, however, a relevant fact that the first election decided by the adult population (less only the women in their twenties) in their new roles as electors[49] was an overwhelming majority for the Coalition which had won the war. Whatever their intentions or their motives, the sequel was an experiment in cross-party politics which was never subsequently repeated. Other coalition governments were formed thereafter. But they did not, and were not expected to, replace the customary practices of peacetime politics or even suspend them for more than a limited and exceptional period. Only Lloyd George seriously attempted to create a lastingly bipartisan institutional context for the conduct of national policy. This involved on the one hand an attempt to bring the two sides of industry together in a spirit of 'Whitleyism' and on the other an attempt to achieve a 'fusion' of the Conservative and Liberal parties in Parliament. But for reasons to be analysed in chapter 3, both failed, and the resumption of party conflict not only deprived the remaining would-be 'centrists' of electoral support but discredited the whole notion of 'national unity'. After 1922, British politics evolved into a contest for votes between nationally organized parties presenting alternative policies to the enlarged electorate in successive General Elections, and both the practices and the doctrines of late-Victorian and Edwardian politics came to seem increasingly remote. Economic issues and related appeals to class-based interests had not been entirely absent from electoral politics before 1914. But issues such as Welsh disestablishment, rural smallholding, temperance, the House of Lords, and the franchise itself disappeared from the agenda; not only the House of Commons but local councils (Chandler 1991, p. 105) became increasingly dominated by career politicians rather than local notables or wealthy industrialists; the power attaching to the role of Prime Minister, now increasingly supported by personal patronage, remained greater than it had ever been; and the old practices of extra-parliamentary appeals to a limited and presumptively well-informed audience through the provincial press were replaced by politics 'packaged for consumption' (Matthew 1987, p. 54) by readers of the popular national newspapers, radio listeners, and in due course viewers of television.

The roles constitutive of national political institutions can, admittedly, differ significantly from those constitutive of local ones. It has often been at the local

---

[49] The 1918 register was, however, 'notoriously bad' (Butler 1953, p. 172 n.2): only 56.6 per cent of the enlarged electorate cast their votes as compared with 71.3 per cent in 1922 (adjustment being made in these percentages for two-member constituencies).

rather than the national level that the carriers of mutant practices have been most active. In the late-Victorian and Edwardian period, as I pointed out in section 5 of chapter 1, there were some thoroughgoing Socialists in municipal government, and Sidney Webb, in the *Fabian Essays* of 1889, had seen in the 'gas-and-water' and other services of the municipal authorities the extent to which 'our unconscious Socialism has already proceeded' (1962, p. 82). Labour candidates in local and municipal elections had scored some notable victories in the years immediately prior to the First World War, and did so again in 1919 when public opinion first began to turn against the Coalition. It was at local level that there emerged, between the wars, the threat of Labour councillors in East London winning elections by promising their poor constituents generous relief to be paid for by 'milking the wealthy rate-payers in the west through the Metropolitan Common Poor Fund' (Deacon and Briggs 1974, p. 352); that Liberal candidates were relentlessly displaced by Labour even when there was a revival of support for the Liberals at national level (C. Cook 1975, p. 168); and that in the early 1980s a new generation of radical Labour councillors emerged out of the dissatisfaction of community activists with traditional Labour policies – councillors, moreover, of whom many combined their roles as councillors in one district with roles as employees of a different authority in another in the cause of maximizing the usefulness of local government as a base from which they could 'translate Socialism into practice on the ground' (Gyford 1985, p. 59). But as the inter-war Labour Party strengthened in both organization and support, so did the roles of its municipal representatives become increasingly subordinated to its national priorities; the threat of the 'pauper vote' receded before central government had to take the measures, including disenfranchisement, which Chamberlain had been quite prepared to contemplate; the Labour candidates who replaced their Liberal predecessors became in their turn the entrenched incumbents against whom the 'New Left' of the 1970s were to mount their rebellion; and when and where members of the New Left came to occupy local-governmental roles, not only their policies but the standard of the services which they provided alienated many of their working-class constituents – notably 'the un-young, the un-black and the un-gay' (P. Jenkins 1987, p. 245). The story of local politics since universal suffrage is thus one which again reflects an unmistakable change from the late-Victorian and Edwardian period, but not one which ever seriously threatened the institutional consensus on the scope and nature of the British version of 'mass' parliamentary democracy.

'Consensus', like 'corporatism' and 'racism', is a term too ambiguously theory-laden to be used to report the state of English society's culture or structure. But to the sociologist concerned only with changes in the mode of the distribution of power, the moral to be drawn from the debates about 'consensus', whether in the age of Baldwin, in the years after the Second World War, or in the post-Thatcherite 1990s, is that there always coexisted uniformity of standards and assumptions with diversity of doctrines and styles. There was always 'consensus' in the sense that the rules which governed the practices defining the roles of the enlarged electorate and their elected representatives alike remained unchallenged except by a handful of extremists, either in 'fringe' parties which never secured more than a tiny fraction of total votes cast or in the constituency associations of the major parties (notably the 'Militant Tendency' in the Labour Party in the 1970s and 1980s). But there was never 'consensus' in the sense that there were always strong divergences of opinion not only between professional politicians but between that proportion of the electorate which voted for the policies of the Left and that which voted for the policies of the Right as these were defined in the particular circumstances of successive elections. The exaggerated parliamentary majorities produced by a first-past-the-post electoral system are not evidence of large-scale conversions to the ideology or programme of the winning party: even in the 'landslide' of 1931 Labour still secured an average vote per candidate of 33 per cent and even in the 'landslide' of 1945 only reached just over 50 per cent (Butler 1953: Table 23). For all the erratic fluctuations in the opinion polls since their introduction just before the Second World War, and for all the startling reversals of fortune in by-elections from East Leicester in 1922 to Chelmsford in 1945 to Orpington in 1962 to Newbury in 1993, the enlarged electorate consistently divided between Left and Right somewhere between 60:40 and 40:60 (the Liberal vote being assumed by psephologists to divide, if no Liberal candidate is standing in the given constituency, in favour of the Conservatives).

There was, however, a lasting difference between national politics after the Fourth Reform Bill of 1918 and between the Third Reform Bill of 1883 and the Fourth. All the participants were now aware not only that the support of working-class electors had to be actively sought and retained by any party which aspired to be a party of government but also that the working-class interest was now inextricably integrated into the process of policy-making at national level. That interest was no longer, as in the late-Victorian and Edwardian period, articulated through parliamentary representatives functioning as ancillaries to the TUC but through a national party organized under the banner of its constitution of 1918. To the extent that trade-union representatives dominated both its national executives and its local constituency bodies, the economic and political roles of the representatives of the working class were now fused. The industrial and political wings of the Labour movement never came together in the way that Arthur Henderson, for one, had hoped that they would do, any more than all working-class electors voted

Labour – a sociological fact which continued to be interpreted by rival commentators in accordance with their own mutually incompatible presuppositions.[50] But the systactic interest (however defined) of the working class was now promoted or thwarted or diverted or appeased, as the case might be, within the institutions of a new sub-type of England's democratic mode of coercion.

§11. Although the actions of the adult members of English society in their roles as voters are the most obvious manifestation of conflict between systactic interests by which a change in, or even of, the mode of coercion might be brought about, they are of course not the only one. Behind the alternation of rival incumbents in ministerial roles and the succession of appointed entrants into Civil Service roles, there continued to function the practices and roles through which the means of coercion were brought directly to bear. Our hypothetical observer from section 18 of chapter 1 needs to see not only what changes there have been in the way in which the power attaching to the roles of electors and their elected representatives has been exercised, but also what changes there have been in the roles of soldiers, police, and the directors and agents of that part of the so-called 'security services' responsible for internal surveillance and control.

In section 12 of chapter 1, I stressed the extent to which, throughout the century, the use of force by the police, backed up by the threat of the use of force by the army, has been at least tacitly accepted as legitimate by public opinion. But the practices defining the roles of the police did, nevertheless, mutate after the First World War. Traditionally, the police outside of London were locally organized, locally commanded, and answerable to the 'watch committee' of their local authority. But between the recourse to troops in the miners' strike at Tonypandy and Penygraig in 1910 and the 'Battle of Orgreave' between miners' pickets and mounted police in the South Yorkshire coalfield in 1984, use of the means of coercion was progressively centralized under the Home Office. Relations between the civil and military authorities continued to be conducted on the basis of an explicit distinction between their roles, with troops only to be used in specific circumstances and under specific constraints for tasks which both sides (for different reasons) agreed were not

---

[50] The contrasting presuppositions are well exemplified in the exchange quoted by McKenzie and Silver (1968, pp. 14, 69) between Peter Shore, writing in a Labour Party Educational Series pamphlet in 1952 ('How is it that so large a proportion of the electorate, many of whom are neither wealthy nor privileged, have been recruited for a cause which is not their own?'), and the rejoinder to him in a Conservative Party pamphlet published in the same year ('It may seem strange to Mr. Shore, but it is fortunately true that large masses of the British People are not animated by class hatred or selfish personal greed, but are inspired by a sense of patriotism').

properly theirs. But the autonomy of local police forces was progressively restricted, and the response to local disorders taken increasingly out of their hands. Such initiatives had met with only limited success prior to 1914: any help given by one police authority to another was at their discretion, however much the Home Office might seek to encourage it. But links to central government were tightened during the war, and although the recruitment of some quarter of a million special constables (including a special reserve force of some ten thousand men with Territorial or regular army experience) during the General Strike could be said to be a response to a unique set of circumstances, the number registered stayed in six figures until the Second World War. At the same time, the chief constables, although still notionally answerable to their local authorities, increasingly saw their roles in terms of answerability to the central government alone, particularly when, as in the 1930s and 1980s alike, they doubted the commitment to 'law and order' of Labour-controlled authorities. By the time of the miners' strike of 1984, the role of Home Secretary could, as I put it in section 13 of chapter 1, be said to have evolved into that of Minister of Police; and by the time that a new police bill was being debated by Parliament in 1994, the issue was whether more than token delegation to local police authorities would still remain (Jones *et al.* 1994).

The police had always, as much in the late-Victorian and Edwardian period as after it, been resented in working-class communities. 'In every direction', as Stephen Reynolds put it in seeking to convey to his middle-class readers a working-class point of view, 'inside his own home as well as out, the working-man's habits and convenience are interfered with, or are liable to be interfered with, or his poverty is penalized, by the police' (1911, p. 86). Or as a later historian puts it, 'What the nineteenth-century and early twentieth-century urban poor experienced was the daily imposition upon them of disciplines which were both alien in origin and coercive in application' (Gattrell 1990, p. 284). Whereas in middle-class communities the police were seen as protectors of property and preservers of the peace, in working-class communities they were seen as fellow-members of the same systact of origin who clubbed strikers, sheltered blacklegs, and worked while others were on the parish (Meacham 1977, p. 18). In this respect, there was no difference between the late-Victorian and Edwardian period and the period after the First World War.[51] The change was that there attached to the roles of an increasing number of administrators and officials as well as police enhanced powers of detention, eviction, investigation, and withdrawal of benefits. Supervision and instruction now extended

[51] Use of the Special Branch (formed in 1883) to monitor 'subversive' groups likewise pre-dates the war (Barnes 1979, p. 941): its target was the Fenians 'strewing their infernal machines about the metropolis' (Adam 1931, p. 165).

beyond the occasional visits of the late-Victorian and Edwardian district nurse, factory inspector (including, from 1893, 'lady inspectors'), school attendance officer, and middle-class philanthropist to the compulsory decasualization of labour, the imposition of 'seeking work' tests on the unemployed, the means testing of households in receipt of benefit, and the removal of children into local authority care, while for the vagrant in the casual ward, the supervision of the 'tramp major' (L. Rose 1988, pp. 114–15), or, for the inter-war unemployed, of the 'ganger' in the labour camp (Humphries and Gordon 1994, pp. 138–9), could more accurately be reported as bullying than as supervision. These intrusions proceeded alongside the relaxation of many of the ideological constraints on the behaviour of the working class which the middle-class philanthropists of the late-Victorian and Edwardian period had sought, however unsuccessfully, to impose. But the powers of coercion attaching to the roles of the police and security services, once enlarged, were never diminished. From the Police Act of 1919 to that of 1964, and thence to the Police and Criminal Evidence Act of 1984 and the Police and Magistrates Courts Act of 1994, the corporate power of the police force, with its own internal hierarchy of roles and its own ideology of accountability to the law rather than the public, was progressively strengthened at the same time as the regulations governing its exercise were (at least in theory) tightened. The fact that, with the exception of the miners' strike of 1984, industrial disputes became less overtly violent should not be taken to license an inference that strikers or rioters who confronted the police were up against anything less than 'a far more formidable instrument for central government, in confronting labour, than could have been foreseen at the turn of the century' (J. Morgan 1987, p. 278).

This increase in the power attaching to roles in or answerable to central government extends, moreover, across the range of functions nominally assigned to local government. At the time when Sidney Webb was proclaiming the unacknowledged Socialism of the municipal authorities, English local government was in its late-Victorian and Edwardian heyday as institutionalized by the Local Government Act of 1888. But after the First World War, as expenditure on housing, health, education, transport, and poor relief steadily rose, so was central government control over that expenditure steadily tightened. There came to attach to the roles of ministers and officials, including district auditors and ministry inspectors, novel powers to override what had previously been the autonomous decisions of the local authorities. The change was institutionalized in the Local Government Act of 1929 in much the same way as the 1888 Act had institutionalized the change from the mid-Victorian period. The power of central government could, to be sure, be used either way: where a Conservative Government in 1926 suspended the Boards of Guardians of West Ham, Bedwellty, and Chester-le-Street, a Labour government in 1974 retrospectively indemnified the councillors of Clay Cross against surcharges arising from refusal to implement the Conservatives' Housing Finance Act of 1972. But there was no question where the power now lay. From the perspective of central government, the sanctions available to curb intransigent local authorities might still seem inadequate. Education, in particular, was an area in which the proportion of expenditure coming out of central funds – itself a matter of dispute from the Fisher Act of 1918 onwards – could be said not to be reflected in a corresponding degree of central control. But there could be no doubt about what the central government could do if it chose, including direct intervention in negotiations over teachers' pay in 1931 and again in 1986. The Thatcher government's abolition of the Greater London Council and the Inner London Education Authority, whether according to your evaluative presuppositions it was a good thing or a bad one, is clear testimony to the extent of the difference from the roles and practices by which the relation of central to local government had been defined prior to 1914.

§12. The augmentation and concentration of executive power in the hands of central government became, indeed, something of a truism from Lloyd George's prime ministership onwards.[52] There were, and continue to be, disputes between rival observers over the nature and extent of that power. Where some saw the prime minister's role as increasingly unfettered by either back-bench MPs now subject to the control of the party whips or public opinion now increasingly vulnerable to manipulation and the concealment of information, others saw it as constrained by the need for electoral popularity, the influence of senior civil servants, and the demands of industry and the trade unions. Similarly, where some saw the Civil Service as increasingly bureaucratic, increasingly solicitous of its members' own corporate interests, and increasingly unanswerable to Parliament, others saw it as increasingly passive, increasingly subservient to ministers, and capable only of interpreting rather than initiating policy. But there could be no dispute either about the increasing concentration of the power attaching to the roles of ministers, officials, and their agents or about the increasing scope and volume of legislation enacted by Parliament. It is true that this legislation, whether in the areas of public and institutional law or in areas concerned with the regulation of the behaviour of the members of British society in their private capacities, was not always enforceable, and that in the relation between employers and

---

[52] The sanction of dismissal of Cabinet colleagues gives the role power over, as well as on behalf of, central government – more so, in one academic observer's opinion, than 'anywhere else in the democratic world' (A. King 1991, p. 31). Cf. Grigg (1988, p. 168) 'whereas Lord Salisbury had far more clout with foreigners than Mrs. Thatcher has, she has far more clout with her own compatriots'.

employees, in particular, it sought not to impose but rather to 'regulate, to support and to restrain' (Kahn-Freund 1977, p. 6). Direct recourse to the means of coercion was both selective and sporadic. But there was never any suggestion that the power attaching to the roles of ministers and officials might be cut back to what it had been before 1914.

At the same time, this change was accompanied by an increase in the activities of what came to be known as 'pressure groups'. It was not until after the Second World War that academic observers began to analyse their functions in any detail. But as one American observer had pointed out between the wars, 'Britain Has Lobbies Too' (Herring 1930);[53] and an accelerating trend in their direction was, like so much else, first clearly visible under Lloyd George's Coalition when there was a marked increase in direct approaches to ministers on behalf of special interests by associations formed explicitly to represent them (K. O. Morgan 1979, p. 168). Such associations had not been unknown to late-Victorian and Edwardian or indeed mid-Victorian politicians: Gladstone had always had to deal with 'faddists' such as the members of the teetotal United Kingdom Alliance or the antidenominational Nation Education League. But after 1918, the practices of pressure-group politics burgeoned in the new institutional environment of mass parties and adult suffrage. The associations formed came to range increasingly widely in membership and objectives from the National Council for the Unmarried Mother and Her Child to the Electoral Reform Society to the British Iron and Steel Federation to the Africa Bureau to the British Legion to the Campaign for Nuclear Disarmament to the National Association for Mental Health to the Child Poverty Action Group to the Sunday Freedom Association. Some pursued their objectives directly through Parliament, some through the media, and some by the mobilization of active supporters. Some, inevitably, met with more success than others. But it would be unwise to infer directly from their existence that political power had been devolved to them to any significant degree. Even groups representing the systactic or corporate interests of sets of roles to which considerable power attached already might function more as outlets for the expression of grievances than as influences on either the formulation or the execution of policy. Thus, neither the Federation of British Industries, established in 1916, nor the National Confederation of Employers' Organizations (NCEO), established three years later, ever had the power to persuade the government to do what they wished even in the final period of Lloyd George's government when, in trade-union eyes, the claims of its spokesmen that it represented equally the interests of capital and labour had

---

[53] It is not that British academics were unaware of the practice of lobbying. But the orthodox response (e.g. Muir 1933, cited by Alderman 1983, p. 16) was to deplore the by-passing of Parliament by 'sundry forces' organized to bring pressure on government directly.

been exposed as fraudulent.[54] Between the wars, when the NCEO was often outspoken in its opposition to Baldwin, such limited concessions as the government made to business interests were at its own timing and on its own terms. Later still, when the Thatcher government was being denounced by the trade unions in terms at least as vehement as their predecessors had ever applied to Lloyd George, the FBI's successor organization, the Confederation of British Industries, was even more resolutely ignored than the FBI had been by Baldwin or Chamberlain. Conservative governments could and did consult business organizations and trade associations before passing legislation, appoint individual businessmen to sit on government bodies, and favour the interests of employers against unions to the extent that their own view of national or party interest might require. But the roles of the representatives and spokesmen of industry, even when they had the wholehearted backing of their constituents, never carried political power as such. Nor did those of the members of the General Council of the TUC, even when granted as privileged access to Labour ministers as they briefly were under the Wilson government of 1974. Persistent and wide-ranging pressure-group activity was symptomatic of an evolution from one to another sub-type of the democratic mode of coercion. But activity was never a guarantee of success.

The proliferation of pressure groups can, therefore, like the concomitant changes in the structure and culture of the political parties, be reported as evidence of an increase of a kind in the power attaching to the role of citizen as such. But it was matched by the increasing power now attaching to the roles of ministers and officials. The government had, by the end of the First World War, a wholly unprecedented power to control the labour of its citizens, whether by employing them directly, conscripting them into the armed services, or indirectly influencing the terms and conditions of their employment with private firms. But for this power to be effectively applied, some accommodation had to be arrived at with the representatives of those whose labour was being controlled. When, in 1915, the government passed the Munitions of War Act, it not only banned strikes (and lockouts) and imposed compulsory arbitration but introduced 'leaving certificates' which placed so much power in the hands of employers that the Act was nicknamed the 'Slavery Act' by union activists (Wrigley 1987a, p. 31). But in January of 1916, the hated section 7 of the Act whereby workers who changed their employer without a leaving certificate would be out of work for at least six weeks was amended in direct response to union representations (A. Reid 1985, pp. 54–6).

---

[54] Sir Allan Smith and the Parliamentary Industrial Group did have some success between 1921 and 1923 with their interventionist and mildly reflationary programme for meeting the challenge of socialism, but it turned out, ironically, to be politically counter-productive (Rodgers 1986, p. 1102).

This sort of compromise between powers taken by Parliament with the theoretical sanction of the legitimate use of force and what is sometimes called the 'veto power' of organized interest-groups has been repeated time and again since 1915. All pressure groups confronting, or seeking to negotiate with, the government of the day could, given a sufficient appearance of support, get their proposals onto the agenda of government. But the willingness to consider them was within an institutional environment taken as given. However successful in delaying, diluting, or frustrating measures which ministers wished to enact, the practices defining their roles stood no chance whatever of undermining the capitalist-liberal-democratic mode of the distribution of power.

The specific use which successive governments have made of their augmented powers and the degree of support or opposition which they have provoked among the incumbents of the roles affected by them will naturally be differently judged by observers with different evaluative presuppositions. But from the perspective of the dominant ideology, the liberties of the law-abiding citizen were sometimes diminished and sometimes enlarged. If the state moved to require all eighteen-year-old males to serve in the armed forces in peacetime, or to restrict the freedom of movement of workers in one place seeking to support fellow-workers on strike in another, or to curb the right of entry to holders of British passports, so did it also move to provide workers with paid holidays, to protect the general public from atmospheric pollution, and to remove from consenting adult male homosexuals the threat of prosecution and thereby of blackmail. On no theory could it any longer be reported as 'neutral' in the sense once proclaimed by the 'old' Liberals and still hankered for by many of the 'new': never again could the metaphor of 'holding the ring' apply in the way that it had before 1914. But 'the state' was still a relatively weak one. The power attaching to the roles of ministers and officials remained from the First World War onwards both much greater than it had been before it and much less than it would have been in either an authoritarian or a socialist mode.

MOBILITY, INDIVIDUAL AND COLLECTIVE

§13. Thus far, such changes as there have been during the twentieth century in the structure and culture of English society have been reported by reference to the roles by whose itemization its modes of production, persuasion, and coercion are defined. But roles are not only parts performed according to institutional rules but vectors in a three-dimensional social space. Their incumbents are constantly moving to them from various systactic origins (or as immigrants from other societies) and leaving them on emigration or death; many of these people have moved from one role into a higher- or a lower-ranked one (or more than one) during the course of their adult membership of

English society; and many of the roles which they have occupied at any one time have themselves been changing not only in their location in social space but in the content of the practices defining them. Social mobility as such is not a defining characteristic of the mode of the distribution of power.[55] But our hypothetical observer needs to be made aware of whatever facts about both collective mobility (i.e. of roles in social space) and individual mobility (i.e. of persons between roles) may help to explain the changes which have or haven't taken place in the modes of production, persuasion, and coercion; and, as will be described in chapter 4, mobility (or its absence) is a significant aspect of the subjective experience of the representative incumbents of different roles.

Although the statistically rigorous study of individual mobility in English society dates only from after the Second World War, it was a topic of which many observers were aware long before that. It was not just that stories of long-range upward mobility of the kind celebrated in Samuel Smiles's *Self-Help* and *Lives of the Engineers* continued to appeal to the popular imagination. Contemporary observers of the late-Victorian and Edwardian social structure were also well aware of the expansion in the number of non-manual occupational roles which was going on around them and the consequent need for recruits to be drawn from working-class families to fill them. D'Aeth, in the analysis of the Edwardian class structure which I took as a starting-point in section 5, commented that 'individuals usually remain in the group into which they were born, but passage into other groups in both directions is common' (1910, p. 272). Given that in the late-Victorian and Edwardian period four-fifths of the population were being born into the working class, the first part of his conclusion was no more than a matter of arithmetic: even with a higher rate of increase in the number of non-manual occupational roles than in fact occurred between the censuses of 1901 and 1911, and a sharper fall in the middle- and upper-class birthrate, the chances of upward mobility for a working-class child could only be minimal. But since there was no institutional barrier to such mobility except to the extent that some occupations were closed to women, there was bound to be a minority of working-class households within which the experience of individual upward mobility was not unknown, and an increasing number of families where one spouse occupied, if only temporarily, a higher systactic location than the other. Moreover, contemporary observers were able to supplement their anecdotal observations with calculations based on the statistics of income distribution which supported a quasi-deductive inference to the same effect. The number of incomes below the income-tax threshold but above the wage-earning working class rose far

---

[55] Not that mobility rates, or 'permeability', cannot be used to define a typology of societies (Svalastoga 1964). But where does it lead? Not, wherever else, to a set of validated hypotheses explaining why their modes of production, persuasion, and coercion have evolved as they have.

faster between 1880 and 1914 than did the total number of occupational roles, so that if, as was assumed, there was an inverse correlation between fertility and class, individual upward mobility out of the working class must have been more frequent still.

This tendency for an expanding non-manual workforce to be increasingly recruited from the children of working-class parents was confirmed by more systematic research carried out several decades later. But before the findings of that research are summarized, readers should recall from chapter 3 of volume II the concept of a 'reproduction ratio' – that is, the proportion of members of a society who at any one time occupy roles located neither above nor below those occupied by their parents at the date of their birth. This, as I pointed out, is an 'inflow' measure: by giving the percentage of children in a given systact who were born into it, it generates comparisons of *absolute* mobility rates. But it will not be the same figure as the percentage of children born into a given systact who have remained in it, which is an 'outflow' measure generating comparisons of *relative* mobility rates. The source for these calculations is in either case a matrix in which a sample of the society's adult population is distributed among cells whose columns denote the respondent's current systact and whose rows denote his or her systact of origin. But the apparent precision of such matrices can entice the unwary reader into quasi-deductive inferences which are not sustainable on closer analysis. There is not only the technical problem that the numbers in the cells are constrained by the marginal totals (and the totals for parental origin are not a report of the distribution of the population in any one year). There is also the methodological problem that the reproduction ratios are a function of the number of systacts into which the total sample is divided, and the researcher's decision about this will be theoretically pre-emptive in the sense discussed at length in volume I. What is more, there is also the further technical problem that some respondents, at least, will not be telling the truth about their parents' systactic location at the time of their birth (or whenever else the investigator may choose).

The two most important studies of individual social mobility in twentieth-century Britain are that undertaken by Glass and associates in 1947 (Glass 1954) and that undertaken by Goldthorpe and associates in 1972 (Goldthorpe 1980). But their presuppositions and purposes are different from each other, their results cannot be directly compared, and neither divides the population systactically in the same way or by the same criteria as is done in this volume.[56]

---

[56] Like the Registrar-General's census classification, the Goldthorpe classification has perforce to be used by sociologists who disagree with his criteria, even though his sample could in theory be recoded into mine (or anybody else's). The theoretical point at issue, however, is not a trivial one: not only should classes be defined in terms of the location of their constituent roles in the economic dimension of social space independently of the duration of individual role-

Moreover, the Goldthorpe study is restricted to employed men aged between twenty and sixty-four in 1972, and it may be hazardous to draw population-wide inferences from a sample drawn from only a proportion of that proportion of the adult population aged sixty-four or less who are in paid employment of some kind in a given year. Notwithstanding all these reservations, however, there can be no dispute between rival observers that there has been a consistent trend in upward individual mobility measured in terms of absolute inflow combined with persistent disparities in relative outflow. Overall, the pattern is one of little long-range downward mobility,[57] modest but increasing long-range upward mobility, and considerable short-range inter- and intra-generational mobility in the middle of the occupational structure. Of Goldthorpe's 'service class' – roughly, my 'upper-middle' and 'middle-middle' classes – the majority were, by the 1970s, sons of fathers who, at whatever date the sons were aged fourteen, had been in occupational roles located below those now occupied by their sons. Of men in Glass's Status Category I ('professional and high administrative') over half were already sons of lower-ranked fathers (although none were sons of unskilled manual workers), while of men in Goldthorpe's Class I (higher-grade professionals, administrators and officials, managers in large industrial establishments, and large proprietors), almost three-quarters were sons of lower-ranked fathers (and an eighth sons of unskilled manual workers).

On the other hand, when the *relative* chances of sons born into different classes of rising into a higher one are calculated, Goldthorpe's sample, like Glass's, shows a predictable inequality between the working classes and the classes above them. Given the distribution of roles between classes as the researchers define them, this could not, for inescapable arithmetical reasons, be otherwise.[58] But the inequality is particularly marked in regard to mobility into

incumbency, but similarly located roles should be assigned to the same class whichever of the three functionally equivalent criteria of economic power – ownership, control, or marketability – applies to them. The apparent exceptions, like the management trainee or boss's son doing a token stint on the shop floor, aren't 'real' incumbents of their roles (cf. section 1 of chapter 2 in volume II).

[57] It is no surprise to find only one Wykehamist born between 1900 and 1922 in a manual occupation in the 1960s (Bishop 1967, p. 61). Cf. Zweig's 'public-school man, a qualified engineer of forty-five' who was working as a fitter with London Transport in 1946–7 (1948, p. 68).

[58] It remains, however, controversial among sociologists why there is not more 'exchange' mobility than there is. It may be because there are structural and cultural constraints on the replacement of middle-class by working-class sons and daughters, or it may be because middle-class sons and daughters are more able and ambitious, or both. Neither the Glass nor the Goldthorpe studies collected the evidence against which the 'meritocratic' hypothesis could be tested; but nor does a fit between the findings of these studies and predictions based on IQ validate it, since any attribute normally distributed with a regression to the mean will fit the mobility data equally well (Saunders 1995, p. 37).

the élites of economic class, social status, and high political or administrative office. Neither Glass nor Goldthorpe offer any data on this. But Tawney, in his Halley Stewart Lectures for 1929, commented on the very high proportion of judges, bishops, senior officials in the home, foreign and imperial services, bank and railway directors, and successful candidates for the administrative grade of the Civil Service who were drawn from the higher classes and more select public schools (1952, pp. 72–4); and similar calculations a generation later disclose a very similar pattern – 62% of senior civil servants, 80% of high court and appeal judges, 67% of bishops, 80% of clearing bank directors and 83% of directors of major insurance companies were educated at public schools (I. Reid 1981, p. 226, Table 6.14 and the sources there cited).[59] It is true that this degree of closure applies more to the topmost status-group than to either the economic or the political élite: the proportion of 'new rich' increased in the middle of the century to the point that of those millionaires who died in the 1960s nearly a third were self-made (Rubinstein 1974, p. 163), and the Labour Party, despite the considerable representation of sons of middle-middle and upper-middle class fathers in its Cabinets, did also provide more openings at both national and local level for sons (and sometimes daughters) of manual workers than the Liberal Party had ever done. But the hopes of egalitarian reformers such as Tawney that changes in the educational system might significantly improve the chances of working-class children rising into élite roles were disappointed. Heath (1981, p. 77) estimates the chances of a man from a working-class home getting into *Who's Who* at 1/5000 as compared with 1/5 for a man from an élite home; for a 'white-collar background' his estimate is 1/500, and for a 'higher professional and manage-rial home' 1/200. Even the proportion of incumbents of higher-grade roles in the Civil Service whose fathers were manual workers, which had increased from 7% in 1929 to 9.1% in 1939 and to 20% in 1950, fell back again to 17% in 1967 (Kelsall 1974, p. 174).

When women as well as men are included in the overall pattern of individual mobility, the analysis is complicated by the number of those who either have no occupational as opposed to household role or have an occupational role lower (or, more rarely, higher) than that of their husband or household head or cohabitee. But despite the continuing disagreement among sociologists over whether or not households rather than individuals should be taken as the unit of class composition, for the purposes of this volume it is merely an instance of the familiar fact that although societies are defined by the itemization of their constituent roles rather than of their individual members, their individual

---

[59] Moreover, the overwhelming majority of these continued to be men: a survey of the top hundred British companies in 1994 found no female chairman, one female managing director, and two female finance directors (*Sunday Telegraph*, 4.9.94).

members can, as I remarked already in section 2, simultaneously occupy more than one role. Genuine two-career families are a rarity (Payne and Abbott 1990, p. 173). But both men and women in occupational roles who are also either hypergamous or hypogamous may need to be assigned to their cell in a mobility matrix in accordance with the higher-located of the two. A copy-typist, for example, who marries a middle-middle class professional or manager has clearly to be assigned to a higher class than one married to a manual worker (Goldthorpe 1984, p. 494); and so, in the same way, has a man in a lower-middle-class occupational role who marries the heiress to a substantial family business to be assigned to a higher class than one married to a copy-typist.[60]

It is true that where the subjective attitude of the person and the potential for collective action which his or her sense of relative deprivation may generate is at issue, the lower-ranked of the two roles may turn out to be the decisive one. But there is no reason to presuppose that such discrepancies will promote a systactic consciousness allying the person with either the lower- or the higher-ranked systact. In twentieth-century English society, the number of women whose marital or household role determines their systactic location, whether because of hypergamy or because they have no occupational role at all, is very much greater than the corresponding number of men. But the inclusion of women in the analysis of individual mobility patterns does not greatly modify the conclusions suggested by analysis of the pattern for men. The two facts to notice are first, that in terms of their domestic roles women are more likely to be upwardly than downwardly mobile through marriage or cohabitation, and second, that their pattern of relative occupational mobility is the same as men's at the same time as they are disadvantaged in absolute mobility: to some extent, therefore, men's upward mobility 'is bought at the price of downward mobility for women' (Payne and Abbott 1990, p. 168).

Finally, in reporting to our hypothetical observer the pattern of individual mobility, the relatively high rates among men born into the lower-middle class call for particular attention. This applies to women's exogamy rates[61] as well as to men's occupational mobility rates; and it applies to men's intra- as well as inter-generational mobility. Analysis of the 1972 sample in terms of 'three-point' mobility from father's class to respondent's first full-time occupation to respondent's occupation in 1972 discloses that men of 'intermediate' origin are rather more widely dispersed than men born into either the upper-middle and

---

[60] Perhaps surprisingly, however, data from the General Household Survey for 1979 and 1980 show that many men who are downwardly mobile from the middle class 'far from retrieving their class position through marriage, appear to consolidate their class status by marrying women in the lower manual classes' (G. Jones 1990, p. 118).

[61] See the diagonals in the matrix in Table 10.2 (p. 283) of Goldthorpe's second edition of 1987, in which the figures are derived from the General Election Survey of 1983.

middle-middle classes or the working classes; that those who are inter-generationally stable are likely to experience a good deal of intra-generational mobility both within and outside of the range within which they were born; and that a 'rather large' proportion of men found at any one time in either the working class or the upper-middle and middle-middle classes will have had an 'intermediate' occupational role at some other time in their lives.[62] One qualification, to which I shall be returning in chapter 3, is that self-employed members of the lower-middle class are comparatively likely to be the sons of men who at some previous time have also been self-employed. But here, too, there is much intra-generational fluidity; and there is no support for the suggestion that a tendency for higher-ranking occupational roles to be filled by those with suitable educational credentials has closed off the opportunities for promotion for the incumbents of lower-ranked ones. This, as I have just pointed out, does not apply to élite positions. But it does emerge from the analysis of different birth-cohorts so far as concerns the upper-middle and middle-middle classes. There can be no question both that inter-generationally, the reproduction ratio is much lower than anything remotely approaching a 'castelike' model and that intra-generationally, there is a great deal more mobility than could be reconciled with the hypothesis that the intermediate classes are a ' "buffer zone" between the middle class and working class proper' (Parkin 1971, p. 56) by which ascent into the higher-ranked roles is con-strained.[63] What counts as a 'high' rate does, admittedly, depend on the observer's theoretical presuppositions; but it would be an unconvincing 'buffer' which failed to prevent more than a third of men who had followed their fathers into working-class roles from rising subsequently into middle-class ones (Goldthorpe 1980, p. 42).

§14. These patterns of individual mobility, both inter- and intra-generational, have changed (or persisted) simultaneously with a pattern of collective mobility whose change (or persistence) may be even more indicative of a change (or not) in the mode of the distribution of power. Some of these changes have been reported already. But it would be a mistake to infer from them that there has been a steady compression of social distance in English society throughout the course of the century, any more than there has been a steady polarization. The fact of the matter is that there has been no uniform trend in either direction.

---

[62] See pp. 257–8 in the first edition, and cf. p. 334 in the second.

[63] Cf. the 'fair amount of short-term class mobility' found by C. N. Gilbert (1986, p. 389) in the 1981 Labour Force Survey, and in particular the mobility from manual into non-manual roles through sales work (particularly for women). If, however, 'salesgirls' should be assigned not to the lower-middle but to the unskilled working class, then Gilbert's inference should be qualified accordingly.

As I emphasized in chapter 2 of volume II, not only can polarization of compression be quickly reversed, but they can both be taking place simultaneously in different areas of social space within the same society – which is just what has happened in twentieth-century England.

In the late-Victorian and Edwardian period, polarization was indeed taking place. At the top, the owners of the large capital fortunes paying tax on their incomes of no more than 1s 2d in the pound were growing steadily richer both through capital accumulation and through increasing returns per unit of investment; and the same seems to have been true of the high-feed professionals of the upper-middle class. Below them, the middle-middle and lower-middle classes and the artisans of the upper working class were in general holding their own. But the steady rise in the cost of living was threatening the earnings of the 'artisans' and 'operatives', even when fully employed; casual and seasonal labourers were becoming more rather than less vulnerable to short-time working and unpredictable lay-offs; and the limited legislative measures being taken to improve the condition of the underclass license an inference to increasing public awareness of a need for protection of sweated labour, the unemployed, and the aged poor.

The First World War brought many changes, not merely in terms of the welfare of the relatively disadvantaged – of which more in chapter 5 – but in terms of the distance between roles in all three dimensions of the social structure. But since some of these changes were only temporary, comparisons with 1914 need to be made by reference not to 1919 but to 1924. By that time, when it was clear both that many of the gains made by the working classes during the war had been eroded and that large-scale unemployment was a problem which could not be dismissed as merely temporary, the argument for polarization as the norm and compression as the exception began to seem increasingly plausible. The failure of the promise of 'homes fit for heroes', the weakening of the bargaining power of the trade unions, the decline of the old staple industries (with real wages in coal mining due still to fall by 6 per cent between 1924 and 1929), the limited level of state benefits, and the continuing political ascendancy, despite universal male and in due course female suffrage, of the Conservative Party seemed to many contemporary observers to point firmly in the direction which the Marxists had predicted for so long. When, in the 1930s, the problem of unemployment worsened yet further, half-hearted intervention by government was having little visible impact on industrial stagnation, and Conservative ministers seemed as unwilling as Labour ministers had seemed unable to take effective responsibility for the welfare of the most disadvantaged, liberal theorists of (in a phrase of Mill's) the 'lowering of the powerful and raising of the low' began to seem even to some of themselves to have lost the argument for good.

Looked at more closely, however, the pattern is altogether more complicated. For a start, by no means all of the gains made by the unskilled working class during the war were eroded after it. I have reported already both the shorter working week and the lifting of the roles of the underemployed casual labourers of the late-Victorian and Edwardian period out of the underclass into the unskilled working class; and the unskilled working class was able, even after the collapse of the post-war boom, to earn pay-rates significantly closer to those of the skilled. Arthur Bowley, who had warned in 1921 that the then rate of minimum wages would not long remain in equilibrium relative to those of the artisans (1921, p. 108), nevertheless concluded ten years later not only that minimum wages were still, in contrast to 1914, above the poverty line but that the wages of unskilled manual workers had increased 'greatly' relative to those of the skilled, even after the flat-rate reductions of the early 1920s (1931, pp. 162–3, 148). Above the working class, the growing numbers of lower-middle- and middle-middle-class salary-earners were on average better off in real terms than they had been before the war, while still remaining below the level of income at which they would become liable to tax (pp. 142–3). And tax rates remained, as we have seen, very much higher than they had been. Bowley calculated (p. 138) that the number of 'the rich' which he defined at £10,000 a year in 1914, had shrunk, once the rise in prices is taken into account, from 3,500 to 1,300 by 1925, and he commented too on the sale or closure of country houses and the sale of farms to their sitting tenants. Moreover, if women in employment are considered separately from men, it is clear that in the 1920s not only did the number of administrative and clerical roles open to them show a marked increase but the wages of women in manual work had levelled up relative to those of men.

In much the same way, the evidence which in the 1930s pointed to a continuation of wide disparities in the degree of economic power attaching to the roles at the top and at the bottom of the class structure could not be claimed to support the inference of relentless polarization and lower-middle-class proletarianization which commentators on the Left were disposed to draw. It is true that studies like the Pilgrim Trust's *Men Without Work*, the Carnegie Trust's *Disinherited Youth*, or Tout's *The Standard of Living in Bristol* were hardly evidence to support liberal presuppositions of progressive compression of social distance, least of all when contrasted with the maintenance by the upper and upper-middle classes of a life-style not all that different from that of their late-Victorian and Edwardian predecessors. But collective mobility, strictly defined, was in fact minimal in either direction during the 1930s. Within the upper class, there was not so much an accelerated concentration of wealth in fewer and fewer hands as a broadening of the range of upper-class roles as money made out of land and finance was joined by new money made out of retailing, entertainment, and urban property. Within the middle classes, despite the downgrading of routine clerical roles, even the less well-paid salary-earners enjoyed greater security of employment than manual workers and retained their more favourable work-situation within the office as contrasted with the shop-floor. In the skilled working class, collective downward mobility of the shrinking workforce in the old staple industries was counterbalanced by collective upward mobility of new roles in electrical engineering, chemicals, motor vehicles, aircraft construction, building, distribution, and retailing. And in the unskilled working class, where unemployment was most severe, the provision of relief, although variable between one region or local authority and another, was nevertheless such as to confirm the view of the Pilgrim Trust researchers that the old, pre-war distinctions between artisans and the unskilled were continuing to be levelled out.[64]

After the Second World War, and the election of a Labour government pledged to wide-ranging social reform, compression between the upper and middle classes on one side and the working classes and underclass on the other looked altogether more pronounced and more lasting. But the contrast was not, as I have already pointed out, by any means as sharp as many contemporary observers believed: by the mid-1950s the relative location of the upper, middle, and working classes and the underclass could be seen to be much as it had been before. Charles Madge, who conducted a study of the wartime pattern of earnings and saving for the National Institute of Economic and Social Research, found no evidence of a permanent restructuring of the pattern (Madge 1943), as well as commenting that manual wage-earners 'do not seek to emerge from their group by acquiring property or a small business of their own' (p. 16). Although a few 'skilled' workers such as printers had become '£1,000-a-year-men' by the early 1950s, the workers in the munitions, aircraft, engineering, and motor industries who had enjoyed the highest increases in the war had not become '*embourgeoisés*' in any sense whatever; and working-class 'affluence' measured in terms of possession of consumer goods, although a journalistic commonplace, was largely the result of the opportunities for employment available to working-class wives. Full employment, mass marketing, and the institutions of the 'welfare state' benefited lower-middle-class and middle-middle-class households no less (and perhaps more) than working-class households; and upper-middle and upper class households, even if permanently deprived of pre-war levels of domestic service, transferred their

---

[64] 'Indeed it has been said that "unemployment is a great leveller" – that while it reduces severely the livelihood of those who are accustomed to some degree of comfort . . . yet there are others, whose value in the labour market is low, for whom unemployment assistance, by providing a steady income at a rate well above that of the lowest wages, definitely raises the standard' (1938, p. 101).

excess spending power into other areas of more or less conspicuous consumption (Barna 1959, p. 38).

After the mid-1960s, there begins a period in which a steady decline in international competitiveness was accompanied by a sharp increase in inflation: if the cost of living is measured against a 1930 (and, after a slight fall and rise, 1937) baseline of 100, the increase from 197 to 305 between 1951 and 1964 looks modest by comparison with the increase from 305 to 1,443 between 1964 and 1980. But the change during that period in the relative position of different classes, or fractions of them, was still not a uniform compression of social distance. The best contemporary source for the distribution of income and wealth is the Royal Commission set up in 1974, whose reports disclose that there was no consistent or lasting relative improvement in the position of the unskilled working class, any more than there had been between 1964 and 1970. The upper and upper-middle classes suffered a reduction in net unearned income; middle-middle-class proprietors, managers, and certain professionals lost ground relative to skilled manual workers; lower-middle-class earnings also increased more slowly than those of manual workers in the early 1970s, although they subsequently recovered; and women gained relatively to men in managerial and manual occupations, but not in public sector administrative and lower professional roles (Noble 1985). Once again, it is the relative inflexibility of the pattern of social distance between roles and systacts which is more striking than the marginal evidence of collective mobility. Such changes as there were were a function more of relative bargaining strength within sectors of the labour market. At the top, the upper and upper-middle classes continued to escape taxation of wealth as opposed to realized capital gains, while at the bottom the relative position of the underclass hardly changed at all. By the end of the period, the most striking change was in the overlap between occupational and household roles within the working class. Already by 1979, the Inland Revenue estimated that the 'black economy' represented $7\frac{1}{2}$ per cent of the national total,[65] and polarization between the members of multiple-earning households and the members of households where nobody was in work at all was on its way to becoming a sociological commonplace (Pahl 1984, pp. 313–14).

In the subsequent decade, as the Thatcher government put the policies of the previous administration deliberately into reverse, it became increasingly clear that the rich were becoming relatively richer and the poor relatively poorer. The incomes after tax not only of the upper class but of the high-feed professionals and high-salaried managers of the upper-middle class rose

---

[65] No precise figure is obtainable, for obvious reasons: a market research agency estimated £66bn for 1994, as against studies by the Revenue and Institute for Fiscal Studies which suggested a figure of between £40bn and £55bn (*Financial Times*, 10.6.95).

sharply, while the underclass became increasingly concentrated in inner-city areas of 'concentrated' poverty (Green 1994), inferior housing, and chronic un- or under-employment. Between 1979 and 1989, the real income of the poorest tenth of the population fell by over £400 per annum while that of the richest tenth rose by nearly £14,000.[66] But this still did not widen the total span of inequality in real net incomes between top and bottom deciles to what it had been in 1914, and in the middle of the class structure, many skilled working-class as well as lower-middle and middle-middle class roles (and households) improved their position relatively to those below them. Apart from the spread of property-ownership already discussed, real earnings growth overall recovered between 1979 and 1985 to more than three times what it had been between 1973 and 1979, while the proportion of total household income classifiable as 'rentier' (chiefly pension and life assurance benefits) rose from a tenth to more than a quarter between 1977 and 1987. Despite an unmistakable repolarization between upper class and underclass, it would not be accurate to report an overall flight from the mean. Conversely, whatever the rise in the living standards of the employed working class it did not amount to an overall compression of social distance between working-class and middle-class roles. In other words, Marx and Mill were still as mistaken as each other in predicting a single uniform trend either way.

§15. Social mobility, however, whether of persons between roles or of roles as such, can take place without any disturbance whatever of the modes of production, persuasion, or coercion. To our hypothetical observer whose interest lies there, rather than in the topic of either individual or collective social mobility as such, the reported facts are of importance more because of what they imply for the answers to two further questions which are closely related to one another: first, what practices are carried by the roles of the upwardly or downwardly mobile by which the mode of the distribution of power might, if significant competitive advantage attaches to them, be changed? and second, how far do the upwardly or downwardly mobile share a common consciousness of a systactic interest and a common sense of relative deprivation such as might, in that event, favour the diffusion and replication of practices defining such alternative roles?

Mutant or recombinant practices can be carried in a double sense when they are not only diffused and replicated among an increasing number of adjacent

---

[66] This was the conclusion of an inquiry into income and wealth by the Joseph Rowntree Foundation (1995). But individual mobility needs also to be taken into account: the households in the bottom decile in 1989 will not be the same as ten years before. Moreover, if household spending rather than household income had been calculated over the period, it is likely that it would be found to have risen.

roles but are introduced into more distant areas of social space by persons who are either geographically or socially mobile or both. There is no lawlike generalization to be cited about the effects of such mobility: it depends, as always, on the net phenotypic effects of the relevant practices in the particular institutional environment. But there are many cases in the historical and ethnographic record where immigrants from one society and culture (or region and sub-culture) to another bring with them practices which modify the institutions of the society (or region) into which they move; and there are likewise many cases where social mobility, with or without geographical mobility, introduces novel practices into existing economic, ideological, or political institutions – or all three. Indeed, English society itself offers many examples during the course of its long evolution, from the modification of the Anglo-Saxon institutions of land tenure and military service by the Norman invaders through the commercialization of the early modern economy by socially mobile yeomen and geographically mobile wage-labourers up to the 'plutocratization' of the late-Victorian and Edwardian upper class by financiers and entrepreneurs of whom a significant minority were foreign or colonial immigrants. But when the pattern of mobility in twentieth-century English society is examined from the same perspective, it is striking how few signs of similar processes are to be found.

Despite the continuing differences between region and region, England – if not Britain – was by 1900, as I have already pointed out, a much more homogeneous society than it had been a generation before. But at the same time, the differences between structurally separate systacts were in some ways wider. As religious and residential ties declined in strength, the distinctiveness of upper-class, middle-class, working-class, and underclass sub-cultures became more marked. The increasing numbers of working-class children who rose into the expanding middle class were moving into roles defined by practices very different from those which defined the roles of their parents (or of themselves, if their first occupational role was a manual one). Yet it was not as if, like immigrants from a close-knit foreign community determined to preserve their distinctive way of life in their new environment, they sought to import working-class practices into middle-class roles. The upwardly mobile, although they might well retain associational ties with members of their systact of origin, were likely to adopt unchanged the practices defining the roles into which they moved. There is, for twentieth-century England, no evidence that, as some sociologists have argued, individual upward mobility is accompanied by tensions of a kind which lead to anomic or disruptive behaviour. Nor, where mobility is through hypergamy rather than change of occupational role, is there any evidence that upwardly mobile spouses refuse, in the overwhelming majority of cases, to conform to the norms of their spouses' systact: on the contrary, the wives in the sample of Marshall *et al.* tend to conform to their husbands' class position as regards both self-rated class and voting intention (1988, pp. 134–5).[67] Nor, finally, is there any evidence that men or women who are upwardly mobile from the working class bring with them 'proletarian' attitudes to trade unionism: although Goldthorpe regards this supposition as 'not implausible' (1980, p. 276), he offers no evidence in support of it,[68] and the surprising proportion of women in Goldthorpe's Class I in Marshall's sample who are union members (63 per cent) is readily explained by their likelihood of occupying roles in teaching, social work, and local government where union membership is already the norm.[69]

There is, accordingly, no prima facie support for a hypothesis that the reported pattern of individual mobility is potentially subversive of the central institutions of twentieth-century English society. But there remains the possibility that this pattern carries implications for the practices constitutive of the roles of the *im*mobile which might be relevant to the stability of the modes of production, persuasion, and coercion. On Goldthorpe's figures, the reproduction ratio of the male working class in 1972 was 71 per cent – that is to say, of men aged between twenty and sixty-four then in manual occupational roles over seven out of ten had fathers who were themselves in manual roles when the men in the sample were aged fourteen. Of the rest, the great majority were the sons of fathers in Goldthorpe's Classes III to V (my 'lower-middle' class), into and out of which there is considerable intra-generational mobility from and to the working classes, while less than 1 in 20 are sons of fathers in Goldthorpe's Classes I and II; and conversely, the chances of a son of a working-class father being found in Classes I or II are just under 1 in 5. This is a pattern which could be argued on social-psychological grounds to be optimal for stability: as in the numerous findings which show that a sense of relative deprivation is less widely (and perhaps less intensely) felt among groups or categories whose prospects are lower rather than higher, this rate of outflow from a working class which is still largely self-reproducing may be at the same time high enough to satisfy the more ambitious of those born into it and low enough not to cause undue resentment and frustration among the rest. The subjective experience of both the mobile and the immobile is, as we shall see in chapter 4, closely bound up with what they perceive their chances of mobility

---

[67] The contrasting effects of upward and downward mobility on voting behaviour had already been widely studied: Butler and Stokes (1969, p. 100) found the middle-class children of working-class Labour parents significantly likelier to become Conservatives than the working-class children of middle-class Conservatives to become Labour.

[68] The supposition is in fact deleted in the second edition.

[69] Marshall *et al.* (1988, p. 128). A word of caution is in any case in order about sample size: there are only 20 women in Marshall's sample in Goldthorpe's Class I, of whom one is self-employed.

to be. But whatever the hopes of left-wing observers or fears of right-wing ones, a working class with a pattern of social mobility like this is no more likely to be as revolutionary as predicted by Marx than to be as assimilated as predicted by Marx's critics.

INTER-SOCIETAL DECLINE

§16. As I emphasized throughout volume II, there is no society whose evolution over the course of its history can be fully understood (in the secondary, explanatory sense) without reference to its relations with other societies, whether more powerful or less. But for the purpose of this volume, our hypothetical observer is interested only in the possible influence of the changes after 1914 in the inter-societal distribution of power on England's modes of production, persuasion, and coercion. The undisputed fact of Britain's decline in the global rank-order had many interconnected causes and generated many far-reaching effects. But if we ask what concomitant changes took place in the central institutions of English society, the answer is: virtually none.

The loss of inter-societal hegemony can be dated accurately enough to the stage of the First World War at which Britain's ability to continue the war at all became dependent on American finance.[70] But if this affected the modes of production, persuasion, or coercion of English society, the effects were not such as could be inferred from a simple comparison between England in the Indian summer of late-Victorian and Edwardian imperialism and England in the traumatic aftermath of the Suez debacle of 1956. Inter-societal decline was, as I remarked at the very beginning of chapter 1, already visibly under way in the late-Victorian and Edwardian period. But it took place in a context of steady increase in the absolute amount of resources available for distribution within English society itself. Whatever might be the pressure of foreign competition on such industries as textiles, shipbuilding, coal or – later – machine tools and motor vehicles, it bore only on certain geographical regions and certain clusters of occupational roles within them. Whatever the consequences of diminishing military and even naval strength relative to the armies and fleets of other nations, there was never any question of British institutions being altered under threat of coercion from any other society. And whatever the loss of national prestige as the superiority of English manners and mores came to be more and more critically questioned by the peoples of other societies (including its own dependencies), its internal status-system was only marginally affected, if at all.

---

[70] Skidelsky (1983, p. 335) says of the words of a memorandum of 10 October 1916 by Keynes that they 'fix the moment when financial hegemony passed irrevocably across the Atlantic'.

The same can be said of the steady weakening of British power relative in particular to the United States. Our hypothetical observer could hardly fail to be struck by the drain on Britain's resources in the two world wars or to appreciate how enormously more powerful the United States of 1945 was than had been the United States of the Spanish–American War of 1898. Indeed, the two world wars could be said to have strengthened the United States *pari passu* with their weakening of Britain: as Britain liquidated its overseas investments, was forced out of its former markets, and turned increasingly to imports for the supply and replacement of the materials of war, so did the United States strengthen its position as lender, extend its commercial influence abroad, and further increase its lead in technology and industrial production. But even in 1945, when British officials were advising their ministers that without an American loan the country was effectively bankrupt,[71] there was no thought in the minds of either themselves or those whom they were advising that the country would have to evolve into a different mode of the distribution of power. With hindsight, it is easy to see that successive governments were over-sanguine both about Britain's ability to maintain its traditional strategic and military commitments and about its international trading position once the countries of Western Europe and Japan had recovered from the immediate after-effects of the war. But they were quite right in assuming that even if the most pessimistic forecasts were to turn out to be well-founded, the attendant difficulties and hardships would be dealt with as best they might within a still capitalist mode of production, a still liberal mode of persuasion, and a still democratic mode of coercion.

The loss of inter-societal hegemony was, admittedly, reflected in a few perceptible changes in both the structure and the culture of English society. In the late-Victorian and Edwardian period, Britain had been the hub of an international system of trade and finance which had at the same time channelled much of its financial resources overseas and concentrated much of its resources in plant and labour in industries whose profitability was dependent on exports. This system, despite the best efforts of politicians, financiers, industrialists, diplomats, and officials (Cain and Hopkins 1993), was impossible to recreate after the First World War. But if the pattern of roles bound up with it was altered, it was only in two areas of the social structure. Since the staple export industries were also strongholds of apprenticeship and the 'craft' unionism of the skilled trades, the loss of overseas markets was bound to be one of the factors compressing the social distance between the Edwardian 'artisans' and 'operatives'; and since the opportunities for overseas

---

[71] Once again the moment can be dated to a memorandum by Keynes, who circulated the first estimate of the post-war deficit in the international balance of payments on 13 August 1945 (Cairncross 1985, pp. 78–9).

investment before 1914 had been partly bound up with Britain's predominance in the international financial system, the roles of the bankers and merchants who had depended on it were bound to be correspondingly weakened. It followed that in the regions where the staple export industries were concentrated, unemployment among 'craftsmen' was particularly severe (Burgess 1980, p. 205); and in the City of London, the careers of financiers like Weetman Pearson, the first Lord Cowdray (nicknamed 'the member for Mexico') or of Sir Ernest Cassel (half helped and half hindered by the Foreign Office in his dealings with China, Turkey, and Egypt) could not happen again (Thane 1986). But these are on any theory very minor changes within England's sub-type of capitalist liberal democracy.

§17. After the Second World War, the decline of British power proceeded in an approximate parallel to the withdrawal from empire. It continues to be debated among historians how far the empire, for as long as it lasted, represented an accretion of power to the metropolitan society rather than a drain on its resources not compensated by any net inflow once the costs of defending it had been met. However impressive to the proverbial man-in-the-street the Victory Parade of 1919 or the British Empire Exhibition at Wembley in 1923, they concealed behind a facade of global strength and united purpose weaknesses in strategy, manpower, technology, and trade which were to be fully exposed in the decades ahead and had been discernible already during the course of the First World War. But until after the Second World War, not only did British policy-makers persist in regarding the rising antagonism of nationalist sentiment in dominions and colonies alike as 'not an historical inevitability but a temporary and curable disorder' (Darwin 1980, p. 679) but large numbers of British people occupied roles which, without the Empire, would not have been there to be filled at all.

In the late-Victorian and Edwardian period, India had been the jewel in Victoria's imperial crown. For the daughter of a family with an already established tradition of either civil or military service, it was a matter of course that 'one's brothers, one's friends' brothers and so on were all either in the Civil Service in some part of India, or in the forces or the police or in something else' (C. Allen 1975, p. 37). But there were also many thousands of families outside of this tradition of imperial service whose members were involved through the roles which they occupied, whether at home or overseas, in trade, administration, education, or defence in relation to some part or another of the territories which the schoolroom atlases still coloured in red. This lasted through and beyond Britain's withdrawal from India, the Middle East, Africa, and the Far East as the practices by which the old imperial roles had been defined mutated from relations of command to relations of consultancy and the power of patronage passed from the metropolitan government and its officials to the roles of the members of the new élites of now independent ex-colonial states.

The question: what happened to all the incumbents of the old imperial roles? cannot be answered at all precisely (or if it can, the source has escaped me). Some stayed on, whether in retirement, or in the service of a newly independent government, or in the employment of a commercial firm which retained its position, albeit under tighter restrictions on its freedom of decision. Some returned, as they would have done in any case, to homes already purchased in the suburbs and seaside towns of the mother country. Some transferred their skills and experience into other occupational roles within the institutions either of England or of some other English-speaking country, sometimes retaining and sometimes not a connection with the territories where they had once exercised, or at least been protected in their roles by, imperial power. As late as the 1990s, for example, British ex-naval personnel were still to be found manning the private yachts of the Sultan of Oman. Whatever became of them all, however, they did not form a group whose consciousness of a common systactic interest might have made them carriers of practices significantly favourable to a change in England's mode of the distribution of power. The practices which had defined their imperial roles were as unlikely to be subversive of the domestic mode of production or persuasion as of coercion. They were no more a distinctive class than they were a homogeneous status-group or a faction of like-minded voters whose shared sense of relative deprivation might, if enough of them settled in the same parliamentary constituencies, have ensured the election of candidates favourable to their cause.

Although, therefore, the gradual elimination of imperial roles after 1945 meant that many of the people who would have occupied and performed them had perforce to find others instead, the social mobility which this implied was more likely to be lateral than vertical. The doctor, administrator, and engineer who might have been found together up-country in India or Malaya or the Gold Coast in the 1920s or 1930s, would, in the 1970s or 1980s, be performing their same occupational roles in the domestic economy; and if their households were in consequence without domestic servants, that was a difference between themselves and their parents or grandparents in England as much as between themselves in their actual domestic and their hypothetical imperial roles. If there was any single group or category whose location within English society was directly affected by the withdrawal from empire, it was that fraction of the upper and upper-middle classes which up to 1914 had derived the largest benefit, net of taxes, from the subsidized commerce between the metropolis and the empire (O'Brien 1988, p. 195). But it could hardly be argued that this change was more than marginal to the subsequent changes in the mode of production or that rentiers whose investments were no longer in companies whose profits derived from an imperial connection came on that account to be located in a different class.

As always, changes of structure must not be considered in isolation from changes of culture, and the gradual disappearance of imperial roles was bound to make their last incumbents look (and sound) increasingly anachronistic.[72] This had already been true, well before the time of Ernest Bevin, of arch-imperialists like Milner and Curzon; it was true of Leo Amery and, for that matter, of Churchill himself in the 1930s; and by the 1960s, it was truer still of Lord Salisbury in his die-hard defence within the Conservative Party of white settler interests in what was still – but not for much longer – being called Rhodesia. Yet it was not as if domestic political opinion had ever polarized between a whole-heartedly imperialist Right and a whole-heartedly anti-imperialist Left. From the days of Blatchford, the Webbs, and the Liberal Imperialists to the days of Attlee and Bevin ('the imperial Micawber'[73]), there had been solid supporters of the Labour Party who wished to maintain as much as possible of British domination, or at any rate influence, over dominions and colonies alike; and there had always been Conservatives as well as Liberals who were suspicious of the cost, and sceptical of the benefits, of the overseas bases and garrisons allegedly necessary to protect the commercial lifeline running from the Mediterranean through Suez to India and the Far East. No doubt the withdrawal from empire was, for those whose lives were directly affected by it, as momentous an event as was the Second World War itself. But, as with the war, it does not follow that any significant change in either the structure or the culture of English society must have either accompanied or followed it. The anonymous wit who, some time in the 1960s, first said that the British had 'ceased to be Romans and become Italians' was right in one way and wrong in another; right in that the practices and roles which gave the overtones of 'Roman' their authentic descriptive flavour had indeed disappeared; but wrong in that no qualitative change in England's mode of production, persuasion or coercion was involved in the process.

§18. Yet there is more to the story of the British Empire in the twentieth century, even for the limited purposes of this volume, than the changing

---

[72] The career of Cromer's son, Evelyn Baring, later Lord Howick, is doubly symbolic: first, as 'truly the last of the proconsuls – born to be a viceroy' who 'came to be a lonely figure on the old imperial Olympus' (Douglas-Home 1978, p. 324); and second, as Chairman of the Colonial Development Corporation for twelve years following his return from Kenya.

[73] Gallagher (1982, p. 146), quoting Dalton's account of Bevin saying to him in 1948 that 'if only we pushed on and developed Africa, we could have the United States dependent on us, and eating out of our hand, in four or five years'.

content and diminishing number of roles defined by practices dependent on its existence. For, as Engels was so well aware, the consciousness of being citizens of the nation on whose empire the sun never set extended far further down the social structure of England than those for whom it represented jobs or titles or an opportunity for travel, adventure, and a more enjoyable middle-class life-style than England itself could offer them.[74] Working-class children in the elementary schools who never read the novels of G. A. Henty, let alone Seeley's *The Expansion of England*, still absorbed from teachers who *had* read them an ideology of imperialism to which they were much more responsive than they were to any form of religious instruction (Humphries 1981, p. 41); and however many of the various imperial propaganda societies may have failed to achieve their stated objectives 'nonetheless they ensured the central and continuing role of an imperial world view in public propaganda, entertainment, and above all in education' (J. M. Mackenzie 1984, p. 171). Nor was there any necessity for newly enfranchised working-class electors to be opponents of imperialist policies abroad: as a German Socialist reported of the early weeks of the first Labour government, 'among the workers, in a circle stretching far beyond the party organization and the Socialistic electorate, there prevailed a naive and rapturous pride that by men of their class, and in their name, the mightiest empire of the world was ruled' (Wertheimer 1930, p. xii).

This aspect of the experience of empire touches on the same complex issues of psychology to which I referred in section 9, and there is unfortunately no well-validated psychological theory to which to appeal for explanation of the causes and consequences of xenophobia at the level of individual attitudes and behaviour. But the consciousness of superiority which Engels so deplored in the late-Victorian and Edwardian British working class[75] defined, sociologically speaking, a rank-order in the ideological dimension of power whereby the role of 'Englishman' carried prestige as such. There is no way of discovering how far this assuaged what would otherwise have been a sense of relative depriva-tion directed towards higher-ranked status-groups within English society itself. But the sense of national identity defined both a relationship of assumed fellow-feeling with the inhabitants of the dominions and a relationship of assumed condescension towards the inhabitants of the colonies – with India arousing, as it had done since the days of Macaulay and before, attitudes both ambivalent and conflicting among those English 'sahibs' and 'memsahibs' who

---

[74] ' "I believe there's quite a future in bugs in the colonies," said father. "What do they call those fellahs? Entomologists? Good open-air life in the colonies, jolly good time, high pay, lots of servants. Wish I had my time again. That's what I'd plump for." ' (Ommanney 1966, p. 56.)

[75] An attitude shared, it is worth noting, at the very opposite end of the ideological spectrum: Curzon, as Viceroy of India in 1903, equally deplored 'the racial pride and the undisciplined passions of the inferior class of Englishmen in this country' (K. Rose 1979, p. 343).

experienced at either first or second hand its bewildering agglomeration of civilizations and creeds.

Likewise, the spontaneous outburst of patriotism which followed the country's entry into war in 1914 reflected a similar sense that England not only had, but deserved to retain, its place in the inter-societal hierarchy. Socialist observers who had been startled by the rejoicings in the East End of London on Mafeking night were hardly less startled at the rush to enlist which, within six months of war's being declared, raised a volunteer army of nearly two million men from all ranks of English society including manual workers from every industry and region. The volunteers were not just the shiftless, the unemployed, or the semi-criminal (although some of course were). They were miners and mill-hands, clerks and shop-assistants, labourers and artisans, who came forward in such numbers that the military authorities were unable to cope with them.[76] It was the more remarkable because of the anti-militarist tradition in England which, as I remarked in section 13 of chapter 1, kept the regular soldiers who manned the Empire almost a race apart from their compatriots at home; and perhaps it would not have happened at all if those who came forward so readily had envisaged something closer to the protracted carnage of the American Civil War than to a decisive season's campaigning which would take the Allies to Berlin by Christmas. But it testified not only to what was to seem in retrospect an irrecoverable innocence, but also to a deep-seated national pride which eventual victory was, for all the disillusionment suffered on the way to it, to sustain.

It was, perhaps, less surprising to observers from the Right of the political spectrum who had never doubted the loyalty to the Crown of even the most intransigent proletarians. As it was put in a War Office memorandum of 1921, 'there are many people, especially in the hereditary criminal classes, who respect and would die for the old flag but would not on any account give information on any subject to the police' (Jeffery 1981, p. 386). But the experience of those from the 'officer class' whose personal relationships with members of the working classes were limited to those of master to servant or employer to employee left many of them with a respect for the courage, endurance, and humour of the British working man which affected their attitudes for the rest of their lives. It did not necessarily make them imperialists or militarists: if it was true of Oswald Mosley on the Right, it was equally true of R. H. Tawney on the Left and – mid-way, as it were, between the two – Harold Macmillan. But it did to this extent transcend differences of political allegiance as well as systactic origin. It is a sociological fact almost too obvious to mention that the roles of

---

[76] They were, however, more likely to be single than married, and the over-representation of volunteers from banking and commercial roles can plausibly be attributed to the later age of marriage of non-manual than manual workers (Winter 1976, p. 549).

officer and soldier are defined by practices very different from those defining the roles of employer and employee, even if the social distance between the two is the same in both cases. Its implications, however, are perhaps less obvious. It was not merely that the junior officers of 1914–18 shared with the 'other ranks' a common paymaster, a common enemy, and a common risk of mutilation or death. It was also that the imperialist, public-school, 'muscular-Christian' ideals which informed the rituals and mores of the territorially based regiments of which the British army consisted gave the relation between officers and 'their' men something of the relation between prefects and junior boys. This relation may (it has been argued) have extended to a kind of latent homosexual eroticism of which some, at least, were explicitly aware (Fussell 1975, chapter VIII). But for the purpose of this volume, its relevance lies in the practices and related attitudes which united the incumbents of military roles across the normal peacetime lines of conflicting systactic interest.

In this, as in other ways, the Second World War was very different from the First. Not only had the innocent patriotism of 1914 been lost, but so had the respect for military authority which the experience of those who survived the carnage of the trenches had destroyed as much in the eyes of the general public as of themselves. Moreover, the mutual resentment between those on the Left who regarded their opponents as anti-democrats fighting to defend a discredited social order and those on the Right who regarded their opponents as pro-Bolsheviks willing only to fight, if at all, as allies of the Soviet Union was muted, not dissipated, by the succession of Churchill to Chamberlain and the common pride engendered by the Battle of Britain. Once, therefore, the war was over it might have been expected that the subsequent withdrawal from empire, and with it the steady loss of remaining illusions about Britain's international influence and standing, would have encouraged left-wing internationalists on the one side and right-wing imperialists on the other to see in those events a vindication of their own doctrinal preferences for a more socialist or a more authoritarian mode of the distribution of power. There certainly were such: the Labour MPs who persistently denounced the foreign policy of Attlee and Bevin were matched by the Conservative MPs who persistently denounced the colonial policy of Macmillan and Macleod. But in both cases, the antagonism was directed against their own parties. The Left disliked the fact that a nominally Socialist government was retaining an imperial presence overseas, and the Right disliked the fact that a Conservative colonial secretary was betraying, as they saw it, the interests of British settler communities in Africa. Despite the debacle of Suez in 1956 and the deep-seated divisions of political opinion aroused by it, the repercussions of the withdrawal from empire were negligible by comparison with the repercussions of Ireland. Not only was there no disaffected faction of ex-colonials with any influence in the government of the day; there was no threat of military or para-military refusal to obey orders equivalent to the mutiny at the Curragh in the summer of 1914, when the brigadier-general commanding, together with fifty-seven other officers, chose to abdicate from their roles rather than to accept orders to take part in active operations against Ulster. However great the difference in attitudes and assumptions, as well as in the place of Britain in the inter-societal rank order, between 1914 and 1956, it generated no significant selective pressure favouring mutant practices whose carriers might have altered the domestic mode of the distribution of power. In the explanation of such modifications as did occur, the withdrawal from empire can be treated as a virtual irrelevance. Yet again, the description of what it felt like to those who lived through it is a very misleading guide to the explanation of the structural and cultural changes to English society which were (or weren't) taking place.

CONCLUSION

§19. The evidence reported in this chapter will (I trust) have been more than sufficient to confirm that between the first and last decades of the twentieth century there was no change in the structure and culture of English society amounting to an evolution out of one mode of production, persuasion, and coercion into another, but that there unmistakably was an evolution out of the late-Victorian and Edwardian sub-type of capitalist liberal democracy into a new and different one. The task of the following chapter, therefore, is to bring the theory of social selection expounded in volume II to bear on this evidence in such a way as will identify both the selective pressures which brought about the changes which did occur and the contradictions or constraints inhibiting those which might have occurred but didn't. But neither this chapter nor the next should be taken to imply a prediction of any kind about what may or may not happen next. It may be that by the first quarter of the twenty-first century, English society will have evolved into a 'post-industrial' mode of production in which self-employment is the norm, trade unions are a thing of the past, and the seven-layered class structure is no longer recognizable, a 'post-modern' mode of persuasion in which the previous criteria of status and legitimacy have entirely lost their hold, and a 'post-statist' mode of coercion in which the previous power of central government has been dissipated among a range of both sub- and supra-national institutions and roles. But my, or any other sociologist's, guess is no more than that – a guess which may well be wider of the mark than your own. This volume is about what has happened to English society up to the closing decade of the twentieth century, not about what may or may not happen after it.

CHAPTER THREE

The case explained

SELECTIVE PRESSURES AND INSTITUTIONAL CONSTRAINTS

§1. The evolution of any society from one to another mode or sub-type of production, persuasion, or coercion results from a process of interaction between the mutant or recombinant practices which define the society's constituent roles and the selective pressures in their environment which bear on them. The process can, as I have emphasized already, be influenced by any number of individual decisions taken by the incumbents of both more and less powerful roles. But these, for the sociologist's purposes, are random inputs to be taken as given, however alien this may seem to readers accustomed to historical and biographical narratives about the aims, ambitions, and strategies of policy-makers and their opponents and allies. Human decisions are not, of course, random in the same sense that genetic mutations are random. But in the explanation of social evolution, they might as well be (cf. Cavalli-Sforza and Feldman 1981, pp. 65–6 on cultural mutations). The contingent causes of the introduction of mutant practices by particular role-incumbents can never furnish the explanation of the systemic outcome of which the mutation was a necessary condition, any more than can retrospective diagnosis of the cunning of Lloyd George, the emollience of Baldwin, the pragmatism of Attlee, the deviousness of Wilson, or the hubris of Thatcher (if that is what you think they were). It is true that this volume is concerned only with relatively small-scale changes in English society over a relatively short period and that these changes have sometimes originated in the deliberate decisions of individual policy-makers.[1] But the underlying process of

---

[1] I do not, for example, doubt that the success of government ministers and Treasury and Inland Revenue officials in securing public acceptance of Britain's distinctive tax system was due to deliberate decisions of policy (Daunton 1996), although I do query the success popularly attributed to Margaret Thatcher in bringing about a decline in British trade unionism for the simple reason that union decline is simultaneously observable in a wide range of other 'advanced' capitalist societies (Western 1995). But in either case, institutional change results if and only if the relevant mutations of practices are favoured by specific features of their environment – which, as in the theory of natural selection, has to be empirically demonstrated.

social evolution is no different here from what it is in any of the larger-scale historical examples discussed in volume II. It is, as in all societies, the functions for the roles which carry them of the practices defining those roles which account for the modes of production, persuasion, and coercion of twentieth-century English society being what they are.

I cannot recapitulate here the rationale for this approach as applied across the range of human societies in volume II. But readers to whom the notion of 'social selection' is antipathetic a priori may find it useful to have a very short summary of my answers to the four objections which have most frequently been put to me since volume II appeared.

The first objection comes from those who believe that the attempt to construct an evolutionary sociology has already been discredited by the failure of Historical Materialism on the one side and Social Darwinism on the other. The answer is that the reasons for which they have both been discredited, far from undermining the extension of Darwinian theory into the study of human societies, have helped to show how it can and ought to be done. The process of 'descent with modification' is, as can hardly be disputed, continuous from the evolution of chemical compounds through to the evolution of human institutions. But it cannot be explained by invocation of some presumptive end-state towards which it is progressively tending, any more than by the invocation of a 'skyhook' – that is, some imaginary ' "mind-first" force or power or process' (Dennett 1995, p. 74) of which, in sociology, Durkheim's *conscience collective* is perhaps the most familiar example. It can only be explained by analysing observed mutations in the basic ingredients of the objects under study, whether these objects are cells, organisms, minds, species, cultures, or societies, and the phenotypic effects which determine their subsequent probability of diffusion and replication; and this in turn depends on an analysis of their interaction with the ecological, demographic, and institutional environment within which they have occurred.

The second objection comes from those who accept that the process of 'descent with modification' is continuous, but argue that the disanalogies between natural and social selection outweigh the analogies. The answer is that although there are indeed significant disanalogies,[2] and although the units of

---

[2] One which sometimes gives rise to misunderstanding is that whereas natural selection involves increasing or decreasing frequency of mutants in successive populations, in social selection mutations can have an influence independent of their frequency. In twentieth-century English society, the unemployment benefit legislation of 1921 was more important than that of 1946 not because of the number of beneficiaries but because of the precedent set by the novel practice of 'uncovenanted' benefit. By contrast, the diffusion of the right to vote in 1918 was important precisely because of the much increased number of voters and its effect on the behaviour of the parties competing for their support. As a *reductio ad absurdum*, 'Generals are much rarer than privates, but what would it mean to say that they had less "fitness"?' (Hallpike 1988, p. 56 – a

selection are indeed different things in both social and cultural from biological evolution, it is still a selective process and the form of explanation is, therefore, still the same. Some human behaviour is 'evoked' (i.e. an instinctual response to environmental stimulus), some is 'acquired' (i.e. transmitted by imitation or learning), and some is 'imposed' (i.e. governed by institutional rules). But any qualitative change in a reported pattern of social behaviour involves the displacement of some units of selection by others, whether these units are genes, traits (or 'memes'), or practices, and for this to happen some feature of the environment must confer a competitive advantage of some kind on the carriers of the mutants which accounts for their success.

The third objection comes from those who accept that cultural and social selection are analogous but not reducible to natural selection, but insist that analysis of the workings of human societies calls for motivational as well as, if not instead of, functional explanation. The answer is that the two are not mutually exclusive. Explanation of many well-documented patterns of behaviour – for example, voting behaviour and its correlation with social class – obviously calls for some account of the agents' motives. But this is not in conflict with a functional explanation of why, for example, the policies of rival parties under universal suffrage tend to converge towards the middle ground. Nor is there any necessary incompatibility between the theory of social selection and rational-choice theory, which seeks to extrapolate social outcomes from the presumptive disposition of individual agents to realize the self-interested goals attributed to them. It depends on what exactly you are trying to explain. This chapter is concerned with explaining why English society's modes of production, persuasion, and coercion have changed neither more nor less than they have during the course of the twentieth century, and for that purpose analysis of individual agents' motives has much less to offer than analyses of the unintended consequences of their actions. But it is a question to be settled by appeal to the evidence how and to what effect agents' motives, whether 'rational' or otherwise, enter the ongoing process of 'descent with modification'. If, in this volume, motives are given less attention than some readers may feel they deserve, that is because they have made as little difference as they have to the competitive advantage which turns out to have been conferred by some rather than other practices on the roles which have carried them.[3]

book which rightly attacks the idea that institutions are selected for their own adaptive advantages, but fails to consider the alternative that practices are the units of selection and adaptation is by the roles which are their carriers.)

[3] For a discussion in these terms which considers the replication and diffusion of a single practice across a range of societies rather than mutations of different practices within a single society, see my plenary address to the 13th World Congress of Sociology, where the practice discussed is wage-labour itself (Runciman 1995a).

The fourth objection, finally, comes from those who question what, if anything, is added to commonsense narrative explanations by rephrasing them in Darwinian terms. If, for example, bureaucratization of clerical work can be shown to have caused higher rates of trade-union membership among the employees concerned, why rephrase the hypothesis in terms of an enhanced probability of diffusion and replication of the practice of collective negotiation in response to selective pressure? To this, however, the answer is that, as I argued in chapter 3 of volume I, in the social as in the natural sciences, causal hypotheses provisionally validated by the evidence against which they are tested need to be grounded in a theory which explains why the causal connection holds. To repeat the example which I used there, the well-validated hypothesis that the boiling-point of water varies with altitude above sea-level could not be fully understood before the invocation of the notion of atmospheric pressure. Only (I believe) a theory of social selection analogous but not reducible to the theory of natural selection can account for the underlying process by which societies of one kind evolve into societies of another, and it is, therefore, only in the terms of that theory that hypotheses about the causes of particular institutional changes in particular societies can be given adequate grounding. This volume cannot demonstrate by itself that I am right in my belief. But it is for those who dispute it to show what alternative explanation grounded in a rival theory does better.

§2. Although it is only with hindsight that well-validated explanations from within the theory of social selection can be arrived at, this does not prevent contemporary participant-observers who have no conception whatever of 'mutation' or 'replication' or 'selective pressure' from seeing for themselves that their environment is changing and wondering what the impact on them is going to be. At the turn of the century, as since, commentators of all persuasions could and did point to a readily visible range of internal and external influences acting on the institutions of which their various roles were a constituent part. Inter-societally, the difficulty of sustaining British economic, ideological, and political power was, as I remarked in section 2 of chapter 1, only too apparent throughout the late-Victorian and Edwardian period. Intra-societally, employers and workpeople alike were aware not only of the conflicts of interest between them over wages, conditions, and hours but also of the demands imposed on both of them by technological change and shifting markets. And at the individual level, competition for vacant roles was as manifestly intense among the new plutocracy as among the aspiring entrants to both the old and the new professions, the starch-collared clerks jostling for promotion in the counting-houses, the would-be apprentices to the restricted number of openings in the 'skilled' manual trades, and the underemployed casual labourers vying with one another for the favour of the contractor or foreman. Governments, meanwhile, were being pressed increasingly in the direction of constitutional as well as electoral reform; demands for female suffrage were becoming more and more insistent; both socialists and syndical-ists were diffusing their potentially subversive doctrines among the more disaffected fractions of the working class; and middle-class propagandists were becoming increasingly vociferous about the 'social question' and the dangers which could ensue if governments failed to take action, as much in their own interest as that of the underprivileged to whose welfare their attention was being directed. To anyone who had grown up in the mid-Victorian 'age of equipoise' the pre-1914 'sense of an impending clash' (Phelps Brown 1959, p. 330) could well seem to point an alarming contrast between internal stability and external strength then and internal instability and external weakness now.

But if all these pressures were as visible to informed participants as to subsequent academic observers, so equally was the strength of the central institutions of a society whose capacity to resist violent change was by now proverbial. The outbreak of industrial unrest which continued through the last years of the late-Victorian period might seem to some to presage an impending reversal of the domination of capital over labour. But those who remembered the sudden upsurge and hardly less sudden relapse of the 'New Unionism' at the beginning of the period might think there was reason to be more sceptical. If, at a time of near-full employment and falling real wages, membership of trade unions and the number of working days lost through strikes were both on the increase, was that not to be expected? Whatever short-term concessions employers might be compelled to make, would they not be reversed by a downturn in the business cycle and a concerted managerial counter-attack of the kind which had been mounted in the 1890s? In any case, the regional and sectoral differences reported in section 3 of chapter 2 were such as to suggest very different predictions, for those rash enough to offer them, about the likely future state of English society as a whole. To an observer of the mineworkers of South Wales, it might seem that working-class unrest would soon be beyond the control of the civil and even the military authorities. But an observer of the mineworkers of Northumberland and Durham would be unlikely to think likewise; and an observer of the ironworkers in Stanley Baldwin's family firm in Bewdley would be likely to conclude that the tradition of stable paternalism in English industrial relations was as strong as ever. Both commentators on the Left, who deplored it, and commentators on the Right, who welcomed it, could point not only to the large sectors of the economy where trade unionism had still made no inroads at all but to the moderation of union officials in the greater part of the unionized sector in support of the view that the unions, far from constituting a threat to the established order, were among its staunchest friends. However differently they might put it to themselves, they did not need to have been taught anything about sociological theory, neo-Darwinian or otherwise, before they could detect that the practices defining the roles of the trade-union leaders might be functioning not merely to preserve but to strengthen the institutions of the capitalist mode of production.

It was much the same in the ideological dimension. Apprehensive as the middle classes might be of the danger posed by the rising self-confidence of organized labour to their hard-won sense of superiority of status, might it not be equally plausible to predict that assimilation of life-styles would be as much a safeguard as a threat to the established mode of persuasion? There was more of an affinity in attitudes and tastes between late-Victorian and Edwardian working men and many Conservative back-benchers than many of the leaders of the Labour movement (Masterman 1909, pp. 142–4). The music halls, which gave perhaps the most characteristic expression to the *Weltanschauung* of the late-Victorian and Edwardian working class, expressed in their jokes and lyrics an attitude to the hierarchy of social prestige which, while by no means deferential, was humorous, escapist, and patriotic (F. M. L. Thompson 1988, p. 324).[4] It might be that by the turn of the century the self-improving mid-Victorian artisan with his provincial newspaper, his regular attendance at church or chapel, and his *Pilgrim's Progress* on the bookshelf was a fast-receding anachronism. But if control of the means of persuasion was about to pass from the Churches to what would later be called the 'media', and the growing number of working-class readers were to prefer the *Daily Mail* and *Daily Mirror* to Dickens and Macaulay, it did not follow that the new institutional environment would be any more favourable to the diffusion and replication of socialist than of authoritarian practices. The popular taste for scandal, sport, and sensationalism might be as distasteful to Lord Salisbury, who famously denounced Northcliffe's newspapers as being written by office boys for office boys,[5] as to the intellectuals of the radical Left. But value-judgements are, as always, neither here nor there in the analysis of the selective pressures at work. For the sociologist's purpose, the point is that rising standards of working-class literacy might turn out to sustain the liberal mode of persuasion rather than subvert it.

---

[4] Bailey (1994, p. 168) calls it a culture of 'competence' rather than 'consolidation', but concludes that 'the counter-discourse of music-hall knowingness was limited to the infraction rather than the negation of the dominant power relationships and, as its echo of official idiom demonstrated, it was compromised between challenge and collaboration'.

[5] A gibe which Kennedy Jones, one of his most successful editors, cheerfully accepted (LeMahieu 1988, p. 20). Cf. Ensor (1936, p. 313): 'But the public which liked them was extremely wide and by no means all poor . . . Harmsworth rightly divined that the favourite paper in the boudoir and in the kitchen would be the same.'

This applies still more clearly to the pressures of which observers of both Left and Right were fully aware for further electoral reform. The putative consequences of the extension of the suffrage to women as well as to all adult men had been debated time and again for many years before they were put into effect in 1918, but there was no agreement either between the political parties or within them as to what they would be. On the whole, party managers were more apprehensive than hopeful (Close 1977, p. 894). Even if they did not seriously believe that an enlarged electorate would at once fall prey to unscrupulous demagogues preaching instant revolution, they did seriously fear that uneducated working men – and their wives – would be less open to rational argument and more easily swayed by appeals to short-term self-interest. Nor was progressive intellectual opinion much less ambivalent. Graham Wallas, who published his *Human Nature in Politics* in 1908, was a firm believer in democracy as the best method of government; but this did not prevent him from being anxiously concerned that working-class electors should be properly guided from above or from worrying at the prospect that the emergence of Labour as a political force would bring with it sectionalism, laxity, and corruption (Clarke 1978, p. 139). It is hard to decide what the various practitioners of, and commentators on, late-Victorian and Edwardian politics would have found most surprising about the politics of the period between the General Elections of 1922 and 1992. Would it have been the eclipse of the Liberals, or the survival of the Conservatives? The collapse of Labour in 1931, its triumph in 1945, or its unexpected loss in 1970? The failure of the Conservatives in 1964 and 1974, or their run of successes in 1979, 1983, 1987, and 1992? Or would they have been most surprised of all by the fact that the practices of the parliamentary system should have been replicated with so little change of either substance or style for so long after the enlargement of the franchise in 1918?

It would be easy, with the help of selective quotation, to show how seriously misguided, and often spectacularly inaccurate, contemporary observers of all persuasions have been in their diagnosis of the condition of English society. By the same token, it would also be possible to find occasional examples of what came to look like an uncanny prescience. But the prescient-seeming guesses were guesses just as much as the misguided ones. Once the underlying process which governs social evolution has been recognized for what it is, there must follow the recognition that any forecast of a major change of, or in, the mode of production, persuasion or coercion will be vindicated only by accident. Sociology, as I insisted in chapter 3 of volume I, is not and never will be predictive science. The competitive advantages which practices confer on the roles which carry them only manifest themselves after the events have occurred which furnish a quasi-experimental contrast between the environment which has favoured them and the different environment which might have, but didn't, favour others instead.

§3. That said, it is time to return for the purpose of explanation and not merely of reportage to the contrast between the aftermaths of the two world wars. It is a twofold paradox that after the First, as I remarked in section 3 of chapter 1, English society should evolve into a different sub-type of capitalist liberal democracy despite all the rhetoric about a return to 'normalcy', only to remain after the Second within the same sub-type despite all the rhetoric about a 'social revolution'. The rhetoric can, as I suggested, be explained easily enough. After the First World War, it suited both Left and Right to pretend for opposite reasons that nothing had changed – the Left presenting it as a bad thing and the Right as a good one. After the Second World War, it suited both to pretend for opposite reasons that a great deal *had* changed – the Left presenting it as a good thing and the Right as a bad one. But what were the selective pressures acting on the practices defining the society's constituent roles which caused the Second World War and its aftermath to make as little difference to the modes of production, persuasion, and coercion as in fact it did, when the First World War and its aftermath had made so much?

The contrast disposes, for a start, of any explanatory presupposition that wars as such cause the societies engaged in them to evolve in any inevitable or consistent direction. Wars may generate, reinforce, and accelerate changes of various kinds which are relevant not only to any account of the subjective experiences of those who lived through them but to many of the broader themes of the economic, social, and political history of the period. The disruption of accustomed routines, the reversal of inherited assumptions, and the emergence of new relationships between the incumbents of different roles can all be documented as well for the Second World War as for the First, and 'total' wars – wars, that is, which impinge on the entire population and not simply on a set of professional combatants – cannot but promote both individual and collective mobility as new roles are brought into being, existing roles are modified, and the new roles are filled by incumbents whose peacetime roles have therefore to be left in abeyance. But as I argued in volume II, practices which are replicated and diffused because of the competitive advantages which they confer on the roles which carry them can be, and often are, *mal*adaptive for the society constituted by those roles at the level of inter-societal competition. Of course, there are innovations which arise in response to a perceived need for efficiency as that is defined, rightly or wrongly, by those in charge of policy at the time. But they are likely to be those whose function disappears when peace returns. The Ministry of Munitions in the First World War grew to a prodigious size and drew into direct employment many women, in particular, who would otherwise have had no occupational (as opposed to household) roles at all. But a Ministry of *Munitions* was, as one historian has aptly put it 'hardly likely to be viewed as a suitable model for the post-war world' (Kirby 1987, p. 128).

If the lasting effects of the First World War on the modes of production, persuasion, and coercion of English society are to be validly explained, they must be analysed as a response to selective pressures generated only partly by the war itself and as much if not more by its immediate aftermath. This is nowhere more clearly discernible than in the introduction of 'uncovenanted' unemployment benefit in 1921, whose long-term significance as a mutant practice I hinted at in section 6 of chapter 2. It had been preceded not only by 'out-of-work donations' to ex-servicemen in 1919[6] but by a series of demonstrations in different parts of the country. At the same time, local authorities on whose rates the cost of assistance would fall were increasingly anxious for central government to assume as much of it as possible. Accordingly, there was a threefold pressure against the practice of paying unemployment benefit only out of insurance contributions in the way that the pre-war legislation had envisaged. Nobody anticipated either the suddenness of the economic collapse in the summer of 1920 or the steepness in the subsequent rise in the number of insured workers unemployed – over 2 million by March 1921. The response of ministers and officials was characteristically bewildered and hesitant: although they had assumed that a short-lived rise in unemployment might have been generated in the immediate aftermath of the war by the influx of ex-servicemen into the labour market, it had never entered their minds that demand, particularly in the 'staple' export industries, would fall so far as to leave towns like Stockton or Jarrow or Barrow-in-Furness or Brynmawr with nearly half of their insured workers jobless. But the result was that the insurance principle, once breached, was never fully reinstated. It offers a classic example of social evolution under selective pressure where the mutation of previous practices had not been intended and its long-term consequences were not foreseen.

In a similar way, the dismantling of controls, which Tawney (1943, p. 14) was to deplore as a precedent for the return of power and profit to the owners of the means of production at the expense of the working class, left behind a set of economic institutions which had been lastingly modified to an extent which nobody recognized at the time. Although, for example, the government abandoned the proposal that the Ministry of Transport should be empowered to nationalize the railways, the 120 separate operating companies were never-

---

[6] These in themselves are symptomatic of how much had changed since the late-Victorian and Edwardian period. There had, after all, been out-of-work ex-servicemen after the Boer War; but for them, the state had done nothing at all.

theless reduced to 4 by the Railways Act of 1921; and this was a reflection of the impact of the war on a railway system thereby shown to be too fragmented in its existing form. Indeed, the railways furnish a characteristic illustration of the unimportance of the source of the initial proposal for change. The idea of consolidation into four (albeit not the same four) systems had been put forward as long ago as 1872; but it only came about after the creation of a Ministry of Transport, and a Ministry of Transport only came about because of the war (Simnett 1923, pp. 13, 26–7).

The same holds for the spate of trade-union amalgamations which followed the Armistice. Amalgamations had taken place before the war and continued during its first years. But in 1917, the Coalition government passed a Trade Union Amalgamations Act which, although it fell short of what the unions wanted, still made amalgamations considerably easier to achieve than they had been. There followed, in 1918, seven major federations. But it was after the war was over that interest in amalgamation 'grew into a fever' (Clegg 1985, p. 304). For a variety of contingent causes, some failed where others succeeded. The post-office workers came together, whereas the shipbuilding and construction workers fell apart. The foundry workers refused to talk to the engineering workers and the plasterers withdrew from talks with the brick-layers, whereas the bookbinders joined the printers and the carpenters joined the cabinet-makers. But this was the institutional environment out of which there emerged the Amalgamated Engineering Union and the General and Municipal Workers' Union, and Bevin's own formidable role at the head of the Transport and General Workers' Union. Once again, as with the amalgamations of companies on the side of the controllers of the means of production, the mutations of practices which led to larger associational structures and greater specialization and hierarchy in the pattern of their constituent roles, having initially occurred under the exceptional circumstances of the war, continued to confer competitive advantage on their carriers in an environment to which so-called 'normalcy' had returned.

The increasing power attaching to the roles of ministers and officials in the regulation of the economy and the administration of welfare was likewise the outcome of similar selective pressures. The political institutions of 1918 and thereafter could not evolve backwards, so to speak, to the late-Victorian and Edwardian sub-type, no matter how much the incumbents of ministerial and official roles wished that they could or pretended that they had. Thus, the Ministry of Labour, whose creation in 1916 was due no less than the Trade Union Amalgamation Act of the following year to Lloyd George's short-term need for trade-union support, survived, as I reported in section 6 of chapter 2, the recommendation that it be abolished. But even if it had not, the functions which its officials by now performed would have had to be performed by the incumbents of analogous roles in some other government department. In addition to its conciliatory and legislative functions in the field of industrial relations, it was inextricably involved, despite criticism from the TUC, the Conservative Party, and the popular press alike, in the administration of unemployment relief whose nature and scale were both unprecedented. Similarly, the Treasury, for all that its officials continued to see their roles through, so to speak, Gladstonian eyes, was inescapably involved in decisions about the management of the economy which had never arisen for their late-Victorian and Edwardian predecessors. The environment of a self-adjusting, free-trade system based on an international gold standard worked by the City of London and the Bank of England, for all its strong and continuing appeal to practitioners and theoreticians alike (Clarke 1990, p. 197), was as irrecoverable as was a domestic economy in which income tax at over 10 per cent was unthinkable. Policy decisions about interest rates and the parity for sterling, as about unemployment relief and the number of civil servants needed to administer it, were now conducted in an environment where the persistence of practices and roles which had emerged in consequence of the war was an incontrovertible testimony to the strength of the selective pressures continuing to favour them.

Why, then, is it that there is, by contrast, so relatively little institutional change to be explained in the aftermath of the Second World War? From 1940 to 1945, the economy was once again controlled directly by ministers and officials with the same powers attaching to their roles. But they had little if any more scope to carry these powers through into peacetime, even if they had wanted to, than had their predecessors of 1915–18. They abandoned physical controls within two years of the war's end. Their most durable innovation was the implementation of a set of improved techniques for the conduct of macro-economic policy which, unfamiliar as they were, found general acceptance by officials and public opinion alike (Cairncross 1985, p. 19). But the differences were differences of policy, and only of policy,[7] within a set of roles and institutions which remained unchanged. It was generally recognized that earlier policies in the institutional areas covered by the term 'welfare' had been less effective than they should have been. But the 'genuine search for bipartisan agreement' on better ones (Lowe 1990, p. 180) involved no change in the relations between the institutions of capital, labour, and the state, and it makes no difference to the sociologist concerned to explain the evolution of English

---

[7] Or in the support of policy changes by people previously opposed to them. The most striking of such changes is the Labour Party's conversion to the principle of family allowances, which the trade unions had previously resisted. Among Conservatives, the attraction of family allowances was as a means of 'giving money to those who needed it without increasing wages' (Lewis 1980, p. 232).

society's modes of production, persuasion, and coercion whether this is viewed, as by commentators on the Left, as a betrayal of Socialism or, as by commentators on the Right, as evidence of the sound common sense of the British people. The First World War had, in other words, already done the work which the Second might otherwise have done in generating the selective pressures which brought about an evolution from one to another sub-type of capitalist liberal democracy. The intense political debate which preceded, accompanied, and followed Labour's tenure of power between 1945 and 1951, whatever it may have felt like to those engaged in it, concealed more than it revealed about how little institutional change was actually taking place.

MUTATIONS AND THEIR FUNCTIONS IN THE MODE OF PRODUCTION

§4. To explain in more detail why the capitalism of the 1920s and thereafter was neither more nor less different from that of the late-Victorian and Edwardian period than it was, it needs to be shown what mutant economic practices were or weren't selected for the advantages which they conferred on the roles carrying them. To observers on the Left, it was obvious that the roles of the active members of the Labour movement, both industrial and political, were the carriers of practices which would sooner or later bring about an evolution to socialism. To observers on the Right, the power attaching to the roles defining the existing institutions of capital and the state was palpably enough to halt any such evolution in its tracks. But neither realized at the time the extent to which the practices defining the roles constitutive of 'the Labour movement' would function to keep British capitalism relatively stable at the same time as the practices defining the roles constitutive of 'capital' and 'the state' function to carry it forward into a different sub-type of the capitalist mode of production.

The conservatism of trade-union leaders was, admittedly, something of a commonplace to contemporary observers. J. H. Thomas's performance of his role in 1919 and 1920 was the extreme case – visits to Cliveden as the guest of the Astors, personal contacts with Lloyd George behind the backs of his colleagues, and deliberate obstruction of any attempt by his executive to mobilize the Triple Alliance in support of the railwaymen. But the roles of union officials, hostile to both employers and government as they might be, functioned more as a bulwark against, than a spearhead for, those whom Lloyd George, writing to Bonar Law, called 'hotheads and feather-brains' (K. O. Morgan 1979, p. 214). More dismaying – or, depending on your evaluative presuppositions, encouraging – was the power now visibly attaching to the role of shop steward through the mutant practice of local shop-floor representation.

In the late-Victorian and Edwardian period, the term 'rank and file' had normally been used to mean either the ordinary run of union members or, sometimes, particular groups seeking greater influence within their particular unions. But after the upsurge of wartime militancy under shop-steward leadership, it conjured up the prospect of mass mobilization against the official leadership of the union movement as a whole. It was, as we have seen already, a prospect which continued to alarm governments, employers, and moderate union leaders alike. In the inter-war period, there were confrontations with, for example, groups of London busmen,[8] cinema projectionists, engineering workers in the aircraft industry, and even a 'Railwaymen's Vigilance Movement' formed under Communist direction inside Thomas's own National Union of Railwaymen. But they might have been less alarmed if they had concentrated on the function of the mutant practices defining the shop stewards' roles rather than on the ambitions and motives of the leaders of the 'rank-and-file' movements. Plant-level bargaining, conducted by stewards who were normally elected unopposed and ready to call local strikes in defiance of agreed procedures for the settlement of disputes,[9] might result in losses of production which government and employers would equally like to avoid if they could. But by no stretch could the practice be claimed to be subversive of the mode of production itself. The mutation helped to generate a pattern of industrial relations qualitatively different from that which had prevailed between 1880 and 1914. But precisely because the power attaching to the shop steward's role was local only, it could never function to radicalize the leadership of nationally organized unions. The national leaders might use the power attaching to their roles to break the rank-and-file movements, as Bevin did with the busmen. But more often, they used it to accommodate them. The eventual incorporation of shop stewards into the official machinery of trade-union government has been called 'the most important reform within the unions since the 1920s' (Clegg 1979, p. 226);[10] and it was systematically assisted by employers hoping, like the Engineering Employers' Federation, 'to contain stewards by putting them under tighter union control and making

---

[8] The defeat of the busmen's strike in 1937 was blamed by its supporters on Bevin's determination to crush the rank-and-file movement. But in 1958, when Frank Cousins as the incumbent of Bevin's role supported the strikers, it was defeated once again – this time, in the eyes of its supporters, 'betrayed by the TUC' (Fuller 1985, p. 227).

[9] The Royal Commission of 1965–8 found that 74 per cent of the stewards sampled in its survey said that strikes which had occurred during their incumbency of the role had occurred without agreed procedures having been exhausted (1968, p. 99).

[10] In the Amalgamated Engineering Union, the enhanced role of the shop steward was officially acknowledged as early as the constitution of 1920, in which they 'were recognized as having a direct right to assist in policy-making, instead of being confined – in rule – to "policing" old members and recruiting new ones' (Jefferys 1946, p. 193).

them subject to what they termed "constitutionalism" ' (Gospel 1987, p. 165). It is true that after the collapse of the post-war boom, some employers sought to reassert the power attaching to managerial roles along the lines of the counter-attack against the unions in the 1890s. But in the changed institutional environment, recourse to 'free' (i.e., 'blackleg') labour was no longer an option: even the Shipping Federation now adapted to it by formalizing the shipowners' relations with the seafarers' unions on a national basis.[11]

The sanction which continued to underlie the power attaching to the roles of national union officials and local shop stewards alike was the withdrawal of their members' labour, and strikes continued to be viewed with as much dismay by commentators on the Right who saw them as symptoms of impending anarchy as they were viewed with satisfaction by commentators on the Left who saw them as symptoms of solidarity among an increasingly class-conscious proletariat. There were some observers like Orwell, as quoted in section 2 of chapter 1, for whom strikes were an obviously intrinsic feature of a capitalist liberal democracy like twentieth-century Britain. But after the Second World War, as the maintenance of international competitiveness came to seem an increasingly pressing problem, politicians and journalists alike came to regard the alleged 'strike-proneness' of British industry as a significant part of it. At the same time, academic commentators became increasingly divided between those who explained strikes as an occasional safety valve for frustrations which the institutionalization of collective bargaining have failed to accommodate and those who explained them as symptoms of the irreconcilable conflict between the owners and controllers of the means of production and workers with only their labour to sell (Hyman 1972, chapters 3 and 4). The two are not, however, mutually exclusive. The function of the practices involved in the withdrawal of labour either by decision of national officials or by decision of shop stewards at plant level is both adversarial in the relations between managers and employees and supportive of the powers attaching to both sets of roles under the existing mode of production. Strikes vary widely in their extent and duration, their incidence is uneven across different industries and regions, they may occur at any stage of the business cycle, they can be directed against other unions as well as the employer, and both their immediate and their longer-term causes are complex and multiple. But their function is to protest over one or more issues where the employers have, in the view of those who call the strike, tried to impose a decision against the wishes and interests of the employees concerned. To this extent, therefore, they are an attack on the

---

[11] The establishment of a National Maritime Board was triggered by unofficial strikes on four transatlantic liners in Liverpool in September 1917 (Waller 1981, p. 272) – another example of unintended consequences of a chance event which would not have happened but for the war; thereafter, centralized wage-bargaining in the shipping industry lasted until the 1980s.

power attaching to the roles of the owners and the controllers of the means of production by those whose roles place them, in the analogy used by Flanders (1964, p. 235), in the position of being 'never more than a permanent opposition' against managers who represent 'the government of industry'. But the collective sense of relative deprivation which finds expression in a strike is, for that very reason, reactive rather than proactive: the overwhelming majority of strikes are of short duration and are called in an attempt to secure an increase in a tabled wage offer, the reinstatement of a dismissed colleague, the preservation of threatened rules or customs, the retention of practices favouring the perceived interests of workers, or the retraction of a refusal of improved conditions within the existing pattern of roles and distribution of power.

Quasi-experimental confirmation of this diagnosis is provided by the near-total failure of the alternative practices carried by those who hoped thereby to transform the relations between wage-earners and the owners or controllers of capital from one of domination into one of cooperation. Even in the inter-war depression, when union density was falling back below its late-Victorian and Edwardian levels, the number of union officials did not decline in step with the decline in the number of members (Clegg 1985, p. 449), while schemes of co-partnership, co-ownership, and profit-sharing were no more successful than they had been when first promoted in the late-Victorian and Edwardian period.[12] It was not that the practices defining such schemes were categorically incapable of replication. But such short-term success as they ever had was due either to particular local circumstances[13] or to the personality and determination of a particular employer.[14] There was a direct contradiction, in precisely the sense of that term expounded in chapter 3 of volume II, between the practice of collective negotiation and the practice of profit-sharing on terms and conditions controlled by the owners of the means of production. It was not just that the roles of union officials were undermined but that workers' interests were better served by bonus payments of a standard kind. If they suspected, as many did, that a willingness to be drawn into co-partnership schemes when times were good would be turned against them when times were

---

[12] Cf. Matthews (1988, p. 232) on the practices introduced by Sir George Livesey in the gas industry: 'As a partnership, co-partnership was hopelessly one-sided. Initiated by capital, capital kept firm control on decision-making as well as profits. The schemes were in no sense examples of industrial democracy and were never more than paternalistic attempts to control the workforce.'

[13] For example, the Meriden Motorcycle Cooperative of 1975 would never have existed without not only the 'implacable refusal' of the workforce to accept closure but the appointment of Benn as Industry Minister (Oakshott 1978, p. 111).

[14] See Perks (1982) for an unusually successful experiment which effectively died with its founder in 1925.

bad, they were probably right. But once again, it makes no difference whether the employers' motives were benevolent or cynical. A practice functional for managerial or proprietorial roles for which mobility is individual rather than collective could not be functional for workers whose roles gave them an interest in collective mobility only.[15] Only in small, face-to-face, privately owned, non-unionized firms could the practice be found of undeclared cash payments to workers in prosperous times (and for obvious reasons it is undocumented in the academic literature).

At the same time, however, the difference between the late-Victorian and Edwardian pattern of industrial relations and that which evolved after the First World War reflects the selective pressures favouring the professionalization of roles on both sides. The Webbs may have been mistaken in their vision of a world in which union officials would, like lawyers, perform a service which 'could, with equal propriety, be rendered to either client' (1919, p. 196 n.1; Hobsbawm 1964, p. 266). But they were not mistaken in seeing that the function of a bureaucratic mutation of the practices defining hitherto adversarial roles might be a relatively greater degree of structural stability. This mutation of practices took place not only at national level, where it was most visibly symbolized by the Mond-Turner talks of 1928, but also at plant level, where the role of 'personnel manager' evolved out of that of 'social secretary' – as the role of the handful of welfare workers in industry had usually been labelled before the First World War – and the inter-war years witnessed an evolution from 'welfare by way of employment' to 'labour management' (Niven 1967, pp. 21, 80). Just as the war enhanced the power attaching to the roles of trade union officials in ways which outlasted the return to 'normalcy', so did it enhance that attaching to the roles of salaried managers. John Lee's 'venturesome essay', as he called it, on *Management* published in 1921, with its assertion that 'the real managers' are an 'expert professional class' (p. 2) is (so far as I can discover) the first explicit claim to a new-found systactic identity. The formation of professional associations to represent such new or modified roles as those of office managers, cost accountants, works managers, and production organizers both reflected and accelerated a trend towards what came to be called, after the Second World War, 'credentialism'.[16] That war

---

[15] In the steel industry, where there was – atypically – limited upward individual mobility within the manual workforce, the roles of union officials were affected in just the way that the theory of social selection would suggest: the practice of collective negotiation on an industry-wide basis lost its traditional function in the 1920s, and 'in everything but "the most general sense" the union leadership became divorced from the particular interests of individual members and irrelevant to the bargaining strength, or lack of it, of individual branches' (Wilkinson 1977, p. 130).

[16] The trend to professional qualifications was already well under way in the late-Victorian and Edwardian period: compulsory examination for members of the Institute of Chartered

likewise accelerated the trend, as the perceived need for an efficient and well-motivated civilian labour force led to a 'vast' expansion in social services in the munitions and other essential industries, including industrial nurses and factory canteens as well as welfare and personnel officers (Stevenson 1984, p. 191). The process of professionalization of middle-class roles was, moreover, self-reinforcing. The relatively small numbers of members of the new professional associations were of much less sociological significance than the mutations of practices which gave their roles an advantage out of all proportion to the direct influence on industrial or political policy of those associations as such.

By contrast, in the area which was the object of greatest public concern, the selective pressures which brought the 'dole' into being conferred no competitive advantage on the roles of those who might have been thought (and often thought themselves to be) harbingers of radical social change. As we have seen, provision for the unemployed on a basis and a scale unprecedented in the late-Victorian and Edwardian period was a response to short-term pressures generated by the immediate aftermath of the First World War. But once it had occurred, it functioned not only to appease working-class discontent but to channel it towards claims for 'work or maintenance' rather than attempts to subvert or replace the existing mode of production. This, it might be argued, was not bound to be the case: might there not have evolved a set of institutions within which the strategy of the NUWM would have had very much more effect? But in the institutional environment of the inter-war period, the response of other and more powerful systactic interests to the selective pressures generated by the war and its aftermath offered little scope to the carriers of revolutionary practices even where they succeeded, as some did, in diffusing and replicating these practices among the working classes and under-class. Cripps's often-quoted remark to the Labour Party Conference of 1931 that 'the one thing which is not inevitable now is gradualness' was as striking an illustration as any on record during the period of the extent to which a well-informed contemporary participant-observer could misunderstand (in the secondary, explanatory sense) the process by which the evolution of his society's central institutions was being determined. He, like many other policy-makers (or would-be policy-makers), entirely failed to recognize the selective pressures which were giving competitive advantage to the carriers of practices other than those which seemed to him to portend an evolution into either an authoritarian or a socialist mode.

§5. But what about the 'bourgeoisie'? In the changed institutional environment

---

Accountants, for example, dates from 1880. But it did not extend to management as such until the introduction of a 'National Certificate in Commerce' in 1939, which then evolved into 'Business Studies' in 1961 (Millerson 1964, chapter 5).

of the 1920s and thereafter, the members of the middle classes, as of the upper class, were fully aware of the increased economic power of the state on the one side and of organized labour on the other. The sense of relative deprivation which saw expression in the formation of the so-called 'Middle Class Union' of 1919–22 (Gleason 1920, p. 17; cf. K. O. Morgan 1979, p. 300), in the protests voiced against Attlee's government after 1945 by spokesmen for middle-class interests (Lewis and Maude 1949, chapter 12), and in the formation of a 'Middle Class Association' in 1974 in the face of a 'catastrophic decline of asset values and an actual fall in disposable income' (Middlemas 1991, p. 13),[17] was a response more to a perceived than to an actual threat to the location of the middle class in the structure of a still capitalist-liberal-democratic society. But it was true that the working classes now had a much greater degree of economic power than before 1914, even in recessions as severe as those of the 1930s and 1980s when unemployment affected manual much more than non-manual workers and their families. No more in the middle than in the working classes were the attitudes, hopes, and fears to be described in chapter 4 a reliable guide to the mutations of practices and selective pressures acting on them by which the systactic structure of English society was in fact being changed. But middle-class observers were right in supposing that the new institutional environment of big corporations, well-organized trade unions, bureaucratization, collectivism, and an increasingly interventionist state could not fail to have an effect of some kind on middle-class roles and the competitive advantages conferred by the practices defining them.

From the perspective of the theory of social selection, it is the lower-middle class which is of particular interest here. This is partly because of the joint processes of proletarianization and feminization which were at work from the 1920s onwards and partly because rates of individual mobility were so high in one fraction of that class and so low in another. As I remarked in section 15 of chapter 2, small proprietors – those, that is, whose roles locate them above the 'penny capitalists' of the working class but below the middle-middle-class businessmen who employ non-family members and manage, rather than work alongside, them – are significantly more likely than the incumbents of other similarly located lower-middle-class roles to be succeeded in them by their sons.[18] But of clerical workers, by contrast, of whom some are men with good

---

[17] The Middle Class Association was in the event very short-lived. But the 1970s also witnessed the emergence of a less ephemeral National Federation of the Self Employed and National Association for Freedom (Elliott *et al.* 1983), of which the second is said by Nugent (1979, p. 76) to be entitled to claim to be 'one of the more successful pressure groups of recent years'.

[18] The reference to males is not because the same may not also apply to women but because the study on which it is based was restricted, as I pointed out in section 14 of chapter 2, to men aged between twenty and sixty-four in 1972.

prospects of early promotion,[19] many are women who are likely to be short-term employees (who, if they rejoin the workforce, will do so in routine occupational roles), and some are men promoted shortly before retirement from manual into clerical roles, are a clear example of the kind of systactic fraction whose members, as discussed in chapter 2 of volume II, will seldom be capable of acting as a class '*für sich*' which thereby becomes the carrier of mutant practices which are successfully replicated and diffused. Moreover, this difference gives rise to intra-systactic as well as inter-systactic conflicts of interest: clerical workers and small proprietors may share a common class and status location and a common resentment of the claims of organized labour while at the same time differing markedly from each other in their dependence on one rather than another set of governmental policies with regard to company, tax, and labour law. But in neither case was the sense of relative deprivation thereby generated such as to pose a challenge to the new sub-type of the capitalist mode of production. The practices defining the roles of the proprietorial middle class were never selected out in English society by hyperinflation or any other endogenous or exogenous pressures. Conversely, however intense the sense of relative deprivation of those clerical, technical, and sales workers who failed to achieve individual mobility into the middle-middle or upper-middle class, they were too small a proportion of the workforce for any collective action which they might be disposed to take to alter the fundamental distinction between skilled working-class and lower-middle-class roles.

'Bureaucratization' and 'managerialization' did, undoubtedly, reinforce the likelihood of replication of some mutant practices. In particular, the increasing size of organizations (and of separate establishments within the same organization) brought salaried middle-class employees together in larger work-groups with less individual autonomy and less particularistic relationships with their employers. But in this new environment many routine clerical functions were abolished entirely, while at the same time mechanization (and in due course computerization) generated requirements for new and different skills. Outside of banks and insurance companies (Crompton and Jones 1984), the number of lower-middle-class roles per establishment remained, even in the 1970s and 1980s, too low for thoroughgoing bureaucratization: particularistic relationships, relative autonomy in the performance of tasks, and a degree of contact and thereby involvement with the exercise of managerial authority continued to characterize the roles of even the lower grades of clerical, administrative, and technical employees. Taken together with the pattern of individual mobility, therefore, the defining practices of the roles which made up the non-

---

[19] Over four out of five in the estimate of Stewart *et al.* (1980, p. 161).

proprietorial lower-middle class functioned both to preserve the hierarchy of differentiated grades and to identify the interests of those pursuing careers within it with the new sub-type of the capitalist mode.

The obvious objection which might be made to this is that from 1920 onwards there was a marked increase in the level of union density among non-manual employees, whether male or female and whether in public-sector or in private-sector employment, culminating, as reported in chapter 2, in 1979. This, it might be argued, is *prima facie* evidence in favour of a 'proletarianization' hypothesis whereby all non-manual employees will be driven to identify their interests with those of the Labour movement as such. But that hypothesis fails in face of the evidence that the significant correlation is not between class (let alone income) and union density but between union density and size of work-group, organization, or enterprise. There is an extensive literature on the topic, and although the correlation is well substantiated its explanation has been disputed between observers of the so-called 'industrial relations' and 'Marxian' schools. Both, however, are agreed that bureaucratization of employment relations is the critical variable: where they differ is over whether or not bureaucratization entails proletarianization. As Lockwood rightly points out (1989, p. 231), the reverse is unquestionably true. But even if 'bureaucratization' is operationally defined in terms of specialization of tasks, external control over the work-group, and central direction of the enterprise (Prandy *et al.* 1983, p. 57), it does not follow that the roles in question have been assimilated to those of the working class in lack of autonomy and remoteness from managerial decision-making, let alone low probability of upward intra-generational mobility.

If the mutations in the practices defining non-manual occupational roles and consequent changes in the nature and extent of the economic power of the lower-middle class since the 1920s do not amount to a 'proletarianization' of more than a small minority of clerical, sales, and administrative roles, it follows that union density among non-manual employees cannot be explained in these terms – particularly since sales employees, however unskilled, are seldom unionized at all. The apparent paradox dissolves when the nature of the competitive advantage conferred on non-manual occupational roles by the practice of collective negotiation is examined rather than the class-consciousness of non-manual workers on the one hand and the policies of governments, employers, and union activists on the other (Runciman 1991). Once this is done, it becomes apparent that there is no contradiction between rising union density among non-manual employees and stability in the relative systactic location of the working and lower-middle classes. The function which the practice of collective representation performs for 'careerless' roles can just as well be performed for middle-class roles where an interest in individual upward mobility is consistent with an equal and simultaneous interest in a 'fair' institutional environment within which the careers in question can be pursued (Price 1983, p. 175).

Each white-collar trade union, like the sector of industry within which it operates, has its own individual history, and it is not in dispute that a significant proportion of the variance in union density at any given stage of the business cycle can be accounted for by the actions of individual employers (including governments) on one side and of union activists on the other. But these are variances within a general pattern which is determined by the degree of competitive advantage conferred on different occupational roles by different institutional environments. Airline pilots offer a good quasi-experimental example. In no remotely plausible sense can they be claimed to have been 'proletarianized'. But they reach the peaks of their careers at a relatively early age and they all have the same interest in securing the best terms they can get (not least in their pension arrangements) from employers of whom many operate a tacit cartel. The practice of collective negotiation, therefore, clearly gives competitive advantage to their roles, however little they may feel themselves to have in common with manual workers and however little they may sympathize with the goals of the Labour movement.

To point this out is not to deny causal significance to both the rate of change in salaries relative to the cost of living and changing risks (or perceptions of risk) of redundancy. But again, these do not explain the correlations which persist through the ups and downs of the business cycle and changes of government policy; and of these, the most important is not specialization, external control, or central direction but the imposition of common conditions – or, conversely, withdrawal of particularistic relationships with employers – which is in turn a function of employment concentration more than any other single variable. This feature of the institutional environment is the source of the selective pressure favouring the practice of collective negotiation, and it explains not only why union density among non-manual employees has steadily risen since the First World War but also why it is found in the particular sectors where it is. Sometimes, as with the local government officers, identification of interests with the employer delayed the growth of union membership, so that it was only after the Second World War, following 'the subordination of local particularism in working conditions to a set of national standards common to the service' that over 90 per cent of local government clerks were NALGO (National and Local Government Officers Association) members (Lockwood 1989, p. 145). Sometimes, it was a combination of wartime collectivism and government encouragement of 'Whitleyism' which overcame the resistance of recalcitrant employers (Bain 1970, p. 182). In the case of schoolteachers, differences of interest according to qualifications, type of school, and career prospects meant not that the practice of collective negotiation failed to be replicated and diffused but that separate associations were formed (Coates 1972, p. 2). But whatever the motives and tactics of different employers and employees, common employment conditions consequential upon increasing work-group and enterprise size always favoured the replication and diffusion of the practice of collective negotiation. Only at the level of the upper-middle class did the high-feed professionals continue to combine in associations whose function was to control entry and maintain standards rather than in trade unions whose function was to negotiate over pay and conditions with employers.

Meanwhile, the employers themselves remained unable to mount a direct assault on the power of organized labour of the kind that their predecessors had done in the late-Victorian and Edwardian period. The explanation is not that they had become, even two generations later, more conciliatory by disposition: employers of the 1920s, 1960s, or 1980s proclaiming the 'right to manage' were as strongly motivated as their counterparts of the 1890s and 1910s to retain their control over the means of production, to secure the labour which they needed as cheaply as they could, and to increase or at least maintain their margins of profit to whatever extent the market would allow. The difference was that the power of organized labour, however much less than its leaders might wish it to be, was enough to deprive the practices of organized strike-breaking and the hiring of 'free' labour of the competitive advantages they would have conferred if either employers' associations or the government of the day had been capable of affording the support which they had done before the First World War. The employers' associations, on the other hand, whatever their function in bringing employers together for consultation and lobbying of government, did nothing to reduce competition between them either through collaboration or merger; and ministers whose incumbency of their roles was dependent on the votes of a fully enfranchised working class would gain nothing, however eager they might personally be for wage restraint, from applying the means of coercion at their disposal to an all-out assault on the rights of combination and withdrawal of labour which the unions continued to enjoy.[20] Among small employers, relations with employees (who, as we have seen, were on that account unlikely to be trade-union members in any case) remained close and paternalistic, even if not particularly cooperative. Fire-breathing anti-unionists of the unreconstructed late-Victorian and Edwardian kind (Fox 1985, pp. 187–8, 196) were comprehensively selected out of British industrial relations. The explanation of the surprising reluctance of Clydeside

[20] This may be disputed by those (like Fulcher 1995) who see the legislation of the 1980s as putting the clock back to 1906; but see, in direct response to Fulcher, Runciman (1995b).

employers in the First World War to be drawn into Lloyd George's attack on craft controls, as of the surprising repudiation of the Industrial Relations Act of 1971 by the Director-General of the CBI in 1974, lies here. The practices defining employers' roles, no less than those defining the roles of trade-union officials, functioned to sustain a system which, although 'managerial' rather than 'proprietorial', still left control of the means of production firmly in the employers' hands.

§6. But there remains to be explained the changed function of the 'state' itself. We have seen how, after the First World War, mutations of the practices defining the roles of ministers and officials drove them, often against the wishes and public proclamations of their incumbents, in the direction of intervention in the economy of a kind inconceivable in the late-Victorian and Edwardian period. But what exactly was it about the 1920s and 1930s which made that happen? And once it had, why did it not go further than it did?

Ministers and officials, whatever the party in power, were as well aware in the 1920s as in the 1980s (or any decade in between) of both the exogenous and the endogenous pressures acting on the British economy. But they could neither predict nor control them. Their influence on the processes of social selection was limited to a choice between a narrow range of alternative policies whose reception by those affected by them might be very different from what they had expected and whose potential for changing the direction in which the mode of production was evolving was marginal at best. Decisions to devalue sterling against the dollar and if so by how much, to raise or lower interest rates, to subsidize directly or indirectly one sector of industry rather than another, and to risk higher inflation for the sake of lower unemployment or higher unemployment for the sake of lower inflation, all had potential consequences for the electoral fortunes of the party in power as well as for the subjective experiences of the members of the different classes, or fractions of classes, affected by them. But to the sociologist, they are a textbook example of random inputs into an institutional environment where the mutant practices of the aftermath of the First World War were unlikely as a result either to gain or to lose the competitive advantage which they conferred on the roles which carried them. They might sometimes furnish a quasi-experimental test of the strength of the selective pressures favouring some practices over others. But to the extent that they influenced the mode of production as such, it was through their unintended long-term consequences, not through the motives or purposes which had inspired them.

The irony here is that the strongest of the selective pressures which, in the inter-war years, altered the roles of ministers and officials in a direction which they sought to resist came from the market, although it was the ideology of the market which the very same ministers and officials were ostensibly seeking to uphold. In the 1920s and 1930s, as again in the 1960s and 1970s, the combination of foreign competition and shifting consumer demand caused industries in which British firms had once seemed securely established to be increasingly willing to consider government help and governments to be increasingly willing to give it. In the process, the roles of the leaders of the industries in question functioned more like those of lobbyists than of entrepreneurs and the roles of ministers functioned more like those of non-executive directors representing shareholders' interests than of party politicians. The extent and nature of government intervention in the workings of the economy varied with the nature of the selective pressures acting on the economy: the pressures favouring direct intervention by ministers and officials were always stronger at times of national than of international difficulty (A. Booth 1982). But even then, the function of their altered roles was to influence the market, not to undermine, and still less to replace it. This was no less true when the need was perceived to be for support for traditional industries through periods of recession than when it was perceived to be for injection of risk capital into industries whose success depended on the exploitation of new technology. And it was no less true when a Labour government was in power and its supporters had to overcome their ideological hostility to private enterprise than when a Conservative government was in power and its supporters had to overcome their ideological hostility to central planning.

To some observers, it was only after the Second World War that the joint pressures of full employment and strong trade unions combined to require government action to restore profit levels (Panitch 1980, p. 174). But as we have seen, these concerns were present to ministers and officials in the aftermath of the First no less than of the Second World War, and the formal institution of consultation between representatives of government, industry, and the unions dates from those years. The lesson of the experience of the Labour governments of 1945, 1964, and 1974 is in this respect the same as that of Lloyd George's Coalition of 1918 – namely, the strength of the constraints imposed by the market on any evolution towards 'corporatism' in a strong sense, even when (or precisely because) the government was seeking to redirect it. Market practices – that is, the free exchange of goods and services, the free borrowing and lending of capital, and the free hiring of labour – conferred advantages on their carriers which became all the more clearly visible as the attempts of ministers to replace them with 'corporatist' practices furnished the necessary quasi-experimental contrast on which the theory of social selection can be brought to bear. It is merely a further irony that Harold Wilson, whose 'bonfire of controls' under the Attlee government was a symptom of precisely this, was the Prime Minister the failure of whose 'social contract' of 1974 demonstrated more unmistakably still that the mode of production of mid-twentieth-century England conferred no competitive advantage on roles defined by 'corporatist' rather than market practices.

But there is one area of the economy which, quite apart from its importance to the themes to be addressed in chapter 5, exemplifies particularly well how the unintended consequence of a mutation of practices initiated by the government of the day came to confer advantage on one set of roles over another with lasting implications for the class structure: housing. I pointed out in section 5 of chapter 2 that the steady trend towards not only middle-class but working-class home-ownership goes back, like so many others, to the aftermath of the First World War. But the explanation of what subsequently happened lies not in the conscious acceptance by ministers and officials of responsibility for housing policy, but in the virtual extinction of the role of the private landlord investing in accommodation for rent; and this was due to the selective pressures which combined to undermine the economic advantage which the practice of private letting had conferred on landlords during the late-Victorian and Edwardian period.

Here, the critical mutation was the introduction of rent control in 1915 – a measure intended, like so many others, to be short-term only and inspired by the perceived requirements of a centralized war economy and the need to placate the working class. But the housing shortage which followed the end of the war meant that if control was abolished the government's popularity would suffer from the sharp increase in rents which would be bound to follow. It was therefore left in place, subject only to a few permitted increases between 1919 and 1923 (Hamnett and Randolph 1988, p. 69). The result was that landlords with sitting tenants were faced with a drop in the value of their property and prospective landlords had an evident interest in placing their funds elsewhere. Meanwhile, the building societies, to whom much of the money was lent which might otherwise have gone to the purchase of housing for rent, had no outlet for their funds other than business generated by transfers into owner-occupation of houses previously rented (Pawley 1978, p. 66). The inter-war house-building boom, therefore, in which over $2\frac{1}{2}$ million houses were built for private sale on terms within reach of the best-paid manual, as well as all but the worst-paid non-manual, workers was a joint function of the availability of competitive building society mortgages on the one side and rising real incomes on the other. When, in addition, building costs started to fall from the mid-1920s onwards, the remaining private landlords could neither offer what the building societies were offering nor secure an adequate return on their capital if they did (Hamnett and Randolph 1988, p. 74). None of this was either planned or foreseen. It happened because and only because the selective pressures acting on the practices which defined the private landlord's role deprived it of the competitive advantages it had enjoyed in the very different institutional environment of the late-Victorian and Edwardian period.

At the same time, as reported also in section 5 of chapter 2, the state continued to be involved in the provision of housing for rent by local authorities, and after the Second World War both Labour and Conservative governments encouraged the building of council houses to the point that over a quarter of households in England and Wales were council tenants. But this again turned out to favour the spread of home-ownership in a way that had been neither planned nor foreseen. As the real incomes of working-class households continued to rise, and the mortgage relief available to income-tax payers became relevant to an increasing number of them, so did the trend to owning rather than renting increasingly manifest itself. This does not license an inference, any more than does any other symptom of supposed *embourgeoisement*, that the social distance between working-class and middle-class roles had therefore disappeared. But it did mean that the Labour Party came to abandon its ideological commitment to council housing as such and that rented accommodation came more and more to be a residual category for either transient occupiers or for those too poor to be able to take advantage of the incentives to own. As it is summarized by Saunders (1990, p. 38), 'What seems to have happened is that policies which originated with no intention of supporting home ownership have nevertheless over time come to have this effect, and as owner-occupation has spread, so governments have found it difficult to amend them.' The final irony, so far as government policy is concerned, is the unintended consequence of the Conservatives' attempt to recreate a market in privately rented housing: as housing subsidies fell, the cost of housing benefit rose, thereby increasing the very dependency on social security which Margaret Thatcher and her ministers were seeking to reduce (Timmins 1995, p. 436).

This example, it might be objected, is merely an instance of the familiar mismatch between the objectives of politicians on the one hand and the impediments to their realization on the other. But the objection is misplaced. Not only is the sequence of shifts and reversals of policy a symptom rather than a cause of the society's evolution (or not) from one to another mode or sub-type of the distribution of power, but the extent and nature of the mismatch between aims and outcomes is precisely what the theory of social selection so well explains. Seen from the policy-maker's point of view, the aims of policy are the constant: not the aims but the obstacles to their achievement are the random inputs by which the course of events intended by the far-sighted innovator is deflected or checked. But the reality which the theory of social selection discloses is that the relation is the other way round. The effects of Lloyd George's housing policy have to be explained in just the same way as those of Attlee's welfare policy, of Wilson's incomes policy, or of Thatcher's trade-union policy. It is not that the initiatives of politicians make no difference to the evolution of the society within which they exercise the power attaching to their roles. But where they do, it is because and only because the mutations of practices which they introduce have the functions which they do for the roles which carry them.

The qualitative change in the relations between the economy and the state in the aftermath of the First World War is thus a reflection of the competitive advantages conferred on the one side by unchanged market practices and on the other by mutant practices redefining the roles of ministers and officials and, in consequence, those of the owners and controllers of the means of production themselves. The systactic redistribution of power which this involved was not – even if, to many observers and participants, it felt as if it was – a victory for one or the other side. As so often, it was less a zero–sum transfer of power from one set of similarly located roles to another than a coalitional readjustment. There was a visible identity of interests between representatives of government and representatives of economic interest-groups whereby the interest-groups received certain benefits in return for their acceptance of certain policies. But this is no more to be explained as an accretion of power to potentially authoritarian or socialist governments than as a devolution of power to either the TUC or the CBI. It was the result of the joint advantages to the roles which carried them of the practices first, of a free market in which both employers and workers were forced into larger group-ings, and second, of a new sub-type of liberal democracy which exposed ministers to demands which they could not, electorally speaking, afford to ignore.

MUTATIONS AND THEIR FUNCTIONS IN THE MODE OF PERSUASION

§7. In narrating the changes in the mode of persuasion of twentieth-century English society in section 7 of chapter 2, I said that there would be no serious inaccuracy if the roles in question were initially, at least, reported in terms of economic class; and likewise, when explanation rather than reportage is at issue, adherents of all theoretical schools can agree that in a capitalist society a mutation of practices which changes the economic location of a role is likely to cause some change also in its location in the ideological dimension of the social structure. In their roles as consumers, working-class families in the inter-war period became radio-listeners and cinema-goers as middle-class families did. After the Second World War, they became motorists and foreign holiday-makers in the way that only middle-class families had been between the wars. As purchasers of clothes, both evolved, so to speak, into wearers of jeans from Marks & Spencer, and thus symbolic equals in a manner inconceivable to the cloth-capped manual and starch-collared non-manual workers of the late-Victorian and Edwardian period.

It would, however, be a mistake to suppose that the changes which took place in the ideological dimension of the social structure can be explained entirely as a function of changes in the economic. 'Deference' is yet another of those sociological terms which, like 'consensus' or 'corporatism', can function as a term of reportage, explanation, description, or evaluation as the presuppositions and purposes of the observer who uses them may dictate. But if, in accordance with section 5 of chapter 2 in volume II, 'deference actions' (Shils 1968, p. 117) are taken to be constituted by intentions and beliefs about differences of power in the ideological dimension, then the failure of practices falling under this heading to be replicated as they used to be – the vocative use of 'sir' or 'madam', the curtseying and cap-doffing of pre-1914 Banbury, and so on – has to be related to the change in their functions for their carriers in the different institutional environment. Some of the selective pressures at work were indeed economic. But by no means all of them were.

The status-system of late-Victorian and Edwardian England had been sustained in part by inequalities in the distribution of income and wealth which, as we have seen, declined thereafter. But it was sustained also by an ascriptive ideology of status by birth, a persistence of face-to-face relations of patronage in stable local communities, and the moral authority of an established Church long identified with a hierarchy of ranks in which clergymen were no less 'gentlemen' than lawyers, doctors, or naval or military officers. In that environment, deferent practices were functional for the roles of client and patron alike. Repudiation of the legitimacy of the traditional criteria of prestige conferred no advantage to the carriers of practices symbolic of it. The 'despondency and unrest' which Rowntree and Kendall (1913, p. 315) observed among farm labourers in the villages of rural England could not be translated into collective self-esteem based on a countervailing ideology. Conversely, new entrants into stable communities who failed to conform to the conventional ideology were countered with the classic sanction of ostracism: Roper Power (1937, p. 398), in his account of inter-war Hertford, contrasted its fluidity and anonymity with its structure in the late-Victorian and Edwardian period, when 'Prestige attached to individuals who were known personally and imitated directly. The newcomer was faced with the task of accommodating attitudes and behaviour patterns to the fairly definite conventions of town society if he wished to secure social acceptance, and without such acceptance his range of contacts was very limited.' Only after the churches had lost their authority,[21] both geographical and social mobility were steadily increasing, face-to-face relationships between employers and employees (including domestic servants) were declining, and the now fully legitimated trade unions and Labour Party provided the focus for alternative criteria of working-class self-esteem, did practices which were also 'deference actions' cease to be functional for either side.

The evolution away from deference towards Gleason's 'manner of jaunty equality' moved, as I have remarked, at a very different pace in one part of the country from another. But the difference furnishes another quasi-experimental contrast whereby explanatory hypotheses framed by reference to the different selective pressures acting on the practices symbolic of deference can be tested. In country districts, the institutional environment remained, even after the Second World War, much closer to what it had been in the late-Victorian and Edwardian period: Newby, who studied a sample of agricultural workers and their employers in East Suffolk in 1972, found that the 'unavoidably personal nature of the relationship between farmer and worker' (1977, p. 420) required farmers still to legitimate their authority by ascriptive criteria, not least because their ownership of their land has come to them by birth and the possibility of a farm-worker rising to become a farmer is virtually non-existent. The difference from the late-Victorian and Edwardian period was that the loyalty which the farmers sought could no longer be secured by birth alone: it now required tactful social behaviour which could be perceived as 'gentlemanly' in more than a purely ascriptive sense. Conversely, the manual workers whom other researchers have found, as I reported in section 3 of chapter 2, to repudiate the traditional criteria of status which place them below non-manual workers in the ideological dimension are all urban. To some extent, this is a function of market relationships. Agricultural workers are significantly less well paid than their urban counterparts, and thereby denied the same degree of approximation of life-styles which in itself narrows the social difference between employer and employee. But on no theory can the continuing importance of ascriptive criteria of status in rural as opposed to urban communities be explained by reference to wage-rates alone.

The outcome was a conjunction, from the First World War onwards, of declining social distance between manual and non-manual workers and their families and a rising sense of relative deprivation of status within the working

---

[21] Koss (1975, p. 125) regards it as a 'commonplace' that the First World War 'dealt a shattering blow to organized religion. The churches never recovered from the ordeal, either in terms of communicants or self possession.' Cf. e.g. the Marchioness of Londonderry (1938, p. 254): 'Religion of any sort seems to have been dispensed with.'

class (Runciman 1966).[22] The mutations of practices involved, as always, both sides of the relationship. As members of traditionally higher-ranked status-groups adopted more 'democratic' manners, so did their supposed inferiors abandon deferential forms of behaviour and address; and the two reinforced each other. To be sure, the evolution in this direction did not continue beyond a certain point. Employees who, in the late-Victorian and Edwardian period, would all have called their employers 'sir' did not, after either the First or the Second World War, start to call them 'comrade'. But once the ideology underlying the traditional forms of deference had been challenged with visible success, those incumbents of the subordinate roles whose interest was in challenging it further could hardly fail not only to resent it more but also to see it as more susceptible to such challenge.

The process underlying this modest but irreversible evolution in the mode of persuasion was repeated when the heightened sense of relative deprivation of ideological, as well as economic and coercive, power among women and non-white ethnic groups found expression in organized movements of protest and countervailing ideologies. The explanation of this further narrowing of social distance between traditionally higher-ranked and lower-ranked roles is much the same as for the narrowing of that between working-class and middle-class status-groups. Individual deference actions and practices symbolic of ideological inequality ceased in the same way to function to the advantage of women in their relations with men and non-whites in their relations with whites. This was partly, but only partly, linked to the shift from individual to collective mobility. Although more women of middle-class as opposed to working-class upbringing and more men brought up in Asian (if not Afro-Caribbean) sub-cultures entered roles which had previously been restricted to white middle-class males, their ambitions were at the same time fuelled by an increase in collective self-esteem. But here too, the selective pressures which favoured less deferential practices did not produce change sufficient to assimilate the lower-ranked to the higher-ranked roles. Women did not become the full status-equals of men, and still less non-whites the full status-equals of whites; and this likewise calls for explanation by reference to the countervailing selective pressures simultaneously at work.

§8. Part of the answer lies in the maintenance by the incumbents of higher-

---

[22] Goldthorpe *et al.* (1969, p. 144 n.1) have argued that their findings are 'not, in general, supportive' of this view. But their objection is based on a misunderstanding. The heightened sense of relative deprivation accompanying a narrowing of social distance can equally well take the form *either* of regarding middle-class aspirations as more realistic than hitherto *or* of regarding middle-class norms as less relevant or legitimate in the face of a collective self-esteem now more confidently held.

ranked roles of differentiation of status through the conventional exclusionary practices – refusal of commensalism, status-group endogamy, and denial of social interaction on symbolically equal terms. But as always, the explanation of their success lies not in how strongly they felt relatively deprived of their traditional social location or how vigorously they tried to recover it, but in the institutional environment which gave the roles carrying exclusionary practices a competitive advantage in the ideological dimension of the structure of English society.

In the late-Victorian and Edwardian period, the ideology underlying the Poor Law had, as I remarked in section 14 of chapter 1, begun increasingly to be both questioned and resented. But the irony was that the moral obloquy which the Poor Law ideology attached to relief out of public funds was, as it is put by F. M. L. Thompson (1988, p. 554), 'so effectively ingested into social canons of respectability, even while the physical sanctions grew less harsh, that it became more and more necessary to devise ways round or outside the Poor Law for supporting the respectable poor without damaging the respectability which derived, antithetically, from "the principles of 1834" themselves'. The legacy of 'bourgeois' respectability which Queen Victoria bequeathed to Edward VII included, as we have seen, not only middle-class norms of sobriety, thrift, and hard work but working-class norms of communal assistance in times of need, repudiation of middle-class paternalism, and avoidance by all available means of the stigma of pauperdom. The 'irrational' expenditure on funerals and Sunday clothes, the ambivalent attitudes to the pawnshop, and the preferred recourse to neighbours and kin are all explicable as responses to an institutional environment in which acceptance of the norm which stigmatized reliance on either public or private charity had been functional for working-class households where there remained any prospect of employment for the (usually male) breadwinners. To observers of Marxian presuppositions, this is to be explained as the exercise of ideological hegemony by the bourgeois state on behalf of the capitalist class in the interests of social discipline. But this way of putting it attributes much more efficacy to conscious policy, and much less to its unintended consequences, than the evidence warrants. By 1900, those would-be policy-makers who were most anxious to reinforce the old ideology were less, not more, influential on public opinion; and the fine gradations between status-groups which had by then evolved in urban working-class communities were much more the result of intra-systactic selective pressures than of ideological domination by agents of the state. Within those communities, repudiation of the norm of respectability conferred as little competitive advantage as it did in the villages of rural England where, as we have seen, face-to-face relations between employers and employees were governed by more explicitly ascriptive criteria. The counter-ideology of the defiantly unrespectable conferred no gain in social esteem in the eyes of members of respectable working-class, any more than middle-class, status-groups. In contrast to the rural communities, there was little or nothing deferent about the practices defining the status distinctions of working-class urban communities. But households of families which 'lowered the tone' were exposed to the same ideological sanction.

It is only by reference to this environment, and the selective pressures generated by it, that it is possible adequately to explain the attitudes which stigmatized the role of the so-called 'scrounger' which emerged in the 1920s after the critical mutation which made possible the receipt of benefit by the unemployed irrespective of contribution record. The negative stereotype propagated by the incumbents of middle-class roles who saw the idleness of the scrounger as subsidized by the taxpayer was matched by the recognition among the employed working class that the contributions of those with jobs were paying for the benefits going to those without them. These attitudes, which will be described in more detail in chapter 4, did not displace the genuine concern felt among all systacts about the plight of the long-term unemployed. But they functioned to encourage a 'surreptitious mobilization of the employed against the unemployed' by the Conservative Party (McKibbin 1990, p. 281), which was to be repeated again in the 1980s when it turned out that equally high levels of unemployment were not as damaging as was widely presumed to a Conservative Party now propagating the ideology of an 'enterprise culture'.

In the inter-war period, the most striking illustration of the advantage conferred in the mode of persuasion by practices which the dominant ideology defined as 'respectable' is the much-publicised Jarrow March of 1936. Jarrow was a single-industry town dependent on shipbuilding, and the impact on its workforce of the closure of its shipyard was predictably dramatic. But it was not this in itself which enabled the Jarrow marchers to achieve the favourable image in the eyes of the media and the general public which they did. The explanation of the altogether greater impact on public opinion of the Jarrow March than of the NUWM's march in the same year (or, for that matter, its earlier one of 1932) was that the way in which it was conducted was 'ultra-respectable' (Stevenson 1975, p. 163). The marchers cooperated with the police, refused to allow any Communist speakers to share their platform, and conducted themselves peaceably when admitted into the House of Commons. The sympathy which they aroused was further aided by the public relations skills of Ellen Wilkinson MP. But without their 'ultra-respectability', her efforts to gain that sympathy would have been in vain.

The ideological advantage conferred by 'respectable' practices applied no less to the roles of the members of women's or ethnic movements than to those of the members of trade unions or of the NUWM. Although militancy did, on occasion, pay off in competition for economic or political power, collective social mobility in the ideological dimension was possible only through the achievement of social esteem by the conventional criteria. When feminism revived in strength, the success which it achieved was principally due to the recognition which it was 'morally impossible to deny to women who had proved their worth by intellectual ability and practical competence' (Perkin 1989, p. 430). Likewise, ethnic groups whose collective sense of relative deprivation of social esteem had been similarly heightened could achieve it only by way of practices approved by the dominant ideology. Practices defined by the dominant ideology as deviant might function for some of their carriers as a means of self-esteem and 'a way of surviving, protesting, and forging an identity for ourselves' (Mullard 1973, p. 152); 'crime', as the dominant ideology defines it, may occasionally offer higher ideological as well as economic rewards than conformism. But the simultaneous effect was to reinforce the stereotypes held by the dominant majority and propagated by the popular press, and to sharpen the dilemma faced by the fellow-members of their communities who wished to maintain mutual solidarity without sacrificing collective respect. There was also the alternative adopted by some of the 'quietist variant of resistance' (Dench 1985, p. 131). But whatever the psychological function of 'quietist', as of 'criminal', practices for their individual carriers, the sociological function of their phenotypic effects was to leave the distribution of ideological power undisturbed.

It can plausibly be argued that the constraints imposed by the dominant ideology would have been weakened and perhaps entirely demolished if Britain had been defeated in either the First or the Second World War. But, as many commentators have observed, victory conferred additional legitimacy on the dominant criteria of prestige and additional popularity on the institution of a hereditary monarchy. That popularity was both a symptom and a reinforcement of an underlying consensus on patriotic values, and there is no way of demonstrating precisely the relative causal significance of each (Birnbaum 1955, p. 12). But the institutional environment continued to favour practices consistent with the established values and conventional norms of conduct which appeared to have served the nation so well through the years of trial to eventual victory.

§9. The dominant ideology – an ideology, that is, explicitly legitimating the central institutions of English society – continued to be propagated after both world wars through the media and the educational curriculum alike. But although rival observers might all agree with this as a statement of an obvious social fact, they differed sharply about its consequences. Observers on the Left were inclined to overstate its immediate significance (in order to support their attacks on the existing system) and understate its more lasting effects (in order to support their predictions of the system's demise). Observers on the Right were inclined, for converse reasons, to do the opposite. But the answer is that although the schools and the media exercised a continuing constraint on the replication and diffusion of iconoclastic practices and doctrines, it was not sufficient to prevent the evolution of the mode of persuasion from one to another sub-type of the liberal mode.

In the relatively less hierarchical institutional environment which evolved in the inter-war period and thereafter, there was little dispute about the value of educational reform. There were some predictable differences between those on the Right who looked to parents willing to pay rather than to unionized elementary school teachers as the purveyors of universal secondary education and those on the Left who thought the National Union of Teachers much less radical than it ought to be; and there was an acceptance across the political spectrum that economic constraints prevented the early realization of the recommendations of the authors of successive reports from Fisher onwards. But the children of working-class parents were almost universally seen as entitled to enter their first adult role with the benefit of as much of an increased investment in their education as the state could afford. The Hadow Report of 1926 envisaged the provision of universal secondary education in accordance with ability, and its recommendations, like those of the Robbins Report on university education a generation later, were accepted by all parties. There remained the difference that reformers on the Left were more likely to emphasize that working-class children who had missed out on secondary education should have the opportunity to enrol in classes run by the Workers' Educational Association or by extra-mural university departments, while reformers on the Right were more likely to emphasize that there should be scholarships or assisted places for working-class children with the potential to go on to university by the normal route. But it was an uncontested aim of policy that working-class children should be more adequately represented in relation to their numbers in the institutions of both secondary and higher education. Sceptical observers might see the aim as acknowledged more by lip-service to the ideology than by practical achievement: even after 1944, it was the children of skilled rather than unskilled manual workers who were better represented in the grammar schools (Himmelweit 1954, p. 158), and the children of middle-class parents remained far more likely than those of working-class parents to receive both secondary and university education. But lip-service is as reliable evidence from which to infer a change in the mode of persuasion as is practical achievement. The qualitative change from the educational ideology of the late-Victorian and Edwardian period is unmistakable, and the advantage conferred on the carriers of mutant educational practices and doctrines correspondingly clear.

But the reformist policies which brought the scholarship boys (and some girls) into the secondary schools, enlarged the adult education classes, and opened the universities to a progressively larger proportion of successive age cohorts were in no way subversive of the established hierarchy of esteem. As the Spens Report and the White Paper which followed it explicitly recognized, the grammar schools and their university-based curriculum enjoyed an overwhelming prestige in the eyes of parents and public (Barnett 1986, p. 297). Likewise, when after the Second World War the Robbins Report led to a significant further increase in the number of universities in Britain, its unchallenged assumption was that any individual secondary school pupil with specified exam qualifications – two 'A' levels – was thereby qualified to study for a degree in the subject of his or her choice.[23] 'Parity of esteem' implied the attempt to raise the less traditionally prestigious academic disciplines to the level of the more, not to reverse the traditional criteria by which roles in the institutions of secondary and higher education were ranked. Technical and vocational education never overtook academic, or applied science pure, in social prestige.[24] In consequence, entry into university by a child of parents who had not themselves had a university education continued to involve individual upward mobility into a status-group as alien as ever to his or her systact of origin. Whatever the hopes of the policy-makers who promoted the abolition of the grammar schools in favour of comprehensives and the conversion of Colleges of Advanced Technology into universities, they had no more effect than the reformers of the inter-war years on the social distance between the roles whose defining practices they sought to modify.

Much the same is true of the democratization of cultural standards in general which followed (if it did not, indeed, begin during) the First World War. No contemporary observer could be unaware of the change: men and women from all systacts and milieux went to see the films of Chaplin and Hitchcock; the *Daily Express*, whose circulation exceeded 2 million by the mid-1930s, drew its readers from all social groups;[25] jazz, in the words of a music

---

[23] The report did not, however, say (as *The Times* implied in its editorial comments) that all who were qualified should go to a university (Layard *et al.* 1969, p. 27).

[24] A nationwide study of mechanical engineers carried out in 1962 concluded that 'to a school-leaver the stereotype of the scientist is much more attractive than that of the engineer, and there is, in addition, a widespread feeling that intellectually, engineering is a low-grade activity suitable for boys who are not very good at mathematics or physics' (Gerstl and Hutton 1966, p. 165). A generation later, nothing had changed (*The Times*, 9.3.92, editorial 'Rebuilding the Engineer').

[25] A. J. P. Taylor (1965, p. 310), who adds the comment that 'Beaverbrook, its Canadian proprietor, was not confined by the English social system and had the New World view that there was no difference between rich and poor except that the rich had more money.'

critic who published an early book about its appeal, 'has permeated through all "strata" of society. It shows, so to speak, no respect of persons or classes, but exercises its stimulating or disturbing influence on rich and poor alike' (Mendl 1927, p. 83). But once again, the change did not result in a reversal, but only a modification, of the traditional criteria by which 'highbrow' books or films and 'quality' newspapers were distinguished from 'lowbrow' and 'popular'. Middle-class cinemagoers did not go to the same cinemas as working-class cinemagoers (or if they did, they did not sit in the same seats); few readers of *The Times* and *Daily Telegraph* also read the *Daily Herald* and *News of the World*; jazz supplemented rather than displaced the 'classical' music enjoyed by middle-class radio-listeners and concert-goers. In their roles as consumers of entertainment, the members of working-class households could now command a range of choice which had not been available to them in the late-Victorian and Edwardian period. But they thereby supplemented rather than displaced the practices and roles by which the dominant status-groups continued to distinguish 'mass' culture from 'élite'.

This is a difficult area in which to measure, even with the benefit of hindsight, the strength of the selective pressures which determined how, and to what extent, the previous mode of persuasion could be modified. But as it happens, the BBC in the 1930s provides something very close to a quasi-experimental test. The chance combination of regular sound broadcasting from 1922 onwards (itself made possible by technological advances stimulated by the war), the appointment of John Reith to be in charge of it,[26] and the decision of the Conservative Government to turn over to a public corporation the assets of what had hitherto been the British Broadcasting Company, placed in the hands of one man a monopoly of the most widely influential single means of persuasion; and that one man was explicitly committed to the preservation of a 'high moral tone'. As a result, the BBC was seen by both those who approved and those who disapproved as systematically upholding conventional values, imposing 'élite' standards of culture, and censoring the expression of un-orthodox or potentially subversive opinions and tastes. But however success-fully Reith appeared to contemporary observers to have achieved his aims, as a test of the theory of social selection it is his failure which is instructive – not his failure to prevent the introduction of commercially sponsored broadcasting, which he was to liken in 1952 to the introduction of smallpox, bubonic plague, and the Black Death (H. H. Wilson 1961, p. 107), but his failure to keep the content of programmes as he wished it in the 1930s when the power attaching to his role was, to all appearances, more than adequate for him to do so.

[26] The coincidences which led to his appointment included the death of a friend in America but for which he would have left England before the general managership had been advertised (Reith 1949, p. 80).

By the early 1930s, the BBC was presenting itself as a bulwark of British culture in a world increasingly dominated by American, comparing itself favourably with the Bank of England, *The Times*, and the Royal Academy, and demonstrating to the government and its audiences alike an unassailable respectability: 'Reith's ideal of public service translated itself into programming which uplifted the Corporation and the medium, as much as the vast audience it strove to serve' (Le Mahieu 1988, p. 189). Yet by the end of the 1930s the programming had been transformed: religion, educational talks, and chamber music concerts went down; variety programmes went up; light music and jazz were scheduled at peak listening hours; human-interest stories and American-style audience-participation programmes were allowed; and by 1939, the BBC's own *Handbook* was proclaiming that 'no one whose business it is to supply things to people – least of all those who supply entertainment – can afford to be ignorant about what people want' (quoted Le Mahieu 1988, p. 290). The change came about, despite Reith's strong personal preferences and autocratic style of management, in response to a set of specific pressures (Cardiff 1983, p. 382): complaints to *Radio Times* (particularly about the mixing of highbrow with popular programmes on the same channel, which Reith strongly favoured); newspaper polls; competition after 1933 from continental stations; the concern of the Radio Manufacturers' Association to sell more sets; and the beginnings of systematic in-house audience research. Reith, in consequence, lost and the consumers won. The power attaching to the roles of the carriers of the practices by which the dominant ideology was defined was now visibly less than they and many contemporary observers had believed, and it remained so thereafter. The vicissitudes of public taste and the shifting content of popular entertainment are a topic for the theory of cultural rather than of social selection: popular music, in particular, offers a paradigm example of the mutation, replication, and diffusion of 'memes'. But in the new sub-type of the capitalist-liberal-democratic mode, it was the consumers who both literally and metaphorically called the tune.

MUTATIONS AND THEIR FUNCTIONS IN THE MODE OF COERCION

§10. To answer the question why the mode of coercion of twentieth-century English society changed neither more nor less than it did after 1918, there need to be tested hypotheses not about the origin of the mutations of practices from which there emerged the institutions of parliamentary democracy but about the consequences of the diffusion of the practice of voting for rival parliamentary candidates to all adult citizens in their roles as such. This, as I said at the beginning of section 10 of chapter 2, amounted by itself to an evolution from one to another sub-type of the democratic mode. I also said that its importance to the replacement of the Liberal by the Labour Party as the principal parliamentary opposition to the Conservative Party was irrelevant to the arguments of this volume. But the extension of the franchise did turn out to constrain the behaviour of the principal party of opposition to the Conservatives, whether Liberal or Labour, much more closely than had been generally expected, whatever the motives and ambitions of its leaders and whatever the slogans under which they presented themselves to the enlarged electorate.

In the late-Victorian and Edwardian period, the anti-Conservative portion of the semi-enlarged electorate of adult males could no longer be mobilized, as the mid-Victorian electorate had been, into a dominant inter-systactic coalition united by regional and religious interests and an ideology of Gladstonian radicalism. But nor could it be reassembled into a dominant coalition between working-class trade unionists and sympathetic middle-class intellectuals and professionals; the working-class trade unionists were too much divided between those who would and those who would not operate within a still recognizable Gladstonian tradition, and the anti-Conservative intellectuals and professionals were too much divided between those who did and those who did not accept the 'statist' premises of the 'new' Liberalism. It is true that at the time when the Edwardian Liberal Party was visibly divided over issues of social policy and the role of the state, and the fledgling Labour Party visibly split between its socialist-intellectual and trade-unionist wings, the Conservative Party was no less visibly at odds with itself over tariff reform. But the Conservatives could always rely on the votes of a majority of the salaried and/ or propertied middle classes and of a significant minority of the working classes, whatever the differences among their leaders over doctrine or tactics. The Liberals, by contrast, had been faced even in the late-Victorian and Edwardian period with the dilemma that they needed both to be and not to be the party perceived as standing for the interests of labour as against capital: they needed to retain working-class votes on other than purely regional and sectarian grounds, but they could not afford to lose middle-class votes by conceding too much to the unions and their intellectual allies.[27] Voting behaviour was never determined simply by the ostensible systactic interests of the voters. But whatever did determine the results of successive General Elections under the enlarged franchise, it was evident from 1918 onwards that formidable difficulties now stood between the Liberal Party and a victory at the polls of the kind it had won in 1906. Quite apart from the division in its leadership which had resulted from the war, a party which had been

---

[27] Thus, for example, Campbell-Bannerman's concession to Labour on the Trades Disputes Bill in 1906 was 'another defeat for the purer principles of the New Liberalism and for the concept of a communal good to which sectional interests had to be deemed subordinate' (Powell 1986, p. 392).

represented in the House of Commons in 1914 by 105 businessmen but only 8 manual workers was 'hardly the kind of party which could have kept Labour at bay indefinitely' (Searle 1983, p. 55). Although the war may have done little to diminish, and much to exacerbate, the union leaders' distrust of government interference, they could not be brought back into a 'Lib-Lab' fold once they had a national party of their own.[28]

In any event, whatever the might-have-beens by which the electoral fortunes of the Liberals could have been restored, the Labour Party in 1918 was an independent national party with a network of some 400 affiliated local bodies and an irreducible fifth or so of the total vote (depending on the number of constituencies which it chose to contest); and it was a party which the trade unions controlled. This was a trend which could be said to date back to the decision of the Miners' Federation to join the Labour Party in 1909. Moreover, the success of the Labour Party in the period up to 1914 had been due not just to the performance of its parliamentary representatives but to the impact on the country of 'local stalwarts', who, in some constituencies, were helped in establishing themselves in that role by the intransigence of the local Liberals (K. D. Brown 1985, p. 12). But it was in and after 1918 that the role became critical to the development of Labour as a national party capable of fielding candidates in virtually every parliamentary constituency. It was not just that effective organization in the constituencies called for money that only the unions were in a position to provide. It was also that the roles of local party agent and voluntary party worker were as important as that of parliamentary candidate, and these too could, for the most part, only come from the unions (McKibbin 1974, p. 242). To observers on the Left who foresaw the radicalization of the unions in the face of intensified exploitation sanctioned by Liberal and Conservative policies alike, this was a help rather than a hindrance to the 'forward march' towards Socialism. But diffusion and replication of the practices defining the roles of the politically active trade unionists were constrained by the same selective pressures as had, before 1914, prevented the Labour Party from evolving into an ideologically and politically exclusive proletarian party with its own Marxist sub-culture. Labour did displace the Liberals 'from the Left' in the sense that it could more readily command the electoral loyalty of anti-Conservative working-class voters. But its success was also due to its ability to take up progressive and reformist causes such as anti-imperialism and working-class education which had been championed by the Liberals in the late-Victorian and Edwardian period. In a constituency-based

---

[28] This is not to question the adverse impact on the Liberal vote of Asquith's decision to allow Labour to form a government in 1923. But even in 1923, the Liberals' share of the vote per opposed candidate was, at 37%, less than Labour's 41% and less than the 38.4% it had been in 1922 (figures for all constituencies taken from Butler 1953, p. 175).

electoral system where the winners were the candidates securing the largest share of the vote, Labour could only hope to form a government if it could win a sufficient number of seats outside its traditional working-class strongholds; and provided that its candidates were not outflanked by a Communist (or, later, a Militant), it could appeal to middle-class progressives without risking the loss of working-class support. In other words, to succeed as a national party Labour would need, even before the decline in the size of the working classes relative to the middle classes reported in section 2 of chapter 2, to be a moderate party in both its practices and its doctrines.

The selective pressures which, however unexpectedly, followed the enlargement of the franchise bore just as strongly on the roles of Conservative as of Labour Party managers and activists. The need to mobilize popular support in the constituencies had already been apparent in the late-Victorian and Edwardian period – so much so, indeed, as to generate fears among some observers that 'caucus' practices might lead to the domination of the parliamentary party by the National Union (McKenzie 1955, p. 584). But after 1922, the function of the organizers' roles was to deliver the vote to the party's leadership, not to formulate the policies on which leaders were to ask the voters to decide. The parliamentary party itself became more formally organized and more tightly disciplined: candidates who deviated from the party line and members who defied the party whips did so at the peril of their careers. But the sanctions were imposed from above, not below; and the leaders of the Conservative, as of the Labour, Party were always more moderate in their views than were the constituency activists on whom they depended. Observers who had doubted whether the enlarged electorate would be capable of acting 'responsibly' in the sense presupposed by democratic theory could, therefore, be said to have been vindicated in one sense. The new electorate of 50,000 or more voters per constituency was, they could claim, not so much exercising an informed and rational choice between alternative sets of policies as responding to the appeals of rival organizations directed to tapping their collective loyalties and prejudices through the 'media', supplemented in due course by the techniques of opinion sampling and market research. But this is a very different outcome from a gullible and volatile mass electorate at the mercy of charismatic demagogues and fire-eating revolutionaries seeking to overturn the mode of coercion from below. Far from giving greater competitive advantage to roles such as these, the political environment as it evolved after 1922 selected them out in favour of practices whose advantage to the roles which carried them depended on their function in securing cross-systactic support.

The strength of this selective pressure is as clearly demonstrated in the virtual extinction of the role of the independent member as in the failure of militant practices to be diffused beyond the fringes of the major parties. There were still a few successful independent (or minor-party) candidates after the extension of the suffrage – 57 between 1919 and 1951 (Butler 1953, p. 165) – just as there were still a few successfully rebellious militants. But neither independents nor militants ever commanded sufficient influence to threaten a change to another mode or even sub-type of the democratic mode of coercion. The nearest approach to such a threat was at the Labour Party's conference of 1980. But in the event, the outcome was a split in the Labour Party and its heavy defeat in the General Election of 1983, when its share of the vote fell below 28 per cent. Thereafter, the Labour Party was only able to restore its electoral fortunes by repudiating the programme which had caused the Social Democrats to break away in the first place. It was the nearest to a quasi-experimental test since Mosley's career between the wars of the hypothesis that the new sub-type of the democratic mode conferred no selective advantage on roles carrying 'extremist' practices and doctrines.

§11. But whatever the moderation of successive governments in matters of national policy, the power attaching to the roles of ministers and officials became, as we have seen, altogether greater than it had been before 1914. The adult members of British society might now, in their roles as voters, have a collectively restraining influence on how that power was used. But they were at the same time increasingly subject to it in their daily lives. It might be mediated through departmental devolutions and reshuffles,[29] and flouted or evaded by those with the opportunity and motive for doing so. But it has still to be explained why it increased as much as it did and why, having done so, it did not increase further still.

The first question is easier to answer than the second. The increasing number of tasks assumed by the state in and after the First World War, together with the increasing resources from taxation with which to fund them, brought into being, as we have seen, a burgeoning Civil Service whose members' roles were defined by 'bureaucratic' practices both in their relations with each other and in their dealings with the public. The new generation of career civil servants was sometimes accused of self-interested power-hunger. But the accusation dissolves on closer examination of the function of the practices defining their roles; much of the advice which they tendered was such as to diminish rather than enhance their influence (Lowe 1986, p. 245). As one contemporary academic observer put it, 'Not their own motion, but the general motion of politics, has enlarged their duties and widened their powers' (E. Barker 1937, p. 30). Their roles might be, and often were, resented by the

---

[29] Devolution does not, however, imply diminution; cf. Newsam (1954, p. 26), quoted by McKenzie and Grove (1957, p. 228): 'although the Home Office from time to time surrenders to other Departments some of its functions it remains, like the widow's cruse, always full'.

public, whether recipients of welfare dependent on the whim, as they saw it, of petty officials or owners of property subjected to the interference, as they saw it, of remote and arrogant 'gentlemen from Whitehall' in their private affairs. But there was little the public could do about it. In their roles as citizens, they had no countervailing power against the decisions of appointed officials except in the few cases where a complaint to the courts, or the special commissioners of taxes, or a Member of Parliament, or a newspaper, or (once the role had been brought into being) an ombudsman might secure reversal or redress. Admittedly, the power of the Civil Service was, as I remarked in section 2, corporate only to a limited degree. Not only did the practices defining its members' roles sometimes function to diminish as much as to augment their own influence, but much of their power was 'secondary' in the technical sense – that is, they derived it from the roles of their departmental ministers. But from the citizen's point of view, this meant simply that the Parliament into which they had voted their elected representatives had a large and well-disciplined army of subordinates to administer whatever measures the government of the day might decide. Moreover, after the First World War the practice of delegated legislation made it increasingly inaccurate to speak of Parliament as the decision-taking body. Ministers' power to make rules and regulations without putting through primary legislation is 'essentially a twentieth-century device, justified by reference to the necessity for speed (particularly in emergencies), flexibility (in revising legislation to take account of changed circumstances) and complexity (because Parliament does not possess the necessary technical skills or specialist knowledge)' (Alderman 1983, p. 10).

Yet the constraints which limited this power are explicable too. In the first place, there is an inherent contradiction between the practices defining the roles constitutive of central and of local government. This does not mean that ordinary citizens were on that account freer to do as they pleased. But the power which continued to attach to the roles of local-government officials, whether elected or appointed,[30] meant that those roles might function to thwart rather than to reinforce the power attaching to the roles of central government ministers and their officials. The erosion of the power of local institutions reported in chapter 2 was accompanied not only by a rhetorical commitment to local participation (D. S. King 1989, p. 206) but by a recognition that the roles of local politicians and officials could never be done away with altogether. It was not simply a matter of central government's

---

[30] The role of 'town clerk' evolved after the Second World War into that of 'chief executive'; but they remained just as likely to be solicitors – 84% in 1974 (Rhodes 1988, p. 217) – as when the Royal Commission of 1929 had been exercised about whether or not they needed to be legally qualified (Thornhill 1971, p. 296).

inability to decide on its own criteria and apply them with sufficient rigour (Beloff and Peele 1980, p. 278). Even if ministers were determined, as they saw it, to bring irresponsible or intransigent local authorities to heel, the practice of administrative delegation conferred on the roles of its local carriers a degree of power impervious to the practices of a bureaucratic 'command code' (Rhodes 1988, p. 411) whose unintended consequences might include a repoliticization of roles at the local level. It was at the very times that central government was most determined to impose control that the hypothesis of a contradiction in the technical sense is given its closest approximation to a quasi-experimental test. Whatever the aims and motives of Margaret Thatcher and her ministers, the failure to impose a community charge or 'poll tax' is as striking as the failure of either the Heath government's industrial relations legislation or the Wilson government's 'social contract'.

Equally important, however, was the pressure-group activity reported in section 12 of chapter 2. As I pointed out, the mere existence of a pressure-group does not license a semi-deductive inference that there attaches to its members' roles the power to change ministerial decisions. But nor, on the other hand, does it license an inference that the society in which they have emerged is 'divided against itself' (Beer 1982, pp. 35–7). In some cases, no doubt, diffusion of the practices defining pressure-group roles should be seen as symptomatic not so much of a changed distribution of political power as of 'the frustrated powerlessness of those who could not get the ear of government, still less their positive action – no matter what they did or did not do' (Dearlove and Saunders 1984, p. 70). But there are also cases where pressure-group activity did result in action by government, whether in moving ministers in a direction in which they were already willing to go or in restraining them from moving as soon or as far as they and their advisers had previously planned. Why, therefore, did the new sub-type of the democratic mode of coercion not bring about the transfer of more power than it did from the roles of ministers and officials to those of the leaders of organized groups representative of significant fractions of the enlarged electorate?

The answer is that the lobbyist's role is another instance of one whose power is more coalitional than systactic. Pressure groups have, by definition, some common interest of which their members are collectively aware, even if the support which they mobilize comes from all classes, status-groups, and factions.[31] But their chances of success are a function of the extent to which the incumbents of governmental roles are prepared to listen to them, not of a constitutional entitlement to be heard. Even where they do succeed, the

---

[31] The objective (and the sense of relative deprivation) may, of course, be vicarious: the Child Poverty Action Group campaigns for increased resources for its clients, not its members (Whitely and Winyard 1987).

response of those whom they have influenced is likely to be grudging acquiescence rather than willing endorsement. But the state of mind of the protagonists is as irrelevant as ever to the nature of the selective pressures which determine the competitive advantage attaching to their roles. However much of a nuisance to individual ministers and officials, pressure-groups function, institutionally speaking, as a convenience to both sides. So much is this so that it has even been said by one observer that 'if an organised group does not exist, the government helps invent it' (Potter 1960, p. 32). The examples which can be cited to illustrate this remark range from the British Iron and Steel Federation in 1934 to the British Institute of Management in 1945 to the Woodland Owners' Association in 1956 to Motability in 1981 – the last being a registered charity managed by a seconded civil servant. The practice of consultation between the incumbents of governmental and pressure-group roles, like the practice of collective bargaining between managements and trade unions, was diffused and replicated because of the advantages which it conferred on both sides. On the lobbyists' roles it conferred, if not political power, at least the possibility of a modest degree of political influence; and on the roles of ministers and officials it conferred, if not an increased degree of political power, at the least the possibility of winning enhanced legitimacy for their decisions.

Thus the new distribution of power between governors and governed evolved out of selective pressures working simultaneously in opposite directions. The pressures favouring participative practices and thereby openness in decision-making reinforced the pressures favouring concentration and secrecy – and vice versa. This is not the paradox it may appear to be: as I reported in section 12 of chapter 2, the outcome was, as so often in social evolution, not a crisis but a new equilibrium between the roles on either side of a systactic divide. The institutional environment of the period after 1922 might be as strange to late-Victorian and Edwardian ministers and those who sought to influence them extra-parliamentarily as it would have been to Gladstone and the mid-Victorian 'faddists'. But there was no inherent contradiction in the evolution of a new sub-type of the democratic mode of coercion which, in the event, gave both more power to the people and more power to the state.

§12. The same holds where the means of coercion were brought directly to bear. It is true that in the area of criminal justice relations between the police and suspected offenders continued, as I remarked in section 11 of chapter 2, largely unchanged: there was the same imbalance of power against poorer and less privileged suspects, the same ambivalent relation between police officers and professional criminals, and the same obstacles in the way of redress for victims of police malpractice at the hands of magistrates or juries. But across the range of contact between police and public, the pressures for more vigorous and wide-ranging enforcement of the law were balanced by pressures for greater disclosure and more effective curtailment of perceived abuses. The power attaching to the role of the special branch detective was, so to speak, mirrored in the power attaching to the role of the investigative journalist, and mutant practices which made the mode of coercion less 'democratic' emerged in parallel with others which made it more so.

One important qualification, however, needs to be made. Selective pressures of a different kind acted on the roles stigmatized by 'public opinion' – that is, by the dominant ideology as expressed by the controllers of the means of persuasion. The actions of the controllers of the means of coercion and their agents might be more open to scrutiny and criticism. But if those against whom coercive sanctions were applied were the incumbents of roles identified as 'subversive', public opinion offered little defence. As we have seen, even before the First World War, surveillance of such groups had been institutionalized through the Special Branch; and after it, large-scale contingency plans for the control of both industrial unrest and political agitation became and remained an inherent component of the policies of governments of all parties. What is more, the need to control organized crime of a steadily more sophisticated and less localized kind not only favoured practices by which police power was increasingly centralized but increasingly concentrated its application on roles perceived as deviant.

In the inter-war period and the early years after the Second World War, the tensions which were thereby generated were, as we have seen, largely free of ethnic or racial overtones. But from the 1960s onwards, the increasing numbers of young black males who were charged with offences rendering them liable to imprisonment led to accusations that the police were deliberately discriminating against them. By the 1980s, it was evident that Afro-Caribbeans, in particular, were represented in the prison population out of proportion to their numbers as a percentage of the population as a whole. To commentators on the Left, this was in itself proof of police discrimination. To commentators on the Right, it was proof that Afro-Caribbeans were more often engaged in crime. Despite a burgeoning research literature on the topic, there was no way of accurately testing these two propositions against each other (Fitzgerald 1992). But it is plausible to suppose that both are correct, since the practices defining the roles on the two sides of the relationship reinforced the diffusion and replication of each other. As reported in section 9 of chapter 2, black people were visibly disadvantaged within English society not only in employment but in housing and education. It was therefore only to be expected that young black males would become disproportionately involved in street crime and that they would become the targets of aggressive policing (Reiner 1985,

p. 136). Even if, for the sake of argument, we suppose that all inner-city police officers had been themselves recruited from minority ethnic groups, it would have remained the case that young black males would invite disproportionate attention from the police and that constables and detective constables in inner-city areas would stop, search, question, and arrest them more than either young whites or older members of any particular ethnic group.

Whoever the targets of surveillance and coercion, the question *quis custodiet?* remained on the political agenda, with commentators on the Left calling for greater accountability to elected officials at the same time that commentators on the Right were calling for stronger police powers. Once again, however, the actual outcome is readily explained in terms of the selective pressures acting on the roles of police and ministers alike after the police strike of 1921 and its threat of a systactic alliance between unionized manual workers and disaffected policemen whom Parliament had deprived of the right to belong to a union at all. The Police Federation, although its members might have lost the right to strike, was if anything more strongly placed than if they had kept it when it came to negotiating over pay and conditions; and it was able to secure a Discipline Code far more favourable to its members than either the practices defining the rights of civilian employees on the one side or those defining the rights of members of the armed forces on the other. Whatever measures might be taken to protect the rights of suspects held in police custody, culminating in the creation of the role of 'custody officer' in the Police and Criminal Evidence Act of 1984, police officers suspected of malpractice could expect to be supported by their colleagues, defended by expert barristers, safeguarded against 'double jeopardy' according to the criminal burden of proof, and offered either early retirement or medical grounds for discharge as an alternative. Furthermore, when police officers were charged with committing a criminal offence, they were likely to gain from the character of the witnesses on whose testimony a conviction by the jury would depend.

This pattern of exogenous pressure for greater accountability on the one side and endogenous pressure for greater self-protection on the other explains in the same way the changes in the roles of the agents of the security services. Sociologists and historians are inevitably hampered in this area by the lack of reliable evidence against which their hypotheses can be tested; there is no way of finding out how far covert operations drawing on the full means of coercion at the disposal of MI5 or MI6 were successfully deployed without even the most astute and experienced investigative journalists knowing anything about them. But such evidence as there is[32] tends to validate the hypothesis that the

---

[32] From the 'Zinoviev letter' episode of 1924 to the 'Spycatcher' episode of 1986, the evidence available has tended to come, directly or indirectly, from incumbents of roles within the system who have a personal motive for seeking to discredit one another.

pressure for accountability functioned to reinforce the competitive advantage attaching to secrecy and loyalty to immediate colleagues within the service. The lifting of the veil by the Major government to the extent of allowing the names of the heads of the security services to be publicly known was not going to make any material difference to the functions of the practices defining their members' roles.

It is, therefore, readily explicable why the relative power attaching both to the roles of the agents of the state and to the members of the public in their roles as enfranchised citizens should remain as it was in the areas of administrative and of directly coercive decisions alike. There was no lack of people on both sides of the relationship who tried to make it otherwise. To senior police officers, the institutional safeguards afforded to suspects or defendants guilty of criminal offences were a serious impediment to the ability of their forces to protect the public as the public would like. To the members of libertarian pressure-groups, the legal powers and the resources in technology and manpower in the hands of the police were an instrument of oppression of underprivileged citizens by the over-mighty state. Neither was ever going to persuade the other. But a significant evolution of the mode of coercion was equally unlikely in either direction.

ADAPTIVE AFFINITIES

§13. Explanation of the changes which have taken place in the modes of production, persuasion, and coercion of twentieth-century England depends, I have argued, on identifying the practices which the process of social selection has selected because of the competitive advantage which they confer on the roles which carry them. Adaptations, if that term is to be used, are *for* the replicators, that is, the practices, *by* the roles which are their carriers. But roles are located in a three-dimensional social space, and although modes of production, persuasion, and coercion are analytically distinct they are always empirically interrelated. Not only do the institutions constitutive of each influence the institutions constitutive of the others, but the roles which make up those institutions are often defined by practices of all three kinds. At the risk of wearying readers who have also read volume II, let me repeat once again that the evolution of a society's modes of production, persuasion, and coercion is not a process of 'adaptation' by the society as such, and that the units of selection are not individuals or groups or systacts or institutions but the practices defining the roles of which the society consists. Adaptations, accordingly, are adaptations by roles whose defining practices confer continually shifting competitive advantages on their carriers in a continuously changing distribution of economic, ideological, and political power. But the success of some rather than other roles and the consequent enhancement of the probability of replication and diffusion of their defining practices depends not least on whether those practices augment or diminish the competitive advantages conferred by each other in the three separate dimensions of social space.

It can plausibly be argued that the practices defining the roles constitutive of a capitalist mode of production, a liberal mode of persuasion, and a democratic mode of coercion will, other things equal, systematically reinforce one another – or to put it in the metaphor which Max Weber liked to borrow from Goethe, that there is some sort of 'elective affinity' between the three. Indeed, we have seen in some detail how the changes in the mode of production after the First World War were related both to the extension of the franchise and to the weakening of traditional criteria of deference. But the articulation of the modes of production, persuasion, and coercion had been equally important to the preceding sub-type of capitalist liberal democracy. Late-Victorian and Edwardian England was capitalist in a fashion more proprietorial than managerial, liberal in a fashion more individualistic than egalitarian, and democratic in a fashion more inclusionary than plebiscitary. The elective affinity between the three is as evident in the roles of the provincial businessmen sitting on the Liberal back-benches in the House of Commons as in those of the respectable trade unionists on the Labour Representation Committee.[33] The war, when it came (or rather, when it lasted as long as it did), altered the modes of production, persuasion, and coercion in ways which likewise reinforced each other. But the new sub-type of capitalist liberal democracy which had evolved by the time of Lloyd George's fall from power was, at the same time, less radically different from that of the late-Victorian and Edwardian period than it would have been if the affinity had not continued to be as close as before.

It is, accordingly, time to look yet again at what took place in the period between 1915 and 1922 in order to understand more fully how it came about that the mutations of economic, ideological, and coercive practices reported in chapter 2 had the effects which they did – unperceived, unpredicted, and undesired as those effects might be. The selective pressures generated by a protracted war favoured the carriers of a connected set of mutant practices whose functions could, as I have remarked already, be expected to lapse when the war was over. And so, in the event, many of them did. But some did not; and even some that did bequeathed to the institutions within which they had emerged an influence which outlived them. Thus, as we have seen, the women who returned from the labour market to full-time roles as housewives retained not only the franchise (or, if under thirty, gained it a few years later) but also

---

[33] Arthur Henderson's combination of the roles of union functionary, local councillor, lay preacher, and temperance reformer (Leventhal 1989, p. 8) was, so to speak, as quintessentially late-Victorian and Edwardian as a Gilbert and Sullivan operetta.

some, at least, of their improved social status in relation to men. The roles of
the officials in the Ministry of Labour who had been principally concerned
with the need to placate the unions on whose members' labour the maintenance
of the war effort depended were adapted to deal with the unprecedented levels
of unemployment which followed the collapse of the post-war boom. Shop
stewards whose roles had been enhanced by the controversies over dilution and
leaving certificates were absorbed into the organization of their unions in
functions which reinforced the trend to plant-level bargaining irrespective of
wartime conditions. Employers who had come together in associations whose
function was to coordinate their responses to wartime direction of the economy
by the state maintained those associations to coordinate their resistance to
organized labour as well as to continue to lobby governments in peacetime. It is
in this amalgam of interconnected and sometimes contradictory-looking effects
that the answer is to be found to the much-debated question of the extent to
which the First World War 'shaped the progress' (J. Turner 1992, p. 2) of
twentieth-century Britain. To say (*ibid.*) that 'closer inspection reveals both
revolution and counter-revolution going off half-cock in the heat of war' is
perhaps an overstatement. But it is a useful way of drawing attention to the
extent to which selective pressures brought into being by the war simultaneously heightened the probability of diffusion and replication of practices
threatening to, and of practices supportive of, the capitalist-liberal-democratic
mode of the distribution of power.

To contemporary observers with 'reconstructionist' presuppositions, the
involvement of the state in the direction of the economy over the heads of both
capital and labour was an irreversible change.[34] But the reconstructionists
might have been more cautious in their predictions if they had asked
themselves exactly what were the competitive advantages conferred on the
roles which carried them by the mutant practices of Lloyd George's 'war
socialism'. Trade-union members had undoubtedly gained economically,
ideologically, and politically from the accretion of power to the roles of their
leaders and spokesmen. But after 1918, the functions of those roles reverted to
what they were bound to be in time of peace in a capitalist liberal democracy.
The rhetoric of the National Industrial Conference of 1919 was soon exposed
for what it was. In the mode of production, the practices which now mattered
were those defining how negotiations were conducted with employers, how
union members were recruited and retained, and how relations between unions

---

[34] Cf. Sanderson Furniss, the Principal of Ruskin College, Oxford, as quoted by Newton and
Porter (1988, p. 51): 'We know that the state can do many things in a time of emergency which
many people thought it could not do at all without very serious consequences; and there now
seems no reason to doubt that, with public opinion behind it, what the state can do in a time of
emergency it can do when times are normal.'

were regulated by, or through, the TUC. In the mode of persuasion, the related practices which now mattered were those defining how trade-union officials were publicly perceived and portrayed and the degree to which, in their dealings with employers and officials of government, they were treated as social equals. In the mode of coercion, the related practices which now mattered were those defining how the activists in the unions and the Labour Party mobilized their supporters and coordinated their readiness to take collective action in support of the party's and the unions' political aims. And there was just as much elective affinity between the three as there had been in the different institutional environment of the late-Victorian and Edwardian period, as the careers of Bevin, Citrine, and countless lesser statesmen of the Labour movement abundantly illustrate.

At the same time, the process was mirrored on the other side of the systactic divide between labour and capital. Lloyd George's 'war socialism' had not only given political influence, ideological legitimacy, and economic bargaining-power to the roles of the trade-union leaders. It had also undermined the social prestige and political influence, as well as the wealth, of the owners of the means of production. Keynes was exaggerating when he wrote in 1919 that 'The terror and personal timidity of this class is now so great, their confidence in their place in society and in their necessity to the social organism so diminished, that they are the easy victims of intimidation' (quoted by Perkin 1989, p. 298). But even those of them who were ready to acknowledge Lloyd George's achievements in prosecuting the war to a successful conclusion were resentful of the concessions which organized labour had won, sceptical of the rhetoric of consensus, and suspicious of continuing governmental intervention. So far as concerned the power attaching to their roles, they had good reasons to be so. But once the selective pressures acting on those roles and their defining practices were those of peacetime, their roles, like the roles of the trade-union leaders, adapted to them. Reassertion of managerial control, affirmation of an ethos of professionalism, and collective representation to government on matters of policy through associations formed for the purpose all went hand in hand. And again, the elective affinity between the three can be illustrated in the careers of many lesser industrialists besides Mond or Weir who, like them, recognized that they could not have recourse to the tactics which their predecessors had employed in the late-Victorian and Edwardian period.[35]

Just as the random input of the character and ambitions of Reith provide a quasi-experimental test of the strength of some of the selective pressures at

---

[35] Hence, for example, Weir's explicit concern in the 1930s that profiteering in the expanding aircraft industry would put at risk 'all Private Enterprise' (Wrigley 1987b, p. 118).

work in the mode of persuasion, so does the random input of the character and ambitions of Lloyd George provide one for the strength of those at work across the modes of production, persuasion, and coercion together. In the immediate aftermath of the war, his reputation in Parliament and the country at large was unchallengeable, and he sought to use it to entrench his role as a leader above party who would bring all but the extreme Left and extreme Right together. The sincerity or otherwise of his sentiments, about which rival biographers and historians continue to debate, is immaterial. To the sociologist, the question is why the mutant practices which the success of his aspirations presupposed turned out to be irreplicable. Continuation into peacetime of a coalition government claiming to reconcile the conflicting interests of all classes, status-groups, and factions presupposed not only cooperation in the mode of production but agreement in the mode of persuasion and reconciliation in the mode of coercion. Lloyd George tried them all, and in all of them failed.

That failure can be (and often has been) narrated in terms of the sequence of stratagems by which he sought to hold the coalition government together and protect his own role as its head. But from the perspective of the theory of social selection, its interest lies in the functions of the roles of those who opposed him and the reasons for which, despite his best efforts, they were successful in doing so. Once 'normalcy' had returned, collective bargaining was increasingly likely to displace cooperation in the interests of the war effort between unions and employers; partisan propagandizing was increasingly likely to displace the rhetoric of national unity; electioneering under conventional party labels was increasingly likely to displace the alliances contrived in support of 'fusion'; and the three sets of practices were increasingly likely to reinforce one another. The inherent conflicts of interest between trade union-ists and employers, between spokesmen for left-wing and right-wing ideolo-gies, and between party activists operating within rival constituency organizations had been difficult enough to suppress while the war was on. After it, cooperative practices could function only to diminish the power attaching to the roles which they defined. However unpredictable the outcome of the conflicts between them, the conflicts themselves were predictable enough. The militant Left, reinforced by the nominally socialist doctrines of the post-1918 Labour Party and the upsurge of support for it in the constituencies, was matched by an intransigent Right eager to uphold the ideology of *laissez-faire* against 'Bolshevism'. The strength of the selective pressures now favouring the diffusion and replication of adversarial rather than cooperative practices is demonstrated precisely by Lloyd George's inability, for all his formidable skills, to hold them at bay.

This explanation of what did and didn't happen in the mode of the distribution of power between 1915 and 1922 is, once again, confirmed by what did and didn't happen between 1945 and 1951. Seen from the policy-makers' viewpoint, the lessons of 1915 to 1922 had been learned, at least to the extent that the ministers in Churchill's coalition government neither wanted nor expected the coalition to continue beyond the conclusion of the war with Japan. But as always, it is not the aims, ambitions, and strategies of the policy-makers which account for the competitive advantage conferred on the critical roles by the practices defining them. The resumption of party-political conflict could not have been avoided even if the Prime Minister of the coalition government had been a Conservative of a more centrist reputation than Churchill, and even if the leaders of the Labour Party had been more willing than they were to defer a contested election. As I pointed out in chapter 2, unanimity on the need to win the war had concealed the diversity of aspirations for its aftermath, and the 1945 election was as fiercely contested as any. As the war drew to a close, the rank-and-file Labour activists correctly saw that power was within their grasp (McCallum and Readman 1947, p. 23); and the practices of which they were the carriers and advocates implied not only the mobilization of their electoral supporters but the displacement of deferential by more egalitarian modes of conduct and the diminution of the control exercised by large private employers over significant parts of the means of production. The elective affinity between the three was as evident to their opponents as to themselves.

But just as the result of the election of 1918 concealed from contemporary observers the strength of the selective pressures which favoured the carriers of adversarial over cooperative practices, so did the result of the election of 1945 conceal the strength of those which favoured the carriers of cooperative practices over adversarial. It is true that some Labour politicians were aware that 'socialism' would mean, once Labour had won, demand management rather than a command economy, an ideology appealing to workers 'by brain' as well as 'by hand', and retention of a parliamentary majority rather than evolution into a one-party state. But their conviction that the system over which the National and Conservative governments had presided in the 1930s had been irrevocably discredited implied its replacement by some new and distinctive set of 'socialist' institutions for which the electors had given a mandate. The lack of difference made to the modes of production, persuasion, and coercion by the measures enacted by the Attlee government was, therefore, as little expected by activists on the one side as on the other. Both recognized, and rightly so, how much enthusiasm on the Left and resentment on the Right those measures were generating. But neither recognized how wide was the discrepancy between attitudinal and systemic change.

Once again, the elective affinity between capitalist, liberal, and democratic practices conferred a greater advantage on the roles which carried them than the mutants which the institutional environment of a nominally socialist government might have been expected to favour. The trade unions, as we have seen, were at the same time essential to the electoral success of the Labour movement and a guarantee of the failure of any attempt by a Labour government to suppress or supersede the practices of free collective bargaining. Similarly, the enthusiasm of the electors for the assumption by the state of responsibility for the provision of health care, accommodation, and a minimum standard of subsistence for all its citizens was articulated within an ideology of freedom of choice which tolerated rationing and physical controls only as a temporary expedient imposed by the post-war shortages. Churchill's notorious election broadcast, in which he conjured up the unlikely spectre of a Labour 'gestapo', was generally regarded as not only rhetorically implausible but electorally counter-productive. But the sensitivity of Labour to the charge that it hankered after a centralized bureaucracy with compulsory powers coloured much of its internal debate during the 1950s and 1960s. 'Fair shares for all' within the institutions of a free market in labour and commodities was a slogan far more appealing to all but a very small minority of its ultra-Fabian or near-Communist supporters. Just as, after 1918, the inherited context of capitalist-liberal-democratic institutions generated pressures which selected out the practices of coalition as envisaged by the 'reconstructionists', so after 1945 did it generate pressures which selected out the practices of 'socialism' as envisaged by the pre-war Left. The aftermath of the Second World War exemplifies as clearly as the aftermath of the First both the adaptation by the carriers of mutant practices to their changed institutional environment and the affinity between those practices in all three dimensions of social space.

§14. Meanwhile, however, as mutant practices altered the relative location of the roles which carried them, increasing numbers of English people moved from one to another role or entered the social structure in a different systact from the one in which they were born. Although, as I have emphasized, mobility rates do not define modes of production, persuasion, and coercion as such they can undoubtedly affect them. As I argued in more detail in volume II, movement of persons between roles, no less than movement of those roles themselves in social space, is by definition a change in the distribution of power, and may therefore influence the probability of replication and diffusion of the practices defining the roles into and out of which the mobile have moved. But not only a high rate of individual mobility but even a significant degree of collective mobility is quite compatible with institutional stability. There does come a point where this no longer holds. But it is then the increase in social mobility which is explained by the change in the mode of production, persuasion, or coercion, not the other way round. Suppose that it had somehow come about that all incumbents of higher-ranking roles in twentieth-century English society who were the children of higher-ranking parents were replaced by children of lower-ranking parents. On any theory, it would be a very different England from the one reported in chapter 2. But it could only have happened after a revolutionary institutional change whose occurrence would have to be otherwise explained.

The relevance of mobility rates to a society's evolution from one to another mode of production, persuasion, or coercion is and only can be through their effect on the net selective value of the practices defining its constituent roles. There may well be such an effect, but it is never easy to trace. Perhaps the most obvious instance in twentieth-century English society is on the topic of voting behaviour. But the relationships are far from straightforward. We know that the upwardly mobile are more likely to adopt the practices and attitudes of their systact of destination than retain those of their systact of origin. From this, it presumably follows that the higher the rate of outflow from the working into the middle classes, the more difficult it is for Labour to retain its percentage of votes cast in General Elections. But then how did Labour achieve the 'landslide' of 1945, or recover from the successive Conservative victories of 1951, 1955, and 1959? Would a reduction in the number of middle-class roles which had to be filled by children of working-class origin have kept Labour in power after 1979? Not only may middle-class voters be more radical, under some conditions, than working-class electors, but notionally right-wing parties in a parliamentary democracy with universal suffrage may have a greater appeal in some areas of policy to working-class than to middle-class electors. It is plausible to suggest that the steady expansion in the number of middle-class roles in twentieth-century English society which have had to be filled by working-class children has further diminished the selective value of the phenotypic effects of 'militant' practices in both the political and the industrial wings of the Labour movement. But if so, it is because it has diminished the likelihood of there developing within the Labour movement the kind of systactic consciousness *für sich* which would provide a favourable environment for the diffusion and replication of militant practices and the doctrines legitimating them.

Rates of individual mobility, therefore, bear on the concerns of this chapter less because any institutional changes have resulted directly from them than because of what I have called 'the subjective aspect of all this' – that is, the collective sense of relative deprivation which can, under certain circumstances, augment the power attaching to roles carrying practices subversive of the existing mode of the distribution of power. If dissatisfaction with the existing modes of production, persuasion, and coercion is becoming increasingly intense and widespread, this may not immediately, or ever, increase the probability of replication and diffusion of subversive practices to the point that their carriers will overcome the resistance which they meet from roles which function in favour of the status quo. But it is entirely possible that prospects of mobility (or lack of it), both individual and collective, may directly influence both the frequency and intensity of the sense of relative deprivation to the point that some mutant practices are more widely diffused and more success-fully replicated. Part of the story is that, as I pointed out in section 2 of chapter 1, potential leaders of the economically, ideologically, and politically subordi-nate have been upwardly mobile out of their systact of origin into roles within the élite. But there are likely to be other potential carriers of similar practices to replace them. More important is the function of the pattern of mobility reported in chapter 2 in at the same time offering the prospect of a middle-class career to ambitious children of working-class parents and leaving a largely self-reproducing working class to experience a modest degree of collective upward mobility. If the sense of relative deprivation can be expected to be least widespread where there is neither too much nor too little opportunity for upward mobility, it is still less surprising that twentieth-century England's institutional environment has been as unfavourable as it has to the carriers of practices which the dominant mode of persuasion labels 'extremist'.

In section 16 of chapter 1, I suggested that in late-Victorian and Edwardian England individual upward mobility was still sufficiently rare for the sense of relative deprivation among the incumbents of working-class roles to be predominantly directed towards collective mobility. There is not the evidence which would validate this conclusively. But it is plausible to suppose that as the number of middle-class roles which would have to be filled by working-class children increased, this not only satisfied the individual ambitions of those who moved into them but diminished the collective dissatisfaction of those who remained in their systact of origin. If this hypothesis is taken together with the lack of evidence which would support the rival hypothesis that upward individual mobility is subversive of the existing mode of the distribution of power, then it seems safe to conclude that the pattern of social mobility in twentieth-century England has in general helped to create an environment supportive of the practices defining the roles constitutive of the existing modes of production, persuasion, and coercion. But the pattern of mobility is, as I emphasized in chapter 2, by no means uniform. Not only has there not been a consistent trend towards either polarization or compression of social distance, but there are areas of social space where individual mobility, both inter- and intra-generational, has been significantly lower than elsewhere, and where there is, therefore, a sub-systactic cluster of roles whose high reproduction ratio may at the same time favour the replication but inhibit the diffusion of the practices by which those roles are defined.

The first area is that where the élite's high reproduction ratio combined with the consistency in the ranking of its constituent roles makes it close to being a 'stratum' in the technical sense defined in section 6 of chapter 1 in volume II. As I have emphasized already, it is not and never has been entirely impermeable. Nor has its consistency of ranking in the three dimensions of the structure of English society ever been complete. In consequence, the scope which it offers for absorbing new entrants whose careers might otherwise have functioned to subvert the existing mode is almost self-evidently supportive of it. But this conclusion does presuppose that the new entrants discard the practices which defined the roles out of which they have moved rather than causing a mutation of those defining the roles into which they enter. 'Elective affinity' is discernible once again: the alternative hypothesis to be tested is that the new entrants (the 'players') modify and displace the norms which governed the behaviour of the old (the 'gentlemen'). But 'gentlemen' could behave like 'players' if they had to (Coleman 1973); and 'players' tended to come from grammar schools which shared the values and assumptions of Oxbridge and the public schools (Rubinstein 1986, p. 203). Just as, in the late-Victorian and Edwardian period, old and new wealth had merged into a single 'plutocracy', so in the more professionally and managerially minded culture of the later twentieth century did the 'gentlemen' and 'players' merge in 'the top echelons of a complex structure of service employment, revolving around London and the Home Counties, which reached even farther down into the world of white-collar employment than before' (Cain and Hopkins 1993, p. 24). Whatever might be the effect on English society's performance in inter-societal competition, the rate of individual inter-generational mobility into the élite did not diminish the net selective value of the phenotypic effects of the practices by which élite roles were defined.

The second such area is that fraction of the lower-middle class whose systactic location is a function of ownership rather than marketability or control. As I pointed out in section 5 of chapter 3, the contrast is particularly marked between clerical workers and small proprietors. If clerical roles are too few, and their incumbents too transient, for the development of a systactic consciousness *für sich*, might it not be that 'petty bourgeois' roles will be those likeliest to be the carriers of increasingly militant practices? But in twentieth-century English society, the answer has been no. It is possible to imagine an environment in which a strong political movement of a Poujadist kind would have emerged and flourished. But the role of the small proprietor was deprived of competitive advantage not only by economic concentration and political centralization but also by the ideology of individualism itself. The little firm and the family on whose labour it depended was as much on the defensive in the era of information technology and professional marketing as it had been in the era of the late-Victorian and Edwardian tailor sitting cross-legged in the gallery over the corn exchange without a telephone. As always, some prospered while others failed, and the relative inter-generational stability of successful small businesses coexisted with a high intra-generational turnover of unsuccessful aspirants (Bechhofer et al., 1974). To the extent, therefore, that the 'petty bourgeoisie' constitutes a distinctive stratum, its high reproduction ratio may function to transmit and reinforce the distinctive attitudes and beliefs of its members;[36] but it has not, in the institutional environment of twentieth-century England, functioned to enhance the economic, ideological, or coercive power attaching to 'petty bourgeois' roles.

The same holds (but for different reasons) for those working-class communities where a high reproduction ratio has been combined with geographical isolation – which means, in particular, the mining industry on whose distinctiveness I have remarked several times already. That they should turn into 'little Moscows' (and that, to look for a moment North of the Border, the West Fife coalfield should elect a Communist MP) may be partly explicable by the transmission of a deep-seated ideological hostility to managers, owners, and governments alike from politically conscious fathers to sons who expect to follow them down the pit. I shall come back to the miners, for the purpose of description rather than explanation, in chapter 4. But the steady decline in their number in itself diminished the power collectively attaching to their roles within the Labour movement. Even when the influence of the National Union of Mineworkers had been at its height, it was less than it might have been precisely because the reproduction ratio within homogeneous and isolated communities precluded the lateral diffusion and subsequent replication of militant practices in other working-class communities. It was in the new and expanding motor industry, by contrast, that the recruitment of labour from other regions and communities imported the practices of militant trade unionism (Whiting 1983, pp. 66, 70, 102).

In the underclass, finally, the inter-generational replication of practices stigmatized as deviant will increase rather than diminish the selective value of their phenotypic effects. Where practices are stigmatized, individual social mobility will effectively eliminate them. Indeed, intra-generational mobility will have the same effect as inter-generational: without some stability of membership, 'there would be no underclass: only a working class, some of whom are temporarily out of work' (D. Smith 1992, p. 5). If, therefore, both inter- and intra-generational mobility (which, by definition, can only be upward) are low, the phenotypic effects of the practices defining underclass

---

[36] It is worth noting that G. Marshall et al. (1988, p. 186) found a higher proportion of respondents here who thought the distribution of income and wealth 'fair' – 44 per cent as against 29 per cent for their sample as a whole.

roles will favour them quite strongly, and a so-called 'dependency culture' will begin to perpetuate itself. But this does not mean that the size of the underclass will necessarily increase, and still less that the modes of production, persuasion, or coercion of English society will be altered in any way. Moreover, as pointed out by Rutter and Madge (1976, p. 304), 'familial cycles are an important element in the perpetuation of disadvantage but they account for only a part of the overall picture', since 'over half of all forms of disadvantage arise anew in each generation' and 'continuities are much weaker over three generations than they are over two'.

It accordingly follows, perhaps surprisingly, that rates of individual social mobility explain relatively little about the evolution of the modes of production, persuasion, and coercion of twentieth-century English society. It may well explain a good deal more about cultural than about social evolution – that is, the replication of ideas, values, and beliefs and their vertical and lateral diffusion not only within families but also within schools, workplaces, and voluntary associations. But this, like the evolution of popular tastes, manners and mores, is a topic outside the scope of this volume.

§15. In the theory of social, as of natural and cultural, selection, explanatory hypotheses can be quasi-experimentally validated only in hindsight by reference to the difference which *would* have been made to the evolution of the society in question *if* the characteristics of the environment favouring the carriers of the mutant or recombinant practices constitutive of a significant change had *not* been present. It has been implicit throughout this chapter that English society might have evolved after the First World War in a direction which, if neither socialist nor authoritarian, would still have made its modes of production, persuasion, and coercion more like those of some other sub-type of capitalist-liberal-democratic society. What, therefore, would have had to happen for England to become more like, say, Sweden, or Japan, or the United States? A serious answer would require a detailed exercise in comparative sociology as long as this volume itself. But simply to raise the question reinforces the conclusion that the selective pressures acting on the roles constitutive of twentieth-century England's modes of production, persuasion, and coercion were such as to make its evolution more distinctive rather than less.

To talk of hypothetical alternatives in terms of national labels (*Japanese* capitalism, *American* liberalism, *Swedish* social democracy, etc.) may look like a despairing recourse to discredited stereotypes of national character. Ought not the alternatives to be framed by reference to Linnaean distinctions between one mode and another in which defining institutional characteristics are specified as such? But where the institutional catchment area whose constituent roles are under study is a nation-state with a distinctive history, its name is a convenient shorthand for an institutional environment which has persisted long enough to constrain the range of outcomes to which alternative mutations or recombinations of practices might have led. To say that England's modes of production, persuasion, and coercion did not evolve in a more socialist or authoritarian (or any other) direction than they did because it was *English* capitalism, liberalism, and democracy is not as explanatorily vacuous as it may appear. It is, rather, a way of encapsulating the elective affinity between England's particular subtypes of all three.

Suppose, accordingly, that a Labour government had remained in power in the 1950s and 1960s, or even that a Labour government with an overall parliamentary majority had been elected in the 1920s: was there not, it might be asked, a potential for English society to evolve in the direction of 'Swedish' social democracy – that is, a variant of the capitalist-liberal-democratic mode in which the organized working class is accorded a direct influence on both government policy and the policy of industrial and commercial companies, collective bargaining is centralized, education is comprehensive, and un- or under-employment is subsidized by steeply progressive taxation of those in work? But the speculation is implausible twice over. In the first place, the Swedish system has been substantially modified under both endogenous and exogenous pressures of a kind which would have been even more difficult for England (or Britain) to resist; and in the second, the evidence already presented in this volume is enough to show how little competitive advantage would have been conferred, in the English institutional environment, on the carriers of the practices involved in a 'Swedish' mutation. How would the unions ever have been brought to a similar degree of subordination to a central body or the employers to a similar degree of shared control? How could the dominant liberal ideology have been modified to accommodate the egalitarian presuppositions by which a similar 'historical compromise' would need to be legitimated? How could a political party committed to a system of this kind avoid defeat at the hands of an electorate constituted as the British electorate has been? However stable (at least for a few decades) the Swedish sub-type, and however difficult to disentangle the different selective pressures acting on the practices defining the English one, to ask these questions is enough by itself to disclose the unlikelihood of a convergence of pervasive roles and central institutions even if a rejuvenated, Swedish-minded Labour Party had been re-elected in 1951.

Convergence with a 'Japanese' sub-type may seem more fanciful still, given the acknowledged uniqueness of Japanese culture and the obvious differences in its history up to and including the Second World War. But it is not totally implausible to imagine the British system of industrial relations evolving in the direction of the Japanese (Dore 1973), or a progressive reinforcement of vertical ties within an increasingly ascriptive ordering of status-groups, or the dominance of a single right-wing political party within which rival pressure-groups would be the vehicles for competing systactic claims. The strongest argument against it is that the roles constitutive of Japanese society as it evolved after 1945 are explicable by reference to practices whose continuing replication reflected the selective pressures at work throughout the long Tokugawa peace. Without a similar antecedent history how could English society have furnished an institutional environment favourable to the practices of patronage and clientship and hierarchical differentiation of roles character-istic of post-Meiji Japanese capitalist liberal democracy? I have, after all, emphasized that the similarities between the late-Victorian and Edwardian sub-type and the different sub-type into which it evolved are in some ways as striking as the differences. Whatever the similarities – including, not least, a hereditary monarchy – between English and Japanese society, their histories from the mid-seventeenth century onwards are too widely divergent for a mid-twentieth-century convergence.

Then what, finally, about the United States? Here the similarities are altogether closer, and there have been many observers who have seen in twentieth-century American society a vision of what the future would hold for England. An uninhibited market economy, an ideology of individualism similarly qualified in regard to ethnicity and gender, and a two-party democ-racy responding to the swings of mood of a media-conscious mass electorate: is not this a far stronger case for *de te fabula narratur* than nineteenth-century England ever was in relation to nineteenth-century Germany? But the 'first new nation' (Lipset 1963) entered the twentieth century unencumbered not only by an aristocracy on the European model but also by a European-style labour movement. The evolution of English society, as we have seen, has to be explained by reference as much to constraints on the workings of the market as to the diffusion and replication of market practices, and as much to traditional criteria of deference as to a traditional ideology of individualism; and whole books have been written about the contrast between the political and legal systems, the armed services, and the police of Britain and the United States. Whatever the historical might-have-beens between 1900 and the present, the institutional differences which had already evolved were too wide for any mutation or recombination of practices to bridge them.

Adequate examination of these, or any other, hypothetical alternatives would, as I have said, require a much more detailed comparative analysis of the modes of production, persuasion and coercion of the societies which might have, but didn't provide the model for English society to follow. But even in default of such detailed analysis, there is a concluding sociological moral to be drawn. To emphasize the continuing distinctiveness of English, as of Swedish or Japanese or American, society might seem to imply that the function of the practices which define their constituent roles is to maintain their pervasive roles and central institutions as they are – which would merely be to resurrect 'the now thoroughly discredited kind of "functionalism"' to which I referred in section 3 of chapter 2 in volume I. But the continuing distinctiveness of different societies within a common mode is not to be explained by identifying whatever features of the institutional environment currently favour (as no doubt some of them do) the replication of their existing practices. On the contrary: in the theory of social, as of natural and cultural, selection, what matters is always the continuous Darwinian process of 'descent with modification'. The environment in which those practices initially emerged has changed in ways which, as we have seen, at the same time continue to sustain a capitalist-liberal-democratic mode and to favour mutant practices defining roles constitutive of a different sub-type. National labels reflect genuine taxonomic differences to the extent that the different histories of the societies concerned have caused them to evolve different economic, ideological, and political institutions through the relation between different mutations of practices and the different selective pressures acting on them. In sociology, as in biology, 'Linnaean' similarities and 'Darwinian' differences march hand in hand, and new forms are continuously evolving whose ancestry both constrains them within specifiable limits and permits their divergence in unforeseeable ways.

CONCLUSION

§16. It is fundamental to the methodology of this treatise that, as I insisted throughout volume I, agents are taken to know what they are doing but not why; and in any case, as we have seen, it is to the functions more than to the motives of their behaviour that we must look in order to account for the institutional changes which do or don't take place in their society. The disjunction between the explanation of a society's evolution and the perception of it by the members of the society themselves is bound, accordingly, to be all the more marked if the explanation is derived from a theory of which they know nothing and which they might well find counter-intuitive if they did. In Marxist sociology, this disjunction was supposedly resolved by the fusion of the theory from which a prediction of the inevitability of socialism was derived with the increasingly revolutionary *praxis* of a class-conscious proletariat. But once it has been recognized that social evolution is inherently unpredictable, and that sociological explanation is possible only with hindsight, it follows that the disjunction is inescapable for Marxists and their opponents alike.

Throughout this chapter, the account of how changing selective pressures have determined the advantages conferred by economic, ideological, and political practices on the roles which carry them has been counterpointed by evidence of the unawareness of it on the part of the incumbents of those roles, including not least the makers of policy and formers of opinion. In the following chapter, therefore, where the experience of representative incumbents of roles within different systacts in English society is described as they saw it – or, where necessary, redescribed in more authentic terms – the disjunction will be accentuated yet further. But that is an inescapable consequence of the combined conclusions of volumes I and II. Description of what it has been like for 'them' is bound to be an altogether different exercise from explanation by 'us' of why 'their' experience has been of what it has and not of a different sub-type of the capitalist mode of production, liberal mode of persuasion, and democratic mode of coercion which might have evolved but didn't.

CHAPTER FOUR

The case described

AUTHENTIC EXPERIENCES AND REPRESENTATIVE BIOGRAPHIES

§1. On the evening of 11 November 1918 David Lloyd George and Winston Churchill dined at 10 Downing Street with F. E. Smith and Sir Henry Wilson, listening to the celebrations of the crowd which had earlier in the day included Virginia and Leonard Woolf drifting about in the rain near Trafalgar Square feeling steadily more depressed (Woolf 1965, p. 256). It was a day at once of triumph and of sadness: Robert Graves, who had been invalided back from the trenches to cadet-battalion duty in Wales, reacted by 'walking alone along the dyke above the marshes of Rhuddlan (an ancient battlefield, the Flodden of Wales) cursing and sobbing and thinking of the dead' (1957, p. 278). The war had not only cost Britain three-quarters of a million lives but affected in one way or another the experience of the entire population; and whatever changes in the modes of production, persuasion, or coercion the post-war era might or might not be going to bring, it could not be expected to feel other than radically different from the era which had ended in August of 1914. Leonard Woolf and others like him were to look back to the years before 1914 as not merely a different era but in some ways a better one; and true as it might be that the loss of able-bodied men in battle had been less than the loss through emigration would have been if it had continued at its pre-war rate, there were many observers who shared the conviction of J. B. Priestley that 'the generation to which I belong, destroyed between 1914 and 1918, was a great generation, marvellous in its promise' (quoted by Howarth 1978, p. 16). However unreliable a guide to the underlying processes of social evolution the opinions and attitudes of contemporaries may be, no description of twentieth-century English society can be either authentic or representative which does not reflect the pervasive sense that life could never feel the same again after what was, to 'them', not the 'First World' War but the 'Great' one.[1]

---

[1] Hence the appearance of 'pre-1914' as a descriptive concept: when, for example, the novelist

But from whose point of view is the description to be drawn? A boy born just soon enough to remember the rejoicings in the East End of London at the relief of Mafeking would have been too young to vote in the two General Elections of 1910, but old enough to serve in the trenches of the Western Front and to be able thereafter to contrast the England of 1914 with the England which voted Lloyd George out of office in 1922. He would still be in his forties when he heard Neville Chamberlain broadcasting to the nation that there was once again a state of war between Britain and Germany; and if he lived on through the electoral triumph of Labour in 1945 and the steady retreat from Empire, he would, in extreme old age, witness the Conservative Party returned to power in four consecutive General Elections, one of which took place in the aftermath of a victorious colonial war. But what boy – or should it be a girl? – are we to choose to tell us what it all felt like? From what systact of origin, in what occupational or other role, from what district or region, and in what sub-culture and milieu?

For all the changes in the years since 1845 when Disraeli, in *Sybil*, had spoken of the 'two nations' of rich and poor, it was a metaphor as authentic in late-Victorian and Edwardian as in early- or mid-Victorian England. The life of 'Darkest England', as the nation of the poor was described in a book of that title by General William Booth of the Salvation Army, was as remote to their comfortable compatriots as the jungles of the Congo, and the difference between them in *Weltanschauung* hardly less than the difference between the Grossmiths' immortal nobody, Mr Pooter, and the islanders of the South Seas whom Robert Louis Stevenson had so eloquently described to his puzzled and often indignant middle-class readers. There was, it might be said, an element of exaggeration in General Booth's description,[2] as in Jack London's description in his *People of the Abyss*. Nor was it only a tiny band of intrepid explorers who had found out at first hand what the lives of the underclass of late-Victorian and Edwardian England were actually like. Well before either General Booth or his namesake Charles, not only social statisticians and professional philanthropists but clergymen, doctors, policemen, publicans, pawnbrokers, and municipal officials were well qualified to describe the conditions in which the poor of London and other major cities were compelled to beg, borrow, and steal. But to the uninitiated voyager from the upper-

---

Anthony Powell first met fellow-novelist Ivy Compton-Burnett, he described her as 'a quite unmodified pre-1914 personality' (Spurling 1984, p. 186).

[2] Thus, for example, one of his informants from among the unemployed is reported as saying from his 'own lips': 'And I struggled until hunger stole my judgement, and then I became a Thief' (1890, p. 34). But do you believe that is *really* what the informant said? And even if he did, the capital T can only be the General's own.

middle class, the shock was indeed the shock of an alien culture made all the more disconcerting by its proximity.

At the other end of the scale, meanwhile, the life of a Duke of Westminster or Northumberland was just as remote from the paupers and vagrants of Limehouse or Shoreditch as that of a Nizam of Hyderabad or a Maharajah of Cawnpore. Towards his own tenants and domestic servants, or the labourers housed in the 'model' cottages on his estates, a 'good' duke might exercise a benevolence both active and informed. But of the teeming warrens and ill-lit alleys of the slums of a great city in which he might also be a substantial landlord, he would know still less than their denizens knew of Eaton Hall or Alnwick Castle. By the turn of the century, moreover, a capitalist employer who, in the mid-Victorian period, would have lived within walking distance of both his workplace and the homes of his workpeople, was likely to travel in from a residential suburb and to employ workers who might themselves have travelled by tram from back-streets which their employer would never have seen. In the cities of late-Victorian and Edwardian England, rich and poor had come to live apart by both preference and circumstances.

No remotely adequate description of the changes in the modes of production, persuasion, and coercion in English society over the course of the twentieth century can possibly be given through the eyes of only a single participant-observer from within a single region, systact, and milieu; and those few who made the transition over the course of their lifetimes up from somewhere close to the apex of the inverted pyramid to incumbency of a role among the élite were, for that reason, unrepresentative in the extreme – as Ernest Bevin said of himself, 'a turn-up in a million' (Bullock 1967, p. 103). Yet however unrepresentative, their reminiscences may be not only authentic but illuminating on that very account. The subjective experiences of men and women born and brought up in late-Victorian and Edwardian England who were subsequently mobile across large social distances are just as deserving of inclusion in a descriptive sociology of their society as those of the immobile incumbents of their first adult roles. Ben Tillett's biographer well conveys the value to the descriptive sociologist of a career like Tillett's when he says of him 'Pugnacious, mercurial, ambitious, he was not a representative figure, but at one time or another he represented, and was unsurpassed as spokesman for, nearly every current which moved the British working class' (Schneer 1982, pp. 2–3). Indeed, it is the changes in Tillett's attitudes before and after the First World War which make him at the same time so unrepresentative as an individual role-incumbent and so representative as a systactic spokesman: by turns organizer, firebrand, patriot, and conciliator, his successive responses to the mode of the distribution of power in English society convey just as much about the working-class experience of it as do those of the cloth-capped, blunt-spoken, uncompromising, North Country union negotiators of the type of Herbert Smith.[3]

Anything approaching an adequate description of twentieth-century English society has, accordingly, to be conveyed to its readers through the eyes not only of representative members of different systacts and milieux but also of both upwardly and downwardly mobile men and women whose experiences may encapsulate a sense of changes (or lack of them) in England's structure and culture in a way that the experiences of those who stay put can never quite do. The representatively immobile will come into their own in due course. But by way of introduction to this chapter, I have chosen the lives of three people born and brought up in the late-Victorian and Edwardian period whose atypical mobility across social space conveys much about what it was like to experience both the permeability of the structure and the stability of the culture of twentieth-century English society. The first is a man downwardly mobile from the upper-middle class; the second is a woman upwardly mobile from the unskilled working class; and the third is a son of the manse who rose by way of an Oxford scholarship, a spell of colonial administration, the bar, a prolific literary output, a lieutenant-colonelcy in the First World War, and a seat in the House of Commons to end his career as Governor-General of Canada.

§2. The man downwardly mobile from the upper-middle class is Geoffrey Brady, who was born in Stockport in 1898 and died in 1968. His early childhood was spent in a status-group precisely located between the aristocracy and gentry above it and the local shopkeepers and managers below:

> What we called county people i.e. landed gentry and the lesser aristocracy out in Cheshire would never have made friends with the professional people and mill owners in the towns. It didn't worry us in the slightest. Similarly, although we were perfectly polite and friendly towards local shopkeepers, and respected them immensely as 'honest tradesmen', we didn't ask them to come and play whist or tennis and I am sure they would have been astonished and embarrassed if we had done so. (T. Thompson 1981, p. 125)

Geoffrey was the second child of a then fairly prosperous millowner, and the family's life-style corresponded to his father's role. There were two maids, a gardener one day a week, and a washerwoman who came every Monday. His father was a member of the local club (for men only, of course), and his mother received visitors 'At Home' on the third Thursday of every month when they would be 'grandly shown in' after putting their cards in a silver tray in the hall.

---

[3] Not that Smith should be taken as a representative stereotype: an illuminating contrast from the Scottish Left is provided by John Wheatley MP who 'unlike Smith reacted against his early experiences by becoming a very smart dresser' (A. Reid 1987, p. 237).

The family would entertain jointly by holding musical evenings, or inviting their friends to play croquet at the weekend. But when Geoffrey was ten years old, all this came abruptly to an end. His father's business collapsed, the family had to move to 'a tiny little house with hardly any garden at all', entertaining was out of the question, and Geoffrey's pocket money was a penny a week – enough for a quarter pound of sweets.

He had been sent to the local grammar school at the age of eight, but after the crash his only chance of staying on was to win the single scholarship awarded to the hardest-working boy in the school. This he achieved; and although he now had no prospect of leaving at twelve to go to a public school as several of his friends did, his ambition was still 'to struggle along and get a scholarship if I could to Oxford or Cambridge'. But when he was fourteen, he allowed himself to be persuaded by his father to be apprenticed to a firm of flour merchants in Manchester where, because of the cost of travel from and to his parents' home, he was paid £15 for his first year, which was £5 more than the other apprentices were getting. His father was able to supplement this with a shilling, or perhaps two, a week for pocket money. But his midday meal in Manchester cost him tenpence, an occasional visit to the early cinemas sixpence, and standing room at a Hallé promenade concert was a still rarer treat costing a shilling. He was now virtually cut off from his former friends, and his recreations were almost entirely restricted to cycling, walking the family's dog, and reading books which could be borrowed free from the Stockport Public Library.

Straitened though his circumstances were, Geoffrey's apprenticeship was one of those which might have led in due course to a partnership: he was understudying a salesman rather than being 'out in the general office entering up ledgers', which would have led only to a senior clerkship. But then the war came. Geoffrey felt bound to volunteer but was unwilling to use the fact of his mother's cousinage with the colonel of the local infantry battalion to procure himself a commission. After he was demobilized in 1919, his attempt to set up in business with a partner failed, and he was reduced to commercial travelling until he was able to find a position with a firm of grain brokers in the City of London. But he found that he disliked the City, and after the Second World War he made a second attempt to set up on his own, this time as a nursery gardener in Surrey. Again, although the business survived, it only just did so, and he began to suffer from heart trouble. He was accordingly forced to sell out at a loss and return to the City until the onset of his final illness two years before he died.

From the perspective of this volume, there are two morals to be drawn from Geoffrey Brady's life story. The first is that for descriptive as opposed to explanatory purposes it would be quite wrong to ignore the cases of downward mobility, however infrequent they may be. English society during his lifetime may have been generating a steady increase both in rates of upward individual mobility and in average real income per head. But behind the statistics, there lie stories not only of enrichment and success but of ambitions thwarted and disappointments endured. Geoffrey Brady's life was not one of either abject poverty or spectacular failure. But it was one in which the standard expectations attaching to his first occupational role as a fourteen-year-old adult in a little grey suit and bowler hat were not to be fulfilled. However irrelevant this may be to an understanding in the secondary, explanatory sense of the modes of production, persuasion, and coercion of English society in the twentieth century, it, or another life like it, is essential to a full understanding in the tertiary, descriptive sense of the experience of the English upper-middle and middle-middle classes.

The second moral, however, is the strength of the hold of the values of the milieu in which Geoffrey Brady was brought up. His own description of his life makes clear that he unquestioningly accepted not merely the practices which defined the boundaries between his status-group and those above and below it, but the standards of conduct conventionally implied by them. But Geoffrey might have resisted his father's pressure on him to go into business, just as he might have wangled a commission when he went into the army; and when, in the winter of 1947–8, his nursery-garden business was struggling to survive, he kept all of his employees on full time even though it was against his interests to do so. Whether he is to be admired on that account or not is up to you. But wouldn't you agree that there is, so to speak, something archetypally 'English' about him – in, of course, a 'bourgeois' sense?

§3. The woman upwardly mobile from the unskilled working class is Kathleen Dayus, who was born in 1903 and in about 1970, at the suggestion of her youngest granddaughter, began writing the story of her life. Her childhood, in the slums of Edwardian Birmingham, was as typical in its way as Geoffrey Brady's very different childhood in Salford. But when she too was old enough at fourteen to go out to work, there was plenty of it in the local factories at weekly rates substantially higher than what was paid to Geoffrey Brady by the firm of flour merchants in Manchester. Kathleen learned the hard way, through a succession of more and less arduous, dirty, or tedious jobs, not to count on taking home the nominal wage-packet, not to work so hard as to get the piece-rates reduced, and not to assume that someone like herself would be allowed to learn enough about any chosen trade to set up in competition with 'the existing gaffers'. But by changing jobs in order to be trained in different processes, she gradually learned the whole of the enamelling trade and was in steady work until, in 1920, the boom in the metal trades came to an abrupt end in Birmingham as everywhere else.

In 1921, she married – being three months pregnant – and in 1922 her second son was born. But her husband was out of work; her father was taken into the workhouse after a stroke and died there; one of the sons was knocked over and killed by a butcher's van; she quarrelled with her mother; her husband's continuing difficulty in finding work was compounded by drink and poor health; and when he died in 1931, she was left a widow of twenty-eight with four small children, no money, and (because her husband hadn't a sufficient record of national insurance contributions) no widow's pension. She had no option but to go 'back on the parish'. But the food vouchers which were all that she was entitled to were too little for the five of them and she took such odd jobs as she could in order to earn an extra few undeclared shillings. Informed on and summoned to the relief office ('You know we can prosecute you for this deception, don't you?'), she took the decision to put her children into the care of Dr Barnardo's. She hoped that if she could find work ('I remember thanking the matron and promising that I would work night and day to get back on my feet, and I really meant it') she would soon be able to provide a home to which she could have her children back. But it took her eight years to become an independent businesswoman with six employees living in a rented three-bedroomed house and driving a second-hand Austin Seven, by which time her son had been sent into the navy at the age of eleven and after a disastrously ill-advised attempt to snatch her youngest daughter away from Barnardo's, she was refused access to her children entirely.

As in the First World War, Kathleen went first into factory work and then back into enamelling as one of ten women employed by a Mr Hart. When Rose, the chargehand, took against her and was caught by Mr Hart putting salt in the frit to spoil Kathleen's enamel, Rose was sacked on the spot and Kathleen promoted into her role. This, together with some experience of office management when Mr Hart was out 'on business' (i.e., at the races) enabled her to get to know the enamelling trade inside out; and when she quarrelled with Mr Hart and left him she was easily employable at Mr Butler's where she'd worked before. Here, as she puts it, 'the tide turned for me. My opportunity arrived at last.' A large order came in for more different kinds of badges and motor plates than Mr Butler had experienced workers to cope with, and he allowed Kathleen to do some of the filing at home with Nell, her landlady, who had a small back room where the two of them would sit after supper filing the badges with carborundum stones and singing to the gramophone. Two years of this enabled Kathleen to save £100. It was not enough to enable her to have her children back, but with the promise of outwork from Mr. Butler it was enough to enable her to let a top-floor shop for 12s 6d a week, invest £50 in materials, and put up a notice for experienced enamellers. The shop was cleaned up and fitted out with second-hand tables and three-legged stools. Kathleen would arrive at 7.30 in the morning and leave after 7 most nights. In the mornings, before the girls came in, she would drown in a bucket the rats for which she'd baited traps the night before. After a while, the work from Butler's went slack but it was soon enough replaced from other customers. She was now K. FLOOD, ART ENAMELLER TO THE TRADE and banking money every week after covering the girls' wages and all the overheads. Her daughters were returned to her.

The first and most obvious moral which her story suggests is the determination that a person like herself required to be able to achieve mobility from the unskilled working class into the self-employed fraction of the lower-middle. Besides, if she had been setting up as an enameller to the trade in the conditions of 1931 – or for that matter 1921 – instead of 1937, who knows whether she would have come through? But her determination not to give in is combined with something very close to fatalism in the tacit acceptance of the alternation of boom and slump, war and peace, and the lack of any collective sense of relative deprivation or systactic consciousness *für sich*.

The second impression which her account leaves is of an outlook comparable in its way to Geoffrey Brady's. Her standards of 'respectability' did not prevent a strong temper from finding outlet in behaviour which those at the receiving end, whether family, employers, or agents of public authority, no doubt described to themselves as shamelessly rude. But it is a rudeness directed precisely against violations, as she sees it, of the conventional norms of decency and fellow-feeling. A selfish mother, a jealous workmate, an ill-tempered employer, a lecherous doctor, an exploitative money-lender, or a condescending and punitive relief worker are resented not for their roles but for a performance of them which falls short of what English people are presumed to be entitled to expect in their dealings with one another.

But let me leave Kathleen Dayus to give her own conclusions in her own words:

> Like me Mary [her sister] wanted to better herself and neither of us had any reason to be ashamed of wanting to join the ranks of the employers. We'd been downtrodden, starving even, ourselves, and there was little chance that we would forget that in our dealings with our people. There were plenty of Brummies, born in poverty, who pulled themselves up by their own bootstraps. One, now a scrap-metal millionaire, had been sweet on Mary in the old days. Perhaps she should have encouraged him. There was Joe Lucas, who founded the engineering firm, who still lived in Carver Street in those days and who my Dad could remember selling tin bowls and kettles from a wheelbarrow. There were plenty more like these. I knew many like them. We didn't have parents who could give us a start in life, nor government grants, nor even social security, when we were at rock bottom; just hard work and sink or swim. Unfortunately, Mary never made it but it was not for want of trying. I haven't got any answers, but the

grinding poverty of the old slums did breed some very determined people. (1985, p. 225)

§4. The son of the manse who rose to occupy the role of Governor-General of Canada was, as many readers will no doubt have realized, John Buchan. His particular combination of a literary with a political career was an exceptional one. But because so much of his own political and social outlook was more or less directly expressed in his fiction, he is an illuminating witness to a set of attitudes and assumptions shared not only by a substantial section of the upper class but also – as can, up to a point, be semi-deductively inferred from the sales of his books – by substantial numbers of his fellow-citizens outside of it.

The descriptions given by his family and friends of his appearance and manner when, after the First World War, he settled in a manor house outside of Oxford with his wife and four children and a domestic staff of six (plus auxiliary gardeners and grooms) suggest almost a caricature of a person of relatively modest systactic origin acting out his role as a member of both the landed gentry and the governing élite. In a memoir by his son William, he is depicted setting out to be driven by his chauffeur to catch the London train complete with pearl tiepin, stiff collar, double-breasted waistcoat, silver cigarette-case, flower in the buttonhole, brass-locked briefcase with the Royal cipher, and 'rather grand' umbrella with an engraved gold band and a tortoise-shell handle (1982, p. 28).[4] But there is nothing inauthentic about it: that, given who one was, was what one wore. The Conservative member for the Scottish Universities who had, as a boy, walked every day to Hutchesons' grammar school through the Gorbals felt himself to be as much at home talking to the Clydesiders in the tea-room of the House of Commons as to the herds and ploughmen in the Peeblesshire constituency he had nursed before the war. His sense of his and his interlocutors' location in an established ranking of roles was unquestioning; when he became Governor-General of Canada, he accepted and followed the ritual practice whereby even members of his family bowed to him in public. But his manners to those in different walks of life whom he met and talked to on his tours of the country were, by all accounts, accepted within those constraints as authentic. In the same spirit, his son William, in his memoir, is at pains to assure us that he and his brothers and sister regarded their father's servants as 'our real friends' and that there was a genuine 'loyalty and affection between master and man' (pp. 34, 32). A sentiment like this concedes the hierarchy in the same breath as it proclaims

---

[4] I have not been able to find a photograph of him in this attire which could serve, for the purpose of description, as well as the one of 'Ian Hay' which was reproduced in section 14 of chapter 4 in volume I. But Janet Adam Smith's *John Buchan and his World* has the soft collar and pearl tiepin in the frontispiece, the double-breasted waistcoat in a photograph taken in 1936 (1979, p. 95), and his 'London uniform', including spats, in a *Spy* cartoon (p. 85).

the friendship across it. Does William Buchan really suppose that he and his brothers and sister would be described by his father's servants from *their* side of the relationship as 'friends'? But it would be a misapprehension to dismiss it out of hand as nothing but upper-class bullshit.[5] For William Buchan, as for his father and many others like them, there was no sense of inconsistency in reconciling the two.

Buchan's politics – which is to say, his particular brand of moderate Conservatism – was entirely of a piece with his conception of the structure and culture of English society. Stanley Baldwin, naturally, was the man he most admired. Ramsay MacDonald he regarded as having put country above party. He disliked die-hard reactionaries as much as affluent vulgarians. Middle-class intellectuals he distrusted. Women he romanticized. Experts he respected (although he had no interest in technology himself). Ordinary people he liked, unless he had reason to do otherwise. He wanted to hold office under the National Government, but Baldwin, who agreed with Tom Jones that there was 'something diminutive about his personality' (Middlemas 1969, II, p. 161) never offered it to him. He never lost the faith in the Empire which he brought back with him from his time in South Africa as one of Milner's young men, and he brought to his role of Governor-General of Canada an unequivocal enthusiasm for the common ideology still, as he believed, binding the people of the English-speaking dominions to the Mother Country.

If, in his *Weltanschauung*, there was a good deal of anachronism – and whether that implies a pejorative value-judgement or not is up to you – it was a subjective experience in which he was by no means alone. Among writers, it is as true in their different ways of Kipling and T. E. Lawrence as it is of Buchan, just as among politicians, it is as true in their different ways of Kipling's first cousin Baldwin as it is of Churchill. As I remarked in section 2 of chapter 1, the sense that Britain's once dominant place in the world was under threat was a tacit tribute to the achievements which had made that dominance possible; and it was therefore inevitable that suggestions for reform should be voiced as strongly by the advocates of a return to what had (in their view) made the nation great as by the advocates of a thoroughgoing break with the institutions of the past in order to preserve as much of that greatness as possible. The ethic conveyed by Buchan's career and writings alike is one of worldly success achieved for reputable ends by honest means in accordance with traditional values. It is an ethic which, in the British context, could not but find expression in a certain snobbery of achievement which substitutes for the overt worship of wealth, social status, or political office the cult of the gifted amateur who moves

---

[5] Readers surprised by the appearance of this vernacular term in a work of academic sociology are referred to section 4 of chapter 4 in volume I.

with effortless ease from one role to the next; and it risks confusing the trappings of power with the reality. Buchan's heroes are conventionally splendid fellows, talented, courageous, self-effacing, and humane. They can be described without irony as 'men to go tiger-shooting with'. But how many readers of this paragraph would choose them to lead their society through the economic, ideological, and political challenges thrown against it by the world as it evolved after 1918? They reflect an outlook which, to a later generation, is sometimes embarrassingly remote from the realities of economic, ideological, and political power in the middle of the twentieth century. Yet it was an authentic ingredient of many upper, upper-middle, and middle-middle-class Englishmen's idealized descriptions of themselves.

§5. No useful generalization about the subjective experience of social mobility in twentieth-century English society could possibly be derived from these or any other three biographies, however chosen. But there is no misapprehending the strength of the attachment of Geoffrey Brady, Kathleen Dayus, and John Buchan alike to the conventional norms of the period within which they were brought up. Such conservatism in outlook need not make any difference whatever to the practices defining the roles which they find themselves occupying and performing later on in their lives. But for this very reason, it enhances the contrast between their experience of the central institutions of their society as described by themselves and the nature of the selective process by which, unperceived by themselves, the evolution of those institutions was being determined.

The disjunction is, moreover, enhanced by the feeling of luck – both good and bad – which all three of their life-histories convey. Nor could it well be otherwise, since all three are instances of a kind of social mobility which is sufficiently rare that any chosen case of it will be subjectively experienced as a matter more for personal than for institutional explanation. Very few men born into the English upper-middle class experience a succession of business failures both of their father's and of their own; very few women born into the unskilled working class experience the role of self-employed business proprietor; and very few sons of the manse end their careers by experiencing the rituals and trappings of a role like that of Governor-General. The sense which it is likely to give them of being singled out by fate may well make their own descriptions of their experience more illuminating for the biographer than the sociologist; and since people usually compare their roles to those of other people close in social space to themselves, long-distance social mobility can only heighten their awareness of difference from their former equals. They should not on that account be charged with mystifying their own experience: that *is* what it was like to be 'them'. But it does mean that their implicit descriptions of the structure and culture of their society need all the more to be supplemented by descriptions by people whose experiences are other than theirs.

In the rest of this chapter, therefore, the representatively *im*mobile, as I have called them, will be given more of a say. Whether a working class – or, for that matter, an élite or a middle class or an underclass – which is in this sense stable is a good thing or a bad thing is up to you. But whatever the disparity between facts reported by observers and myths adhered to by participants, the myths can, as I pointed out at the very beginning of chapter 1, be more important than the facts when description rather than explanation is the sociologist's purpose.

LIFE AT THE TOP

§6. What, then, was it like to occupy a role in the élite of wealth, social prestige, and political influence – the milieu into which John Buchan gratefully rose, which remained wholly remote from Kathleen Dayus (and hardly less so from Geoffrey Brady), yet which Ernest Bevin, the untutored carter from the Bristol dockside, was able in due course to treat on equal terms? After 1918, when Leonard Woolf was waxing nostalgic about the pre-war world, the Duke of Marlborough proclaiming the old order doomed, Keynes pillorying the upper class for its timidity and loss of confidence, and Rowntree warning the rich of the hostility with which their conspicuous consumption was being eyed by the poor, it felt to many of them that their position had been permanently weakened and the criteria on which it was based irretrievably undermined. But was this authentic self-description? Or was it nostalgic bullshit?

The rhetoric of rank particularly needs to be demystified when the language is that of a dominant systact seeking to legitimate its members' privileges. But inauthentic self-description takes many forms; and in the case of the traditional élite of twentieth-century England, there are two clearly distinguishable variants of it. The first deploys the rhetoric of decline, and the second the rhetoric of tradition. The two are sometimes inconsistent, but not always. If the decline is real, it might seem to follow that tradition can no longer be maintained. But then the maintenance of tradition can be described as a heroic effort to halt decline, and decline presented as a manifest justification for doing what can be done to maintain tradition. Already in the 1880s, the English aristocracy had been vociferous in their fears that the sanctity of property, reverence for the authority of the established Church, and recognition of their inherited entitlement to roles of political leadership were under threat; and their fears were authentic to the extent that 'Never again was the landed proprietor to dominate the social fabric' (G. M. Young 1953, p. 145). But the rhetoric was, and was sometimes intended to be, exaggerated. The old grandees might indeed have lost their political pre-eminence. But the participants in the London Season of 1914 could hardly pretend that either their wealth or their status had so far declined since 1880 that some insurgent new systact had displaced them. In the words of Arthur Ponsonby MP (1912, p. 16): 'Apart from their actual political power, which after all is a mere ghost of what they formerly enjoyed, in the social world they reign supreme, and their supremacy would be maintained here even if they were divorced absolutely from all political power.'

After the First World War, there was indeed an understandable loss of confidence among the traditional élite. 'Socialism' – however they might have defined it if required to do so – was now perceived as a threat to their prestige as well as their pockets. They were well aware that the war had required an unprecedented degree of popular participation and that a price had been paid by Lloyd George's government in concessions to the organized working class. They resented the wealth of the 'hard-faced men' now sitting in the House of Commons and what they saw as the 'torrent of honours bestowed by Lloyd George in return for contributions to party funds despite the unavailing protests of Lord Salisbury and his friends' (K. Rose 1975, p. 88). They deplored the sale of country houses and the break-up of art collections. They regretted that they were less deferentially treated by their social inferiors than they used to be. And although they might or might not regard themselves as having become an anachronism, they could hardly fail to put the question to themselves.[6]

But did they still feel the same in 1939? As the likelihood of another war against Germany increased, so did the sense of *esprit de corps* among young men who expected as a matter of course to serve as officers in the Household Brigade or a 'good' cavalry regiment or to put their skills as amateur pilots at the service of the Royal Air Force or their skills as amateur yachtsmen at the service of the Royal Naval Volunteer Reserve. The mood of the London Season was rather more sombre than it had been in the Season of 1914. But there were the same dashing young men in white tie and tails, the same nubile debutantes in long white dresses under the eyes of the same watchful dowagers, the same liveried servants, the same obsequious gossip columnists, and the same plebeian noses pressed to the window-panes.[7] When it came, the Second

---

[6] A poem of A. P. Herbert's ('Derby Day') written in 1931 contains this description of a Marquis and his thoroughbred: 'See what a wise unwinking pair they stand, The last patricians in a vulgar land, While milord mutters in the mobile ear, "We are back numbers, you and I, my dear".'

[7] 'the very sad and embarrassing situation at 6 Stanhope Gate when the very elaborate and delicious supper was laid out in a room whose (uncurtained) bow window overlooked the street. One could see pathetic faces looking in, pressed against the glass at this scene of splendour and scrumptious food' (The Hon. Anne Douglas-Scott-Montagu, subsequently Lady Chichester, quoted in Lambert 1989, p. 113).

World War turned out not to involve the casualty rates which had decimated the platoon commanders who fought at the Somme and Paaschendaele. But there could be no doubting a similar willingness on the part of the sons of the traditional élite to risk their lives in battle; as Orwell put it, 'One thing that has always shown that the English ruling class are *morally* fairly sound, is that in time of war they are ready enough to get themselves killed' (1941, p. 43). You may or may not agree with the value-judgement. But the subjective experience of a young officer in the Grenadier Guards who had held the perimeter at Dunkirk in 1940, escaped death or capture at Arnhem in 1944, and taken part in the crossing of the Rhine in 1945 was not so very different from one who had survived the trenches of 1916 and 1917 to take part in the repulse of the final German offensive in 1918. Nor were the attitudes and idioms which went with that experience very different either. When the Duke of Northumberland was killed on active service in 1940, his mother complained that 'the Guards are going pink' because the posthumous VC was awarded to a warrant officer; and when the topic of 'war aims' was once raised among officers of the Coldstream Guards as they fought their way up the Italian peninsula in 1944, the conversation was brought to a speedy end by the one who said, 'I know what *I'm* fighting for – a large house near Ascot with millions of servants and everything it stands for.'[8]

After 1945, when Churchill had been voted out of office,[9] death duties were at 75 per cent,[10] domestic servants were almost totally unobtainable even for those who could afford them,[11] and the owners of country houses who felt unable to carry on were rescued only if at all by the National Trust,[12] the loss

---

[8] The wording of this remark has been reconfirmed at my request by my informant Simon Phipps, then a subaltern in the Coldstream and subsequently Bishop of Lincoln.

[9] Harold Nicolson to his son Nigel, 27.5.45: 'People feel, in a vague and muddled way, that all the sacrifices to which they have been exposed and their separation . . . from family life for four or five years, are all the fault of "them" – namely the authority or the Government. By a totally illogical process of reasoning, they believe that "they" means the upper classes, or the Conservatives, and that in some manner all that went well during these five years was due to Bevin and Morrison, and all that went ill was due to Churchill' (Nicolson 1967, p. 465).

[10] And in his 1947 budget Cripps imposed a capital levy – for Chips Channon, in his diary for 6.4.47, 'a monstrous and quite unnecessary piece of class legislation', although two days later 'my chartered accountants seem to think that I shall not be completely ruined by this wicked Capital Levy' (Rhodes James 1967, p. 516).

[11] Not but what they were still there in the House of Lords itself: 'Yesterday [13.11.46] I lunched with Tony (Powell) and his brother-in-law, Lord Pakenham, who's got some sort of job for the Government (Lord-in-Waiting) in the House of Lords. He made us laugh about the House of Lords, most extraordinary institution, which he obviously rather liked, especially the servants, who, he said, were numerous, and made you feel a Lord all the time' (Muggeridge 1981, p. 209).

[12] Like Lord Newton at Lyme Park in 1943: 'Lord Newton is hopeless. The world is too much for him and no wonder. He does not know what he can do, ought to do or wants to do. He just throws up his hands in despair . . . I am already sure that he will not see out his ownership'

of confidence was considerably more serious than it had been after 1918. Nobody was talking now about a return to 'normalcy'. This was the world of the queue, the spiv, the clothing coupon book, the foreign travel allowance, and the five-shilling restaurant meal – the latter circumvented either through the black market or, by the chef at Boodle's, thanks to hampers sent down from their estates by the members out of which 'would come tumbling pheasants, hares, rabbits, grouse, snipe, woodcock, partridges and so on, that all helped us considerably' (Addison 1985, p. 31). This period of continuing austerity, and the accompanying awareness of the country's economic dependence on the United States, gave even those whose fortunes had survived relatively unscathed reason to doubt whether either the national economy or their own position within it could be restored to what it had been before 1939. Yet within a few years, those doubts were being comprehensively dispelled – not, perhaps, about the strength of the economy or about the country's position in the inter-societal rank-order, but about the persistence of both its structure and its culture and the social distance still marking off the top 1 per cent or less of its members' roles from the rest. Orwell's vision (1941, p. 55) of an England in which the Stock Exchange had been pulled down, the country houses all turned into children's holiday camps, and the Eton and Harrow match forgotten was fantastic even before 1951, let alone after. Not only the Eton and Harrow match but Ascot, Henley, Cowes, Glyndebourne, and even Queen Charlotte's Ball reemerged much as before; property values recovered; share prices boomed; the *Tatler's* photographer was back in attendance at society weddings and hunt balls; winter holidays could be taken once more at St Moritz or in the Caribbean; and by the time of Queen Elizabeth II's succession to the throne Chips Channon could write in his diary (for 15.6.53) 'The old world persists, thank God' (Rhodes James 1967, p. 580). True, the stately homes were now open to the public, white tie and tails were no longer worn as they used to be, debutantes were no longer presented at court after 1959, a Conservative government was to introduce life peerages and abandon the creation of hereditary ones, and the dissociation between inherited status and political influence became virtually total. But the fears of 1919 and 1946 had been of something much closer to Orwell's vision of an 'English Revolu-tion' than this.

In brief, the disjunction between description and explanation at the furthest distance from the apex of the inverted pyramid had three doubtfully authentic aspects. The first is rural nostalgia; the second is the wilful confusion of a cycle with a trend such as I touched on in section 2 of chapter 3; and the third is the

(Lees-Milne 1975, p. 273). The relevant statistic, so far as representativeness goes, is that out of the Trust's 207 'stately homes', 54 were still occupied by the donor family in 1994 (*The Economist*, 14.1.95).

failure to distinguish between the movement of people in and out of roles and the movement of roles in relation to each other.

As an example of rural nostalgia, here is the entry in Halifax's diary after the fall of France in 1940:

> Here in Yorkshire was a true fragment of the undying England, like the white cliffs of Dover, or any other part of our land that Englishmen have loved. Then the question came, is it possible that the Prussian jackboot will force its way into this countryside to tread and trample over it at will? The very thought seemed an insult and an outrage; much as if anyone were condemned to watch his mother, wife, or daughter being raped. (Birkenhead 1965, p. 458)

There is nothing inauthentic about the strength of feeling expressed. But it is awkwardly reminiscent of Churchill's 'you who are listening to me in your cottages' remark in an election broadcast of 1945, from which Denis Healey, for one, inferred an 'obvious inability to understand [in, that is, the tertiary, descriptive sense] the men and women he had led in war' (Healey 1989, p. 67). It is not that rural nostalgia is a uniquely upper-class trait. It can be traced as easily through the best-selling verses of Housman or Masefield as through the party-political rhetoric of Stanley Baldwin ('the sight of a plough team coming over the hill . . . the eternal sight of England')[13] or, later, Enoch Powell ('the fields amid which they built their halls, their cottages, their churches, and where the same blackthorn showered its petals upon them as upon us'). Indeed, as more and more middle-class families became car-owners, it became more and more actively disseminated by travel- and guide-books and a whole flood of writings that turned the countryside into an 'extra-urban service centre' (Lowerson 1980, p. 262): well before the Second World War, country landowners had 'made the fortunate discovery that they were part of the national heritage' (F. M. L. Thompson 1993, p. 5). But an awareness that the landed proprietor had indeed, until recently, 'dominated the social fabric', the traditional contrast between the supposed tranquillity of rural and restlessness of urban life, and the continuing attraction of a country house as both an amenity and a symbol of prestige combined to underemphasize within the *Weltanschauung* of the élite the extent to which the 'social fabric' had become ineluctably urban (or *sub*urban). The persistence of these attitudes is quite irrelevant to the explanation of either the changes in the modes of production, persuasion, and coercion which followed the First World War or those which didn't, after all, follow the Second. The practices defining the economic, ideological, and political roles of the mid-twentieth-century élite would have been what they were whether or not Halifax and those like him romanticized

---

[13] Cf. Lees-Milne (1994, p. 5): 'What I remember of my talks with Baldwin was his adoration of Worcestershire which conveyed to him the same ineffably cosy, remote, hay-meadow, apple-orchard, hop-garden nostalgia which it does to me.'

the English countryside quite as they did. But it was an intrinsic part of what their own experience of their roles was like for many of 'them'.

The confusion of a cycle with a trend is still less confined to those at the top. The feelings of the members of the traditional élite who saw their inherited way of life receding into the past and their privileges under increasing attack were matched by those of their opponents who saw in the rise of the mass electorate 'a slow underground social upheaval, moving independently of leaders or organization – propelling a lower strata [sic] of society into a more dominant position'.[14] But it was hardly surprising that in the aftermath of both world wars, a sense of decline should be strongest among those whose systactic location had been highest and therewith most obviously vulnerable. Families who were (or saw others like themselves being) compelled to sell their farms to the sitting tenants, despatch their collections of books and pictures to the auction rooms, and demolish their country houses because they could no longer afford their upkeep were hardly likely to imagine a future in which land could be repurchased, art collections reassembled, and country houses reconverted from institutional to residential use. Nor were those like the Hon. Mrs Eny Strutt (previously Baroness de Briene), who was still talking defiantly in 1948 of 'class and breeding and the necessity for both' (Lees-Milne 1985, p. 17), likely to imagine a future in which that view would come to be shared by the 'new men' risen to eminence in the world of Bevin and Beveridge or the electorate who had voted Churchill out and Attlee in. Yet Evelyn Waugh, who did share that view, and who had written *Brideshead Revisited* as a lament for the aristocratic country-house life,[15] was to concede in the preface to the second edition in 1959 that he had been preaching a panegyric 'over an empty coffin'.

This exaggerated sense of systactic decline, compounded by rural nostalgia, was further intensified by an unwillingness to recognize that a systact is, in Schumpeter's simile, like a bus or hotel – always full, but of different people. It was not just a matter of emphasizing the plight of families who did feel compelled to retrench, or sell up, or emigrate and ignoring the success with which others preserved their social position. It was also a matter of ignoring the

---

[14] Beatrice Webb in her diary for 5.4.27 (M. Cole 1956, p. 138). Cf. the boast of Sir Hartley Shawcross in the House of Commons on 2nd April 1946 that 'We are the masters at the moment – and not only for the moment, but for a very long time to come' – a remark much misquoted subsequently as 'we are the masters now', although hardly reported at all at the time (Howard 1963, p. 29).

[15] That term itself is by no means theory-neutral: some 200 new 'country houses' have been built (as against some 700 demolished) since *Brideshead* was written, but it must be doubtful whether Waugh would be willing to describe them as such. Cf. Hoskins (1955, p. 167): 'The very last country house to be built in England – the last that will doubtless ever be built – was Castle Drogo, built by Lutyens in Devon between 1911 and 1930 for a wealthy grocer.'

recent arrivals – people who, although the sources of their wealth and the uses to which it was put might be different, nevertheless occupied roles whose location was not so very different from that of the old landed proprietors. Intra-systactically, the difference might be perceived much as the intrusion of the new plutocrats had been in the late-Victorian and Edwardian period. But if families whose wealth and position had depended on the rents of land and the dividends of Empire were now being replaced by families whose wealth and position derived from retailing, or motor manufacturing, or the entertainment industry, that did not mean a compression of social distance (or, as those who deplored the idea were apt to describe it, a 'levelling down').[16] Laments for a golden past could be authentic enough if the experience to which they referred was indeed that of long-range downward individual inter-generational mobility (however the fallen heirs to once broad acres and splendid treasures might describe it to themselves). But laments for the disappearance of 'class and breeding' were less so. Life at the top – that is, the privileges of wealth and status attaching to the roles of the most favoured percentile of the population, together with the potential ability of the families concerned to pass those privileges on to their children – was as different from life below it as it had ever been. It was different, to be sure, in a different way from what it had been when Max Beerbohm published *Zuleika Dobson* in 1911. But complaints about a collective 'levelling down' *were* largely bullshit, all the same.

§7. But to assess the authenticity of élite self-descriptions it is not enough just to demystify them as necessary in their own terms. Practices, as cannot be too much emphasized, are units of *reciprocal* action, and the opinions and feelings of the incumbents of the roles which they define can only be fully described when account has been taken of their sense of the attitudes of the incumbents of the roles which interact with theirs. There are, in broad descriptive terms, three different subjective responses to the perceived location of élite roles. The first is the deferential, as evinced by those who not merely accept the power attaching to élite roles but attribute to their incumbents qualifications for them which they may or may not actually possess (McKenzie and Silver 1968, p. 166). The second is the envious, as evinced by those who accept the practices by which élite roles are defined but think that their incumbents should be replaced by the likes of themselves (Thomas 1959, p. 20). The third

---

[16] F. M. L. Thompson (1991, p. 17): 'After 1918, purchasers of the old style, looking on land as a social elevator which would erase their vulgar origins, pretty well disappeared. What was left was a continually replenished group of purchasers who were intent on adopting, in some form, the life styles and possessions of the aristocratic bourgeoisie as those had been developed by the Victorians, that is they aimed at remaining prominent businessmen as well as becoming country landowners.'

is the dismissive, as evinced by those who are hostile to the wealth, contemptuous of the prestige, and impervious to the influence attaching to the roles of the élite independently of any view they may hold of the character of their incumbents.

'Snobbery' is yet another sociological term with too many pre-emptive overtones to be usable in reportage.[17] But it does come into its own in description, for there has never been a shortage of English men and women ready and willing to apply it to the attitudes and behaviour of one another. It attaches almost of its own accord to the views of someone who could write to his wife that he liked his friends to be 'well-read and well bred' and that he regarded 'the territorial aristocracy and the types that have gathered round them in England' together with 'our scholars and intellectuals' as 'the civilized'. This is Harold Nicolson in the 1930s,[18] and these are the authentic tones of someone not all the way 'in' but by no means 'out' of 'society'.[19] The value-judgement to be made is, as always, up to you. But the explicitness is illuminating. According to his son Nigel, 'He knew that he belonged to an élite, an élite more of intelligence and achievement than of birth, and he tended to feel that people outside that élite had something wrong with them: business-men, for example, the humbler type of schoolmaster or clergyman, most women, actors, most Americans, Jews, all coloured or Levantine peoples, and the great mass of the middle and working classes' (1967, pp. 24–5). It is – is it not? – quite a list.

For a diametrically opposite attitude, a good place to start is the Labour Party Conference of 1944 at which Denis Healey, then a major in the Royal Engineers, was denouncing the upper classes 'in every country' as 'selfish, depraved, dissolute, and decadent' (Addison 1975, pp. 255–6). The young radical who ends his career in the role of elder statesman is familiar from all eras of British political history, and it should not be inferred from a speech like this one, any more than from Bevan's celebrated remark about Tories being 'lower than vermin', that it enshrines an authentically felt and fully elaborated descriptive sociology. But it does enshrine the important distinction between seeing a topmost systact as the wrong set of roles and seeing it as the wrong set of people in them. The two could be, and sometimes were, combined. But a categorical repudiation both of the existence of the roles to which significant economic, ideological, or political power attaches and of the entitlement of their present incumbents to occupy them is as relatively unusual as an

---

[17] Cf. Runciman (1970, p. 198): 'Not even an English anthropologist can give a closed definition of "joke" or "snobbery".'

[18] Letters of 4.2.34 and 23.3.33 (Nicolson 1966, pp. 164, 139).

[19] Chips Channon, in *his* diary for 15.11.47, quotes 'Willy' [Somerset Maugham] as saying of 'other' diarists that Harold Nicolson 'was not in society' (Rhodes James 1967, p. 509).

unqualified acceptance of both as the best of all possible worlds. More representative is the attitude expressed by Bevin in 1920 when he said: 'I do not decry education. I lament the lack of it and I curse the other class for monopolizing it' (quoted by Bullock 1960, pp. 132–3). Articulate disrespect for the 'Establishment' was (in England, at least) more often a denunciation of politicians than of politics, of bishops than of religion, of judges than of the law, and of individual members of the élite than of the existence of an élite as such.[20]

But there were, all the same, members of both the middle and the working classes for whom the practices defining the roles of the élite were regarded with unrelenting disapprobation. For the middle classes, the stereotype is Orwell's 'Bloomsbury highbrow with his mechanical snigger' (1941, p. 50). For the working classes, it is Hoggart's 'Us' for whom 'Them' are 'the people at the top', 'the higher ups', the people who 'get yer in the end', 'aren't really to be trusted', 'talk posh', 'are all twisters really', 'never tell yer owt' (e.g. about a relative in hospital), 'clap yer in clink', 'will do y' down if they can', 'summons yer', 'are all in a click [clique] together', 'treat y' like muck' (1957, pp. 72–3). Explicit repudiation of the criteria by which élite roles are defined is easier to find among middle-class intellectuals, while working-class attitudes are likely to be closer to the generalized cynicism which Hoggart describes. But there need also to be described the attitudes of the self-educated working men who took from the writings of Blatchford, Morris, and Henry George (and sometimes Marx) a vision of a better world to which they committed years of their lives. After 1918, moreover, the milieu within which 'ethical' Socialism was sustained and propagated became less exclusively male. The working-class women who joined the Labour Party, the Women's Cooperative Guild, and the ILP shared the 'broadly humanitarian ideals with a strong class emphasis' of the men and the conviction that 'working people, once fully organized, would radically change the nature of society. In the foreseeable future, they would replace competitive capitalism with a new system modelled on the co-operative commonwealth and firmly based on the principles of justice, equality, co-operation, and international peace' (P. M. Graves 1994, pp. 67, 68, drawing on personal interviews). Although the awareness of persistent systactic differences among the overwhelming majority of English people can authentically be

---

[20] As, for example, in this reminiscence of his schooldays in the late-Victorian and Edwardian period by a former tram and bus conductor: 'so then I started reading all different books, an' I read *Old Nobility* by Robert Blatchford . . . And I thought to myself, well, this is the type of people we're supposed to look up to and respect and they'd 'ave been turned out of a decent working street with the capers they cut' (Humphries 1981, p. 43). But contrast Margaret Loane (1908, p. 64): 'It has often surprised me to observe the tolerance, and even sympathy, with which the public amusements and extravagant personal expenditure of the wealthy are regarded by those in the narrowest poverty.'

described as more acquiescent than otherwise, no description will be complete which does not reflect also the perceptions not only of dissident middle-class intellectuals but of many tens or even hundreds of thousands of working-class activists for whom a capitalist economy was immoral, inherited status indefensible, and government by and (as they saw it) for the ruling class illegitimate. They may have done little to undermine the ingrained self-esteem of the élite whose location they sought to attack. But the manifestations of defensiveness, loss of confidence, and sense of the need for a reasoned justification of traditional privilege[21] are all testimony to an awareness that inter-systactic relations had been changed by a self-conscious refusal of acquiescence on the part of incumbents of subordinate roles.

Authentic self-description of the élite, therefore, entails a recognition that it did self-consciously remain an élite after both world wars in both the economic and the ideological dimensions of the structure of English society, even though any lingering illusions about serious political influence had, well before the end of the century, been conclusively dispelled. But its constituent roles, whatever the differences of temperament and attitude among its individual incumbents, could not be described authentically without some reference to an awareness of the mutations of practices responsible for the democratization of manners and mores. The rapacious financiers, galvanic industrialists, and commercially minded landowners, whether old or new, might be just as rapacious, galvanic, and commercially minded as their late-Victorian and Edwardian counterparts. But neither 'plutocracy' nor 'aristocracy' could be used to describe them with quite the same overtones as before 1914. After the First World War, dukes were still dukes; but dukes were not what they had been.

§8. How, then, is the transition, as experienced at the top, from the late-Victorian and Edwardian period to the subsequent modes of production, persuasion, and coercion to be described in summary? Perhaps the best way is to perform the thought-experiment of asking what would be the reactions of a representatively well-endowed nobleman[22] of the 1890s who was returned

---

[21] However little attention it might attract. Cannadine (1990, p. 633) contrasts the reception of the Beveridge Report with the reception of Lord Salisbury's 'brief, dull, and austere manifesto entitled *Post-War Conservative Policy*, which urged the importance of the land, of the established church, and of a reformed and powerful House of Lords', in which 'no one was remotely interested'.

[22] Or woman? 'Wives of Victorian and Edwardian politicians, unlike most women, performed several specific roles in addition to being wives and mothers . . . They were confidantes to their husbands, they participated in electoral campaigns and, from the 1880s, many wives contributed to the women's political associations and the female suffrage campaign' (Jalland 1988, p. 189). But these roles were still a function of 'secondary' rank in the technical sense: for a sense of the difference after the First World War, contrast, say, the role performed by Nancy Astor with that performed by Margot Asquith.

into his same role in English society a hundred years later. This, admittedly, begs the question of what such person is representative: in section 16 of chapter 2 in volume I, I cited the 2nd Marquis of Rockingham (1730–82) as authentically representative of his period and milieu, and perhaps the same could be claimed of, say, the first Earl Brassey (created 1911), son of the great Victorian railway contractor to whose barony he succeeded in 1886, who joined Gladstone's second administration as Civil Lord of the Admiralty in 1880 and was subsequently lord-in-waiting to Queen Victoria, Governor of Victoria, and Lord Warden of the Cinque Ports. But who could say how far his own self-description of his role, let alone his description of a similar milieu a century later, would avoid the risk of over-simplification, exaggeration, and all the other failings by which autobiographical reminiscence can be vitiated? The answer can only be that, as I argued in chapter 4 of volume I, sociological descriptions can achieve their purpose all the better if they are of the form 'it was as if . . .'. In what follows, I am not suggesting that Lord Brassey or any other presumptively representative member of the late-Victorian and Edwardian élite would actually say what is said in the paragraphs which follow. But I *am* suggesting that the sources of the kind on which I have drawn in this chapter license the inference that the paragraphs which follow would be acceptable as authentic by a representative one of 'them'.

Such a resurrected English nobleman could hardly fail to pass comment on both the changes and the continuities which I reported in section 7 of chapter 2. He would probably not be surprised by the extravagant popularity of athletes and pop stars, since he would recollect that in his day professional jockeys had been 'national figures whose only rivals, if even they, were the Queen and Mr. Gladstone' (McKibbin 1990, p. 133); but he might be very surprised that professional jockeys, cricketers, and footballers were now awarded knighthoods. He would probably not be surprised by the political influence accorded to trade-union leaders, since he would recollect that a TUC president had said as early as 1886 that he would 'not be satisfied until we have a representative of unionism within the charmed circle of the Cabinet' (quoted by R. M. Martin 1980, p. 42); but he might be very surprised to see the 'entirely different pattern of ministerial duties from anything remotely prevailing before 1914' in the 'great new departments, like Health, Social Security, and the Environment' (R. Jenkins 1993, p. 137). He would probably not be surprised at the number of *nouveaux riches* at the top of the distribution of income and wealth and least of all at those who were Jewish or Colonial immigrants, since he would have known that the German-Jewish Sir Ernest Cassel had been 'an accepted house-guest of the Devonshires at Chatsworth by the early 1900s' (Thane 1986, p. 80); but he might be very surprised by the burden of taxation which the likes of himself would have somehow to circumvent if he were to preserve, let alone augment, his family's wealth.[23]

Suppose, accordingly, that we take him on a round of visits not just to Cowdray Park and Chatsworth, but to a representative sample of society weddings, hunt balls, grouse shoots, livery company dinners, memorial services, coming-of-age parties, and gala performances at Covent Garden. He might well remark that country-house weekends were not what they had been in the late-Victorian and Edwardian period and that it was a pity to see what had once been the town houses of families whom he knew converted to corporate headquarters or foreign embassies. But he would not find the life-style of the seriously rich any less distinctive than he remembered it; he would be thoroughly familiar with the codes and conventions still governing the giving and receiving of hospitality within the élite; and he would recognize at once the mode of informal speech – allusive, ironic, understated, and self-regarding – in which he and those whom he regarded as his equals conversed with one another on occasions like these. He might be sorry to see that Lord Portman had had to sell up in Dorset to pay estate duty, that the Duke of Westminster had allowed Eaton Hall to be turned into an officer-cadet school (and subsequently demolished), and that Lord Bath had introduced a game park for tourists at Longleat; but then he might also be relieved to find that Lord Portman, the Duke of Westminster and Lord Bath were still worth, even on a conservative estimate, hundreds of millions of pounds (in 1990 money) apiece. Moreover, if his round of visits extended not only to the aristocratic landowners whose grandfathers had been his contemporaries but to the grandsons of the founders of the great pre-1914 commercial fortunes, he would have no difficulty finding Swires, Keswicks, or Cayzers whose relative wealth and standing were visibly undiminished. If he enquired about the best-known names in banking and finance, he would find not merely Rothschilds but Schroders, Kleinworts, Hambros, and Flemings of whom the same was equally true; and he would immediately appreciate the irony of the second and this time fatal over-speculation by Barings Bank in 1995, 105 years after the first.

But having resurrected our late-Victorian and Edwardian nobleman, it is worth keeping him with us for a moment longer. After his round of social visits, let us take him into the studies, the boardrooms, and the accountants' and solicitors' offices where the families of both the old élite and the new organize their financial affairs. This is where he will get the authentic sense that it is not so surprising, after all, that despite the enormous increase since

---

[23] Thus, he might find life at Cowdray Park not changed wholly out of recognition; but if he remembered that £40,000 a year (say £1.5 million in 1990 money) was what the first Lord Cowdray regarded as enough 'to live quietly at Cowdray' (Beard 1989, p. 46), he would realize that things were not, after all, quite the same as before 1914.

his time in the burden of taxation in all its forms, families with a modicum of commercial good sense and experienced professional advice could ensure that they, at least, did not join the downwardly mobile. He would immediately recognize the soft-footed, sharp-eyed descendants of Dickens's Mr Tulking-horn; he would appreciate without difficulty the combination of luck and judgement which lay behind the decisions to break an entail, switch into equities, form a private limited company, let out the sporting rights, or hang on, even at the cost of servicing borrowed money, until the art market recovered or small parcels of land could be sold for development at fancy prices. He would sympathize with the families whose indolent or foolish children dissipated their inheritances as much as he would share the satisfac-tions of those whose children spent carefully, invested wisely, and married well. And if he asked how it was that the avoidance of tax had not been made more difficult than it had, he would readily grasp the significance of what we could tell him about gifts *inter vivos*, insurance policies, covenants in favour of grandchildren, and above all discretionary trusts. Indeed, he might find it particularly pleasing if he were to be shown the concluding paragraph of Professor Titmuss's chapter on 'Tax, Time and Kinship in the Arrangement of Income' (1962, p. 99) where Titmuss quotes from Pollock's summing up on family settlements in 1894: 'there is nothing, perhaps, in the institutions of modern Europe which comes as near to an *imperium in imperio* as the discretionary settlement of a great English fortune'.

UPPER-, MIDDLE-, AND LOWER-MIDDLE

§9. The literature of academic sociology contains far fewer studies of the middle than of the working classes. But once description rather than explana-tion is the task in hand, there is an abundance of source material in the form of biographies, memoirs, and novels; and as I remarked in section 7 of chapter 1 in volume I, 'novels *are* sociology to the extent that their authors make them so', just as anthropologists or descriptive sociologists are in a similar sense 'authors'. If you want to understand in the tertiary, descriptive sense what it was like to be the incumbent of a representative middle-class role in late-Victorian and Edwardian England, go to the novels of Bennett, Conrad, Forster, Galsworthy,[24] Gissing, and Wells. The overwhelming impression left by the sources, both factual and fictional, is that the upper-middle, middle-

---

[24] George Lyttelton to Rupert Hart-Davis, 14.3.56: 'I agree about Galsworthy. Anybody ought to be able to see how good his picture is of late Victorian times, and indeed of Victorian figures; those Forsytes are *very* true to life – some of them hardly distinguishable from relations of mine' (Hart-Davis 1985, p. 101).

middle, and lower-middle classes in the years before the First World War were all acutely aware of being, indeed, in the middle.[25]

That said, however, there were then, and increasingly thereafter, large differences in the subjective experiences and attitudes of representative members of different sub-systacts and milieux *within* the 'middle': indeed, these differences could be said to be the point of (for example) Forster's *Howards End*. They are not easy to describe authentically. In the first place, English people themselves, although they often distinguish in their own speech and writing between 'upper-middle' and 'lower-middle', seldom if ever use 'middle-middle' as a vernacular term;[26] in the second place, they consistently use the term 'class' to stand for differences of social prestige as well as, or rather than, of class in the strict academic sense of the relation of a role and its defining practices to the mode of production; and in the third, the vernacular language of 'class' systematically obscures the difference in the subjective experience of men and women, even when they occupy similar roles. 'Middle-class' roles can be distinguished in terms both of differences in the amount of economic power conferred on them by their defining practices and of differences in its source. But the subjective experience of a late-Victorian and Edwardian male household head living off his holding of railway shares and government bonds was very different from that of his unmarried sisters who were doing the same; the subjective experience of a male clerk in a banking or brokerage house was very different from that of his female counterpart; and the subjective experience of a male general practitioner was very different from

[25] Chesterton (n.d., p. 13): 'One peculiarity of this middle-class was that it really was a class and it really was in the middle. Both for good and evil, and certainly often to excess, it was separated both from the class above it and from the class below.' Cf. Macqueen-Pope (1948, p. 11): 'They began with the professional classes and they ended with the small shopkeeper and skilled artisan. There was, it is true, a sort of froth on the surface of this great mass of humanity, a foam which lapped against the side of the upper classes but really never got beyond the high-water mark of Middle Class – which called itself the Upper Middle Class. But it really only existed in its own imagination.'

[26] Lewis and Maude (1949, p. 16n): 'Some would urge the inclusion of a somewhat nebulous third stratum in between the upper- and lower-middle classes. But such refinements could be indefinitely extended. There is no dividing line, but numberless gradations between the extremes.' They do, however, cite a Gallup Poll of 1948 (p. 17) in which 6% of respondents described themselves as 'Upper Middle', 28% as 'Middle', and 13% as 'Lower Middle'. Cf. Geoffrey Grigson's remark on the children in A. A. Milne's *When We Were Very Young*, published in 1924, that they 'come of families comfortable, secure, self-certain, somewhere above the middle of the middle class' (quoted by Thwaite 1990, p. 264); or Hope (1971, p. 13) on Orwell: 'Most Eton collegers would have gone to Eton without a scholarship, or to another large public school with one if they had failed the exam. They begin in the middle of the upper-middle class, whereas Orwell, with scrupulous accuracy, described himself as *lower* upper-middle class.'

that of one of the 212 'lady' doctors enumerated in the census of 1901, or the 500 enumerated in the census of 1911.

How, therefore, can a brief description be given of the subjective experience of the English middle classes in the decades after the First World War? As it happens, there is one immediately revealing aspect of that experience which made no difference whatever to the evolution of England's modes of production, persuasion, or coercion, but was acutely felt by the numerous middle-class males who were affected by it: 'deofficerization'. The term is taken from a memoir by a self-styled 'semi-professional' and 'hereditary provincial bank clerk' (Mottram 1969, pp. 72, 84) who had been commissioned as a 'temporary gentleman'[27] and like many others felt not only demobilized but 'de-officered' when it was all over (p. 73). The problem for these men was not so much that jobs were hard to find (although they often were) as that they did not confer either the authority or the prestige that an army commission did. The 'ex-officer problem' was recognized as such at the time by ministers and officials as well as by middle-class opinion in general. But nobody had a solution for it. *A Temporary Gentleman* was the title of a successful West End play of 1919 whose evident message was that ex-officers 'whose status had been artificially elevated by war must now recognize that having held a commission was no automatic passport to the gentlemanly ranks of peacetime society' (Petter 1994, p. 133).[28] There is nothing new in the sense of bitterness and frustration felt by ex-soldiers of all ranks who return from a war in which they have been lauded as heroes to a peace in which they feel their achievements unremembered, their sufferings unacknowledged, and their capacities unused. But in English society as it was in 1919, this bitterness and frustration was compounded by a sense of relative deprivation of the status conferred by the traditional equation between the roles of 'officer' and 'gentleman'. The 'gor-blimey' officer who had come up through a Cadet Battalion for which he had been selected on grounds of merit found himself, after demobilization, patronized by his fellow-officers who had been drawn from the upper-middle class and resented by his fellow-members of the lower-middle class who had remained in the ranks. It was a very different subjective experience from that of the civilian beneficiaries of the expansion in the number of professional and

---

[27] To a cadet from the traditional officer class who joined in 1917, by which time still more 'temporary gentlemen' were being promoted from the ranks, 'Part of my distress during the first days of my training at Bushey was due to my finding myself in a room with six companions whose habits, interests and subjects of conversation differed so entirely from my own. This was really no very great hardship, but it was one to which I was not used' (Cooper 1953, p. 66).

[28] Cf. Lewis and Maude (1949, p. 24): 'Nothing was at once so heartlessly obtuse and yet revealed so clear an understanding of human nature and of the social problem as the coinage of the upper middle-class phrase "temporary gentleman" in the 1914–18 war.'

administrative roles which needed to be filled by the sons of lower-middle-class or working-class parents.

The difficulty of finding employment commensurate with their expectations did also extend to some demobilized ex-officers drawn from the traditional officer class: the son of a county family who returned from the trenches to find the family house on the market and the estate already sold to the sitting tenants might feel no less resentful than the 'temporary gentleman' unable to find a clerking job at £150 a year. But a descriptive distinction still needs to be drawn between the representative members of the different status-groups. The social attitudes exemplified in say, Ian Hay's *A Knight on Wheels* are very different from those exemplified in Warwick Deeping's *Sorrell and Son*. The first is an authentic expression of the traditional ethos of the traditional officer class by the author of *The First Hundred Thousand*, whose picture, as I have already mentioned, I used in chapter 3 of volume I to exemplify precisely that status-group (and whose portrait, in the uniform of a major-general, still hangs in a corridor of the Garrick Club). The second has been described with little or no exaggeration as 'a grim pot-pourri of middle-class grievances and fantasies' (McKibbin 1990, p. 272). It is an illuminating document of the 1920s not only because of its idealized description of the plight of a virtuous and unfortunate ex-officer but because of its almost hysterical resentment of profiteers and workers alike. But the grievances and fantasies, inauthentic though they may be, appealed to the middle-class readers of forty-nine successive editions because of the implicit legitimation which the fictional narrative gave them – a legitimation derived from a notion of 'gentlemanly' conduct which was a wholly authentic ingredient of the dominant ideology. That ideology was very differently expressed after the experience of the First World War from before it: the public-school poetry of Henry Newbolt could hardly be recited with a straight face by 1930 (Coleman 1973, p. 116). But the ideology survived, even if in an attenuated form, through to the Second World War and beyond. The mingled notions of self-effacing good manners, fair dealing ('an Englishman's word is his bond') and patriotic duty overriding both individual and collective self-interest continued to be transmitted from one middle-class generation to the next by the public schools and the families who sent their sons to them. As I reported in section 13 of chapter 1, the conscripted officer cadets of the Second World War, drawn once again from a similar cross-section of systactic origins,[29] found themselves confronted by the same ritual practices, the same corporate values, and the same hierarchy of ranks. The young men in the passing-out parade at Sandhurst in the 1980s might lack the 'confident sense of

---

[29] Thus Hoggart (1990, p. 9): 'Socially, our most central point of origin was lower-middle to slightly middle-class with a very few from the upper-middle class at one end and a very few from among the respectable working-class at the other.'

god-given superiority' of their counterparts from before the 'Kaiser's War' (Mason 1982, p. 220). But their ethos was the same.

Experiences of war and its aftermath, however, are as illuminating as they are precisely because they are not the experiences of the same people in their normal, peacetime roles. They are experiences of *crises révélatrices* of the kind sought after by anthropologists in the field to illuminate what is otherwise latent in the *Weltanschauung* underlying the routine interactions between the members of the society under study. Yet the theme which runs from the experiences of the demobilized 'temporary gentlemen' through the whole range of peacetime middle-class careers as experienced by their incumbents thereafter is the continuing conflict between the norms of achievement and of ascription. This is yet another pair of sociological terms whose definition is too ambiguous for the purpose of reportage. Nor are they terms which would be used by those whose subjective experience the sociologist is seeking to describe. But as managerial roles came increasingly to displace proprietorial, professional qualifications to displace personal recommendation, and an ideology of merit to displace the ideology of inherited entitlement, so did the representative hopes and fears of middle-class English people come to assume a distinctive mid-twentieth-century form.

The difference extends, moreover, from their hopes and fears for their own careers to their hopes and fears for their children's; and this means above all a preoccupation with their children's education. In families like those of the fictional Sorrell and his son, it implied a willingness to sacrifice other traditional middle-class amenities and enjoyments in order to send a favoured child – almost invariably a son – to a 'public' school. For the families of the lower-middle class, it implied before 1944 the hope that the child could stay on at school beyond the minimum leaving age and perhaps even win a university scholarship. After 1944, it implied the hope of success in the 'eleven plus'. As 'Mrs Clark' of Woodford, whose daughter was already at grammar school, told an interviewer in 1959: 'We don't know how the two boys will do in the eleven-plus when their turn comes, but we're *hoping*. Like most of the parents in this district, we do take an interest in our children. We encourage them all we can. You can see how important it is for them to pass.' Or as 'Mr Hammond' put it: 'Naturally enough, parents worry about it. My wife and I have been giving her exam test papers to do, just a few to keep her up to it and she's come up from twenty-ninth to twelfth in her class last year. But you can't be sure, can you? All parents out here are suburbanites. To hear them talk they've *all* got children who have moved up in the class. I'm afraid Essex is a very competitive county' (Willmott and Young 1960, p. 113).

This increasing awareness of the importance of credentials obtained through competitive examination has an evident affinity with the traditional middle-class ideology of individualism and self-help. Here, for instance, is the poet Philip Larkin's description of the early life of his father, who rose from the lower-middle class to be Treasurer of the City of Coventry and an OBE: 'he was secretary of a chess club, he went for long cycle rides, he studied for examinations and passed them easily, he economized – for in those Edwardian days, money made sense' (Motion 1993, p. 7). Larkin himself was to write in 1976 that 'thanks to my father's generosity, my education was at no time a charge on public or other funds' (Larkin 1983, p. 25); and although the middle classes may in general have been as ready as anyone to accept a hand-out from the state if it was offered to them, it was in the context of occupational roles in which promotion in some form or other was normally in prospect. Indeed, that familar contrast can be described without exaggeration as the biggest single continuing difference between the subjective experience of the working and of the middle classes; and much of the well-documented difference between them in attitudes to education (to which I shall return) becomes better understandable in the tertiary, descriptive sense if it is borne in mind.

But then what about the middle-class rentiers – Campbell-Bannerman's 'quiet people who live on railway dividends'? Rentiers didn't cease to exist after 1918, despite Keynes's famous phrase about their 'euthanasia'. So what did the evolution to a new sub-type of capitalist liberal democracy feel like to them? 'They', in this context, are not a homogeneous group. The rentier living wholly off what he or she might still refer to as a 'competence' existed side by side with the not quite passive director of a small privately owned business, the 'gentleman' farmer whose life-style was subsidized by investment income, the solicitor or accountant or general practitioner fortunate enough to have married a 'young lady of means', the regular army or navy officer not dependent only on his pay, and the otherwise impecunious intellectual whose occasional fees and royalties were supplemented by a legacy or by dividends from a family trust. But all shared a common interest in a mode of production which permitted a not too punitively taxed transmission of wealth from one generation to the next and continuing opportunities for attractive real yields on fixed-interest securities or capital gains on equity shares. The difference from the feel, as it were, of the late-Victorian and Edwardian period was not that these opportunities were no longer there, but that the acceptability of 'unearned' income was increasingly under attack on what would later be called 'meritocratic' as well as 'socialistic' grounds. For the sons (and to a much lesser extent daughters) of middle-class families to be without 'gainful employment' was to invite not only commitment but criticism. Once past working age, no stigma attached: just as the role of 'pensioner' came to imply an entitlement as of right to provision by either a private employer or the state, so did the notion of 'putting by' earnings as a protection against the contingencies of retirement retain its traditional respectability. But the able-bodied male 'doing nothing for a living' did come to be perceived more and more as an anachronism.

How far the able-bodied males in question felt themselves to be so no doubt varied according to temperament, outlook, and political attitude. But I know no more vivid description of a rentier family whose way of life continued almost uncannily unchanged than that given (with perhaps a touch of exaggeration) by Richard Cobb of the Limbury-Buses of Tunbridge Wells. At the outbreak of the Second World War, the family consisted of old Mr Limbury-Buse (who had never done a day's work since leaving Cambridge) and his wife, their son Geoff (who had returned home so as to be 'near his parents' following a brief involvement in the film industry after service in the First World War), and their daughter Olive (who had, by contrast, worked to the extent of being a seasonal winter-sports instructress for English visitors to Switzerland). They lived in a big Victorian house with a maid in her seventies and an overgrown garden, where they maintained a life of 'determined idleness' which success-fully excluded 'such external horrors as wars, civil disturbances, class conflict, or, indeed, anything unfamiliar'. By the 1950s, the parents had died and Olive had gone to live in Switzerland, but Geoff was still taking his daily walk to the Tunbridge Wells and Counties Club for his glass of sherry and game of bridge. Here is Cobb's description of the difference between his own attitude as a young man and that of his mother to the father and son:

> Old Mr Limbury-Buse and Geoff also compelled my admiration for their total lack of *ambition*, as if they had never known the meaning of the word, or had long since forgotten it. In this sense, too, they lived outside the conventional time-scale imposed by education, achievement and promotion. The father had given up at 21, Geoff a bit later. But it was hard to know what had provoked this retreat from active life: it might have been the War, more likely that he had found a form of serenity by living at a very low key, and spending a lot of time, like the rest of the family, including the old maid and the untidy black dog, asleep. 'Poor Geoff', my mother would say, 'he doesn't seem to get much *out* of life, he should *do* more'. My mother was an understanding woman in many ways, but total lack of ambition both puzzled her and shocked her, as flying in the face of some of her most cherished values. For she liked to be able to categorise people by achievement and promotion: an FRCS before he was 35, an LRCP at 40, a consultant at only 42 (a ladder that may also have been leaned in *my* direction; as one who took on his first salaried job at 38, I made rather nonsense of her cherished hurdles). In what category to place the passive, slow-moving Geoff? (Cobb 1983, pp. 87–8)

In what category, indeed? Hardly a representative one[30] – an instantiation of

---

[30] Slightly more representative might be the 'permanent' residents of the large seaside hotels 'draining away the ends of their lives in shabby gentility supported by small private incomes, pensions, and investments' (A. A. Jackson 1991, p. 303).

an ideal type, not of a statistical mean. But authentic, without doubt. For explanatory purposes, irrelevant. If value-judgements are to be made, to be welcomed or deplored according to your own presuppositions. But for descriptive purposes, as deserving of a place as any striving careerist in anything approaching a complete account of the middle classes of mid-twentieth-century England.

§10. As the description of twentieth-century English society moves down the systactic scale, the disjunction with explanation becomes further compounded. Lewis and Maude were quite right in their comment that within the English middle classes 'there are numberless gradations between the extremes'. The categories in terms of which the changing distribution of economic, ideological, and political power has been reported and explained, neutral between rival descriptive theories as they may be, cannot hope to reflect fully these gradations as they are subjectively experienced by the incumbents of the roles to which there attach subtly perceptible (and sometimes illusory) differences of kind as well as degree; and the gradations are further complicated by the experience of intra-generational mobility and systactic exogamy. Thus, to give an obvious example, the subjective experience of a male university teacher born into the lower-middle class who marries a rich wife, writes best-selling history books, ends his career as head of an Oxford college, and is awarded a knighthood is very different from that of one of identical systactic origin who ends his career with a lectureship, a recently paid-off mortgage, no income but his pension, and no public recognition of any kind. Yet it is just such intra-systactic differences as these which would need to be brought out in a complete description of the English middle classes – which is why, once again, any account which a chapter like this one could offer would need to be supplemented, so far as university life is concerned, by an extensive reading of novels and biographies, from the memoir of G. M. Trevelyan by his daughter through C. P. Snow's *The Masters* to Kingsley Amis's *Lucky Jim* and beyond, in which the nuances of 'gradation' in the world of 'higher' education are vividly and illuminatingly explored.

So who, for the purposes of a descriptive summary, *are* the English 'upper-middle' and 'middle-middle' classes? Whose experiences and attitudes are we talking about? Where is the frontier of the 'U-speaking' status-group, and what was it like to be there? One answer, which is more seriously meant than it may appear, is: those very people who are referred to by the cartoonist 'Pont' as 'the British' but ought really (as pointed out by Delafield 1951, p. 7), to be referred to as 'the English' – the people, that is, who invite caricature for their 'fondness for writing letters to *The Times*', their 'failure to appreciate good music', their 'love of dumb animals', and their 'enthusiasm for gardening'. 'They' are the more ('upper-middle') and less ('middle-middle') highly located company directors, business proprietors, civil servants, brokers, lawyers, doctors, farmers, army, navy or airforce officers, bankers, consultants, advertisers, architects, publishers, professors, lecturers, accountants, and their wives (with or without professional careers of their own) to all of whose roles there attaches substantial economic advantage in the labour market, relatively high standing in the conventional hierarchy of occupational prestige, and a potential, at least, for political influence going beyond that attaching simply to the entitlement to vote in local and national elections. The attitudes and values of those employed in the private sector might differ from those employed by the state,[31] just as both might differ in turn from the attitudes and values of the freelance professionals. But whatever their anxieties, resentments, or grievances, there was never anything remotely 'proletarian' about any of them.

Their manners and values remained much the same after the Second World War as they had been in the 1920s and 1930s. The 'Sloane Rangers' of the 1980s, however different – and they weren't all that much – in outward appearance from Pont's 'British', were not significantly different in attitudes to the mode of the distribution of power. But, as I pointed out in section 7 of chapter 2, there was never unanimity. As in all systacts and milieux, conformism coexisted with its opposite. Gerald Brenan's account, for example, of his decision to live in Spain from the 1920s onwards was that 'I was rebelling against English middle-class life. Today in our formless society this seems to me an odd thing to do, but I can assure anyone who has grown up since 1920 that he can have no idea how stifling that life was' (1957, p. 2). Description of what it was like to belong to the upper-middle and middle-middle classes has, accordingly, to extend not only to the skidders and drop-outs but to the committed and sometimes lifelong protesters, ranging from the high-thinking, low-living intelligentsia through the literary expatriates to the active participants in dissident causes and movements, of which support for the Republic in the Spanish Civil War was the most salient before the Second World War (Stansky and Abrahams 1966) and the Campaign for Nuclear Disarmament the most salient after it (Parkin 1968). However little effect they had on English society's modes of production, persuasion, or coercion, their well-publicized opinions and attitudes were as much a part of the subjective experience of their fellow-middle-class contemporaries as of their own.[32]

---

[31] For the young John Maud (later Lord Redcliffe-Maud), as for many like him, 'Neither industry or commerce ever occurred to me' as a career (1981, p. 20), just as to many commercial families 'civil servant' was a term of mild but genuine ridicule.

[32] Andrews (1991), who interviewed a selection of lifelong activists, remarks that 'the role of class-consciousness in the process of radicalization was very different for working-class and middle-class respondents' (p. 135): 'broadly speaking, the working-class respondents talked more about

These experiences, however, need to be descriptively differentiated from the experiences of those born and reared in the *lower*-middle class. The reason is simple enough. Whatever the facts of the distribution of economic, ideological, and political power, the answer to the question 'what was it like for "them"?' depends at least as much in the lower-middle class on 'their' subjective view of the lower-middle-class/working-class boundary as it does in the upper-middle class on 'their' subjective view of the upper-middle-class/upper-class boundary. In late-Victorian and Edwardian England, the 'Suburbans', as Masterman described them, were not merely aware but fearful of the urban working class (1909, p. 68). Returning to the theme in the aftermath of the First World War, Masterman described the typical London middle-class suburb as hating and despising the working classes 'partly because it has contempt for them and partly because it has fear of them' (1922, p. 54). Edward Norman, then chaplain of Peterhouse, Cambridge described himself in 1979 as 'like most English lower middle class people' in having been brought up 'with a savage view of working class life' (quoted by P. Jenkins 1987, p. 82), and an explicitly autobiographical novel of roughly the same period describes 'the distaste and fear with which my mother and father and their friends regarded the workers' (Aldiss 1970, p. 102 quoted by McKibbin 1990, p. 273: 'father was a provincial bank manager given to calling the destitute "our non-banking friends". "Non-washing you mean", Mother said. It was not their financial so much as their hygiene habits she loathed').

Much of the antipathy was mutual. But on the lower-middle-class side of the line it was increasingly defensive. The 'real detestation' of the 1945 Labour Government which was felt in the 'suburban' middle class (Blake 1985, p. 264) was bound up with not only a stereotype of greedy trade unions extorting more pay for less work[33] but also a feeling that the traditional status of lower-grade non-manual labour was being systematically devalued. 'The Town Hall Young Men Are Producers Too' – an article in the journal *Local Government Service* in 1952[34] – conveys this defensiveness well. And among the self-employed – or, as they were apt to describe themselves, 'self-made' – who believed that 'trade unions and the welfare state have undermined the will to work', a

a shared sense of relative deprivation and the middle-class respondents more about identifying with a particular movement or cause'.

[33] Lockwood (1989, p. 104 n.2) cites a Gallup Poll of 1956 in which roughly one in three clerks interviewed about recent strikes and the government's attitude to them 'gave answers which clearly demonstrated their conception of the working class and trade unionism as a threatening and dangerous force which should be repressed'. 'So', as Bonham (1954, p. 55) put it in discussing middle-class voting behaviour, 'we get the idea of "the public" as opposed to the organized manual class'.

[34] *Ibid.*, p. 105 n.4; cf. the other references in the same note, and those cited in Runciman (1966, p. 138 n.63).

respondent 'typical of many' interviewed by Scase and Goffee (1980, pp. 127, 129, 135) complained that 'Nobody can run a country when, all the time, you've got people in unions saying "I *won't* do this". I don't care what country it is – if you haven't got *discipline*, you can't run it' (and this, incidentally, is a farm labourer's son who left school at fourteen to become a farm labourer himself on 10s 6d for a 52-hour week, of which he paid over all but 1s 1d to his mother).

The other side of this descriptive coin is the subjective experience of the increasing number of salaried employees who themselves joined trade unions. But here, the disjunction between description and explanation becomes even more acute. The attitudes and values of a junior commercial clerk or civil servant who, despite a 'social perspective' remote from that of the 'proletarianized worker' (Mercer and Weir 1972, p. 69) is persuaded to join a union in the hope of protecting himself or herself in a threatened occupational role are much closer to those of a writer persuaded that it would be to his or her pecuniary advantage if the Society of Authors were to be registered as a trade union, as 68 per cent of its members decided in 1978 that it should (Bradley 1982, p. 171), than to those of a card-carrying militant on the factory floor. Likewise, the Jaguar-driving, suburban-dwelling, posh-speaking airline pilots might, as explained in section 5 of chapter 3, have good reason to bargain collectively with their employers, but they were as far in attitudes and values from the miners of the NUM or dockers of the T&GWU as any self-employed professional. Conversely, the left-wing activists in the Association of University Teachers might whole-heartedly subscribe to the ideology of the Labour movement, but they could hardly pretend that what it was like to be a university teacher had become assimilated to what it was like to work on the vehicle-builders' assembly lines. Office workers contemplating computerization in the 1970s and 1980s might see it as 'reskilling' as much as 'deskilling' clerical functions,[35] as might their counterparts of the 1920s and 1930s confronting the influx of 'adding machines, folding machines, wire-stitching machines, envelope filling and sealing machines, stamp affixers, letter copiers, machines for opening letters' (Demant 1931, p. 35), even though both might also feel a need for protection against the redundancies to which mechanization or computerization might be going to lead. Likewise, newly unionized civil servants aware that cash limits and manpower reductions were diminishing their prospects of

---

[35] A relevant but, for obvious reasons, not conclusive piece of evidence is Daniel's finding (1987, p. 164) that managers in a national sample of firms perceived new technology as enriching the jobs of non-manual much more than manual workers. For a counter-example to the progressive fear of white-collar job losses following computerization, here is 'Pam' (interviewed by Black 1994, p. 53): 'I always say computers they take away one job but they give another, at least two others I always think.'

promotion did not feel on that account as if they were being reduced to the condition of manual workers with no prospects of promotion at all. Descriptively speaking, a bowler-hatted civil servant on a picket line in Whitehall is as wide a world away from one of Arthur Scargill's striking miners in 1984 as he is from one of Arthur Cook's in 1926.

Description of what it was like to be in a non-manual occupational role does, however, need to distinguish the experience of women from that of men. Of the increasing proportion of the growing number of women in clerical work after the First World War who were from working-class families, many were performing tasks which, although they required a certain minimum of education, were largely routine. Their male colleagues saw them as vain, inattentive, and silly.[36] But sympathetic trade-union organizers who saw in their working-class origins, their conditions of work, and their stigmatization by male employers and colleagues a potential for enrolment in the Labour movement also saw how few of them were likely to feel that way themselves. They did not see themselves as career employees: they were aware that even if they wished to remain at work after marriage, their employers would discourage if not actually prevent their doing so. As employers' attitudes changed over the subsequent decades, so did middle-class men's and women's subjective experiences of employment begin to converge. But the convergence was far from complete. When, in the decades after the Second World War, women were both better able and more willing to return to work after bringing up children, they still felt themselves to be disadvantaged relative to men in terms of promotion even if they returned (as many did not) to full-time rather than part-time work: the only significant exception was if they were returning to the role of teacher (Dex 1987, p. 124).

Subjectively, women who might start in the same lower-middle-class roles as men were aware both that they were likely to abandon them at least temporarily after marriage and that their chances of subsequent promotion would be diminished thereby. Nor, unless they married into a significantly higher class, would they think themselves likely to be able to afford the domestic and child-rearing help which would allow them, if they wished, to continue in work while their children were small. Crompton and Jones in their study of clerical workers in banking, insurance, and local government in the 1980s, found that the younger women were more likely to resent their disadvantage while the older were more likely to acquiesce in it. But both the older and the younger saw equality of opportunity between themselves and their male equivalents as a myth. What is more, when women in the sample *were* exercising a degree of

---

[36] As vividly illustrated in a symptomatic drawing in the Lloyd's Bank in-house magazine of 7 April 1920 (reproduced by Booker 1991, p. 4: 'ledgers support a pretty girl and her vanity bag while a pass-book wallows in spilled ink!').

responsibility, 'if a *man* had been occupying these positions, he would be in a "promoted" grade' (1984, p. 244).

This experience was to some extent paralleled by the experience of women in the middle-middle and upper-middle classes, where the sense of expanding opportunities went hand in hand with a continuing sense of relative deprivation. From 1918 onwards, such women could not fail to be aware that it was becoming easier for them to acquire a university degree, to qualify in medicine and the law, to enter Parliament, to establish businesses of their own, to rise to senior positions in the Civil Service, and to pursue administrative and managerial careers outside of the areas traditionally regarded as appropriate for them. But this expansion of opportunities was at the same time rapid enough to encourage aspirations and not rapid enough to appease the sense of relative deprivation by comparison with similarly qualified men. Moreover, the continuing mismatch in the distribution of occupational roles by gender – over-representation in personal service and under-representation in professional and managerial roles – meant that young women entering on a career continued to feel themselves channelled away from such traditionally male preserves as systems engineering, stockbroking, and works management. A summary of changes in the field of personnel management (Legge 1987), whose professionalization from the 1920s onwards I briefly discussed in section 4 of chapter 3, shows a continuing dichotomy between male specialists dealing with 'industrial relations' and female specialists dealing with 'welfare'. Similarly, a study of the clothing industry following the introduction of computer-aided design found not only that male craftsmen were being replaced by female operatives but that the maintenance engineers as well as the systems managers were all men (Cockburn 1986, pp. 178–9). Any descriptive generalization about middle-class women's subjective experience of the structure and culture of twentieth-century English society has accordingly to present a two-fold contrast. They could not fail to be aware of being regarded far more nearly as equals by their male counterparts than their own counterparts had been during the late-Victorian and Edwardian period, when they would, if Oxford or Cambridge undergraduates, have been ineligible to receive the same qualifications as the men alongside whom they were being taught.[37] But it was not as if it made no difference that they were women and not men: where, for all the individual achievements of a few outstanding women scientists, was the

---

[37] As a small descriptive touch, here is an extract from an unpublished letter from a Newnham undergraduate describing the reading of the Mathematical Lists in 1890: 'Then the dons read out "Women" and raised their caps, an example which all the crowd followed. Two or three voices called out "Ladies, Sir, Ladies", at which the don repeated "Women". This is a standing joke. There was a certain amount of applause at P. G. Fawcett's . . .' [Philippa Garrett Fawcett, whose final marks were above the Senior Wrangler's] (Catherine Holt to her mother, 25.9.90).

'positive leadership from the Hadow (1926) and Norwood (1943) reports to pull, push, cajole, bully or direct girls into maths and science' (Delamont 1989, p. 191)? What was being done about what Nancy Seear, in a survey carried out for the Royal Commission of 1965–8, had called the 'subtle and not so subtle ways an atmosphere is created which still makes it appear peculiar or comical for women to be both feminine and using their capacities to the full' (quoted by Thane 1991a, p. 203)?

§11. 'Despite what some commentators might believe, the plain fact is that manual workers remain excluded from a whole range of privileges that the middle classes have long taken for granted' (Roberts et al. 1977, p. 25). Well – yes. Throughout chapter 2, I emphasized that the changes of structure and culture reported in it have not amounted to a closing of the systactic gap between middle-class and working-class roles, and in this chapter I have emphasized the continuing significance of subjective middle-class expectations of individual advancement and the outlook and life-style that goes with them. But what descriptive generalization are we to draw? Is the litany of middle-class complaint nothing but bullshit? Or is the sense of relative deprivation so consistently voiced by middle-class people since the days of *Sorrell and Son* an expression of genuine experience of England's new sub-type of the modes of production, persuasion, and coercion authentically described?

Here is another of Willmott and Young's informants, a teacher (1960, p. 118): 'I suppose before the war I'd be middle class. Teachers had a high social standing then, but now professional people are the lowest. At least that's in money. Actually, we're a pretty high class.' That quotation succinctly conveys much of the pervasive ambivalence in representative middle-class attitudes to the systactic structure of mid-twentieth-century England. On the one hand, there is the feeling that the esteem for educational qualifications reflected in pay is being eroded, and on the other there is the insistence that the traditional superiority of teaching over better-paid but less prestigious occupations still holds. Teachers, like the clergy, are textbook exemplars of roles in which higher status is seen as compensating for lower pay.[38] But the theme that the rewards, both tangible and intangible, attaching to middle-class occupational roles are less than they should be runs through from the rhetoric of the short-lived but vociferous Middle Class Union of 1919–22 to that of its equivalents in the 1970s and beyond. 'Increasingly sneered at and attacked' (Hutber 1976, p. 103): the resentment is not merely of the gains seen to have

---

[38] As was true between the wars of higher civil servants: the permanent secretary of a major department of state with a knighthood in prospect was paid less than half the salary of the clerk to a county council. By the 1980s, however, salaries more nearly comparable with the private sector were seen as necessary to attract and retain them.

been secured by organized manual workers but of the ingratitude of the country in general and successive governments in particular. Not only are the financial rewards accruing to workers by brain rather than by hand less than workers by brain deserve, but the traditional values of thrift, loyalty, individual effort, and disinterested professionalism are being either ignored or deliberately undermined by the very people who are the beneficiaries of what a commitment to those values has achieved for the nation as a whole.

Much of this sort of talk can be dismissed as blatantly inauthentic, but by no means all of it. The study from which I quoted in the opening sentence of this section collected information about subjective as well as objective aspects of their respondents' 'mobility experiences', and that information 'suggested that, amongst our sample, downward mobility was usually unacknowledged and psychologically quite unacceptable' (Roberts *et al.* 1977, p. 81).[39] As I remarked about Geoffrey Brady in section 2, it would be descriptively wrong to ignore the cases of downward mobility. However small the statistical chances of it for children of middle-class parents, all of them knew that it could and would happen to some.[40] Yet the fear of falling from an initial starting-point well above the apex of the inverted pyramid, and the psychological gymnastics which may be required for those who do fall to rationalize it away, are only one side of the story. The representative incumbent of a first adult role located in the middle classes not only fears to fall but hopes to rise. 'For the majority of white-collar employees, promotion is almost automatically a desired objective' (Goldthorpe *et al.* 1969, p. 73). There are of course exceptions, male as well as female, and even those who have told an interviewer that they are 'interested' in promotion may grow less ambitious as they grow older, or welcome the chance to get out of the 'rat race' if an early pension or an inheritance of capital enables them to do so. But the more representative response is of dissatisfaction with careers which have failed to live up to expectations initially held of them. Richardson (1977, p. 286) says of his sample of middle-class London men: 'One of the most striking impressions of this study was the extent "core" [i.e. immobile] members of the middle class evidenced status and financial deprivation . . . what I recorded were sentiments recognized at least since Orwell was writing in the '30s: that relative to their own past and to the working class of

---

[39] An impression confirmed by Goldthorpe (1980, p. 246); but it would be interesting to know what the wives of the men in his sample would have said if they had been interviewed too, both about their husbands' careers and (if they have one) their own.

[40] Here, for example, is the playwright John Osborne (1981, p. 26) in a characteristically uncharitable but authentic-sounding description of his mother's and father's lower-middle-class families: 'Coming Down in the World was something the Groves had in common with the Osbornes, except that the Groves seemed to feel less sense of grievance, looking on it as the justified price of profligate living or getting above yourself, rather than as a cruel trick of destiny or a creeping army of upstarts Getting the Better of their Betters.'

today, they feel worse off and appear to find ways to reduce these feelings of relative deprivation.'

The sociologist's reaction to evidence of this kind is likely to be twofold: first, to discount the stereotyping implicit in the contrasts drawn with the undeservedly well-paid working class, and second, to insist on the 'whole range of privileges taken for granted' – the better working conditions, the fringe benefits, the premium on age and experience even for the unpromoted, the life-style of family and friends, the access to credit, the insurance and pension provisions, and the proximity to managerial authority. But it does not follow that the sense of grievance is inauthentic. None of the criteria of misdescription set out in chapter 4 of volume I applies to candid avowals of a strongly felt sense of disappointment of expectations regarded as legitimate. The middle-class couple who have restrained their expenditure for the sake of a private education for their children only to find the school fees rising prohibitively in real terms, or have put by a modest capital sum for their old age only to see its value, and that of the husband's occupational pension, eroded by inflation, or have built up a small but prosperous business only to be confronted by the punitive administrative and financial consequences of unforeseen changes in tax, company, and employment law are not to be equated, descriptively speaking, with the university professors whose laments for the decline of civilization could be unkindly construed by A. J. P. Taylor in 1959 as laments for the decline of domestic service (E. H. Carr 1961, pp. 106–7).

But something is still missing – something just as intrinsic to middle-class experience as any of the privileges listed above, but less frequently pointed out and less self-consciously recognized by the incumbents of middle-class roles themselves. It has long been remarked by sociologists and historians that involvement in, and more particularly direction of, voluntary associations is much more characteristic of the middle than of the working classes.[41] The explanation is not entirely straightforward. As Bottomore (1954, pp. 368–9) points out, the leaders of voluntary associations may be chosen because of personal qualities which explain their occupational status rather than because of their occupational status itself. But participation in voluntary associations, particularly but not exclusively when they are of a relatively formal educational,

---

[41] Finlayson (1994, p. 332): 'The vast bulk of voluntary social action in the 1960s and 1970s was done by the middle classes, and there was a lack of any real working-class involvement, especially where the voluntary activity had a philanthropic, rather than a mutual-aid orientation. The evidence produced by the Opinion Survey of 1976 indicated that much the greater contrast in voluntary work related not to age and sex but to social class.' On the evidence of the 1992 General Household Survey, 40% of professional men and 41% of professional women had undertaken some voluntary work within the previous 12 months, as against 8% of men and 14% of women classified as unskilled manual (*Social Trends* 1995, Table 8.4).

cultural, or philanthropic kind, is overwhelmingly a middle-class rather than a working-class experience. This holds, moreover, as much where the aims and activities of the association are antagonistic to the current mode of the distribution of power as where they are supportive of it. Bagguley (1992, p. 39) remarks of the so-called 'new social movements' such as environmentalism, feminism, and the 'peace movement' that they 'are like many other social movements in including many middle-class professionals. They do so because this class possesses the skills and knowledge, in short the social resources, for political mobilization.' This, when it comes to descriptive generalization about subjective differences in experience and attitudes, is the significant point, whether or not those resources are in fact deployed in voluntary activity and whether or not that voluntary activity has any effect at all on the modes of production, persuasion, or coercion.

Middle-class people have, and are so used to having that they hardly notice it, a capacity bound up with their education, their conditions of work, and their informal social networks for articulating, defending, and promoting what they see as the interests of a cause which they espouse. What is more, it has a significance beyond voluntary activities in which they may or may not choose to engage. As the state has continued, in the ways and for the reasons set out in chapters 2 and 3, to encroach more and more on the activities of its citizens, so has the experience of dealing with officialdom in its increasingly varied forms become more and more salient in their lives. The relative difficulty experienced by many working-class families in their dealings with officials was recognized already by middle-class observers in the late-Victorian and Edwardian period: Margaret Loane, for example, was made uncomfortably aware by her visits to (or should they be described as intrusions into?) working-class homes in her role of district nurse of the impossibility of 'natural' conversation across the systactic boundary which divided her from them, even if she then failed to draw from it the inference that she could not therefore 'know' – that is, understand in the tertiary, descriptive sense – the working classes as well as she claimed to do (McKibbin 1990, p. 196). But as working-class and middle-class families alike became more and more involved with the agents of national and local government in health care, education, legal aid, planning, licensing, taxation, and all the institutions and activities of the 'welfare state', so did there increase the subjective difference from the working classes in what David Lockwood calls the 'know-how, demeanour, self-esteem, and persuasiveness which the middle classes can bring to bear in their dealings with the representatives of public bureaucracies, who are anyway their status equals or inferiors'.[42]

---

[42] The quotation is from an unpublished English version of Lockwood (1987).

It might be objected that this is too sweeping a generalization to be equally authentic and representative for upper-middle, middle-middle, and lower-middle-class people alike. Is there not an enormous gap in know-how, demeanour, and self-esteem between the smooth-tongued, worldly wise, well-connected professionals at the top of the range and the fraction of the lower-middle class at the bottom of it who may in any case identify themselves to survey interviewers with the working class?[43] What about the differences in attitude to which I have already referred in earlier chapters between private-sector managers and public-sector officials, or between proprietors and employers, or between the 'credentialled' and the 'self-made'? But differences in economic interests and political opinions could and did coexist with shared assumptions and attitudes. Evidence to support this conclusion which is not merely anecdotal or impressionistic is not easy to find. But there is a test of a kind in the results of the *British Social Attitudes* survey conducted between 1983 and 1990 (Heath and Savage 1994). If there is indeed a difference in assumptions and attitudes between different fractions of the middle class which undermines my descriptive generalization, it should be reflected in differences in the pattern of responses to questions about party-political affiliation. But that is not what we find. On the contrary, 'none of the factors which have been proposed as sources of systematic division within the middle class – sector, employment status or education – divided the middle class into two clearly defined opposing camps' (p. 72). The respondents were, as a representative sample would be bound to be, split roughly in half in terms of supporting the Conservative Party or not and there were also predictable differences in a few 'aberrant' groups which raise the familiar explanatory difficulties: are members of the security forces right-wing because of their occupation, or do they join the security forces because they are right-wing? But there is no support in the data for a conclusion to the effect that there is a less privileged fraction of the middle class whose different subjective experience finds expression in a significantly lower proportion of support for the political party standing for the established order. However wide the individual differences in temperament, character, and talent within the English middle classes, there is, descriptively speaking, a middle-class sub-culture whose continuing existence and distinctiveness the sources on which I have drawn for this chapter overwhelmingly confirm.

---

[43] Of men and women classified as 'non-manual' in a national sample survey (excluding Scotland) in 1962, 12 per cent answered the question 'what sort of people are you thinking of when we talk about "people like yourself"?' in terms coded as ' "working class", manual workers' (Runciman 1966, p. 162 (Table 4)).

WORKERS, MORE SKILLED AND LESS

§12. After the outbreak of the Second World War, when Arthur Exell, a Communist shop steward at Morris Motors, went to enlist with his two brothers, 'I was told to wait. They had been informed from Radiators of the men they expected to recall, which were all their skilled men. That was the first time I knew I was classified as skilled' (Exell 1980, p. 90). It is an illuminating warning of the danger of assuming that evidence about earnings differentials, apprenticeship, 'deskilling', the mutant practices redefining the role of 'artisan', and so forth translates at all directly into the subjective experience of the incumbents of working-class roles. But it is at the same time consistent with the conclusion drawn by Blackburn and Mann (1979, p. 108) from a study of the labour market in Peterborough in the early 1970s that '*The internal labour market is fundamentally an apprenticeship in co-operation*' (authors' italics). Of course, there have always been cleaning and labouring jobs for which not even literacy is required, just as there have always been jobs requiring a high degree of physical exertion and risk.[44] But differentiation by 'skill' is, as I pointed out in section 4 of chapter 2, not always what it sounds like; and what it often feels like, and thus in the descriptive sense is, is a sense of autonomy or responsibility, or of value placed on loyalty or experience, which is not there at all in the 'dead-end' jobs where workers are well aware that they can be replaced at any time at the going rate.

Just as a complete description of middle-class experience of the mode of the distribution of power in twentieth-century English society would have to include all the 'numberless gradations between the extremes' which fall through the mesh of standard sociological categorization, so would a complete description of working-class experience have to include hardly less numberless gradations in terms and conditions of work, in patterns of residence and recreation, and in rates and distances of social mobility. But any descriptive account has to recognize the difference between the subjective experience of the 'skilled' working class as it was from the 1920s on and that of both the lower-middle class above it and the unskilled working class below.

The first is the familiar difference, which I have emphasized already from the middle-class point of view, between the 'job', however 'skilled', and the

---

[44] Willis (1977, p. 190): 'two things are clear. Rough, unpleasant, demanding jobs *do* still exist in considerable numbers. A whole range of jobs from building work to furnace work to deep-sea fishing still involve a primitive confrontation with exacting physical tasks. Secondly, the basic attitudes and values developed in such jobs are still very important in the general working-class culture, and particularly the culture of the shop floor.'

'career'.[45] It remains central to what Hoggart calls 'a felt sense of working-class life' that in his words,

> After the age of eleven, when the scholarship boys and girls go off to the grammar-school, the rest look increasingly outward to the real life which will begin at fifteen, to the life with the group of older men and women which, for the first few years after school, forms the most powerfully educative force they know. Once at work, there is for most no sense of a career, of the possibilities of promotion. Jobs are spread around horizontally, not vertically; life is not seen as a climb, nor work as the main interest in it. (1957, pp. 17, 82)

This does not, as Hoggart also emphasizes, preclude respect for the 'good craftsman'. Nor does it preclude pride in hard work, or regret at the impact of the technology which has, as it were, replaced the master baker with the standard loaf. Indeed, it is intrinsic to the often intense attachment to demarcation in factories and shipyards and the determination of the 'skilled' to maintain their traditional position in the rank-order of manual earnings. Recognition that improvement in pay and conditions depends on collective solidarity more than individual effort is a wholly authentic response to the practices which continued to differentiate working-class jobs from middle-class careers. As a middle-class observer of Edwardian Bermondsey had put it in seeking to convey to his readers the life of the 'working man', he 'sighs neither with hope nor regret. He knows neither the pleasant surprises nor the disappointments of promotion' (Paterson 1911, p. 209). The change which followed the First World War was not that the incumbents of working-class roles came to share middle-class attitudes to work, but only that they gradually became aware that for an increasing minority intra-generational mobility out of the working class into the lower-middle or middle-middle class was starting to be a realistic prospect.

Once more than a third of men who had followed their fathers into working-class jobs were destined subsequently to rise into non-manual careers, a working-class job could no longer be seen as quite the life sentence it used to be. But it continued to be true for what continued to be the substantial majority of working-class men that the prospect of 'betterment' was seen not as a function of individual effort but of a general improvement in living standards reinforced, in the view of some, by the efforts of the trade unions. When Goldthorpe and his colleagues reinterviewed a sub-sample of their respondents

---

[45] 'Careerlessness' does not, however, preclude differences in work histories or strategies 'perhaps giving priority to the more modest goals of stability and job security rather than to advancement' (R. Brown 1982, p. 130). The term 'career' is deliberately used by some sociologists to cover 'the wholly domestic career of the full-time housewife' (Crompton and Sanderson 1990, p. 87). But following section 6 in chapter 2 of volume II, I distinguish 'careers' from 'roles' in terms of institutionalized expectations about future social mobility.

about their subjective experience of mobility (or immobility), they found that
the stable members of the working class, although representing their advancement as in some part the result of their own efforts, still envisaged the process
as 'a collective one, involving the working class as a whole or, at all events,
sizeable sections of it' (Goldthorpe 1980, p. 231). No matter how 'skilled', even
the men most optimistic about the future for their families and themselves
continued to have, as Goldthorpe and his co-authors had earlier described it
for the 'affluent workers' of Luton in the 1960s, 'not so much a belief in their
own individual capacities to "make good" as, rather, a belief in the probability
or inevitability of uninterrupted advance along a broad front' (1968, p. 143).[46]
The 'wages struggle', as the militants were apt to describe it, was a collective
experience for non-unionized workers in smaller plants or firms as well as for
unionized workers in bigger ones; and likewise, protection against unemployment was never a matter of individual provision but something for which even
the most highly paid manual workers looked to their trade union or friendly
society or (from the 1920s onwards) the state.[47]

This common aspect of working-class experience did not, however, override
the difference in what it was like to be in a skilled and in an unskilled or 'semi-
skilled' manual job. Zweig, who interviewed 601 men in four firms in 1958 and
1959, found a 'basic diversity in attitudes to work' amounting to a 'gulf'
between the skilled and the semi-skilled. The skilled men would say things like
'I was always interested in metals', 'I like fiddling with machines', 'It is in my
blood', 'You can always learn something new', 'I like making things', 'It is the
right type of work for me', and 'If I had my time over again, I would do the
same.' They tended to dislike piecework, which the semi-skilled tended to
prefer, and they disliked night work much more than did the semi-skilled.
'The skilled man has a trade which he follows no matter which firm he is
working for; the semi-skilled man looks for a job whose nature often changes
from one firm to another' (1961, p. 66). The semi- or unskilled could never

---

[46] Young and Willmott (1973, p. 159) found that some London manual workers 'considered they
could rise to chargehand, or foreman if they wished' (cf. Willmott 1966, p. 114 for a mirror
silverer with ambitions to become a manager). But the many who expected their living standards
to continue to advance if they remained in work expected them to do so 'not on the steep climb
of the successful young executive but at a more gentle if steady rate as a result of their trade
unions or of competition in the labour market'; and 'most of them knew that there was nothing
much they could do individually, only collectively, to get more money, let alone some of the
fringe benefits possessed by people in the office'.

[47] This is not to say that working-class people could never accumulate capital unless they won the
pools: a London transport driver for thirty-two years who died in 1972 left an estate valued at
over sixty thousand pounds. But he had no children, and his brother-in-law described him and
his wife as having just 'the bare necessities' (*The Times*, 29.2.72). Cf. John Hilton's comment
(1944, p. 49) on headlines of the type of 'In workhouse, but worth £2,000': 'If they weren't
exceptions they wouldn't be in the news.'

expect equivalent satisfaction from changes either from one firm to another or from one job to another within the same firm. As one employee of a big chemical company told an interviewer in the 1970s, 'You move from one boring, dirty, monotonous job to another boring, dirty, monotonous job. And then to another boring, dirty, monotonous job'; or in the words of another, 'You come in here sometimes and you think, "I'd do anything to get out of this" . . . You think, "God, what am I doing this for?" But next day you're back. I think all of us are mad' (Nichols and Beynon 1977, pp. 16, 17).

If left to stand by itself, however, this contrast still oversimplifies the range of working-class people's subjective experience of work. There are not merely the gradations of 'skill' within manufacturing industry but the whole range of jobs which are outside of manufacturing entirely. The shop floor and the assembly line are integral to both the experience and the image of the mid-twentieth-century British working class. But what about the building site, the brewery, the delivery van, the ship's hold, the bus, the dairy farm, the gas works, the storeroom, the municipal garden, the hospital kitchen, the railway line, the bakery, the timber yard, the car park, the furniture repair shop, the laboratory, the lock gate, the post office, the garage, or the fairground? And within all sectors there were differences in what it was like to be employed both across the industry and over time. Work-group relationships, use of technology, and attitudes of managers and supervisors could all vary widely. So too could the experience of deskilling even where, as in the motor-vehicle industry, the trend towards mass production 'on the track' most closely approximated to the stereotype. In Coventry, the practices of recruitment and training for 'skilled' roles and the workshop culture that went with them persisted, with the active consent of management, long after the days when brackets had been handmade and body work handpainted, and craftsmen had ordered their own parts. At Standard Motors, there was even a system of collectively determined piecework: as one man who joined as late as the 1970s put it, 'booking' and the 'rota' meant that 'when work is done, you could sit down and chat with your friends, read a newspaper, drink tea' and the 'shopsteward and the chargehand would get together how much they were going to "book" in terms of payment . . . it gave the worker this added sense of control, and independence on the job' (P. Thompson 1988, p. 63).

'Control' and 'independence'. These two words convey more vividly than any others what was always most important, independently of rates of pay, about the working-class experience of work. It applied equally to the skilled craftsman with his box of tools and to the unskilled navvy who expressed his independence by 'jacking' as and when he felt like it – to the point that, as it is described by a participant-observer who studied a hydroelectric construction site in the north of Scotland in the 1950s, 'There was little doubt, judging by the men's boasting, that the less the reason for jacking and the more sudden the decision to jack, the more effective it was as a gesture of independence' (Sykes 1969, p. 26). In between – on the assembly line or, as it might be, at the docks,[48] or in the garment factory or baking plant – workers continued to use a variety of devices to escape from supervision, to reduce the time needed to earn the same wages, to use their employers' equipment for making things of their own ('foreigners', as they are known throughout the British engineering industry), to cut corners, to manipulate piecework rates, to control output, or to double-book onto two jobs at once. Resistance might sometimes extend beyond 'skiving' or 'fiddling' to the point of deliberate sabotage which might or might not be just 'for a lark' (Humphries 1981, p. 145), or as a relief of tension and frustration (Taylor and Walton 1971). But attitudes towards activities tacitly assumed to be legitimate or at any rate acceptable could usually be distinguished from attitudes towards activities recognized as going too far.

The distinction is not always clear-cut, but it holds across the range of employment. There is nothing particularly 'working-class' about dishonesty: the shipyard worker who walks out of the dock gate with half a generator tied round his neck underneath his muffler is no more of a 'thief' than the booking-clerk who short-changes the rail passengers on Friday evenings, the head chef who loads sides of beef from the hotel kitchen into the boot of his car, the solicitor who holds back his clients' money to spend it on himself, the stockbroker who systematically churns investors' portfolios to generate spurious commissions, or the peer of the realm who fakes a multi-million pound insurance claim.[49] What is distinctive about working-class as opposed to middle-class experience is the 'covert institutions' which 'restore to the worker the autonomy of which the organisation has stripped him' (Mars 1982, p. 206). The middle-class salesman who fiddles his expense account is using the control and independence given him by his role to cheat his employer. But the working-class operative in the bakery manipulating the conveyor-belt process of production is using it to introduce into his role an element of autonomy which the practices officially defining it deny him (Ditton 1979, p. 160). The qualitative difference in the experience of manual wage-work from sales, technical, or clerical work is not just in the physical conditions but in the greater element of '*persistence* [my italics] of different social relations of work in

---

[48] Where the 'unfettered casual could come and go as he pleased, and he was loath, not seeing the shape of things to come, to give this up' (Oram 1970, p. 48, quoted by Turnbull and Sapsford 1992, p. 302).

[49] An ingenious practice to be found in certain sectors of British industry is for a purchasing manager to disclose the tenders of rival sub-contractors in return for 1 per cent of the value of the contract from his contact in the firm that wins it. Cf. Ditton (1977, p. 172) on fiddling as 'a sub-culture of legitimate commerce itself'.

the office' (Lane 1988, p. 92) from which the baking plant, shopfloor, dockyard, coalface, building site, and hotel kitchen are all cut off by an intervening layer of discipline bearing if anything more heavily, even on the 'skilled' worker, than it did on the late-Victorian and Edwardian artisan.

An alternative response was to move beyond the reach of the foreman or supervisor into self-employment, which, although it might not involve any significant change in class location, might involve a much more significant one in subjective experience. But any descriptive generalization must distinguish between the experience of those who valued it as a means towards independence from the experience of those for whom it was a response to lack of opportunity for sufficiently well-paid wage-earning employment. The roles of the 'penny capitalists' of the late-Victorian and Edwardian period had oiled the wheels, as it were, of an imperfectly lubricated mode of production by providing goods and services in places or at prices which their consumers could not find elsewhere, whether in retailing food and drink, building or repairing of roofs and walls, carting of coal or manure, shaving and hairdressing, or bookmaking and moneylending. But many were only doing what they could to 'make a little money on the side' rather than going into business 'with the express intention, at least in the long term, of attaining independence of wage labour' (Benson 1983, p. 130). The distinction continued to be relevant in the mid-twentieth-century sub-type of the capitalist mode of production despite the increase in real working-class earnings and the provision of unemployment benefit by the state. The experience and attitudes of Scase and Goffee's ex-farm-labourer whom we met in section 9 have to be quite differently described from those of a handyman doing part-time jobs while claiming unemployment benefit, or a builder working 'on the lump', or a merchant seaman driving a minicab during his time ashore, or a joiner installing double-glazing at weekends for payment in cash. These practices and roles, while peripheral to the central institutions governing working-class life, were at the same time integral to working-class experience as possible options to be contemplated. But they offer as little support for generalized left-wing descriptions of the homogenization of proletarian experience as they do for generalized right-wing descriptions of working-class individualism, enterprise, and self-help.

The other, and more important, qualification which needs to be made concerns the experience of *not* working. The reported facts and figures are as familiar to academic observers as the subjective experience is to 'them'. In the 1930s, as in the 1980s, skilled manual workers were more likely to be unemployed than clerical, technical, or sales workers, and unskilled workers more likely still. But what cannot be inferred from the facts and figures alone is what it was like to feel at risk of unemployment even if you were one of those fortunate enough to escape it. It is true that at both times there was a minority who, once a minimum level of subsistence was guaranteed by the state, preferred not to work – a state of affairs exacerbated by the 'poverty trap' resulting from the high marginal cost of forfeiting benefits to those who returned to employment in low-paid jobs.[50] But such evidence of representative attitudes as is available points to the inference that the overwhelming majority would work if they could, and that even those who have been out of work for extended periods still share the attitudes and values of their fellow-members of the working class (Heath 1992).[51] The exceptions might be of two very different kinds: 'individualists' who would say to an interviewer things like 'It's an advantage to be able on a nice sunny day to go down on the beach. You know it's nice. Besides I prefer to stay at home', and 'activists' who would say things like: 'I'm lucky in as much as when I was made redundant I didn't drop out of the trade union and I'm in a very good trade union as far as unemployment is concerned . . . Also branch activity and divisional activity within the union can really keep you involved and feel that you're doing something . . . for your class for your people' (Bagguley 1991, pp. 150–1).[52] But it would be unwise to interpret even responses like the first as representative of a 'dependency culture'. Relatively few of the able-bodied unemployed, in the 1980s any more than in the 1930s, hoped never to be in paid work again.[53] Subjectively, there is all the difference in the world between resignation, apathy, and a disinclination to try too hard or too soon to find a job which will offer little more in take-home pay than staying on the dole and a positive decision to join the vagrants, drop-outs, dossers, casuals, and benefit fraudsters

[50] Or not so low-paid. In a case cited by a London Citizens' Advice Bureau in a parliamentary briefing note on the Jobseekers' Bill 1995, 'The husband was ill and off work and the woman was offered a job paying £13,000 per annum which she was keen to accept. The couple had one child but even with the recently introduced child care disregard under family credit, travel costs and higher payments of rent and council tax meant that the family would be at least £40 a week worse off.'

[51] Heath's sample is family units from the 1989 British Social Attitudes Survey where neither partner was in paid employment and at least one member had been in receipt of income support within the previous five years. He offers this as an operational definition of the underclass (p. 33). But that term should, as I argued in section 15 of chapter 1, be reserved for roles *permanently* dependent on charity or the state for the income accruing to them.

[52] Cf. the comment in the Pilgrim Trust's *Men Without Work* (1938, p. 135) on the feeling 'that solidarity with those with whom they had once worked gave them a sort of independent status in relation to the community as a whole' among those of the long-term unemployed who kept up their union membership.

[53] Gallie and Vogler (1993) found that the 22% of their sample unemployed who were receiving benefit but not seeking work had a significantly lower level of work commitment (64%) than either claimant seekers (81%) or non-registered seekers (82%). But the claimant non-seekers included a higher proportion of older workers and younger mothers. Cf. the finding of Wallace (1987, p. 99) about a sample of school-leavers: 'whilst their present life-styles appeared to accept and adapt to unemployment, their views of the future did not'.

who have no intention of taking up permanent employment even when it is offered to them.

Much more representative of the subjective experience of the semi- and unskilled working class in periods of high unemployment was the persistent sense of insecurity attaching to jobs in which workers always knew that they could be replaced at any time. This applied not only in regions where from 1920 on the decline of the 'staple' industries involved the relentless shedding of skilled as well as unskilled labour. It applied equally in the regions where the expansion of new industries kept the rate of unemployment as low as 1 per cent or 2 per cent. In Slough, which was a boom town in the 1930s, the expansion of the food processing and electrical engineering industries might offer unskilled jobs thought particularly suitable for young women (Glucks-mann 1986) and some employers might, like Mars, pay their non-unionized workforce higher than union rates (Clegg 1979, p. 102). But the young women, being readily replaceable, could be attractive to employers precisely in anticipation of high labour turnover; and they were in any case under threat of replacement by young men migrating into the area from South Wales or elsewhere because it was well known to be an area of low unemployment (Savage 1988, p. 233). Similarly, the non-unionized worker on the assembly line at Ford, well-paid though he might feel himself to be, was always conscious of the risk of being told by the foreman on Friday afternoon that he needn't come back on Monday morning. In the steel industry, after the collapse of the post-war boom, to a worker fortunate that 'our place remained a steelworks and never a grass-covered heap of dismantled junk' £3 from alternate weeks on the furnaces and on the dole 'was millions compared to thousands of other steelworkers' incomes' (McGeown 1967, pp. 104–5). In the 1980s, when it was not manufacturing but service industry which provided the best opportunities for recruits, those without technical or computing skills were conscious of the inherent risk that employers would replace them by part-time or otherwise 'non-standard' workers at lower cost (Rubery 1988, p. 266). For some skilled manual workers, the loss of a hitherto secure-seeming job was if anything more painful,[54] as might be the experience of a bank clerk or salesman (or woman)

---

[54] For example, the 47-year-old self-described 'ordinary respectable artisan' included in Beales and Lambert (1934) who wrote about his experience of finding it impossible for a year to find work in his own trade or even, thereafter, outside it: 'I have thrown myself into revolutionary movements from time to time, but it all seems so futile. The one important thing is to get hold of money. I'd steal if I could get away with it. The outlook as far as I'm concerned is hopeless. I've given up dreaming of any return to my former life and work, and just hang on hoping something will happen before I die' (p. 76). Cf. Hilton et al. (1935, p. 327): 'When a lad is set to serve his apprenticeship his parents know that for five years or so he will not be self-supporting. In the past the immediate sacrifice was outweighed by the knowledge that at the end of his time he would be set up for life. Now that security has gone.'

who did lose his or her job, whether in the 1920s or 1980s or, for that matter, in between. In the working class, the experience of the miners in the 1980s is particularly striking. But the miners, for all their importance to the political as well as the economic history of twentieth-century Britain, were, as I have remarked more than once, unrepresentative in several ways of the experience of the working class. For the purpose of descriptive generalization, the pervasive contrast is between the experience of relatively greater security attaching to 'skilled' working-class jobs even in times of high unemployment and the endemic insecurity attaching to unskilled jobs even when times were better.

Thus far, I have described working-class experience in almost exclusively male terms. This order of priorities is, however, descriptively apt, since it mirrors a dominant ideology whereby paid employment is the norm for men and domestic and childrearing work the norm for women, particularly during the period of their lives when they are presumed to have young children to rear. The presumption is as explicit as anywhere in the Beveridge Report. Working-class women who did want to be in full-time jobs, to join a trade union, and to be active in the Labour movement could not but be conscious that they were doing so in an environment in which the traditional doctrine of 'separate spheres' continued to be upheld. It is true that by the 1970s, this had come to be overtly recognized by both participants and observers. But the TUC's charter *Equality for Women within Trade Unions*, published in 1979, 'was found to have had what was euphemistically referred to as "a mixed response" ' (Purcell 1988, p. 176). It was hardly surprising that women should be under-represented in blast furnaces or at the coalface or on deep-sea trawlers. But they continued to be very under-represented in apprenticeships to 'skilled' trades. In the 1980s, despite the increasing awareness of the issue among both employers and prospective employees, researchers still found that 'For a woman to aspire to technical competence is, in a very real sense, to transgress the rules of gender' (Cockburn 1986, p. 185) and that 'women's jobs' were still 'heavily imbued with the maternal and caring elements of the stereotypical female role' (Crompton and Sanderson 1990, p. 162).

The causal relation between this institutional environment and the opinions expressed by the working-class women who have grown up within it is, as always, difficult to disentangle. But however their responses to researchers' questions are to be explained, the data of the 1980 Women and Employment Survey 'suggest that most women accept or accommodate to the sexual division of labour we have described. Only small minorities were very traditional or very radical in their attitudes towards women's roles or position in society' (Martin and Roberts 1984, p. 192). Moreover, women are found to display both a relative indifference, by comparison with men, to trade-union activities

(Cockburn 1987) and a disposition to understate the 'skill' required by their jobs in contrast to the disposition of men to overstate it (Howell *et al.* 1990, p. 211). There is no implication in this that women in working-class jobs could not be radicalized by a common sense of relative deprivation, just as even the most 'respectable' working-class housewives could be radicalized by a threat to their expectations for their families 'by the inter-war means test, for example, by rapacious landlords or cuts in the children's free milk' (B. Harrison 1989, p. 128). But theirs has remained, for all the changes reported in chapter 2, a different world from the world of work as experienced by their fathers, brothers, husbands, boyfriends, and sons, and their attitudes and feelings have to be separately described in any proffered generalization about the working-class experience of work in twentieth-century England.

§13. But work, or the lack of it, is only one aspect of working-class experience. What about the patterns of residence and recreation to which I referred in passing? And what about the distinctions of status within working-class communities on which so many observers commented both in the late-Victorian and Edwardian period and in the decades after it?

There is much anecdotal testimony to the efforts of working-class mothers, even in the least 'respectable' households, to instil some rudimentary 'manners' into their children. Tommy Morgan, born to drunken and violent parents in Blackfriars in 1892, later recalled how he and his siblings were never allowed to put their arms on the table. ' "Get them arms off!" Wallop – you know. Put a knife in your mouth – you got a hiding for that. Oh she taught us good manners as far as she could go' (T. Thompson 1981, p. 17). It is a reminiscence which vividly authenticates – or at least appears to – Margaret Loane's account (1911, p. 221) of catching in working-class homes 'the thousand times repeated warnings of the nurseries and schoolrooms of the well-to-do'. But descriptions like these need to be carefully construed. Gavron (1966, p. 76) says of her respondents 'In conversation the working-class mothers sounded very like the middle class in their attitudes to their children.' But she then goes on to say 'In practice, however, they appeared more aggressive, and less in control, than their words suggested.' There is thus a double risk of inauthenticity. Working-class parents might behave in ways which would lead middle-class observers to attribute to them an aspiration to the standards of the 'well-to-do'. But, as I emphasized in section 14 of chapter 1, working-class norms of respectability must never be assumed to equate with middle-class norms of respectability.[55] The contrast which the descriptive

---

[55] Was rural England different from the towns? Flora Thompson (1939, p. 29) says that 'good manners prevailed'. But this turns out to mean that children were expected to eat what they were given in silence except for 'please' and 'thank you'. Meanwhile, Father might be shovelling

sociologist needs to draw is with what 'respectable' working-class people themselves disapproved of among the 'rough'.

When Richard Hoggart arrived in the barrack-hut in Oswestry which housed his platoon in the autumn of 1940, he observed that:

> Beds were soon exchanged so that the main groups were together. At the far end from the door, and that gave a little time to hide gambling or secret drinking, was the rougher and mainly urban group: getting drunk too often, vomiting on the floor now and again, smoking furtively after lights out, fiddling booze or rations with bent storekeepers, boasting endlessly about 'bints' they had had or proposed to have, refusing to get under the shower more often than every week or two, now and again brawling with similar groups from other huts or within themselves. (1990, p. 6)

As with the middle-class phenomenon of post-war 'de-officerization', the enlistment and basic training of recruits drawn from the whole range of working-class jobs and homes provides an opportunity for a description which the abnormality of the context makes all the more vivid. But Hoggart's description of the contrast between his own life-style and attitudes and those of the unrespectable among his hutmates is a microcosmic reflection of a contrast equally observable in peacetime throughout the communities in which he and they had been born and reared. It is a contrast whose terms are defined from the 'respectable' end: the vocabulary in which the behaviour of the 'rough' is stigmatized is not that of the 'rough' themselves. But it informs the subjective experience of the rough even, or all the more, when they repudiate it.

There is ample evidence that the feelings of contempt and mistrust between the two are mutual (Klein 1965, I, p. 266). But a study of social relations among the working-class inhabitants of the pseudonymous town of 'Winston Parva' in 1959–60 (Elias and Scotson 1965) found not only that the established residents of the 'Village' outranked the newer residents of the 'Estate' in their own estimation but that the residents of the 'Estate' were powerless to retaliate despite the lack of a factual basis for their stigmatization. Most of the 'Estate' families did not have the 'low morals' which the 'Villagers' attributed to them, yet they 'could be put to shame if the "villager" used in their presence a humiliating code word, symbol of their lower status such as "rat alley"' (p. 101). Or, as might be expected, some of the adolescent children of 'Estate' families would try 'to get their own back by behaving badly with greater deliberation' (p. 129).[56] This response was in turn likely to perpetuate the

---

peas into his mouth with his knife, Mother drinking her tea from her saucer and the children licking their plates, which 'passed as a grateful compliment to Mother's good dinner'.

[56] Cf. e.g. Spencer (1964, p. 254) on 'the standards of behaviour characteristic of the "rougher" of two sets' of children involved with an adventure playground on the Upfield housing estate in Bristol.

stereotyping which had caused it in the first place. But explanation apart, the researchers are concerned particularly to convey 'how deeply the consciousness of their standing among others had sunk into the children's consciousness of themselves' (p. 145). These subjective distinctions are just as keenly felt as any between one middle-class status-group and another, and often more explicitly expressed. Here, for example, is part of the first conversation recorded by Tony Parker (1983, pp. 11–12) in his description of the residents of the Providence housing estate in East London – his informant is the driver of one of the mini-vans of the mobile caretakers:

> No I don't live on the estate mate, no I certainly don't thank God. The rubbish of the local authority, that's who lives here if you want my honest opinion about it; and there's no one gets more experience of it than me, I can tell you. Cleaning up shit is all what my job is mostly nowadays: shit from the corridors, shit from the lifts, shit from the stairs . . . But there's still nice parts though too you know, still some very nice parts . . . In one word? If you asked me to sum up the estate in one word, what'd I say . . . what I'd say is 'mixed'. That's the word I'd use . . . Eh, don't get me wrong will you? I don't mind coloureds you know, so long as they're good coloureds – know what I mean?

A descriptive contrast between 'respectable' owner-occupier and 'rough' council tenants became increasingly commonplace after the Second World War. But it needs to be qualified in several ways. In part, it reflects a tension between age-sets: in the words of a long-standing resident of a Liverpool estate, 'when I moved in here in 1929 you needed a letter from the Holy Ghost himself to get a council house . . . Nowadays, they only seem to give houses to layabouts and ex-jailbirds' (M. McKenna 1991, p. 188). But it also reflects the increase in the proportion of working-class home-owners of whom many might be no more 'respectable' than many council tenants. It is true that council estates became increasingly the residual strongholds of Labour Party support: council-house tenants were twice as likely to vote Labour in 1992 as council-house buyers (Garrett 1994, p. 115). But 'respectability' is not to be equated either descriptively or explanatorily with Conservatism. The complex relation of 'respectability' to housing tenure was particularly significant in the early experiences of women residents of new estates like Wythenshawe, outside Manchester, who explicitly insisted that they were not 'slum-clearance' tenants (Hughes and Hunt 1992, p. 88). Later, as differentiation increased between the more and the less 'respectable' council estates, so-called 'sink' estates with their broken windows, weed-choked gardens, and graffiti-covered grilles concentrated together tenants whom both the local authorities and the 'respectable' tenants themselves wished to keep separate. But it merged with, rather than displaced, the late-Victorian and Edwardian pattern of segregation by subjective criteria of status within the working classes which extended not merely to different streets within the same district, but to different ends of the same street (Johnson 1988, pp. 33–4). It could even matter to the extent that, for example, residents of Campbell Road, Islington, between the wars would, if looking for work or getting into trouble with the police, try to 'pass' by giving a false address (White 1986, p. 51). And similar differentiation by status could be observed in rural as in urban England: 'In Wing, as in Exton, the council house "end" of the village is on the outskirts and there are two pubs; the council tenants tend to drink in one, while the owner occupiers go to the posher pub down the street' (Duckers and Davies 1990, p. 132).

Yet through all this, there remains the difference in attitudes and mores consistently separating the working from the middle classes. The social worker on the same Providence Estate commented on it as a place 'where on the whole people have a great sense of belonging' – a sense which was put by one resident himself (who at the time of the interview had been 'off bleeding work six fucking months now') like this:

> I think the best thing or at least it is to me is that our sort of people have what I think's a very easy-going attitude towards life. They don't rush in and pass judgement on other people; they nearly all seem to regard themselves as being in a way part of one big family. This may be just my opinion but I think it's a working-class thing. I don't think you get it with the nobs, they only stick together when they're closing ranks to defend their wealth against other people getting their hands on it. But the working class don't have any wealth in that sense; they do have a wealth but it's more what you might call the enjoyment of the richness of living. That's something which they share among each other, and I suppose because they're so ready to share it that's what makes it what it is. (Parker 1983, pp. 348–9)

This self-conscious invocation of a specifically working-class norm may be thought by some readers to have a touch of specifically working-class bullshit about it. But it is consistent with the equally self-conscious repudiation of lower-middle-class 'pretensions' and 'snobbism' documented by Goldthorpe and colleagues for the 'affluent' workers of Luton (1969, p. 152). Remarks along these lines are always open to the objection that what people will say to an interviewer may not be reflected in the way they actually behave: however sharp the distinction between stereotypical middle-class and working-class attitudes, values, and mores, many English people live their lives on both sides of the line either through individual intra-generational mobility across it or through membership of families which straddle it. But its subjective significance is undeniable. It is vividly authenticated in a study of another of those rituals of the kind which anthropologists are apt to find particularly revealing – the street parties held at the time of the Queen's coronation in 1953. In Birkenhead, where an explicit distinction between 'respectable' and 'rough' coexisted with an explicit view of middle-class areas as 'hoity-toity', the 'respectable' almost all saw themselves as 'working-class' at the same time as seeing middle-class neighbourhoods as lacking in 'neighbourliness':

> While it was known that respectable people in more desirable residential areas tended to consider it 'common' to hold street parties, this did not prevent the more respectable in Mersey ward from organizing and joining in them with gusto, without feeling themselves any the less respectable. While they often described their parties as 'nice', 'refined', 'reserved', or 'decent', these epithets referred to a type of organisation which middle-class people tended to regard with disapproval. (Broady 1956, p. 239)

Spontaneous expression of detailed awareness of the distinctions of this nature by working-class people rather than by middle-class observers are, unsurprisingly, rare in the academic literature. But a 31-year-old upholsterer from Nottingham answered a Mass Observation questionnaire in 1939 in terms which, however unrepresentative, nevertheless describe very precisely what such distinctions can mean in terms of subjective experience. 'Myself I should classify: skilled artisan by trade; middle working class in living habits and manners; round about £3–£4 in income; the W.E.A. study-in-spare-time class, as differing from the pub-and-dance-and-girl class of young men.' And in his social contacts, his stated preference was for 'informed, but respectable working-class people' rather than people of superior background who 'behave in such a mannerly fashion in which I have no training, who have a code which I do not understand' (quoted in Cronin 1984, p. 73). The language may sound a little dated half a century later. But the descriptive point which it makes remains authentic. For all the overlap of middle-class and working-class roles in social space, and for all the movement of individuals between them, neither impressionistic nor survey evidence can sustain a descriptive generalization which fails to convey the two different sub-cultural norms of respectability in terms of which these roles are subjectively experienced by their incumbents.

To complete the description, however, we must go back and pick up the concluding remark of the man in the mini-van on the Providence Estate. 'Racism', however defined, is far from being a universal part of either working-class (or middle-class) experience. In many regions and communities, from the villages of Northumberland to the farmsteads of Exmoor, it has remained as remote during the twentieth century as it was during the nineteenth.[57] But in London and the Midlands, it has been intrinsic to the experience of the ethnic

---

[57] Not that it follows that attitudes and experiences would have been different in the countryside if immigrants had settled there in significant numbers. Alfred Dann, Secretary of the National Union of Agricultural Workers, to George Isaacs, Minister of Labour, 30.10.47: 'We appreciate, of course, that these people are human beings, but it would seem evident that to bring coloured labour into the countryside would be a most unfortunate act' (quoted by Lunn 1985, pp. 24–5).

majority and minority alike; and it has been more salient in working-class than middle-class experience, given not only the concentration of underprivileged ethnic groups in working-class districts but the more overt manifestations of hostility reported from them.[58] In the London of the 1920s, 'anti-alien' attitudes and behaviour were directed principally against East End Jews who were popularly supposed to have evaded military service and profited from the war (E. R. Smith 1989, p. 55). After the Second World War, when as I reported in section 9 of chapter 2, Blacks rather than Jews became the principal targets of hostility, the stereotype fused criminality with the rejection of work (Gilroy 1987, p. 73). Immigrants, whatever their society of origin, always faced the double bind that if they found work, they would be seen as taking it away from the native-born, while if they didn't they would be seen as exploiting the social services – an attitude ('they don't want to work', 'they came here to get all they can') often bound up with a mistaken view of the social services as actuarially based ('they haven't been here long enough to pay in', 'we've been paying taxes all our lives') (Rose and Deakin 1969, p. 571). A detailed description of these attitudes would need to extend to the different perceptions of the sub-culture of different ethnic groups and to the ambivalence of those whose experience of racism is tempered by awareness of having a standard of living 'which many could only have dreamt of back in the Caribbean' (James 1989, p. 237). But that 'racism', however it should be explained and whatever value-judgement you may be disposed to make about it, is what 'they' experience is incontestable; and out of all the literature (including novels and poems) in which this is conveyed, none is more vividly illuminating than that which describes what it is like for children from ethnic minority communities when they first meet it at school. 'My first taste of racism was in the language of white children. As a child I was advised to respond along the lines of

> Sticks 'n stones
> might break ma bones
> but words'll
> never hurt me.

Given that words like "nigger", "paki", "darkie" invariably did hurt it seemed a pity to say they didn't' (Sulter 1988, pp. 57–8).

---

[58] Contrast, for example, the experience of a black West Indian professional ('No one cares if after a hard day's graft the extent of my social pleasures are limited simply because blacks are not allowed; no one cares if I am a professional man when I go to the shops and a white employee has no desire to serve me; no one cares if, as a black professional, I wish to buy a house in a particular area of the city, when the estate agents would suggest an alternative; and no one cares when as a black professional I question the educational output that is being given to my children and to many of the young people I work with') with that of the working-class victims of deliberate skinhead violence (Husband 1987, p. 197 and chapter 4).

§14. Is it then possible to offer any short general description of 'working-class culture' in the sense of representative responses and attitudes to the modes of production, persuasion, and coercion in twentieth-century English society? Any generalization (and I offer two) must reflect not only the disjunction between the processes of social selection and representative role-incumbents' awareness of them but also the ambivalence in the minds of working-class people who are simultaneously aware that their and their families' life-chances are improving and that they remain, all the same, relatively underprivileged within the structure and culture of their society as a whole.

The first generalization rests on the observation that whatever the increase in the rates of individual mobility, whether inter- or intra-generational, it did not become a prevailing working-class norm (Richardson 1977, p. 278). It is this which lies behind the many descriptive accounts of the discouraging attitudes of working-class parents to their children's education. Here for example is the pseudonymous 'Mark Benney's' 'Uncle Fred' (1936, p. 85): ' "What's he want with yer fancy ideas?" he'd ask blightingly when Mother talked of higher education and the Civil Service. "I was earning good money at 'is age! Give the boy a charnce – 'e won't get nowhere by gluing 'is arse to a noffice stool!".'[59] After the Second World War (and the 1944 Education Act), the authors of *Coal is Our Life* still remarked on the view of the miners they talked to that daughters' education was a waste of time (Dennis *et al.* 1956, p. 239). In the early 1960s, a Labour Party official in Luton said to a journalist about the 'affluent' car workers, 'The educational side is lacking, that's where they fall down. When it comes to children, they are quite content to let them go to an ordinary school' (G. Turner 1963, p. 10). Likewise, a study of middle-class and working-class wives in Kentish Town in 1960–1 found that 96 per cent of middle-class wives compared with 44 per cent of working-class wives valued education for their children, that of these 37 per cent said neither they nor their husbands considered education important, and that a further 19 per cent thought education important for boys but less so for girls (Gavron 1966, pp. 77–8). Many felt, as did many of the children themselves, that the academic curriculum was completely irrelevant to the adult roles which the children would occupy: 'Most boys at my school, their attitude was this isn't going to help me when I leave school so I won't bother . . . Maths, history, all that crap' (Willmott 1966, p. 80).[60]

---

[59] As it happens, 'Mark Benney' is the same person as the co-author of Benney *et al.* (1956), a study of voting behaviour in Greenwich in the General Election of 1950: he subsequently published a further autobiographical volume suggestively titled *Almost a Gentleman*. I owe the reference to Martin Bulmer.

[60] An attitude with which some of their teachers sympathized. Thus Partridge (1966, p. 153): 'There seems to be so little relationship between what is taught here and between the work the

In the same descriptive vein, Hargreaves (1967, p. 39) says of a school in a working-class area of a Northern industrial town that: 'In 4A the norm was against working too hard, that is, failing to make full use of opportunities for "messing" which bring relief from work. In 4B the norm is against working *at all*: "messing" is the alternative to work.' Jackson and Marsden, in a study of eighty-eight working-class children who *did* go to grammar school in a Northern city, found that a disproportionate number had a parent who had either had a secondary education themselves or passed their scholarship examination but not been able to take up their place (1962, p. 60); and they also describe in detail the difficulties which many of these children experienced both at the school and in their home communities. Thus, 'when I got to Ash Grange and wore the uniform, the other children used to shout about that. I didn't mind so much. I felt superior. But I had a violin as well, and I used to dread carrying that violin case. I used to plot my way from the yard at home to the teachers, but that violin case seemed to stand out – that brought me more bashings than anything else' (p. 96). One mother in East London told an interviewer how her husband's family were united in opposition to a daughter's scholarship because 'his family were a family of work-people. Some of them said I ought to be ashamed of myself' (Young and Willmott 1957, p. 147). The children's relations with their friends, too, could be affected, both when the friends were at a secondary modern school in their 'clan' and after the age of fifteen when the friends were at work 'and you were still at school and they regarded you as a kind of low life' (Willmott 1966, p. 89). Thus: 'it gets me mad to see these kids working in a fucking office. I just dunno how they do it, honestly. I've got freedom, I've got . . . I can get money, it's hard to explain . . .' (Willis 1977, p. 104).

Remarks like this last one are not always easy to understand in the tertiary, descriptive sense: they may reflect a felt need to repudiate an ambition which, once avowed, could only imply an awareness of failure. But they too have to be seen in the context of the steadily increasing opportunities for upward mobility. Not only was there bound to be, for the arithmetical reasons discussed in section 13 of chapter 2, a combination of high absolute and low relative mobility rates out of the working class but there were also bound to be some working-class parents who actively encouraged their children to take advantage

boys will eventually do and their individual cultural backgrounds . . . The only school activity that does have some relevance to the cultural background of most of the boys here is sport', and Hargreaves (1982, p. 21): 'Many teachers can readily recognize the difference between individual misconduct and counter-cultural opposition, and they often have ambivalent feelings about the latter, having a partial sympathy with it'; or Paul Harrison (1983, pp. 293–4): 'Inner-city teachers with no ultimate power to enforce their will, are all too often tempted to throw in the towel. The sheer pressure of pupil resistance can easily turn them into the unwilling accomplices of children's low expectations, midwives of educational failure.'

of what opportunities they saw.[61] Just as there were always middle-class parents determined to secure for their children the protection which they believed that a fee-paying school could provide against the risk of downward mobility, so were there always some working-class parents eager for their children to 'better themselves' in a way which had been out of the question for them. Those children of working-class parents who remained in the working class had, therefore, an added reason to legitimate their immobility in their own eyes, and their parents likewise. From 1918 on, the increasing number of children of working-class parents who stayed on at school, of whom an increasing proportion went on to university, were undergoing an experience much less anomalous than the altogether exceptional scholarship boys born into the late-Victorian and Edwardian working class who determinedly shed their accents and dialects on the way to the world of 'letters' (Waller 1987, p. 22). But the attitudes of the majority were still the attitudes of men and women who, in sensing that they *were* the majority, were right to do so.

The second generalization, about the experience of underprivilege, follows almost self-evidently from the description already given of those aspects of working-class life which, despite all the changes reported in chapter 2, are hardly less different from middle-class life than they were two or more generations ago. But it too involves attitudes to social mobility, and in particular the subjective aspect of the distinction between individual and collective mobility which I touched on in section 15 of chapter 1. Two distinct responses are open to the incumbents of subordinate roles who feel relatively deprived. The first is to hope for individual mobility – that is, future incumbency of a higher-ranked role. The second is to hope for collective mobility – that is, for the sort of 'advance on a broad front' which will raise the incumbent's present role to equality with a comparative reference group located above it. The two attitudes can of course be combined. Bevin and many other less celebrated figures within the Labour movement rose to positions of influence without abandoning the collectivist ambition for the working class as a whole to which their individual rise was due. But, as I have emphasized already, such careers are very unrepresentative. There are effectively two routes to 'becoming middle-class': the first is to move into a non-manual occupational role (or, alternatively, to acquire a significant capital sum or form a durable attachment to someone who has already done either or

---

[61] There is some anecdotal evidence that working-class mothers rather than fathers have encouraged educational aspirations in their children, but although there is no reason to doubt the authenticity of the anecdotes there is reason to doubt their representativeness: Halsey *et al.* (1980, p. 89), drawing on the Oxford mobility sample of 10,000 men in England and Wales in 1972, found that 'Either or both parents play their part in forming the educational fate of children.'

both of these); the second is to occupy a nominally 'working-class' role such as that of professional sportsman whose location in social space rises to the same level as that of the lower-middle or middle-middle class, or even, as the mode of persuasion evolves, entitles an outstandingly successful incumbent of the role, like the jockey Gordon Richards or the cricketer Len Hutton, to a knighthood.

It is difficult to generalize about working-class attitudes to this choice for the familiar reason that the immobile are less likely to be the articulate. The synopses of working-class autobiographies published in the first half of the twentieth century (Burnett *et al.* 1987) reveal much readily understandable (in the tertiary, descriptive sense) propensity to political activism in youth, followed in many cases by a rise into a middle-class role in middle age. But these need to be set against the subjective experience of working-class people with no more interest in trying to change their lives than in trying to describe them. Here is an account of a meeting with one such by the son of a mining family in County Durham who has gone back to the village which his father thankfully left in order to try to find out what 'their' lives were like:

> Not for the first time since I came to Horden, I thought of the meaning of the phrase, 'The Raising of the Working Class'. It had a fine-sounding ring, but what did it actually mean? It implied that the working class should somehow transform and transcend itself. But from what, and to what? Till now I had naturally assumed it meant getting away from the ugliness and limitation of Horden and the whole East Durham world. According to my grandfather's vision, as I understand it, the working class should 'raise' itself through education. He had made every effort to ensure that my father had the best education available, and my father, like many of his more able fellows, had lost no time in leaving the area and discarding as many as possible of those attitudes and ways of behaving that had made them working class. So was that what was meant by 'the Raising of the Working Class'? That they should simply become middle class.
>
> Here, however, represented by Harry, was a culture not so much at variance with, but simply indifferent to this self-improving ethos – a culture enterprising, virtually self-sufficient and resolutely apolitical, that had no aspiration to be anything other than what it was . . . Here was a man, thoughtful and imaginative, whose considerateness and cheerful stoicism seemed expressive of an innate gallantry, who actually liked many of the aspects of Horden – the betting shop, the Big Club, and doubtless the bingo hall too – that I felt so bitterly that people should want to be raised from. (Hudson 1994, pp. 128–9)

Any descriptive generalization about the sense of underprivilege needs, accordingly, to distinguish not only between those working-class people who hope for individual and those who hope for collective mobility but between both of these and those who have no interest in either; and these have in turn to be divided between those like Harry, about whose attitudes there is nothing which could plausibly be described as 'deferential', and those whose attitudes as recorded by survey interviewers lead them to be described as not merely deferential but 'submissive' (Nordlinger 1967, p. 91).

Where life-style as such is in question, there is even less justification for describing representative working-class attitudes as reflecting an implicit aspiration for assimilation to middle-class norms and values. This is more than a matter of different criteria of 'respectability'. It is a matter also of authentic differences of taste. Although in section 8 of chapter 2 I took issue with those observers who already in the 1930s were reporting an assimilation of middle-class and working-class life-styles, continuing self-differentiation on the part of middle-class people need not be inconsistent with a reciprocal self-differentiation on the part of working-class people who stay away from the antiques market in Farnham not because they would feel uncomfortably out of place but because they have no interest in antiques. Mark Hudson found it to be part of the 'demonology of East Durham' that the one 'posh' estate in Peterlee was inhabited by the kind of people who 'joined the golf club and invited each other to dinner-parties' (1994, p. 207). How is this to be construed? In a world where Durham miners were genuinely separate from but equal to managers and professionals who prefer the golf club to the bingo hall, the difference in life-styles would be a matter of mutual disagreement on level terms. Although there is a tendency in all cultures for aesthetic differences to acquire moral and even political overtones, they can still do so without being tied to a systactic hierarchy of values. Or, in the twentieth-century English mode of persuasion, can they?

The answer to this question leads back once again to education – or rather, school. The values of science and scholarship ('maths, history, all that crap') may be as alien to many children from working-class homes as the values of thrift and useful hobbies were to their late-Victorian and Edwardian grand-parents. But they are the values of the dominant ideology. Few if any working-class (or, for that matter, middle-class) schoolchildren are likely to put it that way to themselves. But that, nevertheless, is what their experience is of. It is not an experience of old-fashioned disciplinarianism so much as of up-to-date credentialism. Even though the formal qualifications come later – tests, exams, diplomas, degrees, and so forth – no schoolchild can fail to sense that the rationale of the curriculum is that it is a ticket to a role in an adult world whose priorities it reflects. Ironic as it may come to seem to a working-class child (Hargreaves 1982, p. 76, quoting from Common 1951) that schools in working-class districts should take pride in how *few* recruits into working-class roles they turn out, that is what the working-class child perceives. The teachers may not seem either to themselves or to their pupils as agents of a mode of persuasion directed to the deliberate subordination of working-class to middle-class values. Indeed, those whose personal presuppositions and purposes are of the Left may, on the contrary, see themselves as actively encouraging their pupils to question the nature and purpose of the system of which they are a part. But as an innovative Scottish schoolmaster put it in the light of his own experience in the early 1960s, within a regional sub-culture where, in contrast to England and Wales, 'working folk treated education with reverence',

> I hadn't realised before the extent to which the education committees of Britain, the convenors, the directors, the inspectors, the professors, have lost touch with this suspicious, potentially generous but uncommitted new generation. I hadn't realised the gulf between these pupils, so responsive to even the smallest efforts to meet their needs, and their elders, conscientious, sincere, but unimaginative, and unaware that the education system has no nourishment to offer them. (R. F. Mackenzie 1963, pp. 31, 138)

Nor is it as if when working-class children emerged, more or less thankfully, from the schoolroom into the adult world they found the dominant ideology any more nearly neutral as between working-class and middle-class priorities and standards. Robert Graves and Alan Hodge commented in *The Long Week-End* on the 'curious class-distinctions' to be observed in the nomenclature of the residential buildings erected between the wars: 'working-class flats formed "tenements", and were usually named "So-and-So Building"; whereas middle-class and luxury flats formed "blocks", and were usually "So-and-So Court" or "House" or "Close" (1940, p. 175). Descriptive nuances like these are, perhaps, more significant to the observer than to the observed, for whom they may be a matter of indifference even when pointed out to them. But the messages purveyed by radio, the cinema, and television could hardly fail to reinforce an impression of a world in which patterns of life-style and consumption were ideologically defined from above rather than below. 'Democratization' of manners and mores might extend to a common taste for jazz and later, rock music, a common style of leisure clothes, and a common enthusiasm for selected cultural inputs from the more populist entertainment industry of the United States. But it did not extend, even among the most affluent working-class households, to a shared life-style of sherry-glasses, water-colours, bridge fours, theatre stalls, thank-you letters, coffee-table art-books, and *haute cuisine*. As it is put by the social worker on the Providence estate from whom I have already quoted in section 12, 'Working-class people are not exactly kept away, but more kept separate from very many things that the middle class take for granted. I have in mind such things as further education, legal services, concepts such as taste and design, and so on' (Parker, 1983, p. 289).

Nor, finally, for all the incorporation of the working class after 1918 into the institutions of the state, did there disappear the difference between working-class and middle-class people's experience of the mode of coercion.[62] In this respect, little if anything changed after either the First World War or the Second from what Stephen Reynolds had sought to describe to his middle-class readers in 1911. Relations between the police and the 'hereditary' or 'professional' criminals – 'Mark Benney's' teenager 'absorbed in crime as an artist is in art' (1936, p. 239) – remained a world of its own. The experience of the detective inspector of the 1990s would have struck his counterpart of the 1890s as different in scale and style,[63] but not in substance. But for working-class men in general, the double function of the police in controlling industrial disputes and in patrolling the streets of working-class districts generated the same antagonisms and the same intermittent recourse to violence. In the words of a Liverpool constable of the inter-war period, 'Policemen in those days, particularly like me who had been away to sea, were a bit rough. We didn't carry batons for ornaments. We used them. You had to do it' (Brogden 1991, p. 107). As Brogden comments (p. 109), oral history is particularly difficult on this topic. But 'An officer who spent his career patrolling a middle-class suburb would only in extreme circumstances be involved in a physical encounter. Conversely, in the inner city, the use of the stick could be a regular practice.' The same could equally well be said half a century later. 'It is easier to police public than private spaces, and so those people who must inhabit the former – young working-class males – are most "at risk"': in the words of an officer interviewed in the same study from which this quotation is taken, 'I tend personally to accept a few scuffles and bruises . . . There are times when to be honest you would charge sometimes to cover yourself because you have to put an injury-on-duty form in' (McConville et al. 1991, pp. 17, 26).

If there was a significant descriptive difference between the inter-war decades and the later decades of the century, it was that the efforts of the police to control street betting were replaced by efforts to control drug-dealing. But in both cases, the targets of policing were working-class rather than middle-class, and in both cases, although the activity in question overlapped with

---

[62] Here is the description by a man arrested on 4 October 1936 of his treatment at the hands of the police in the 'Battle of Cable Street': 'The mounted police was whacking away with laths, whacking away at my legs though they couldn't bring me down, and finally, when I did begin to come down I was just swept behind the crowd. The police was still battering away and one policeman was just about to whack me one on the head so I punched him in the face. Anyway I was arrested and about twelve or fourteen police took me to the station. Well when they got me there they turned me up like a battering ram and they just bashed the charge room door open with my head, beating me with truncheons all shouting out "You yellow bastard!" When I came round I had about twelve stitches in my head and in my pocket was a brick, a file, a bag of shot which were planted on me when I was unconscious.' (Charlie Goodman, in Humphries and Gordon 1994, p. 107.)

[63] Albeit with the same borrowing of 'stylistic devices' by the agents of the state from those whom they seek to control (Hobbs 1991, p. 606).

activity which was authentically criminal, the majority of participants in it saw themselves as doing something which, if it was illegal, ought not to be. The Street Betting Act of 1906 had been spectacularly ineffective, and until betting was taken off the streets after the Second World War into the betting shops of Ladbroke, Mecca, and William Hill it was conducted through a network of agents and lookouts more or less under the eyes of the police, who knew perfectly well who the local bookies were. The policing was conducted in an almost ritual manner: in Salford, for example, the police would arrest the 'dogger-out', as the lookout's role was called in that part of the country, who would not resist arrest and would have his (or her) fine paid by the bookie, so that the police would meet their quota of arrests and the bookies would escape prosecution (Davies 1991, p. 91). A generation later, when drug-dealing on the street had replaced street betting as the target of policing, mutual hostility between police and young working-class males was further compounded by ethnic tension. It is immaterial to the description of this hostility and tension how far the police are justified in explaining it by reference to the greater propensity of the targeted groups to be involved with drugs or the targeted groups justified in explaining it by reference to prejudice on the part of the police. For those involved on both sides, the experience only confirmed the stereotype.[64]

Retrospective descriptions of working-class, no less than of middle-class, experience have always to be construed with care, whether given by participants who may unwittingly exaggerate or observers who may unwittingly romanticize them. But whatever reservations may need to be entered about particular observations or reminiscences, the overwhelming impression remains of a sub-culture which, however different it became after the First World War from what it had been in the late-Victorian and Edwardian period, remained equally different from a middle-class sub-culture which had altered too. To say this is not to cast doubt on the evidence reported in chapter 2 to the effect that the systactic distance between middle-class and working-class roles had narrowed, or that there was an increasingly large minority of

---

[64] Not that the experience of white male working-class teenagers in Newcastle might not be very similar to that of their black counterparts in Notting Hill or Brixton. Cf. e.g. B. Campbell (1993, p. 96), describing the riot of 1991: 'In the year of the riot the absenteeism rate in year eleven was twenty-three per cent in one of Newcastle's West End schools. An average of twenty children were excluded for at least one day for violence. Almost all were *white boys*. Adrift from all institutions, how could they experience themselves in a system, how could they discover the power they might have in a process, the influence they might have through negotiation? For a lad whose culture celebrated a man's authority and power, and lethal weapons as the solution to social problems, the discovery of his own illiteracy or incompetence could, of course, carry the dread that "being inside society" meant "being defeated". That was the scenario some of these lads repeated in the riots, where *power* only meant *brute force*. "They have no idea how society works" says one of their lawyers.'

individuals, households, and families whose location was less clearly determinate than that of their grandparents had been. But any suggestion that the two distinguishable sub-cultures had merged in a single common amalgam of lifestyle, attitudes, and subjective experiences of the modes of production, persuasion, and coercion was as implausible in the year of Mark Hudson's sojourn in Horden as it had been in the year of Priestley's *English Journey*.

LIFE AT THE BOTTOM

§15. Description of what it was like to be in the 'submerged tenth' of late-Victorian and Edwardian English society cannot but centre round the family (or lack of one) and particularly the mothers who kept the family together (Paterson 1911, p. 32). As General Booth, his namesake Charles, Mrs Bosanquet, Nurse Loane, Lady Bell, and Mrs Pember Reeves were all aware, whatever different conclusions about policy they might draw from it, the experience of the majority of those below the 'poverty line' was intimately bound up with the role of the wife and mother in managing the expenditure of the meagre income on which, after the husband and father had reserved 'Dad's whack' for himself, the family's well-being depended. In the environment of the slums, subjective experience varied at least as much as elsewhere with temperament and character. Some wives and mothers were resourceful and energetic where others were apathetic and despairing, just as some husbands and fathers were dissolute and violent where others were helpful and affectionate. But the representative descriptions, whether by middle-class observers or by men and women brought up in that environment who subsequently wrote down their recollections or narrated them to oral historians, all convey a pervasive sense of the inescapability of hardship. As Rowntree pointed out in the well-known paragraph which I quoted in section 16 of chapter 1, even in families with no more than three dependent children and the father in regular work, a weekly income of 21s 6d allowed no margin whatever by a standard which may not have been 'scientific' but could on no theory be described as 'comfortable'. The breadwinner, whose dietary needs to sustain him in that role were often met at the expense of the needs of his wife and children, could not afford to be off work, yet for many the only work available was irregular or seasonal. There was the option of borrowing, but how were debts once incurred to be repaid? There was the chance of an occasional charitable handout, but it was likely to be limited to the odd piece of clothing or pair of boots, or free Christmas dinner, or bowl of soup or mug of cocoa available from a church or school. And the wife and mother, however careful and provident, had no choice but to buy in smaller and therefore more expensive quantities, to give her children food which was filling rather than nutritious, and to rely for an occasional meal with meat on offal sold off at a discount by the local butcher at the very end of the day – all this in a house in which vermin was rife, running water unknown, and good cooking equipment a luxury.[65]

It was not always the husband and father alone on whom the family's budget depended. Mothers and children could and did find work to do. But what work, and in what conditions! Robert Sherard, who published in *Pearson's Magazine* a series of articles 'descriptive of the horrible slavery to which so many thousands of our countrymen and women are subjected' (1898, p. 15) was well aware that many employers believed him to have been 'kidded' by their employees. But his descriptions of the female white-lead workers of Newcastle or chain-makers of Cradley Heath convey an authentic sense not only of long hours, physical strain, and unhealthy surroundings, but of a felt need to earn whatever they could to the point of carrying on until within an hour or two of being confined in childbirth. Moreover, his descriptions are further authenticated by those to be found in the reports of Asquith's 'lady inspectors' (and the employers' resentment of them).[66] No doubt there is always a risk of sentimental, as of censorious, bullshit in middle-class observers' descriptions of the lives of the poor. But contemporary observers' reports are conclusive to the effect that in the late-Victorian and Edwardian period 'Large numbers of married women of the urban poor worked not because they particularly wished to nor because they adhered fervently to the ideals of middle-class feminists, but because they had to' (Chinn 1988, p. 99).

Low-wage factory work was not the only means by which married women in the late-Victorian and Edwardian underclass could alleviate their husbands' lack of regular employment without recourse to prostitution or the workhouse. Some made matchboxes or sewed buttons or took in washing in their own homes. Others worked as charwomen in other people's houses, or minded other people's children, or went out sorting rags or selling lumps of salt. Sons and daughters could also be enlisted to supplement the household's income, whether by similar work carried out in the home or by casual labour or street-selling or totting or hawking or begging ('Carry your bag, Madam?') or thieving

---

[65] Few were in the position of 'Mrs C., with seven children, who succeeded in becoming a tenant of the Duchy of Cornwall and when work for her husband, a painter's labourer, was slack simply stopped paying any rent at all: "The Prince er Wales, 'e don't want our little bits of sticks, and 'e won't sell us up if we keeps the place a credit to 'im" ' (Pember Reeves 1913, pp. 183–4).

[66] Some vivid examples are quoted in Pike (1972, pp. 70–80): for the inspectors' own reactions, see e.g. (p. 72) Miss Tracey in the *Factories and Workshops Report for 1913*: 'when, as is so common now, women are accused of malingering, I often wish that complaints would accompany me on my investigation of cases of accident or poisoning at the workers' homes, for I know that, like me, these people would return in a humbled state of mind, recognizing courage and endurance under circumstances which would break many of us.'

outside it. And there were always some parents willing to see their daughters, or more rarely sons, go into domestic service. But just as the pervasive impression of the role of the unskilled male seasonal or casual labourer is one of chronic insecurity, so is the pervasive impression of his wife's and children's labour one of exiguous reward in uniformly arduous conditions. In country districts, parents were less unwilling to see their children go into domestic service. But both before and after the First World War, factory work was usually felt to be preferable by the daughters of the urban poor. A revealing counterpoise to the complaints of middle-class housewives about the difficulty of recruiting living-in maids even when unemployment was high is provided in the reminiscences of Helen Forrester, the daughter of an upper-middle-class bankrupt who was compelled to bring up his seven children on the dole in Liverpool in the 1930s: 'Neither she [her sister Fiona] or I had ever considered going into domestic service. Even in my most depressed days, when I began to fear I would die from hunger, I had never considered this way out of my misery. Both of us remembered the servants in our own house when we were small' (1981, p. 40).

The middle-class observers of the late-Victorian and Edwardian poor were apt to be impressed not only by the way in which some families seemed somehow to be able to contend with what Kathleen Dayus described as 'a seemingly inevitable cycle of pregnancy, hard work, poverty, and grief' (1985, p. 157), but also by the extent of cooperation between neighbours as well as relations. The 'neighbour role' (Hunt 1935, p. 78, quoted by Ross 1983, p. 6) embraced doing laundry and making fires for the sick, sheltering battered wives, caring for children whose mother was giving birth to another, or taking in families evicted from their homes. At times of death, it extended to laying out the body as well as preparing the funeral tea. In all this, it is important not to forget to describe the scrounging brother-in-law, the grandmother who sells the pawn tickets to buy drink, the daughter who drifts into prostitution, the teenage son already embarked on a succession of petty thefts, and the whole persistent fraction of the 'submerged tenth' who have no interest in an honest day's work even if offered to them. But reciprocity was the norm.[67] As one Lancashire informant put it to an oral historian, 'a little bit of tea, a little bit of sugar, a shilling. But it usually came back' (E. Roberts 1984, p. 191).

The difficulty, for the purposes of this chapter, is that the experience of the wives and mothers of the urban poor may be misdescribed no less pre-emptively by latter-day historians than they were by contemporary observers against whose very different presuppositions the latter-day historian is

---

[67] With one practical qualification: families where 'We had so many addresses, we couldn't pay the rent, we had to keep moving' (P. Thompson 1992, p. 142) could hardly build up and sustain a network of reciprocal neighbourly obligation.

concerned to react. For explanatory purposes, this is neither here nor there. There is no reason to suppose that the working-class women who felt compelled to supplement their husband's earnings with low-paid wage-work understood the selective pressures which bore on the practices defining their roles. Nor, conversely, are they likely to have been aware of why there was such a movement by working-class women in general into unpaid domestic labour during the late-Victorian and Edwardian period by comparison with the mid-nineteenth century (although they can hardly have failed to be aware that the requirement on their older children to attend school reduced their availability as minders of their younger brothers and sisters). But talk of the 'oppression' of working-class housewives is questionably authentic as a description (Burke 1994, p. 164), not because they were not in important respects subordinate to their husbands, as to their employers (if they had one), but because their subjective experience was dominated above all by the struggle for the well-being of their families. Moreover, their own sense of the subordination of their roles to those of their husbands might be diminished either by their sense of controlling a sphere of independent decision in the management of the home, or by their awareness of the value of their own independent contribution to the family's total income, or by both ('a shilling of your own is worth two that *he* gives you'). The value-judgements to be made about the conditions in which they succeeded or failed are, as always, up to you. But pre-emptive middle-class presuppositions must be strictly excluded from the description of what their lives were like for *them*.

§16. Then what changed for 'them', in the terms in which they experienced it, after the First World War? What were the 1920s and 1930s like for the woman quoted in the *Contemporary Review* of October 1915 who told a working-women's club that she 'did not see what difference it would make if the Germans did come and rule England. She had always been poor, and didn't suppose she would be worse with than without them' (Waites 1987, p. 187)? The three big factual differences, as we have seen, were the smaller numbers of dependent children in the families of the poor, the rise in real wages for the unskilled worker, and the provision of relief by the state. But it was the third which represented the most fundamental change in subjective experience of the mode of the distribution of power. It did not do away with the felt need to be able to appeal to neighbours and kin,[68] or to voluntary and charitable agencies. Indeed, the disappointments of Kathleen Dayus and many like her at

---

[68] Notwithstanding the comment of one of Elizabeth Roberts's male informants about the inter-war period: ' "Help." There was a lot of it, but it was gradually dying out. It died away somehow as you got richer' (1984, p. 198). A symptomatic later change after the Second World War was the replacement of the neighbourhood 'layer-out' by the paid undertaker (Roberts 1993, p. 40).

what the state was in practice willing to provide often heightened their sense of relative deprivation and their readiness to flout regulations which they felt to be unjust: the experience of the small proportion of schoolchildren of unemployed parents who managed to qualify for free school milk during the inter-war depression is less representative than that of the many who didn't. But no one could fail to be aware that the state was there as a provider to an altogether different degree from the late-Victorian and Edwardian era. As Bowley and Hogg pointed out after a detailed examination in Reading, where one household out of four in their sample was in receipt of either a pension or unemployment benefit, wage-earners no longer had inescapably dependent on them others besides their own wives and children (1925, p. 26).

From the 1920s onwards, therefore, we are in the world of the 'claimant' and the 'scrounger' – alternative terms for a role defined by practices which were very differently experienced by different incumbents of it and very differently regarded by different incumbents of the roles to which it was institutionally tied. The extent to which the social services can be claimed to have succeeded in meeting the felt needs of those towards whom they were directed is a matter for the following chapter rather than for this one. But to the question 'what was it like to be on the receiving end?' the answer must be 'it depended where you were living'. And to the question 'where was it least disagreeable to be on the receiving end?' the answer must be 'where there were least others like you'. Although local authorities in depressed areas were more likely to be left-wing and therefore in principle, at least, more disposed to be generous, they might not in practice be able to afford to be; and Labour councillors might be as hostile to 'scroungers' as Conservative ones, whether out of conviction or out of concern not to appear to be condoning the expenditure of public money on the undeserving. 'Not surprisingly', therefore, in the inter-war period, 'the few most generous authorities in the official league table, such as Stepney, Coventry and Leicester, paying above 35s for a family of five, mostly lay outside the distressed areas' (Webster 1985, p. 209). Nor was this state of affairs significantly different in the decades after the Second World War, however much more generous benefits may have been in real as well as nominal terms. The poor were still likely to be concentrated in working-class districts in the larger cities where Labour was likely to be in the majority. Not only would this not thereby guarantee them better provision of social services; they would also be more rather than less likely to feel themselves to be 'the victims of the practices of staff in the public services – police, social security, housing and job centre staff, for example, all increasingly strongly represented by trade unions' (Donnison 1982, p. 127).

In this respect, the experience of the many 'genuinely' seeking work was not so very different from that of the few genuinely 'workshy'. Important as it is for explanatory purposes to have distinguished the unstable members of the working class from the stable members of the underclass, for descriptive purposes it may feel much the same for members of the one as of the other when signing on at the labour exchange or queuing for a handout in the benefit office. Indeed, it may even be a worse experience for the former, just as may have been the loss of a better-paid or more highly skilled job which hitherto seemed secure. Anger at the means test was no less intense among the skilled, like John Gorman's father who never forgot being driven to sell his son's two sets of cigarette cards to provide a dinner for the family: 'The desperation that drove a kindly man and a skilled craftsman to sell his little boy's treasured but pathetic collection in order to provide food, seared his pride. Means-tested misery heaped humiliation upon helplessness, creating an anger fuelled by poverty towards the absolute unfairness of capitalism. The hurt was suppressed and seldom revealed, but it remained with him until the end of his days' (Gorman 1993, p. 171). From the 'genuinely seeking work' test of the 1920s all the way to the discretionary 'severe hardship' benefits of the 1980s, the requirement to demonstrate entitlement ('you know we can prosecute you for this deception, don't you?') generated a pervasive, deeply felt, and abundantly documented resentment among those who experienced it.

The old ideology of the Poor Law, whose psychological influence, as we saw, had been most evident at the very time that its sociological influence was arousing most concern, survived intact from the 1880s to the 1980s when striking Yorkshire miners could describe the unemployed to a visiting journalist as 'idle buggers and dole wallahs' (P. Jenkins 1987, p. 231). Donnison, visiting social security offices in the Northwest of England in the 1970s, found that he was attacked even more sharply by the women among the staff than by the men about 'fraud, workshy claimants, feather-bedded claimants, cohabiting claimants, and women who will not go back to their husbands because we give them too much money' (1982, p. 63). A self-legitimating tradition of mutually antagonistic attitudes – incomprehension and resentment on one side and disapproval and distaste on the other – was, and remained, intrinsic to the subjective experience of the institutions of the welfare state from their inception. The latent assumption that only those who have paid contributions are deserving of benefit long outlasted the reluctant recognition by ministers and officials that the contributory principle was a fiction. Hence 'the ideological representation of the taxpayer as a "giver" to the state and the supplementary benefit claimant as a "taker" from the state (and thus, ultimately, from the compliant taxpayer)' (D. Cook 1989, p. 167). Or as Orwell put it in the 1930s, 'why are beggars despised? – for they are despised universally. I believe it is for the simple reason that they fail to earn a decent living. In practice nobody cares whether work is useful or useless, productive or parasitic; the sole thing demanded is that it shall be profitable' (1933, p. 154).

Yet it was not as if fraud and malingering were myths propagated for ideological purposes of their own by politicians, journalists, or administrators. They were endemic from the moment the 'dole' was born in 1921. It is in the nature of such behaviour that the facts of its incidence are impossible to establish precisely, and that academic observers who are either too credulous or too sceptical will find themselves describing what is not really there – or not on the scale or to the extent which they have presupposed – to be described. But, like 'fiddling' at the place of work, cheating the benefit system extends across a range of behaviour from what is condoned as excusable if not legitimate to what is condemned as excessive if not downright immoral. Whatever the statistics which only the recording angel could provide, it is a pattern of behaviour so extensive and so well-entrenched that any description which ignores it would be dismissed by the people engaged in it as pitifully naive. An American researcher visiting Liverpool in the early 1990s was instructed by an informant whom he calls 'Scully' in the dodges and breaks which are bringing the income of himself and the mother of his two school-age children up to somewhere between £900 and £1,000 a month before taking account of 'Scully's' off-the-books job in London from which he returns to see his family and register for the dole:

> Does Scully feel any guilt about anything he's doing? 'The system's there to be fucked,' he said. 'You're soft if you don't.' How unusual is Scully? 'I know more people like me than people who are actually working,' he answered. I asked him to tell me about his friends who were playing the system straight. After a long pause, he said, 'I'm not making this up. I can't think of anyone.' Another pause. 'One person. My mother.' (Murray 1995, p. 23)

This is the sort of anecdote which invites instant scepticism on grounds of authenticity and representativeness alike: isn't it just the sort of bullshit that someone like 'Scully' would particularly enjoy feeding to a visiting American eager to hear it? But what matters for the purpose of description is not how many 'Scullies' the recording angel could enumerate[69] or what are the selective pressures which continue to diffuse and replicate the practices defining 'Scully's' role, but the awareness on the part of both claimants and

---

[69] Cf. the comment of a director of Welfare Services a generation earlier on a man in Gloucester convicted of theft who, the magistrates were told, had not worked for three years and had an income from the state of £17 which could be supplemented by part-time casual labour: 'How many further exploit the state in that way, augmenting their settled income by part-time or casual work – and at the same time invite exploitation by employers looking for cheap labour – no one knows. There can be little doubt, however, that only a small number of them figured in the 1,666 convicted of various types of fraud against the National Assistance Board in 1964' (*The Times* 22.3.66).

non-claimants on the one side, and benefit officials and their supervisors on the other, that such people do indeed exist in substantial numbers. Newspaper stories of extravagant and, by implication, widespread abuse of the welfare system are as familiar from the inter-war period as for the decades after the Second World War. But John Hilton's comment on headlines of the type of 'In workhouse, but worth £2,000', which I quoted in section 11, doesn't quite apply here, for the point of the stories about benefit fraud is not that what they report is unusual but that it is, by implication, by no means as unusual as it ought to be (any more than is tax evasion among the self-employed or expense-account fiddling among company directors and salaried employees). To be sure, they are often exaggerated for polemical purposes. But there is nothing inauthentic about the answer given by a young dosser in the early 1970s to the question 'what do you do for money?': 'That's no problem. If you don't work you beg and if you don't beg you steal and get some assistance, it's all pretty easy. If you get depressed go up to the spike where you can get food and a good clean up' (Page 1973, p. 14).

To which should be added a subsequent comment of the same author's (p. 136): 'At present it is possible to claim virtually anything with only the flimsiest evidence of identity.' No less than with the élite 1 per cent, description of what being one of 'them' is like has to include some sense of *their* sense of how they are regarded by others; and in the case of the underclass, this involves above all the attitudes of those with whom they cannot but come into contact as a function of each other's roles. The subjective difference, however, is that the 'toffs' who are aware of, but repudiate, the attitudes and values of those who detest what they see them as representing can afford to ignore them; the 'scroungers' who are aware of, but repudiate, the attitudes and values of those who detest what they see them as representing cannot ignore them at all. And whatever their personal feelings, the officials of the 1980s were just aware as their counterparts in the 1920s had been that applicants for relief could not be rigorously vetted (Deacon 1977, p. 22). This meant that on both sides of the counter, as it were, there was a pervasive awareness that the rules, more or less stringent as they might be at any one place or time, carried an inescapable element of discretion. This, in turn, was bound to have wider repercussions, as politicians, journalists, pressure-groups, and sometimes the courts argued for different interpretations which might significantly determine what one or another category of claimant would or would not receive. The issues of policy raised are a matter for chapter 5. But for the purposes of this one, there needs to be brought out the extent of the difference between what it was like for 'them' in the late-Victorian and Edwardian period and in the decades from the 1920s onwards. The 'claimant', not yet so called, before 1914 had a relatively much clearer entitlement, whether as an old-age pensioner or an insured worker with a sufficient record of contributions paid, while for those who fell beyond these categories it was, as they were all aware, a matter of charitable, neighbourly, familial, trade-union, or friendly society assistance outside the reach of the state. But thereafter, claimants' claims were themselves discretionary in a way less different than might have been supposed from the way in which the charitable hand-outs of the previous era had been; and it is relevant to a full description of the subjective experiences involved that those exercising the discretion were for the most part, unlike almost all of those over whom they were exercising it, white middle-class males.

§17. The distinction between the scroungers and the genuine claimants is not, however, the only one which needs to be drawn in order to give a generalized description of the subjective experience of those whose roles are closest to the apex of the inverted pyramid. Here, too, there are fine gradations to be drawn which cannot be inferred from the statistics of poverty or the regulations governing the administration of benefits or the reports of investigations into the incidence of abuse. In a view, as his subtitle puts it, from 'one end of Skid Row', Phillimore (1979, p. 34) describes how

> while dossers who are engaged in casual work at Spitalfields Market frequently voice the opinion that they are superior to other dossers, and often label those around the fire as jake-drinkers, a parallel process occurs all the time among the men at the market entrance without the participants having recourse to social categories to express their distinctions. In a word, social distinctions operate at every level, down to contrasts which seem minute to the outsider.

Descriptions of this kind, like descriptions of the relations between criminals and police, have about them a strong flavour of the ethnographic present. However different the bureaucratic world of state provision from the world of the Charity Organisation Society, there is a timelessness about the dosser's life which suggests that General Booth might feel less unfamiliar in Spitalfields Market a century after his time than the hypothetical nobleman of section 8 resurrected for a weekend at Chatsworth or Cowdray Park. Indeed, the Salvation Army Hostels – and the conditions within them as described alike by Orwell in the 1930s and Page in the 1970s – would be there for him to visit for himself. It is not as if the enormously greater involvement of the state had done away with voluntary and charitable agencies who saw themselves, rightly or wrongly, as furnishing a service of a more personal and less censorious kind. Even though the punitive regimes of the late-Victorian and Edwardian work-houses were progressively softened – by the 1920s, gruel and stonebreaking could be described as symbols of a bygone age (Crowther 1981, p. 265) – the same contrast between the attitudes of the officials in the benefit offices and of the Irish nuns in the soup-kitchens was still there to be seen, along with the gradations of status which still distinguished the 'highbrow tramp' or 'gentleman of the road' from those whom he regarded as 'feckless men with no self-respect' (Page 1973, p. 116).

Likewise, personal differences in both circumstances and attitudes remain a perennial theme in descriptions of the experience of families permanently dependent on state support. Mr and Mrs Nelson, living in a four-roomed council flat in a poor district of Oldham in the late 1960s and early 1970s (Townsend 1979, pp. 305–10), had three sons of whom one was handicapped; Mr Nelson was epileptic (with a disability index score of 11) and his wife, who had given up her job as an office cleaner to look after him, suffered from chronic ill-health herself (with a disability index score of 3). They had no carpets, refrigerator, or washing machine; the flat, which was very damp, was heated by a coal fire in the living-room (for which they bought coal in 28-pound bags as and when able to afford it) and a single-bar electric fire moved from bedroom to bedroom. The family's treats consisted of two day-trips in the year to visit Mrs Nelson's sister in Yorkshire and a trip to the cinema to see *The Sound of Music* including ice-creams for each of the children. Asked to describe poverty, Mr Nelson said 'The circumstances we are experiencing now. Poverty is when you are living from hand to mouth and you have no security.'[70] Mrs Nelson said, 'Not being able to buy anything for the kids . . . I'm hoping things will be better for my kiddies in time to come. I never thought life would be like this.' When interviewed in 1972, Mrs Nelson had just learned to her surprise and dismay that she was about to have a fourth child. Mr Nelson died in 1976, aged forty-three. It goes without saying that this is poverty of a kind positively enviable to some of Robert Sherard's interviewees in 1898, to whom a one-bar electric fire and day-trips to Yorkshire would have seemed a vision of bliss. But the experience of poverty always had a relative as well as an absolute dimension,[71] and there is yet another constant which links the experience of family poverty in the era of the welfare state with the experience of it in the era of Booth and Rowntree: number of children. Although, as we have seen, the extent of poverty was significantly reduced by

---

[70] For the aftermath to the changes to the social security system implemented in 1988, cf. e.g. Rashid Chaudry, a former textile worker in Bradford with three young children: 'I just worry about paying the bills . . . I can't think about when the children grow up . . . the worst thing is just not having enough money to pay the bills, buy the goods and look after the children. It's too much from hand to mouth' (Cohen *et al.* 1992, p. 20).

[71] Descriptively, this is vividly apparent in the heightened demands which children make even on low-income parents, e.g. for a home computer for GCSE (General Certificate of Secondary Education) homework like all their classmates appear to have: 'Well, yes, I would like my children to have one but I can't afford it. But it's getting to the stage where it's becoming, I think, essential' (Middleton and Thomas 1994, p. 67).

the smaller families of the 1920s and thereafter, what difference did that make to the experience of those who *were* still the members of large ones? Beveridge himself had been conscious of it, and PEP, in a study of poverty looking back to his Report (1952, p. 25), said that 'Having three or more children before the war in the working class was practically sufficient to guarantee poverty.' After 1945, when working-class mothers could draw family allowances for their second and subsequent children as well as go out to work at rates which, again, would have seemed a vision of bliss to Robert Sherard's informants, it was large families dependent on the state for whom, along with the elderly (Wedderburn 1962, p. 263), provision continued to lag behind felt need (Wynn 1970). And in the 1980s, when unskilled manual jobs for young men like the Nelson sons were increasingly scarce, the experience of large families where the household head was among the long-term unemployed became increasingly like that of the families described by the Pilgrim Trust or Carnegie Trust investigators between the wars.

In the underclass, too, no less than in the middle and working classes, the experience of women has to be described separately from that of men; and this means particularly the experience of single mothers of dependent children.[72] Within this category of roles there was a long-standing differentiation of status between the widow of a lawful husband and the unmarried or deserted single woman whom the father (or fathers) of her child (or children), although still living, refused to support. Widows' pensions, including an allowance for dependent children, date back to the Widows, Orphans and Old Age Contributory Pensions Act of 1925; and inadequate as they may have seemed to many of their recipients, they placed widows, then and since, in a far more favourable position than other one-parent families. But the number of single parents, of which the overwhelming majority were women, steadily rose: by 1992, one in five mothers with dependent children was a single mother (as against one in less than fifty fathers). This would have been inconceivable in the late-Victorian and Edwardian period. But, as with attitudes to the unemployed, the attitudes to single mothers dictated by the dominant ideology outlasted the behavioural change not only among the men behind the benefit counter but among the men on the council estates where they found themselves rehoused.

For all the difference to the condition of the most disadvantaged members of English society made by the increase in provision by the state, the twin themes of stigmatization and helplessness[73] recur all through the decades since the

---

[72] But by no means exclusively – particularly in communities where there is a predominantly male sub-culture of petty (or not so petty) crime (B. Campbell 1993, chapter 11: 'Grafting is women's work').

[73] Or, for those of the seemingly permanently unemployed who finally succeed in finding work,

First World War in representative descriptions of underclass experience. By Thursday the benefit money has been spent, something is borrowed until Monday, and the cycle starts again. I commented in section 14 of chapter 1 on the strength of the ideology of the Poor Law, despite the hostility it aroused, in the late-Victorian and Edwardian period, and the persistent stigmatization of those dependent on others than themselves or their families is reflected no less in the reluctance of the 'respectable' to claim their entitlement when overtaken by poverty or hardship than in claimants' resentment of how they feel that they are treated. Mr and Mrs Ellman, for example, aged eighty-one and seventy, handicapped and living on an income below the poverty line in a four-roomed cottage without mains sanitation (let alone television, a refrigerator, or a washing machine), are 'too independent' to apply for supplementary benefit and believe that poverty is people's own fault (Townsend 1979, p. 329); and there were, and are, many like them. But even those most willing and ready to claim their legal and moral entitlements were aware that the scale of benefits available from the state was not, and was not intended to be, such as to lift them out of the underclass altogether but only to alleviate their condition within it. Benevolence and deterrence were always inseparable, and experienced as such.[74] The moral judgements to be made about those who claim, or don't claim, or claim what they are not entitled to are, as always, up to you. But descriptively, the subjective experience of being confronted with those choices continued to be as different as ever from the experience of those with access, whether direct or indirect, to the rewards of participation in the labour market of mid-to-late-twentieth-century capitalist-liberal-democratic English society.

CONCLUSION

§18. This chapter would need to be at least as long as the volume of which it is only a part if it were to qualify as a full descriptive sociology of twentieth-century English society. At most, it has sketched in outline the range of subjective experiences of the modes of production, persuasion, and coercion across the systactic structure and summarized some of the most vividly perceived differences, from that same perspective, between the late-Victorian and Edwardian period and the decades since the end of the First World War.

---

the feeling that it is a matter of luck: 'Amongst the great majority of those I have interviewed it has become very evident that there is no single "right way" to look for work and what is seen as luck has often tended to dominate the job-search, especially for the unskilled' (Sinfield 1981, p. 44).

[74] Hence the policy dilemma as experienced by ministers and officials with regard to 'casuals': was it the objective to help them to return to 'normal' life, or to deter them from coming to the casual ward in the first place? (Krafchick 1983, p. 204).

It has not explored the private lives of the people on whose testimony it rests; it has almost entirely ignored the differences which can be made to the subjective experience of similarly located roles by the ages of different incumbents; and it has barely touched on the subjective experience of corporate and associational stratification within such semi-autonomous social worlds as the law, the armed forces, the turf, the stage (or more broadly the 'media'), the Churches (or the Freemasons or the Jehovah's Witnesses or the Rastafarians), or the universities and schools – to say nothing of the 'total' institutions such as prisons, monasteries, or long-stay mental hospitals in which a small number of the members of English society may spend the greater part of their lives. Yet it has already begun to encroach on the territory of the chapter which follows, since much of the subjective experience of representative members of different systacts and milieux is bound up with the value-judgements which they are themselves disposed to make about it. It is not the sociologist's business to endorse or to reject the values which inform those judgements. But it *is* the sociologist's business to assess not only the disjunction between 'their' experiences, however authentically described, and the actual process of social evolution underlying it, but also the disjunction between 'their' opinions and attitudes and the actual effects of their society's evolution from one to another sub-type of their society's modes of production, persuasion, and coercion on their well-being (if such it is) as policy-makers have sought to promote it.

CHAPTER FIVE

The case evaluated

SATISFACTIONS AND RESENTMENTS

§1. 'Beautiful, free, generous England': the words are Sigmund Freud's, written in London in June of 1938 as part of a second prefatory note to his essay on *Moses and Monotheism* (1955, p. 70); and in the following year he wrote to H. G. Wells that since he first came to England at the age of eighteen it had been his 'intense wish phantasy' to become an Englishman. He was not the first or the only immigrant Jewish Anglophile of the century. Yet it is not, as we have seen, as if all Jewish, let along 'New Commonwealth', immigrants had found themselves welcomed in England, or liked what they found. There has never been a lack of critics as well as encomiasts of English institutions. 'I know what England is', an immigrant girl in Australia said in 1846. 'Old England is a fine place for the rich, but the Lord help the poor' (quoted from Kiddle 1950, p. 243 by J. F. C. Harrison 1971, p. 177). A hundred years later, there were many who would say the same. The structure and culture which the more fortunate eulogized were the same by which the less fortunate felt exploited, rejected, and oppressed. The sociologist (as opposed to the moral or political philosopher) has to do justice to both points of view without intruding his or her own personal values, whatever they may be. But how?

It is not as if all incumbents of the more privileged roles were satisfied with the mode of the distribution of power in English society or all incumbents of the less privileged roles dissatisfied. In the late-Victorian and Edwardian period, Beatrice Webb was not alone when she spoke, in *My Apprenticeship*, of a 'growing uneasiness, amounting to conviction' among 'men of intellect and men of property' that the system which had generated so much wealth had at the same time failed to provide a decent livelihood for the majority of the inhabitants of Great Britain (1942, pp. 154–5). But there were many working-class men and women who were indifferent, if not downright hostile, to the ameliorative efforts which Beatrice Webb and others like her were making on their behalf. If, contrary to fact, the lines of economic, ideological, and political conflict had been drawn exclusively between a privileged systact wholly satisfied with the existing modes of production, persuasion, and coercion on the one side and an underprivileged systact consistently hostile to them on the other, then sociologists could simply calculate the outcome of a zero-sum game in which one side's loss was the other's gain and their readers could be left to side with the winners or the losers as their personal values might dictate. But the actual state of affairs is a great deal more complicated than that, not only in the differences of attitude which cut across systactic boundaries but also in the reactions of the representative incumbents of different roles to changes which they might have resisted only subsequently to welcome or welcomed only subsequently to deplore.

There is, accordingly, no possibility of drawing up a balance-sheet of the gains and losses accruing to different roles on which observers of all theoretical schools can agree, however disinterested the sociologist who attempts the task and however dispassionate the incumbents from whose testimony such a balance-sheet would be calculated. Different incumbents of similarly located roles may, and often do, take diametrically opposite views of what changes are or are not to be counted as improvements. If, as I quoted from Paul Addison in section 6 of chapter 2, Britain's social services were, taken all in all, the most advanced in the world by 1939, is that not an indisputable reason for satisfaction? But then as now, there were some policy-makers and opinion-formers for whom that level of provision was scandalously low and others for whom it was scandalously high, while at the receiving end some welcomed it, some exploited it, some ignored it, and some refused it. It is not only that the views of back-bench Conservative MPs about welfare policy were, and were bound to remain, irreconcilable with those of their Labour counterparts. They were no further apart, and perhaps less so, than the scroungers like 'Scully' on one side, and on the other Mr and Mrs Ellman who are too proud to claim even what they know they are entitled to.

The best that the sociologist can offer, therefore, is a broad account of how far the changes in the mode and distribution of economic, ideological, and political power which have occurred in English society since it evolved out of its late-Victorian and Edwardian sub-type of capitalist liberal democracy have been welcomed or deplored by significant groups or categories of its members whose welfare policy-makers and their advisers have sought to promote. Whether they are to be admired or deplored for their attitudes is for you, not for me or any other sociologist, to judge. But it *is* for us to set out the evidence which may help you to decide for yourself.

§2. For most people in twentieth-century England, the obvious source of satisfaction has been the steady and indisputable rise in real income per head.

But the lives of the people of England improved not only in the sense that they had more material resources to enjoy but also in the sense that they had significantly longer life expectancy in which to enjoy them – for the United Kingdom as a whole, from 45.5 in 1901 to 73.2 in 1991 for men, and from 49.0 to 78.7 for women. The two went hand-in-hand: 'the long-run growth in average income has been one of the causes of lower mortality through its effects on nutrition, on standards of housing and sanitation, and on health expenditure' (R. V. Jackson 1994, p. 523). At the same time, the increased material resources could be distributed among a smaller number of non-productive consumers, since a rising number of people in employment was combined with a decline in the proportion of dependent children – a bad thing only from the viewpoint of those according to whose values a higher birth rate, whether to provide bodies for Britain or souls for God, was an end in itself.

In the late-Victorian and Edwardian period, a representative woman of twenty could expect to spend about a third of her remaining life in what would, in effect, be a full-time role of motherhood – a figure which in the aftermath of the First World War would fall to about a tenth. Again, this might not be regarded as an improvement by observers for whom motherhood was the vocation to which all women should aspire and who deplored their entry into occupational roles which took them outside their homes. But there is no evidence (known to me, at least) that this is how the women themselves regarded the change. It might pose for them, as for policy-makers, 'a host of new problems' (Titmuss 1958, p. 93). But they were problems which, all the same, they preferred to have. Likewise, there might be some observers for whom the increasing availability of increasingly sophisticated consumer goods to an increasing proportion of English households was to be deplored as leading them into a decadent and selfish materialism. But it is not seriously possible to doubt that for the overwhelming majority of the members of twentieth-century English society, electric light, supermarkets, motor cars, central heating, indoor running water, antibiotic drugs, contraceptive devices, frozen foods, washing machines, clothes 'off the peg', telephones, radio, and television were an improvement in the quality of their lives.

From this point of view, moreover, the increasing involvement of the state in the welfare of its citizens from the First World War onwards can hardly be regarded as other than a net improvement from the citizens' point of view. True as it might be that much of the additional expenditure was grudging in intention, inefficient in administration, and punitive in dispensation, it would be difficult to argue that the recipients would have felt themselves better off without it than with it. However unimaginative some features of the design of the inter-war housing estates and post-Second-World-War tower blocks, slum clearance was universally accepted as a desirable objective. However hard it might be to measure the satisfactions derived from activities pursued in additional amounts of leisure time, the Factory Act of 1937, which restricted the hours which could be worked by the under-16s to forty-four a week, or the Holidays with Pay Act of the following year, which increased the number of wage-earners entitled to a paid annual holiday from 3 million to 11 million, were by any standard beneficent measures. However limited the facilities established with government help in areas of high unemployment under the Special Areas Act of 1935, it was surely better that there should be a thousand of them in operation by the outbreak of the Second World War than that there should be none. And however much less the National Health Service achieved in either preventing or curing illness than many of its advocates may have hoped, the numerous patients who received medical treatment which in both quality and quantity was substantially more than would have been available to them without it had no conceivable reason to be other than grateful.

Another way of making the point would be to compare the prospective well-being of a representative child born to parents without inherited capital or marketable skills in 1900 with one born to similar parents in 1950. The child born in 1950 could look forward to being brought up in a better-furnished and more comfortable house or flat; to attend for longer schools staffed by better-trained teachers; if suitably qualified, to have a better chance of a university degree or professional qualification of some kind; to find a job with less arduous, disagreeable, or dangerous working conditions; in that job, to be better paid for fewer hours' work per week and weeks' work per year; if unable to find a job, to be in receipt of more generous assistance from the state; if drawn into, and convicted of, criminal activity, to be imprisoned under less harsh and degrading conditions; if the victim of ill health, to be better cared for; if destitute in old age, to be better housed in more suitable accommodation; and finally, to be less of a financial burden to relatives or friends when dead.[1] The many politicians, civil servants, writers, researchers, campaigners, and practitioners who had worked in one way or another to achieve these things might not agree about how much credit was due to whom, or about whether more could have been done than was, or about whether what was done should have been done differently. But they would surely agree that much had been done, and that it was good that it had.

§3. Yet that whole story could be, and has been, told from what is virtually the

---

[1] Cf. the suggestion that respondents to a national survey in 1981 who had been in their forties in the 1950s 'perhaps thought themselves four times blessed – receiving state allowances as the parents of young children, benefiting indirectly from the state pensions enjoyed by their ageing parents, living in subsidized dwellings as householders, and receiving free medical services as patients' (Abrams 1983, p. 26).

opposite point of view. By this, I mean not, or not only, the version told by critics of the welfare state for whom, if on the Left, it fell far short of meeting legitimate needs or for whom, if on the Right, it went well beyond what could be justified in providing a basic minimum without sapping initiative, enterprise, and the will to work. It is also a matter of evidence from the recording angel's archives which observers on both Left and Right could not do other than accept about the ways in which the intervention of the state from the First World War onwards failed in what it was supposed to have achieved.

The most vivid *crise révélatrice* of this failure came about through the evacuation of schoolchildren from London and other major cities in September 1939 in the expectation of German air raids. Titmuss, as the official historian of wartime social policy, provides compelling evidence for the extent to which the evacuation not only exacerbated inter-systactic resentments and stereotypes but also disclosed hitherto unrecognized deficiencies in the 'condition of the people': the record is replete with more or less horrified accounts of undernourishment, shoelessness, incontinence, 'rags', head lice, dirt, and in terms of the children's behaviour, aggressiveness, instability, and disobedience. Descriptively, these accounts have to be systematically demystified to take account of deep-seated misunderstandings on both sides: East End children evacuated to Oxford who found that they had to sit down to meals and not run out into the street with a slice of bread in their hands (Macnicol 1986, p. 26) were as understandably baffled as hosts who expected them to benefit automatically in morale as well as in health from a spell of country life. But there was little for the incumbents of ministerial and official roles to be proud of in the 'contradictions between the official facts that were published before the war and the evidence on social conditions that came to light in September 1939 and subsequently' (Titmuss 1950, p. 130).

Nor was it as if those who might be thought to have the strongest claims on the state were always treated as they felt that they deserved. On this, some of the most descriptively vivid evidence is to be found in the letters of servicemen's widows from both of the two world wars (Lomas 1994). Seen from the recipients' end, it was a classic instance of the reluctance of officialdom to 'do the decent thing'. How could it, they wondered, be right that they should be refused a war widow's pension because they married after the husband had been discharged, even where the authorities accepted that his death was the result of his war injuries? Why should war widows', of all people's, pensions be the only war pensions to be taxed? Eventually, as it happened, this was put right – half in 1976 and the other half in 1979. But 'eventually' is the word: the concession was by then too late to benefit most of them.

To cite this example is not to imply that the war widows had an unanswerable moral case: that, as always, is up to you. But, like the more public and immediately effective resentment of the new benefit scales introduced in 1935, it testifies to the sense of an unjustifiable discrepancy between promise and performance which the academic sociologist has to register, whoever's side he or she may be on. After the Second World War, when comprehensive national insurance and a national health service initially free of charge ushered in what was widely regarded as – at last – a thoroughgoing 'welfare state', it turned out, for all the demonstrable benefits which it conferred, to generate disappointments and resentments of a kind which neither the policy-makers nor the prospective recipients had foreseen. Moreover – and more ironically – its left-wing and right-wing critics both came to be proved right. By the end of the period covered by this volume, it had become a commonplace both that expenditure on health and welfare could never bridge the gap between limited resources and unlimited demand, and that even on a strict definition of a 'basic' minimum the safety-net could not be sufficiently tightly drawn to prevent some people from falling through the mesh. Indeed, the prospect of an increasingly large population of increasingly long-lived pensioners supported by a diminishing proportion of the adult population in gainful employment was beginning to call in question even the presupposition that increasing life expectancy was a good thing in itself. What value is to be attached to a protracted old age if it involves a need for continuous attention, costly medical treatment, the erosion of a lifetime's savings, a mounting burden on children and other relatives, and the forced sale of a much-loved and long-inhabited house in order to be able to pay the fees for residential care in an unfamiliar, impersonal, and not always well managed or properly staffed nursing home?

There is a further irony, too, in the steady increase in the proportion of the population dependent on means-tested benefits. This was something which had not merely not been intended by either the supporters or the opponents of the social policies of either inter-war or post-1945 governments, but would have been equally deplored by both of them. To the Left, it implied the continued replication of practices which, as we have seen, had generated a deep and lasting resentment among the working classes of the inter-war period. To the Right, it implied a continuing dependency on the state on the part of a section of the population most of whom were, or should be, well able to look after themselves without it. Yet nobody seemed to know how it could be done away with. How could it be right, even if it were practicable, to provide the whole range of benefits designed to relieve legitimate need free of charge to every citizen, whether needy or not? Yet to apply a test of need was not only to encourage precisely the attitudes and behaviour described in section 16 of chapter 4, but to create an insoluble dilemma about the level at which unemployment benefit, in particular, should be set: if below the going wage-rate, it could not but penalize the thrifty, and if above it, it could not but reward the lazy. Nor had Beveridge, or for that matter anybody else, solved the problem of harmonizing locally variable costs, including rents, with nationally determined scales of benefit – an omission which was to prove 'a continuing Achilles' heel' (J. Harris 1977, p. 399).

At this point, accordingly, we are faced with not merely two disjunctions, but three. The first is the explanatory disjunction between the actions of individual role-incumbents and the selective pressures acting on the practices which define their roles. The second is the descriptive disjunction between the underlying processes of social evolution and the subjective experience of those involved in it. The third is the evaluative disjunction (whatever your own values may happen to be) between the moral and political judgements which have inspired what were conceived of as improvements in the condition of the people and the moral and political judgements which are subsequently provoked by their unforeseen and unintended effects.

MATERIAL PROGRESS

§4. Of all the areas of social policy in which these disjunctions emerge, unemployment relief is the one where they have emerged most vividly since the evolution of English institutions out of their late-Victorian and Edwardian mode. It is not just that neither the policy-makers nor the opinion-formers who sought to influence them could either explain what caused persistent unemployment or predict what might cure it, any more than could those who actually experienced it in their own very different terms. It was also that the measures which were taken to alleviate it produced consequences which were time and again at variance with what either the policy-makers or those affected by their policies had either expected or desired.

Whatever the views of right-wing commentators about the extent to which unemployment is the fault, if not the deliberate choice, of the unemployed, the sociological evidence overwhelmingly endorses the generalization that its psychological effect on them is bad (Warr 1978, p. 115). It is bad not only in the sense that all but a few of them would like to return to work if they could, but also in the sense that it disadvantages them in housing as well as in health, undermines their sense of self-esteem, diminishes their freedom of choice in the conduct of their lives, and exposes them (depending on individual temperament and circumstances) to the risk of serious clinical depression. Observations to this effect had been made by a variety of social investigators during the inter-war Depression, and were repeated on the basis of more systematic studies in the 1980s. The psychology of unemployment, about which there has been considerable academic debate, is outside the scope of this volume – that is to say, I am not concerned with the differences in personality which make some people more vulnerable to stress and deprivation than others or with the reasons for which some but not others translate the experience of unemployment into feelings of apathy rather than resentment. I simply assume, in accordance with the methodological argument of chapter 4 in volume I, that unemployment is to be regarded as an evil which governments of all parties would like to cure if they could – cure, that is, without recourse to solutions incompatible with the ideological presuppositions of capitalist liberal democracy.[2] Unemployment was 'cured', if you like, in 1939 by the outbreak of the Second World War. But nobody seriously argued thereafter that war was therefore to be preferred to peace, any more than that the unemployed should be despatched to compulsory labour camps, or forced to emigrate, or enlisted for 'national service' of indefinite duration.

These, to be sure, were not the only alternatives on offer in either the 1930s or the 1980s. Perhaps it would have been possible to create more new jobs if the labour market had been more flexible, or to re-employ more unskilled manual workers if they had been better educated in the first place, or to have preserved more subsequent opportunities for English-born workers if immigration policy had been more restrictive when the demand for labour was high, or to have kept workers in at least nominal employment by licensed absenteeism and part-time shift-work, or to have encouraged deliberate over-manning by government subsidy, or to have financed extensive public works out of higher taxation without creating more unemployment in other sectors through the reduction of consumer demand. But the answer is irrelevant here. The fact is that whoever may or may not be to blame, unemployment was persistently higher in the 1980s, as in the 1930s, than anybody had wanted it to be. To that extent, therefore, those willing to do an honest day's work but unable to find it could fairly claim that the new sub-type of the capitalist mode of production, for all the increase in GDP per head which it might be generating and for all the increase in real levels of benefit which that increase might make it possible to fund, had nonetheless failed *them*.

Nor was it as if this claim could be adequately answered by pointing out that the level of unemployment benefit was, in real terms, above the average earnings of unskilled manual workers in the late-Victorian and Edwardian period. As average earnings rose, so did benefit levels rise with them, and nobody disputed that they should. For the unemployed themselves, the nature of the choice between living on benefit and finding a job which will bring in as

---

[2] A revealing text in this connection is Keith Joseph's attack in 1979 on 'excessive government spending, high direct taxation, egalitarianism, Luddism, and an anti-enterprise culture' as 'poisons which wreck a country's prosperity *and full employment*' (my italics; quoted by Kavanagh and Morris 1989, p. 19).

much or preferably more net income remains the same. In the 1980s, as in the 1930s, there were some observers who maintained that the level of unemployment benefit was such as to constitute a disincentive to those in receipt of it actively to look for work (Capie 1987). But once again, the most systematic and reliable of the evidence tells against them. Gallie and Volger (1994) found that the work histories of the employed and unemployed are strikingly similar in both mobility and tenure, and that those of the unemployed who suffer greater financial hardship are no likelier to be more willing to take a lower-paid job or to move house in search of work. What is more, they found that differences in attitudes to work among the unemployed correlate little if at all with whether they do or do not re-enter employment later.[3]

Where there *is* a disincentive to work, it is not in the level of benefit but in the effective marginal tax rate imposed by the rules of the benefit system on some of those re-entering work. Hence the 'poverty trap' affecting not only claimants who might lose three-quarters or more of what they gained through finding work because of a concomitant reduction in their entitlement to family credit and housing benefit, but also retired people who could be penalized in loss of income support and housing benefit by increases in their occupational pensions. In particular, a working wife whose husband had been unemployed for a year had every reason to withdraw from the labour market at precisely that point, since her marginal tax rate would jump as a direct consequence of her husband's transition to means-tested benefits from an unemployment benefit linked to national insurance contributions. These consequences of uncoordinated and often makeshift adaptations of the benefit system to meet unpredicted contingencies were not foreseen, let alone intended, by Beveridge or anybody else. But from the point of view of unemployed men and women only too anxious to get back into paid work of a regular and legitimate kind, they were a blatant flaw in a system ostensibly designed to help, not hinder, them in doing so.

No doubt every system of benefits has its anomalies and imperfections, and some element of job insecurity is inherent in a mode of production in which the labour market is formally free. No doubt too it is both a symptom and a cause of material progress for twentieth-century English society as a whole that new technology should make it possible to eliminate many boring and repetitive jobs, that technical qualifications should attract an increasing premium, that the workforce should be more flexible and more mobile, and that opportunities for part-time employment for both men and women should increase rather than diminish. But changes like these are not, and never will be,

---

[3] To be precise, nine months later in a sample drawn from four selected areas in England and two in Scotland.

cost-free, or even a net benefit after costs for everyone affected by them. However preferable, according to your personal values, a capitalist mode of production over a socialist or authoritarian or any other alternative, you cannot pretend that unemployment is not a problem for it or that only a negligible proportion of the population suffers hardship in consequence of it.

§5. But even if we suppose that England's mid-twentieth-century sub-type of capitalist liberal democracy had somehow succeeded in ensuring that unemployment was always short-term, retraining opportunities always available, levels of benefit always sufficient to avert serious hardship, and gainful employment always on offer for at least one member of two-or-more-member families and households – even then, what about the plight of those permanently excluded from participation in the labour market at all?

It would be utopian to suggest that any 'welfare state' could abolish the underclass entirely. Even in periods of full employment, there will always be people of working age who for one reason or another are more or less permanently unable to work. Indeed, as the needs of the mentally and physically disabled became more widely recognized, they raised yet another dilemma of policy: should those needs be met by improving standards of institutional care, or should they on the contrary be met by enabling families and communities to accommodate them – to some commentators an obviously preferable alternative, but to others a simple-minded illusion nurtured by an unholy alliance between right-wing reluctance to spend public money and left-wing reluctance to see vulnerable people incarcerated at the mercy of authoritarian bureaucrats and self-interested professionals? And what about the needs of those friends, neighbours, or relatives forced into the role which the vernacular terminology came to label 'carers'? How far should employers, whether in the public or the private sector, be required to offer employment to men and women whom they would not otherwise select? And what about the 'victims' – if that is the appropriate word – of alcoholism and drug dependency, who might be as much of a menace to their employers and workmates if in work as to their families and communities if out of it? Or the habitual petty criminals fit only to return to their same way of life with their chances of legitimate employment reduced rather than enhanced both by their experience while in prison and by the reluctance of employers to take ex-prisoners onto their books?

All these are problems of social policy which have to be faced by mid-twentieth-century English or any other 'modern' society, whatever its mode or sub-type of production, once they are accepted as in one way or other the responsibility of the state. But on no theory could the same be said about the unintended creation of seemingly inescapable dependency on the state among the incumbents of roles of which the architects of the 'welfare state' had simply failed to take account. How far the failure should be judged as culpable is up to you. But no less in the aftermath of the Second World War than in that of the First, policy-makers had assumed that except during temporary periods of exceptionally high unemployment, male school-leavers would move into full-time employment lasting to retirement age; that women, although they might supplement the income of their households with paid work of their own, would give priority to their roles as wives and mothers; and that although there might be some households with dependent children where there was only one parent to provide for them, these would almost without exception be households where the single parent was a widow. Had this in fact been the case, and had national insurance benefit rates been held above rather than below national assistance rates and the tax threshold held above subsistence level, a combination of contributory benefits as of right with a non-contributory minimum income level might have fulfilled the expectations of policy-makers from 1921 onwards. But so far did this not turn out to be the case that by the early 1990s not much less than one household in two in Great Britain was at least in part dependent on a means-tested form of support, whether income support, family credit, housing benefit, or council tax benefit (Field 1995, p. 90).

This state of affairs was no less puzzling, as well as deplorable, to Labour than to Conservative policy-makers. When the household means test was abolished in 1941, Labour politicians assumed that that was the end of means-testing. But it was no such thing. In the 'heady optimism of the mid-'40s . . . the experience of the war years seemed to indicate that it was possible to provide means-tested assistance which was free of the taint of pauperism and which was claimed by all those who were eligible to receive it' (Deacon 1982, p. 294). But experience was to show not only that many people who were eligible would fail to claim such assistance, but that many would claim it who were not; and as the total expenditure on means-tested benefits inexorably rose, so did it lend support to the criticisms of observers on the Right for whom the 'New Jerusalem' of 1945 was 'a dream turned to a dank reality of a segregated, subliterate, unskilled, unhealthy and institutionalized proletariat hanging on the nipple of state materialism' (Barnett 1986, p. 304). It is not necessary to share the evaluative presuppositions underlying that comment to agree that the outcome of the long evolution of 'uncovenanted' benefits from 1921 through to the legislation of 1946 to 1948 and beyond diverged in unanticipated ways from the intentions of those responsible for it. There is an enormous literature on the history of British welfare policy, and within it there are many interesting counterfactual speculations about how it might have been possible, if different initiatives had been pursued, to avoid some of the most uncontroversially undesirable consequences of those which were. But whatever the answers, an expansion in transfer payments out of government revenues raised from taxation which was beyond the dreams of the reformers of the late-Victorian and Edwardian period had, nonetheless, failed to satisfy anybody that it was being distributed as it should.

§6. What then would Booth, Rowntree, the Webbs, Stephen Reynolds, Nurse Loane, and Maud Pember Reeves have had to say about it? They would not agree in their personal value-judgements now any more than they did then. But all the informed observers of late-Victorian and Edwardian England could, at the very least, agree that it had been 'a society where public health and hygiene came most slowly to those whose need was greatest' (Garrett and Reid 1994, p. 167); and if they had foreseen the steady rise in per capita income and concomitant increase in public expenditure on welfare which took place from the 1920s on, would they not have expected the problem of 'poverty in the midst of plenty' to be much more nearly solved? It is not as if even the most reactionary Conservatives thought that it was a good thing that infant mortality should be kept high, that as many children as possible should go barefoot, that as many houses as possible should be without running water, that the wages of unskilled labourers should be as far as possible below what was needed to sustain their physical efficiency, or that the higher the proportion of the elderly who ended their days in the workhouse the better. However passionate the disagreement on priorities between Left and Right over particular issues of social policy,[4] governments of all complexions wanted to be governing a more rather than a less prosperous population, just as they would all have preferred lower to higher unemployment despite their differences over what it was worth to achieve it. When, therefore, social investigators 'rediscovered' poverty in the 1960s, it was an unexpected disappointment to Right and Left alike. Commentators on the Right might seek to discredit the findings as exaggeration, just as commentators on the Left might claim that if anything they still under-estimated the poverty of the poor. But neither sought to pretend that there was nothing to worry about.

In this context, the most interesting of the reformers is Rowntree himself. He cannot be taken as 'the' representative investigator for the purposes of this chapter, any more than any single English person could be taken as 'the' representative member of even a single systact or milieu for the purposes of

---

[4] Notably in the House of Commons on the evening of 28 June 1923, when Maxton and Wheatley, in a debate on Scottish estimates, persisted in calling Sir Frederick Banbury, the member for the City of London, a 'murderer', and when they refused to withdraw were suspended from the House by 258 votes to 70; they were then followed by Campbell Stephen and George Buchanan, the members for the Camlochie and Gorbals divisions of Glasgow (165 H.C. Deb., cc. 2382–2402).

chapter 4. But not only was Rowntree, as we saw in chapter 1, the most influential of the enquirers into the 'problem of poverty' as formulated by progressive opinion in the late-Victorian and Edwardian period; he also lived long enough to publish, in 1951, a short book written jointly with a research assistant under the title *Poverty and the Welfare State*, in which he sought to summarize the effects of the measures introduced since his second study of York in 1936 on the reduction of poverty. It would be wrong to describe the book as complacent, particularly about the needs of the elderly (Briggs 1961, p. 330). Yet it came to seem so. Abel-Smith and Townsend (1965, p. 9) saw its findings as having encouraged precisely the view that their own findings called into question: 'They seemed to confirm expert as well as popular supposition. The absence of mass unemployment, the steady increase in the employment of married women, the post-war improvements in the social services and the increase in real wages all seemed to point unequivocally to the virtual elimination of poverty, at least as it had been understood in the nineteen-thirties.' Or as G. D. H. Cole put it, 'There are, of course, still immense differences in consumption between the rich and the poor; and despite high direct taxation there are still considerable groups able in one way or another to live lives of conspicuous luxury at the expense of the common people. These groups are, however, a good deal less numerous than they used to be; and – what is much more important – there is much less sheer privation at the bottom end of the social structure' (1956, p. xxiii). Yet there were still some 2 million people living in households with what, to Abel Smith and Townsend, were 'exceptionally low' incomes. And, more ironically still, a very large minority of these were children – thus confirming the continuing importance of the 'poverty cycle' to which Rowntree himself had been the first to draw policy-makers' attention.

The trouble is that, as everyone can agree, 'poverty' is not a theory-neutral term; and Rowntree himself never quite knew what he meant by it. There were always two separate themes in his mind. On the one hand, his aim in 1936, as it had been in 1899, was, as one of his commentators puts it, 'to show scientifically that some poverty was caused by incomes too low even for good managers to live decently on' (Veit Wilson 1986, p. 86). Hence his determination to fix a standard of poverty which could not be criticized as sentimentally generous, his sense of the need to bolster it 'scientifically', and his attempts to relate it to what representative working-class families could realistically be thought to be able to spend. But at the same time, he did not think that what in *Poverty and Progress* he called 'bare *subsistence* rather than *living*' (1941, p. 102) should determine who is to be counted as 'poor'. Hence his raising of his poverty line for 1936 to £2 3s 6d for a family of five – a figure which was deliberately higher in real terms than his poverty line for 1899, and intended to reflect the change since the late-Victorian and Edwardian period in the idea of what constitutes being 'in want'. Both his methods and his conclusions in both studies were open to criticism: he was unexpectedly amateurish in his statistical methods, and oddly reluctant, as I pointed out in section 16 of chapter 1, to use the data on family incomes which he had obtained in calculating the actual extent of 'poverty' in York. But even if his studies had been so designed and executed as to escape any possible strictures of this kind, that would not have enabled him to resolve the dilemma posed by his wish to define poverty in both deliberately generous and deliberately ungenerous terms.

It follows that for all his (and many others') desire to arrive at a genuinely objective assessment of how far the condition of the poor had improved between the turn of the century and either the inter-war period of active state intervention or the post-1945 'welfare state', no such assessment is possible. Nor is it possible, by distinguishing 'primary' from 'secondary' poverty as Rowntree did, to remove the subjectivity inherent in distinguishing the deserving from the undeserving poor. If you believe, with Adam Smith, that 'necessaries' include 'not only those things which nature, but those things which the established rules of decency have rendered necessary to the lowest rank of people', then the standard of 'subsistence' will rise with the growth of the national economy and there will always be a class of 'new poor' for whom the state will need to make provision – with the consequence that the concept of 'primary' poverty loses its meaning. But if you believe that there is a 'scientifically' demonstrable minimum, then as standards rise, you will refuse to count as 'poor' people or households who lack many of the amenities which all the rest of their fellow-citizens take for granted. No doubt Rowntree, were he to have lived to study eleven thousand families in York in 1999, would unhesitatingly have hailed as 'progress' the visible advances in housing, health care, unemployment benefit, and average real wages which had occurred over the course of the century. But he would be no nearer resolving his dilemma about how 'poverty' should be defined.

The dilemma does not, admittedly, arise for those whose evaluative presuppositions dictate either that all 'poverty' is 'primary' or that none is. For observers on the Left for whom poverty is a strictly relative term, there is always a moral case for raising the lower deciles in the distribution of income nearer to the median, however high the median may be. For observers on the Right for whom it is an absolute term defined by an adequate diet and a not insanitary or overcrowded home, any expenditure by the least well-off which is not required for one or other of these is conclusive evidence that they are not deserving because they are not 'in want'. But does any reader of this chapter seriously subscribe to either of these views? The disagreements by which rival observers have been most sharply divided, in the 1990s as much as in the

1890s, are about how, in practice, Adam Smith's dictum ought to be applied. Children running barefoot in city streets weren't the scandal in 1899 that they would be a hundred years later. But then as now, there was ample room for argument about what the 'established rules of decency' require, and ample evidence from which to conclude that money given to those defined by either public bodies or private charities as 'poor' would be spent in part on other things. Whatever the weaknesses in Rowntree's studies of poverty, they can be agreed to have made the dilemmas which any policy-maker must confront more clearly visible than they had been. Thereafter, you must decide for yourself what ought or oughtn't to be done by those whose roles empower them to do so.

RESPECT AND SELF-RESPECT

§7. To ask how far a diminution in social distance in the ideological dimension of the structure of twentieth-century English society is or is not a good thing for the people whose roles are involved is to raise two further questions which are in their different ways equally difficult to answer, even if conflicting value-judgements have been kept out of them. The first is whether the change is reflected in a measurable sense of increased self-worth. The second is whether a diminution of inequality between status-groups in one aspect of reciprocal behaviour may not promote alternative criteria of mutual differentiation by which competition between roles within the same mode and sub-type of persuasion will continue undiminished in other forms.

Discussion of these questions is apt to be further complicated by a well-known argument to the effect that people are better off, psychologically speaking, within a fixed hierarchy of roles where economic, ideological, and political power are distributed according to rules accepted by habit and sanctioned by custom. The argument presupposes on the one hand that *anomie* is a bad thing and on the other that duties as well as rights attach to the higher-ranking roles: those who control the means of production are assumed to act generously and fairly towards their subordinates and employees, those who control the means of persuasion to practice the norms of tolerance and responsibility which they preach, and those who control the means of coercion to expose themselves to the same or greater risks and hardships as those whom they order into battle on the society's behalf. Its strengths or weaknesses as an argument in political philosophy are irrelevant here. But sociologists of all theoretical schools must acknowledge the possibility that the diminution of a long-standing inequality of status may generate novel aspirations whose disappointment will only cause greater resentment in its turn. I pointed out in section 7 of chapter 3 that the selective pressures acting on the practices by which the roles constitutive of the mode of persuasion were defined had, at least for a time, a cumulative effect. But as I also pointed out, the evolution from one sub-type to another ended in a new equilibrium in which differentiation by the same criteria was still at work. Different observers will have different and mutually irreconcilable views not only about the optimal distribution of roles in the ideological dimension of the social structure but about the hypothetical conditions under which the chances of its being attained would be increased. But it is possible, without entering into inescapably inconclusive argument on either of these issues, to ask how far the change which *has* taken place accords with the hopes of the representative members of the status-groups which might be supposed to have benefited from it.

The young Alfred Marshall, in 1873, read a paper in Cambridge entitled 'The Future of the Working Classes' – a deliberate echo of Mill's chapter in his *Political Economy* on the 'Probable Future of the Labouring Classes' – in which he predicted that, although equality would always be unattainable, slow but steady progress would continue to the point that 'the official distinction between working man and gentleman has passed away' (Pigou 1925, p. 102). The presupposition underlying Marshall's way of putting it is that the manual worker has no opportunity for acquiring a liberal education and the 'free growth of his higher nature' which would go with it – an aspiration which would no doubt receive the proverbial two fingers from the working-class schoolchildren whose attitude to the middle-class curriculum I described in section 13 of chapter 4. But a point directly relevant to the concerns of this chapter is, all the same, being made. As hours of work came down, conditions of work improved, real wages rose, and working-class and middle-class life-styles became increasingly assimilated, why shouldn't a manual worker be as much of a 'gentleman' (however defined) as a non-manual worker, or (if you prefer) a non-manual worker as little of one as a manual worker? Why should any distinction of ascriptive status remain between them? And would it not be an unequivocal improvement within the liberal mode of persuasion that any lingering traces of such differentiation should be removed?

But now as then, to pose these questions is not only to highlight the irreconcilable differences between the values of commentators on the Left and on the Right but to expose the ambivalence underlying the opinions and value-judgements of would-be reformers of all theoretical schools. Whatever the conclusion to be drawn from the answer, the question 'what did manual workers themselves think the answer to be?' is one to which a work of sociology ought to be able to contribute by both the results of opinion surveys and observations of the behaviour of working-class people themselves. But, as we have seen, working-class aspirations were never particularly egalitarian, whether in the sense of seeking to abolish internal differentiation within the working classes or in the very different sense of aspiring to middle-class norms and life-styles. On certain questions of policy, there was no disagreement between the official representatives of the working-class interest and their political allies in the *bien pensant* upper-middle class. Of course workers and their representatives should be treated civilly and with respect by their employers and the value of their contribution to the welfare of the nation recognized equally with those of intellectuals, professionals, and entrepreneurs, just as they ought all to be decently housed, properly attended in sickness, adequately supported through periods of unemployment, and suitably provided for in old age. But the aspirations turned out to be more problematic than was foreseen by Laski, Tawney, Cole or any of the reformist intellectuals who, from 1918 onwards, saw in the policies and programme of the Labour Party the best hope for securing for the working classes the respect which the ideology and practices of *laissez-faire* capitalism had hitherto denied them. The cautious hopes for a genuinely more egalitarian future which Tawney voiced in the 1951 edition of *Equality* were no less plausible than Rowntree's cautious welcome for the improvements in the condition of the poor. But just as Rowntree would presumably have been dismayed by the persistence of imperfections and anomalies in the benefit system – all the more because of the proportion of government expenditure absorbed by it – so would Tawney presumably have been dismayed by the persistence of illiberal and inegalitarian attitudes in the working class – all the more so because of the erosion of so much of the old distinction between working-class and middle-class status-groups.

This dismay might have been, and on the part of some like-minded observers undoubtedly would be, bound up with value-judgements about systactic manners and mores. Even those who did not seriously want or expect to see working-class families use their new-found opportunities and resources to assimilate to the world of golf-clubs and dinner-parties might wish to condemn the behaviour of football hooligans and lager louts, or deplore the willingness to defraud the benefit system on the part of the sons and daughters of parents who had been too proud even to claim what they were entitled to, or regret that so much of their disposable income should go on what John Hilton had called 'pints, pictures, perms, pools, smokes, and all manner of fripperies and elegancies' (1944, p. 101). But such judgements are as irrelevant to this volume as the denunciations which could equally well be levelled against the extravagance, snobbery, selfishness, and lack of public spirit observable among the status-groups depicted in the pages of *Tatler*, *Hello!*, or *Harper's and Queen*. The answer to Alfred Marshall's prediction, suitably rephrased, has nothing to do with the apportionment of praise or blame. It has to do with the fundamental and persistent difference, which even a century of growth in per capita incomes could not undo, between occupational roles which are also careers and those which are not, and with the manners, mores, values, and attitudes which go with it.

To reassert, in this context, that the difference remained fundamental is not to minimize the significance of the changes reported, explained, and described in earlier chapters, including in particular the effect of both inter- and intra-generational social mobility in blurring the traditional distinctions between working-class and middle-class life-styles. But in spite of this, and in spite of all the progress (if you are willing to call it that) which has been made over the century in raising educational standards, improving conditions of work, enriching job content, and mechanizing or automating some of the more tedious, routine, and disagreeable 'manual' tasks, there remain occupational roles to which there does not attach 'parity of esteem' for the simple reason that anyone can do them. It is true that, as I pointed out in chapter 4, there are some working-class roles to which that does not apply – those in which, 'careerless' as they may be, there is a genuine requirement for skill or experience, or prestige accrues to the worker because of the dangerous and demanding physical conditions in which the work is done, or there is a degree of independence and discretion which gives the role an element of quasi-professional status. But there are not that many of them. And even if there were, whatever claims might be made for the beneficent effects of the evolution from one to another sub-type of the liberal mode of persuasion, fulfilment of Alfred Marshall's prediction cannot be said to be one of them.

The only such claim that could plausibly be made would be that the growing equality of life-styles on which Orwell, Priestley, Carr-Saunders, and others were already remarking between the wars continued to the point that, as one of Zweig's informants put it to him, 'I am working class only in the works but outside I am like anyone else' (1961, p. 135). Here again, it is important not to forget the reservations entered on this topic in section 14 of chapter 4. But there is no inconsistency in answering 'no' to the descriptive question 'are the subjective experiences of working-class families the same as those of middle-class families with whom they share an increasing similarity in life-styles?' and 'yes' to the evaluative question 'has there been an improvement, from the point of view of working-class families, in the extent to which they feel themselves regarded as status-equals by middle-class families?' The 'gulf', as I described it, which in late-Victorian and Edwardian England divided the music hall, brass band, public bar, and association football match from the 'legitimate' stage, classical concert, hotel lounge, and tennis club had by no means disappeared. But to the extent that it was experienced as a difference in tastes rather than a difference in attributes to be ranked by the dominant ideology as superior and inferior, progress had demonstrably been made – always presupposing that your own values are not such as to commit you to the view that a more castelike ordering of life-styles ought, on the contrary, to have been retained.

§8. But quite apart from the ranking of occupational roles and associated life-styles, the liberal ideology has to confront the differences in the respect accorded by the members of some status-groups to the members of other status-groups on other ascriptive grounds. Recall from section 13 of chapter 4 the remark of a girl from an ethnic minority about her first experience of racism at school. The use of vernacular terms of abuse with the deliberate intention of causing distress will hardly be defended as an indifferent, let alone a desirable, symptom of status-group differentiation even by the most committed defenders of freedom of speech within the liberal mode. Is there then any basis on which it could plausibly be claimed that there has been an improvement in the mode of persuasion here?

Although there have been and are societies in which the ideology of racism is openly endorsed by dominant status-groups and their official propagandists, it cannot seriously be argued, even by those most quick to detect and eager to denounce it, that England since the First World War is one of them. Racism has, from time to time, been outspokenly defended, but its defenders have consistently been marginalized by the controllers of the means of persuasion. It has tended at most to be half-heartedly excused, whether by commentators on the Right who sympathize with the feelings of those who practise it or by commentators on the Left who are ready to blame working-class racism, in particular, on the capitalist mode of production itself. But this, from the perspective of this volume, lends all the more force to the question with which I ended the preceding paragraph. Whatever your own value-judgements about racism, you are entitled to wonder why the liberal ideology has failed to dominate so blatantly illiberal a counter-ideology as effectively as in theory it should. Particularly, indeed, if your own values are those of orthodox liberalism, you may be not only surprised but dismayed that despite rising prosperity, improvement in standards of education, and legislative measures specifically directed to preventing their overt expression, discrimination and prejudice against ethnic minorities in twentieth-century English society are as widespread as we have seen that they are.

As with the failure of the capitalist mode of production to solve the problem of unemployment, the failure of the liberal mode of persuasion to solve the problem of discrimination could perhaps have been prevented under conditions which might have, but didn't, obtain. If immigration policy had been so consistently strict that only descendants of native-born Britons had ever been admitted for permanent residence in the United Kingdom, there could hardly have been occasion for ascriptive stigmatization of immigrants perceived as alien. Or perhaps, if immigration had been more gradual and the immigrants themselves more widely dispersed, they would have assimilated almost imperceptibly within the communities where they settled. But since this is not what happened, policy-makers were faced with attitudes and behaviour which directly contradicted the self-regarding image of English tolerance. Particularly, but not only, in urban working-class communities, the overt hostility and prejudice faced by ethnic minorities and the response of those minorities (including on occasion taking to the streets) were such that no political party could seriously argue that to the extent that there *was* a problem it could be left to resolve itself in the way that the liberal ideology might be thought to imply that it should. It is, no doubt, possible that in time it will, and that demands for equal treatment by members of ethnic minorities will be granted increasing legitimacy even by those who feel their interests threatened in consequence. But for the moment, 'it is difficult to come to any general conclusion other than that relations may have been getting "better" on some measures and "worse" on others' (Banton 1988, p. 113). And for as long as this is so, the dominant liberal ideology is, by its own criteria, on trial.

The same holds for the position of women. The feminist movement, like the movement for racial equality, has often been internally divided, and its opponents have accordingly been able to argue that its own ideology is no less incoherent than theirs: do women want their difference from men to be treated as irrelevant or, on the contrary, do they want it acknowledged as the reason for which they are entitled to more favourable treatment than they get? But whichever the answer, the liberal ideology could not comfortably contain even the late-Victorian and Edwardian version of the doctrine of 'separate spheres'. Then and since, there were anti-feminist women as well as men who agreed with Queen Victoria's view of what she had called 'this mad, wicked folly of "Women's Rights"', and perhaps some readers of this volume (although I suspect not many) agree with her. But when the suffragists made the point that a woman could be a doctor, mayor, factory hand, or teacher and yet be denied the vote whereas a man could be an alcoholic, a criminal, or an imbecile and yet retain it, the 'Antis', as they were called, had to find arguments of a different kind with which to resist them. Needless to say, they did; and not only Marxists like Hyndman and trade unionists like Burns but Asquith himself, like Gladstone before him, remained on their side. But by the end of the First World War, the notion that women were inherently unfitted, by contrast with men, to choose between rival parliamentary candidates had become increasingly implausible, and within a few more years entirely discredited – with the incidental irony that women turned out to be more likely than men to vote for the party which had been the most strongly resistant to enabling them to do so.

Thereafter, as increasing numbers of women came to occupy roles which had previously been restricted to men, so did their demonstrable competence in performing them make it 'morally impossible' (to echo the phrase which I quoted already in section 8 of chapter 3) to sustain the practices of exclusion and ostracism. The fact that despite this increase in numbers women continued to be under-represented, statistically speaking, in many upper-middle-class roles provoked very different responses among observers with different evaluative presuppositions. To some it was obviously right, and to others obviously wrong, that there should therefore be quotas laid down for admission to the House of Commons (or selection for candidacy by constituency parties), entry to the Bar (or promotion into the judiciary), or membership of academic departments or learned societies. But the disagreement was within the terms of an ideology whereby upward mobility, whether individual or collective, could not legitimately be denied to any group or category of persons demonstrably capable of performing the relevant role. Even those women, or their male allies, most dissatisfied that more progress towards complete equality of status with men had not been made since the granting of the franchise did not dispute that such progress as there had been was precisely that – progress as John Stuart Mill himself would have defined it. 'Everything, for a woman, is better now, even if it is still not as good as it could be' (Forster 1995, p. 307).

§9. What, then, is to be concluded about the 'new' liberal mode of persuasion and the ideology which legitimates it? Whether you subscribe to the ideology or not, you are equally entitled to ask whether the liberal mode does or does not enhance the quality of life of the members of English society in the way that the official ideology claims that it does. And since, in particular, it explicitly gives priority to equality of opportunity over equality of condition, both those who do and those who don't share the values which dictate that priority have reason to consider the possibility that there is an inherent contradiction within it.

Its claims have continued to be challenged alike from the Right and from the Left in much the same spirit as they were challenged, as we have seen, in the late-Victorian and Edwardian period by Hegelians on the one flank and Fabians on the other. Individualism has continued to be suspect not because the ideals of personal freedom and the capacity for self-realization are repudiated as such but because of the conflict between the individual's right to advance his or her interests by all lawful means and his or her obligation to respect the interests of the other members of the community to which he or she belongs. As in the late-Victorian and Edwardian debates over the nature and function of the state, it was a conflict reflected on both sides of the Left–Right divide. There continued to be, as I remarked in section 9 of chapter 1, anti-individualists within the Conservative no less than within the Labour Party. The anti-individualism of the Left is easier to follow and document, from Bernard Shaw's Fabian essay (1962, p. 218 n.1: 'All attempts to mitigate individualism by philanthropy instead of replacing it by Socialism are foredoomed to confusion') to similar attacks a century later on the lack of a 'general ethic of distributive justice . . . when laissez-faire liberalism proclaims the virtues of private charity' (Westergaard 1995, p. 72). But there were always Conservatives too whose implacable dislike of Socialism went hand-in-hand with a recognition that 'the extension of "freedom" by the creation of an enterprise culture and a free-market state' would endanger the freedom of the individual if it were to do away with the 'complex assortment of historic rights, laws, traditions, political institutions and corporations' whose importance has been stressed by Conservative theorists from Burke to Oakeshott (Gilmour 1992, pp. 198–9).

To be sure, the solutions put forward by Conservative anti-individualists were not only divergent in principle from, but incompatible in practice with, those put forward by the Left. But whichever way your own values and preferences may incline you, you can agree that equality of opportunity cannot but result in inequality of condition, and that if the result is unacceptable it can only be corrected by diminishing the freedom of choice of some at the same time as enlarging the freedom of choice of others. Consider for example the inheritance of capital. If all members of the society are free to do the best they can for themselves and their families, subject only to the requirement that their activities must be within the law, some families will do very much better than others, and unless some effective form of taxation, whether in life or after death, is strictly imposed, they will transmit the fruits of their endeavours to their children or other heirs. But not only will this progressively widen the inequality of condition between those who do best and those who do least well; it will also undermine the value of formal equality of opportunity. Just as any child of an ethnic minority family subjected to racial abuse in the classroom or playground can fairly ask what good the ideology of liberalism is to him or her, so can any child of underprivileged parents ask what is the value of it to him or her when denied, through the inheritance of capital by the privileged, the prospective benefits of supposed equality of opportunity through no fault of his or her own.

The dilemma is thoroughly familiar both in academic discussion about moral and political principles and in the planning and execution of policies in the areas where it is inescapable in practice, and it depends on your personal values which way out of it you choose. But it has a particular relevance to the concerns of this volume in view of the contrast between the functions of the state in the late-Victorian and Edwardian mode of production, persuasion, and coercion and its very different functions from the 1920s onwards. If there is a single text where its implications for mid-twentieth-century English society are most cogently elucidated, it is T. H. Marshall's lectures on *Citizenship and Social Class* which he delivered in 1949. They are at the same time a brief and lucid summary of the evolution from legal and political rights to civic rights and a warning of the potential for conflict of a different kind to which the exercise of civic rights may lead (Runciman 1996a). They are not an attack on the liberal ideology as such. But composed as they were when the welfare legislation of the Attlee government had recently come into effect, they are at the same time a welcome for the advance, as Marshall unequivocally regards it, over the principles which underlay the welfare legislation of the late-Victorian and Edwardian period and a recognition that to diminish inequalities between citizens of one kind may be to foster inequalities of another. If, with the critics of Marshall from the Left, you would prefer to see greater economic as well as social equality imposed at the cost of greater political inequality between governors and governed, nothing in Marshall's lectures, let alone in this volume, need inhibit you. But even if, on the contrary, you are an individualist of the most uncompromising kind, you will have to concede that there are conflicting objectives which cannot be reconciled within the liberal ideology.

In no area of policy was this more apparent in the decades after 1918 than education. That education is a good thing nobody denied. Nor was it questioned that children would, or at any rate should, benefit from the raising of the school leaving age from fourteen, or that the standard of teaching should be maintained and if possible improved, or that more pupils should be both encouraged and enabled to remain in school for longer if they so wished, and to go on beyond school to some form of higher education if they were qualified to do so. But education in what? And for what? And by whom? The long history of enquiries, reports, commissions, and debates from the Fisher Act onwards is full of detailed proposals as well as strongly held views covering the whole spectrum from infant schooling through to the universities – a history which can only reinforce the conclusion that unintended consequences are more important than intended ones and that the motives and ambitions of politicians and their advisers have singularly little to do with the actual process of social selection by which the future structure and culture of their society is being determined, as it were, under their feet. But whichever side you may be on in the long-running disputes over the public schools, or the grammar schools, or streaming, or the eleven plus, or technical training, or parental choice, or the curriculum itself, you will nowhere find a clear and consistent resolution of the liberal dilemma. Every child should be entitled to as good an education as any other, if equality of opportunity is to be more than an empty phrase. But what if that means in practice that children have imposed on them a curriculum which, as we saw in chapter 4, they neither want nor can put to use? It is not the business of this chapter to offer an answer. But the question itself leads to the answer to the question whether there is an inherent contradiction in the liberal ideology when applied to the choices which face the makers of educational policy. Whatever the educational policy which you would yourself like to see put into practice, the answer to that question is: yes.

'POWER TO THE PEOPLE'

§10. If, as I have said, the extension of the franchise after the First World War amounted by itself to an evolution out of one into another sub-type of the democratic mode of coercion, what can its recipients be said to have gained from it? For a start, by no means all of them took advantage of it at all. The turnout in successive General Elections since 1922 has varied for a multiplicity of reasons: there are sometimes significant regional differences, some eligible voters may have reasons of their own for not being on the electoral register at all, there may have been recent by-elections in some constituencies, the weather may deter some voters from going to the polls, some voters such as soldiers or students may not be in residence at their electoral address, and so on (Butler and Kavanagh 1992, pp. 345–7). But after the 1918 election, when as I pointed out in section 10 of chapter 2, the register was notoriously bad, roughly three-quarters of the enlarged electorate regularly cast their votes in General Elections – or to look at it the other way round, roughly a quarter of adult British citizens still did not choose to exercise the precious right for which democratic reformers had struggled for so long.

Before 1918, as we saw, informed observers, including those who favoured universal suffrage on principle, were worried that the enlarged electorate might be susceptible to the blandishments of unscrupulous demagogues. As the century progressed, and rival governments succeeded one another in office against a background of stable political allegiances and moderate party plat-forms, fears of volatility gave way to concerns about 'apathy'. After the Second World War, when political scientists had available to them the results of large-scale sample surveys as well as detailed local studies in which the opinions and attitudes of voters were systematically examined, it turned out that whatever else might determine their choices it was only in a minority of cases that they conformed to a model of deliberate choice between rival programmes carefully weighed against each other. On the contrary, such is the strength of family tradition, itself often bound up with long-standing occupational, regional, and even (still) religious differences, that it is only a relatively small number of 'floating' voters, so-called, whose changes of mind, whether between one General Election and the next or in the course of a closely fought campaign, determine the outcome. Whether you think it a good thing or a bad one, for the purpose of this chapter it reinforces the point of the question: what is it that the enlarged electorate can be said to have gained?

Later still, it became something of a commonplace that the electorate had grown increasingly cynical. As the age of Attlee and Churchill gave way to the age of Macmillan and Wilson and then in turn to a decade and more of 'Thatcherism', it was increasingly often claimed by political commentators not only that the electorate was less deferential than it used to be but that the democratic process itself was losing the legitimacy which it formerly enjoyed. But whether or not this is so, it does not follow that electors, however apathetic or cynical, derived no benefit from their possession of the right to vote. The change, as I reported it in section 10 of chapter 2, was that the working class as such was now fully integrated into the institutions of parliamentary democracy; and individual members of it could, and did, gain from that change without having themselves to go to the polls or, if they did, being either knowledgeable about the issues affecting them or enthusiastic about the party they chose to support. Just as apathetic or cynical trade-union members might benefit from improvements in wages and conditions negotiated on their behalf without any direct participation by themselves, so might apathetic or cynical electors benefit from policies for which their party could secure a mandate by speaking in their name. That this has, at least sometimes, been the case since 1918 is sufficiently demonstrated by the legislative measures passed by Conservative as well as Labour governments from which the incumbents of underprivileged roles have derived tangible benefits. It is, no doubt, arguable that some of these measures would have been introduced and passed even on a restricted franchise – legislative concessions to the working-class interest were, after all, made not only during the late-Victorian and Edwardian period but even before it. But it would be difficult to deny that some, at least, of the institutional changes reported, explained, and described in chapters 2 and 4 which *did* benefit working-class people were due, at least to some degree, to the extension of the franchise.

But if this is indeed so, was it to the detriment of other systactic interests? Is this an example of an institutional change where the gains accruing to one set of roles is at the expense of another? To any readers who share the view that since 1918 the middle classes have been worse, and the working classes better, treated by the state than they deserve, the answer will presumably be yes; and if you are one of them, neither I nor any other sociologist is entitled to say that you must change your mind. But the sociological question which can still (with the benefit of hindsight) be usefully addressed is whether the fears of those observers who were most apprehensive of the consequences of the extension of the suffrage were well-founded; and the answer is that they were not. Even those who most strongly regretted the displacement of the Liberals by the Labour Party during the inter-war period could hardly feel threatened by the policies pursued by Labour governments under the leadership of Ramsay MacDonald. The sight of Frank Hodges playing golf with the future King George VI (Lyman 1958, p. 14) was not, perhaps, as reassuring in itself as the financial orthodoxy of Philip Snowden as Chancellor of the Exchequer or, more important, the fact that they were governments which lacked an overall majority of seats in the House of Commons. But even when, in 1945, a Labour government was elected with an impregnable majority, the fears of its anti-socialist opponents turned out, as we have seen, to be almost entirely baseless.

This is not to say that they were not genuine fears. In 1945, the electorate could hardly fail to see itself as being invited to choose between two very different visions of what sort of a society post-war Britain ought to be. It is true that some voters chose not to choose between them: out of some 25 million votes cast, over 4 million were cast for parties other than Labour or the Conservatives. But on one side was the party of the status quo and on the other a party committed to its repudiation. How, therefore, could this fail to be the moment when the British people would have to choose between progress and reaction? And if Labour won, would it not be a definitive test of the ideals and policies of the Left? What is more, however irrelevant the rhetoric of the hustings when examined with hindsight (and particularly so when examined from the perspective of the theory of social selection), Churchill really was a bogeyman to many Labour voters just as Laski and Bevan really were to many Conservative ones. Churchill's housekeeper was not the only one who didn't know '*what* the world's coming to' when the result became known (Hennessey 1992, p. 86, drawing on M. Gilbert 1988, p. 111). And thereafter, it continued to be as important to labour politicians to portray themselves as radically different from the 'Old Gang' responsible for the evils of the inter-war period as it was to Conservative politicians to portray them as a dangerous group of irresponsible intellectuals, over-mighty trade unionists, and crypto-communist apparatchiks.

Later on, it suited both sides to pretend that they had not been so far apart after all. The Conservative Party sought to appear friendly to responsible trade unionism, sympathetic to demands for expenditure on social welfare, and ready as ever to place national above systactic interests, while the Labour Party sought to appear competent in the management of the economy, friendly to salary- as well as wage-earners, and forward-looking in its policies for science and technology. Later still, it suited both sides to claim that although there *had* been a post-war consensus, it had been a bad thing rather than a good one – to the Left bad because Socialism had been betrayed, and to the Right, bad because the quest for the New Jerusalem had diverted scarce resources from productive investment into wasteful and debilitating public services. But whichever side you are on, the shifting idiom of party-political rhetoric leaves unaltered the fact that much less changed between 1940 and 1951 than was proclaimed at the time, just as much more than was acknowledged at the time changed between 1915 and 1922. It follows that to commentators on the Left the enlarged electorate culpably failed to gain from their possession of the vote what they could and therefore should have. But only if you go so far as to say, with Proudhon, that universal suffrage is 'a device to make the people lie' can you translate your disapproval (if such it is) of the electorate's preferences into a denial that the extension of the franchise made those to whom it was granted better off in their own terms than they had been before.

§11. Yet, as we have also seen, power to the people as exercised through the ballot box was accompanied by power to the state as exercised by the swelling army of officials serving the new and enlarged departments and the ministers who presided over them. To the extent that they were perceived as using that power in the interests of those affected by their decisions, the new sub-type of the democratic mode of coercion was self-evidently an improvement over the old. But what is to be said to the many English people disposed to question whether they did, and the many commentators on both Left and Right who would have preferred their functions to be performed locally, voluntarily, and with a minimum of interference from either Westminster or Whitehall?

Not, to be sure, that all was well at the local level. Nobody called it a good thing that local government should be as inefficient, wasteful, and even, on occasion, corrupt as in many parts of the country it demonstrably continued to be. From the time when the Webbs had been compiling their exhaustive history of *English Local Government*, observers of all persuasions had worried about the apathy of local electors,[5] the vested interests of local councillors, the difficulty of attracting reliable and competent candidates to stand for local office, and the risks inherent in the entrenchment of single-party regimes in town and county halls. It was a further irony that in the very boroughs where those in need were likely to be concentrated, the quality of services was likely to be inferior, not just because of the lack of resources which I touched on in section 16 of chapter 4, but because of the lack of an effective electoral opposition. Since it was here that the ordinary citizen was most likely to come in contact with the agents of the state, it was here that the shortfall between expectations and performance was likely to be most keenly felt. To say this is

---

[5] Nor is it as if the voters who do turn out in local elections are voting on local issues: 'local election results overwhelmingly reflect national swings of opinion for or against the incumbent government as these are modified by different social bases in different areas' (Dunleavy 1980, p. 136).

not to underrate the role of the constituency MP: Bessie Braddock, for example, calculated in 1963 that she had seen some 75,000 'patients' in her 'surgery' since 1930 (Braddock and Braddock 1963, p. 162). But often constituents who turned to their MP were doing so precisely because of what they saw as the failure of their local authority to deal with a problem of housing, or social security, or the conduct of officials or police. What is more, it was often regimes like that of the Braddocks in Liverpool which attracted blame for an alleged decline in working-class political participation (Hindess 1971, chapter 5). Whatever the relation of central to local government, whatever the party in power, and whatever the mechanisms of selection of either elected councillors or appointed officials, the enfranchised and presump-tively articulate citizen unable to get a council house adequately repaired, or to discover a local authority's housing allocation points system, or even to understand the wording of the leaflets ostensibly designed to explain the workings of the social security system to the uninitiated, could reasonably wonder what exactly were the benefits which this supposedly 'democratic' network of agencies was bestowing upon him or her.

As a sociological as opposed, once again, to a philosophical question, this amounts to asking whether the bureaucratic practices whose diffusion and replication were reported in chapter 2 and explained in chapter 3 were bound to involve the failings for which bureaucracies have been criticized the world over since the days of John Lydus and before. The academic literature on bureau-cracy is huge, and its authors include some of the most respected authorities in the sociological canon. But for the purpose of this chapter, the point to be made is that the traditional criticisms of bureaucracy have been echoed over and over again by a succession of observers who have examined the workings of both local and national government in England since it evolved out of its late-Victorian and Edwardian into its mid-twentieth-century sub-type of the democratic mode. Many of these criticisms were, and will continue to be, couched in terms pre-empted by the evaluative presuppositions which lie behind them. What is more, the rhetoric of political debate encourages members of the opposition party to attack, in the name of 'democracy', the same practices through which they have sought to implement their own chosen policies when in office in the past and will do again if they can persuade the electors to vote them back in the future. But irrespective of the rhetoric, and whatever the value-judgements you may yourself be disposed to make about the power which attaches to the roles of the agents of the state in their dealings with the public, there runs through the discussions of policy-makers, practitioners, and academic observers alike the awareness of an inescapable conflict between the ideals of local participation and democratic decision-making on the one hand and the realities of bureaucratic administration on the other.

The conflict is as clearly articulated in the career of Beveridge himself as anywhere else. He had, after all, been directly involved in the setting-up of labour exchanges and introduction of statutory unemployment insurance in the late-Victorian and Edwardian period, and was to come to believe that it was the obligation of the state both to ensure that unemployment was only seasonal or temporary and to provide a universal and comprehensive national health service. But behind the invocation of 'democracy' in the opening sentence of the final paragraph of his celebrated Report ('Freedom from want cannot be forced on democracy . . . ') lay a conviction that it was for the state to decide on, and put into effect, whatever reformist opinion, backed by research, saw as in the best interests of those on whose behalf it intervened. The contradictions of Beveridge's personality and his sometimes startling changes of view are well-documented. But he was always one of those for whom, as I put it in section 15 of chapter 1, doing good was doing whatever the doers might choose to define as good rather than what might be defined as good by those to whom it was being done. He was a 'democrat' in that he well recognized the need for popular support for his proposals if they were to be put into effect. But he had as little compunction as any Hegelian Conservative or Fabian Socialist about empowering officials to bring about the outcomes which, within the framework enacted by Parliament, officials wished to see. Since, however, this is to some degree, whether you welcome it, deplore it, or are merely resigned to it, inescapable, the question which needs to be addressed alongside the question 'what did the ordinary citizen gain by it?' is 'what redress did the ordinary citizen have against its abuse?' Here, once again, there is evident scope for conflicting evaluative definitions of 'abuse'. But if England's particular mid-to-late-twentieth-century sub-type of the democratic mode of coercion is to be defended in its own terms, then this must be the test to apply. Granted, it may be said, that bureaucracy is inescapable and Beveridge to that extent right, what countervailing power against it does the citizen have?

Whatever the evaluative presuppositions with which you approach that question, the answer must be: not all that much. Defenders of English democracy could, and often did, point to the bureaucracies of other societies to argue that 'our' legal and administrative system was less restrictive of individual liberty, more open to scrutiny and criticism, and better provided with checks and balances than 'theirs'. But for all the importance, in this context, of the roles of the ombudsmen, the tribunal members, the judges, the advice workers both statutory and voluntary, the solicitors acting *pro bono* or with funds from legal aid, the constituency MPs in their surgeries, or the investigative journalists hot on the trail of scandal, the imbalance of power is unmistakable. 'But Parliament is sovereign, and governments, like local authorities, can be voted out of power.' Yes: it is, and they can. But how much choice does the electorate have? We have seen that the membership of 'extremist' parties has throughout the century been, to borrow Orwell's word for it, 'pathetic' – which may, according to your values, be a very good thing or a very bad one. But the choices put before the enlarged electorate are inescapably restricted, whatever the hopes or fears originally entertained by the advocates of universal suffrage. Complaints to the effect that in mid-to-late-twentieth-century England 'more areas of life have been brought under the control of the central state and removed from even the possibility of popular control or influence' (Hillyard and Percy-Smith 1988, pp. 109–10) are factually based, whether or not you share the evident wish of these authors that the facts were otherwise.

§12. The complaint that the mode of coercion is 'democratic' only in name has particular force when levelled at the roles through which the means of coercion are brought directly to bear. What comfort is there in talk about accountability and due process to an unemployed and homeless teenager directly subjected to intimidation and harrassment by the police even though innocent of any criminal offence? It has always been a relatively uncontroversial question to ask, when one society is being compared to another, 'where does the law-abiding citizen have least to fear from the police?' And whatever the answer in comparative terms, for the purpose of this chapter it is therefore relevant to ask: 'did the law-abiding citizen have any less to fear from the police after the late-Victorian and Edwardian period than during it?'

To this second question, the answer is that it became only a little easier, if that, after the First World War for the law-abiding citizen without money or influence to secure redress against malpractice by the police. To be sure, this is very different from saying that Britain is or ever has been a 'police state'. Undoubtedly too, access to free legal aid was an improvement over the 'dock-brief', the creation of a Police Complaints Authority gave an opportunity which had not previously been available for victims of mal-practice to be compensated and police officers guilty of malpractice to be disciplined, and the creation at the very end of the period of an independent Criminal Cases Review Commission enhanced the chances of a person wrongly convicted of a serious criminal offence having the conviction overturned. As cynical commentators were quick to observe, these improve-ments no less undoubtedly brought with them opportunities for abuse by unscrupulous lawyers, malicious complainants, and lying witnesses. For obvious reasons, there will be no chance, even with hindsight, of calculating either the decrease (if it is) in the risks of a miscarriage of justice or the increase (if it is) in the risk that defendants guilty as charged should contrive to walk free. Likewise, periodic scandals about police corruption in London or the Midlands could be interpreted by rival observers either as a sign of the determination of chief constables or the Metropolitan Commissioner to uphold the integrity of their forces or, on the contrary, as the tip of an iceberg of systematic complicity and concealment. The most that can be said is that there was an increase in public concern over the conduct of the police, whether that concern was as misguided as police spokesmen were likely to argue or, on the contrary, as abundantly justified as alleged by civil-libertarian pressure groups.

But this increase in public concern coincided with the seemingly irreversible centralization of control of the means of coercion reported in chapter 2 and explained in chapter 3. If 'democracy' implies the oversight of a multitude of small local police forces by the watch committees and standing joint commit-tees of the late-Victorian and Edwardian boroughs and counties, there is no escape from the conclusion that the mode of coercion was less democratic in the 1990s than it had been a century earlier. What is more, the evolution in the direction of less accountability was endorsed no less by Labour than by Conservative ministers. Explanatorily speaking, this is, as we have seen, as understandable as the accretion of power to the role of chief constable, the increased coordination of local police forces under Home Office direction, and the adoption of increasingly sophisticated equipment and techniques for the purposes of surveillance, investigation, and the prevention or suppression of public disorder. But it has meant that opposition to it has effectively been restricted to the campaigns of libertarian middle-class pressure groups; and although pressure groups are themselves a manifestation of democratic participation, their effectiveness, as I pointed out in section 11 of chapter 3, depends as much on their convenience to ministers and officials as on the commitment and enthusiasm of their members. As on all these topics, it is up to you whose side you are on: in the eyes of the police and those who supported them, the libertarians were themselves to blame for the decline in standards of behaviour which made it necessary for the police to be given more power, while to the libertarians the police were themselves to blame for exacerbating the hostility which they then used as an excuse for demanding it. But just as unemployment poses an unresolved dilemma for the capitalist mode of production and education an unresolved dilemma for the liberal mode of persuasion, so does policing pose an unresolved dilemma for the democratic mode of coercion. In the concluding words of the study from which I quoted in section 11 of chapter 2, 'The dilemma of reconciling effectiveness and control in the conduct of the law confronts social leaders today with the same urgency, uncertainty, and anxiety as it confronted their predecessors a generation ago' (J. Morgan 1987, p. 281).

WELL-BEING OR WELFARE?

§13. Flora Thompson, in *Lark Rise to Candleford*, asks of the vanished generation of country-dwellers whose lives she describes whether they knew 'the now lost secret of being happy on little' (1939, p. 74). Well – did they or didn't they? The question conjures up a familiar set of arguments about false consciousness, authorial prejudice, romanticization of the past, the nature of happiness, and the difference between 'well-being' (as judged by 'them') and 'welfare' (as judged by the policy-makers who are trying to do them good). It is tempting to dismiss it as sentimentality born out of nostalgia by puritanism. But it restates in perhaps its starkest form a difficulty which faces even sociologists who have no wish whatever to impose value-judgements of their own on the people whose well-being they are seeking to assess. *Were* the various social 'improvements' which changed the lives of the people of England almost out of recognition from what they had been in Flora Thompson's late-Victorian and Edwardian childhood *really* a 'blessing'?

The immediate answer must be that just as there is no evidence which would license the conclusion that working-class women in twentieth-century England did not consciously prefer to spend less of their adult lives in full-time motherhood than their own mothers and grandmothers had done, so is there no evidence which would license the conclusion that Flora Thompson's villagers did not consciously prefer to have more money to spend than their parents and grandparents had had. This might not prevent them from subsequently disapproving of what they would come to see as their own children's mis-spending of more money than was good for them, or from wishing that it was possible to reconcile the neighbourly norms of poverty with the selfish pleasures of affluence in some best of all possible worlds. But 'happy on less'? The implication is 'unhappy on more'. But would 'Old Queenie', 'Master Price', and 'poor old Dave' have refused a few more shillings a week if it had been offered them? Or did the later generations of ploughmen, shepherds, and labourers and their wives ever seriously wish that they were living the lives that their parents had lived? Of course not.[6]

The question for this chapter is not, therefore, whether people are entitled to their preferences. They are. But there remains the question whether they might not have preferred yet other alternative improvements to the quality of their lives which could, and therefore should, have been put to them but weren't. The often-quoted remark in Douglas Jay's *The Socialist Case* that 'the gentlemen in Whitehall really do know better what is good for the people than

---

[6] Cf. the temperate autobiographical comment of a working-class girl brought up in London between the wars: 'The supposed disadvantages of today's greater affluence need to be set against those bred by poverty' (P. Willmott 1979, p. 137).

the people know for themselves' (1937, p. 317) is usually construed – derisively – as a candid but deplorable assertion of bureaucratic paternalism of what might be called a 'hyper-Beveridge' kind. But even in the least bureaucratic of large, modern, complex, democratic societies, ordinary citizens cannot be well enough informed about the options in social policy confronting their governments and their advisers to be able to decide which will best accord with the ordinary citizens' own preferences – if, that is, they have even articulated them to themselves. The case for saying that the gentlemen in Whitehall *don't* know better than the people is that the gentlemen in Whitehall take decisions which, however benevolently motivated and thoroughly researched, demonstrably fail to achieve their intended result on the people's behalf. And there is ample material in any textbook history of twentieth-century England to justify the conclusion that the gentlemen in Whitehall often do fail in precisely that way.

Before pursuing this theme any further, however, let me head off a possible objection which some readers might be tempted to take directly from my own methodological injunctions in volume I. I may (it could be said) be right to insist on a distinction between reportage, explanation, description, and evaluation of social events, processes, and states of affairs. But doesn't this tell against my deliberate neglect of appraisals of England's capitalist mode of production, liberal mode of persuasion, and democratic mode of coercion by standards other than its own? The self-legitimation of capitalist-liberal-democratic societies rests precisely on their claim to be giving the people what they want. So am I not surreptitiously endorsing it by failing to confront the arguments of those who believe that some alternative mode of the distribution of power is better whether English people recognize it or not? But the answer to both questions is no. If you detest capitalism, despise liberalism, and regard parliamentary democracy as a fraud, the arguments of this chapter – and indeed, of this volume and of the whole trilogy which it concludes – leave you as free as ever to do so. Likewise, you remain as free as ever to argue that a different kind of society, actual or (if you wish) hypothetical, would satisfy the preferences of its members more fully than twentieth-century English society has done. But that is no reason why you should not be prepared to consider, on the basis of the evidence presented in chapters 2 and 4, how far the changes which those chapters report, explain, and describe have been subsequently regarded by policy-makers or ordinary citizens (or both) as improvements or otherwise.

It can hardly come as a surprise that the gaps between expectations and outcomes should be as wide as they are. It is not only because the hopes and visions of would-be reformers are so often impracticable. It is, in addition, because the behaviour of policy-makers is itself conditioned by the underlying processes of social selection, whether they are aware of it or not. I have said that it is not the purpose of this volume to narrate the careers of individual politicians or to chart the course of their shifting opinions and allegiances. But even the most superficial account of the policies of successive administrations from Lloyd George's to Major's will show, in many other instances besides those to which this volume has had occasion to refer, how arbitrary their conception and wayward their execution has been. It is true that there have always been contemporary commentators ready to point out the mismatches been social reality and political rhetoric and to predict, as it turned out rightly, that Lloyd George's housing policy would fall short of its targets, that Ramsay McDonald would be helpless in the face of high unemployment, that nationalization of the mines and railways would make far less difference to their operation than either its advocates or its opponents supposed, that a national health service could not be free of all charges at the point of delivery forever, that rising levels of income would not cure rising levels of crime, that racial discrimination and prejudice would not be eliminated by legislation, that a so-called 'community charge' or poll tax would be unworkable, and so on. But no commentator can ever predict what the long-term consequences of this mismatch between reality and rhetoric will be. Commentators, academic or otherwise, can only report (and deplore or not as they please) the succession of manoeuvres by which the contenders for political power in a democratic mode of coercion steal each other's clothes, or distance themselves from their predecessors, or rediscover mythical party traditions, or move to reoccupy the middle ground, or promise what they cannot seriously hope to perform, or do whatever else it may be that they, their colleagues, and their advisers believe will put them in position to put their nostrums into effect from the despatch box. There always has been, and always will be, both a gap between policy and performance and a gap between well-being and welfare; but the verdict to be passed on the policy-makers at the end of the day is up to you.

§14. This holds no less on the issue of inequality as such. To some sociologists, it is axiomatic that changes in a society's modes of production, persuasion, or coercion which reduce the social distance between its constituent roles are changes for the better. But what if the incumbents of those roles disagree? As I remarked in section 1, there is so little unanimity on the matter in twentieth-century English society that at no systactic level have all the incumbents of similarly located roles subscribed even to the policies and programmes which most obviously accord with their economic, ideological, and political interests. The sociologist who sets out to report, explain, and describe their conflicting opinions and attitudes is free to question their consistency, correct the information on which their opinions are based, and explore their reactions to hypothetical alternatives put to them. But no sociologist is or will ever be entitled to tell them that their opinions and attitudes ought, morally speaking, to be other than they are.

It is true that the question 'would or wouldn't more people think themselves better-off in a society in which the social distance between roles was narrower?' is in principle an empirical one. But how is it ever to be answered to the satisfaction of observers of rival persuasions? Consider the following exchange between two sociologists whose views about social inequality are self-evidently irreconcilable: the first quotation is from a book whose stated purpose is an analysis of 'the direction British society has taken in this century', and the second is from the rejoinder by a rival sociologist which it provoked.

> Unless they are shown to be relevant to needs, inequalities based on differences of personal quality are no argument against equality. Nor is the familiar argument that incentives necessitate inequality to be taken as a fundamental law of human economic nature. The incentives they assume are the products of present values and interests which arise from our existing institutions, and institutions can be changed. In a fraternal society it could reasonably be expected that any extra rewards to effort and capacity that might be necessary for the efficient division of labour would leave the basic structure of equal citizenship unimpaired. (Halsey 1981, p. 165)

> Of course in a sense he is absolutely right. Other versions of 'human nature', requiring different incentives, *are* feasible. The effectiveness of economic incentives *does* depend on established values and interests.
>
> These in turn do indeed arise out of the existing institutions of the liberal democratic order. And certainly, as the Socialist world graphically demonstrates, these institutions can be changed. The questions that need to be addressed in relation to these possibilities – questions systematically neglected throughout the material used to introduce students to sociology – are these:-
>
> 1. At what cost, economic and political, would such changes be instituted?
> 2. What evidence is there of any desire on the part of the vast majority of people for any such changes?
> 3. Why should it be supposed that the narrowing of equality differentials will not close off the dynamism of liberal capitalism, and result in significantly lowering everyone's standards of living?
> 4. What reason is there to suppose that sociologists' absurd obsession with inequality extends much beyond sociology's own narrow bounds? (Marsland 1988, pp. 152–3)

Taken together, these two passages could almost have been written to order to illustrate the arguments which I deployed in volume I about the need to disentangle the language of the seminar-room from the language of the pulpit. But their authors evidently see no such need, or they would not have written as they have. So on what grounds am *I* entitled to say that *they* shouldn't be doing what they do?

The answer is that they are just as entitled to be doing it as you or I or anybody else. But in doing so, they are not doing sociology as sociology is defined in this treatise. They are doing instead what the 'gentlemen from Whitehall' do when they move from assessing well-being to pronouncing on welfare. Some readers, sociologists included, may be inclined to respond to this remark of mine by asking first, 'But doesn't it need to be done?', and second, 'Aren't sociologists the people best fitted to do it?' – to which my answers are yes to the first question, but no to the second. Policy-makers do have to act on assumptions which are by definition untestable about the different prospective consequences of alternative decisions on the well-being of their fellow-citizens, and if sociology were, or ever could be, a predictive science, sociologists might indeed be the people pre-eminently qualified to advise them. But it isn't, and they aren't. Sociologists are better qualified only to report, explain, and describe what has happened after it has actually done so, and to evaluate it in the limited sense and to the limited extent that they can demonstrate that people themselves feel better or worse than they did in consequence of the decisions which the policy-makers have made.

§15. Then what, finally, about the rate of individual social mobility? More specifically, what about the well-documented increase in both inter- and intra-generational upward mobility which has continued since the late-Victorian and Edwardian period (and, so far as we can tell, was underway already during it)? Since it is plausible to suppose that only a very few members of twentieth-century English society have been downwardly mobile by choice, does it not follow that the higher the rate of upward mobility the better English society can be said on that account to be? But once again, matters are not so simple.

Glass and his associates, in the first of the two major studies on whose findings later sociologists have mostly to depend, adopted as a benchmark an ideal type of 'perfect' mobility which they defined in terms of random association between parental and filial rank across the range of occupational roles. But it is an odd definition of perfection to put forward even from an avowedly egalitarian point of view. In the first place, it pre-empts the question whether it might not be a good thing for children in the children's own terms that they should follow their parents into the same or similar occupational roles. And in the second, it ignores entirely the possibility that random association between parental and filial rank might be less preferable as a goal of policy, even – or, for that matter, particularly – to egalitarians, than collective mobility of the lower-ranked roles to the point that the social distance between the higher- and lower-ranked is negligible. Both these propositions are inherently contestable and there are probably as many different responses to them as there are readers of this paragraph. But would any of you, I wonder, seriously prefer to have been born into an otherwise unaltered capitalist-liberal-democratic society in which the relative location of parental and filial roles was random?

In the later study by Goldthorpe and his associates, Glass's concept of 'perfect' mobility plays no part. But the contrast between the increasing proportion of middle-class roles which come to be occupied by people who were born into the working classes and the relatively constant imbalance in the chances of a working-class child attaining a middle-class role is persistently drawn in such a way as to imply that it is not a good thing. To some degree, as I have pointed out already, it is simply an arithmetical function of the relative size of the different systacts and the fertility differentials between their members. But to imply that it is a bad thing is to be committed to the view that a higher proportion of middle-class (and, *a fortiori*, élite-born) children ought to be downwardly mobile. Now there are several reasons for which you may well agree that they ought. One is that you believe that there is an untapped reservoir of talent in the working classes and that there are many more working-class children who, if adequately trained, ought to displace from middle-class roles the less talented middle-class children now occupying them. Another is that you think the liberal ideology of equality of opportunity would carry more conviction if everyone could see that children born into middle-class families had no better chance, and preferably a worse one, of a middle-class career than children born into working-class families. Yet another is that you would like to see all children of relatively privileged parents begin their adult lives in less privileged roles and work their way up from there. But all of these can, and doubtless will, be contested by other observers who do not dispute any of the numbers in the cells of the mobility matrix but do not share your evaluative presuppositions. Nor are you free to say in reply that you are doing no more than I have myself been doing in this chapter – that is, offering an assessment of how far the change which has in fact taken place has been a good thing from the point of view of the preferences of all those affected by it – since although an increase in absolute mobility rates might be Pareto-optimal, a higher rate of structural downward mobility would quite obviously not be.

Optimal mobility rates, therefore, like optimal social distances between roles and systacts, are for the moral or political philosopher, not the sociologist, to define. The philosopher, like the hypothetical observer whom I introduced in the concluding section of chapter 1, can fairly look to sociologists to provide the evidence for qualifications and credentials, methods of selection and promotion, techniques of obstruction and exclusion, grounds of ascriptive discrimination, ties of patronage and clientship, inheritance of monetary and 'social' or 'human' capital, and the whole range of practices which determine not only how much power attaches to English society's constituent roles but who will individually occupy and perform them. Even, however, if the evidence is as detailed and reliable as it can be, and its interpretation as uncontroversial between sociologists of rival schools as it will ever be realistic to expect, there will never be any more agreement about optimal social distances or optimal mobility rates than there will about the merits or demerits of the capitalist mode of production, liberal mode of persuasion, or democratic mode of coercion themselves.

CONCLUSION

§16. I cannot emphasize too strongly that this volume is 'applied' social theory only in the sense that it applies the theory of social selection expounded in volume II and the methodology expounded in volume I to the particular case of twentieth-century England. It is not 'applied' in the very different sense that medicine, say, is applied physiology. This final chapter, accordingly, can fairly be regarded as no more than an appendix to the reports, explanations, and descriptions which I have given of a society whose economic, ideological, and political institutions have evolved, during the course of the twentieth century, as far and no further than they have. Since there will never be agreement on the aims of social policy of the kind which there is about the aims of medicine, there will never be textbooks of applied sociology to which policy-makers can turn in the way that doctors can turn to textbooks of medicine. Yet it would be a mistake to conclude that sociology has nothing whatever to contribute to policy. Policy-makers who understand, in the secondary, explanatory sense why their society's modes of production, persuasion, and coercion are as they are, and also understand in the tertiary, descriptive sense, what it is like for the members of their society to occupy the roles which they do within it, will be at least a little less likely to take decisions whose consequences are grossly at variance with their stated objectives and inimical to the well-being of those affected by them; and to the extent that their aim is to improve the condition of the people as the people see it, sociology may help them to make their society better than it was before. I have confessed elsewhere (Runciman 1989, p. 13) that when I set out on a career in academic sociology, one of my motives was the hope that sociology could be useful to governments with the broad and uncontentious aim of improving the quality of life of the people of Britain as a whole. As readers of this volume will undoubtedly have detected, I would now take a less naively optimistic view. But I have not abandoned the hope entirely.

References

Abel-Smith, Brian and Townsend, Peter (1965) *The Poor and the Poorest* (London)

Abrams, Mark (1983) 'Demographic Correlates of Values', in Mark Abrams *et al.*, eds., *Values and Social Change in Britain* (Basingstoke)

Adam, H. L. (1931) *C.I.D. Behind the Scenes at Scotland Yard* (London)

Adam Smith, Janet (1979) *John Buchan and his World* (London)

Adams, Henry (1946) *The Education of Henry Adams* (2nd edn, Boston)

Addison, Paul (1975) *The Road to 1945. British Politics and the Second World War* (London)

  (1985) *Now the War is Over. A Social History of Britain 1945–51* (London)

Alderman, Geoffrey (1983) *Pressure Groups and Government in Great Britain* (London)

Aldiss, B. (1970) *The Hand-Reared Boy* (London)

Allen, Charles (1975) *Plain Tales from the Raj: Images of British India in the Twentieth Century* (London)

Allen, G. C. (1966) *The Structure of Industry in Britain* (2nd edn, London)

Allen, V. L. (1957) *Trade Union Leadership* (London)

  (1981) *The Militancy of British Miners* (Shipley)

Anderson, Olive (1971) 'The Growth of Christian Militarism in Mid-Victorian Britain', *English Historical Review* 85

Andrews, Molly (1991) *Lifetimes of Commitment: Ageing, Politics, Psychology* (Cambridge)

Argyle, Michael (1994) *The Psychology of Social Class* (London)

Ashton, D. N. (1973) 'The Transition from School to Work: Notes on the Development of Different Frames of Reference Among Young Male Workers', *Sociological Review* 21

Atkinson, A. B. (1975) *The Economics of Inequality* (Oxford)

Bagguley, Paul (1991) *From Protest to Acquiescence? Political Movements of the Unemployed* (London)

  (1992) 'Social Change, the Middle Class and the Emergence of "New Social Movements": A Critical Analysis', *Sociological Review* 40

Bailey, Peter (1994) 'Conspiracies of Meaning: Music-Hall and the Knowingness of Popular Culture', *Past & Present* 144

Bain, G. S. (1970) *The Growth of White-Collar Unionism* (Oxford)

Bain, G. S. and Price, Robert (1972) 'Who is a White-collar Employee?', *British Journal of Industrial Relations* 10

  (1980) *Profiles of Union Growth: A Comparative Statistical Portrait of Eight Countries* (Oxford)

Banks, James *et al.* (1994) *The Distribution of Wealth in the UK* (London)

Banton, Michael (1988) *Racial Consciousness* (Harlow)

Barker, Ernest (1937) 'The Home Civil Service', in W. A. Robson, ed., *The British Civil Servant* (London)

Barker, R. S. (1986) 'Civil Service Attitudes and the Economic Planning of the Attlee Government', *Journal of Contemporary History* 21

Barna, Tibor (1959) Comment on H. F. Lydall, 'The Long-Term Trend in the Size Distribution of Income', *Journal of the Royal Statistical Society* 122

Barnes, Trevor (1979) 'Special Branch and the First Labour Government', *Historical Journal* 21

Barnett, Corelli (1986) *The Audit of War. The Illusion and Reality of Britain as a Great Nation* (London)

Barr, Ann and York, Peter (1982) *The Official Sloane Ranger Handbook: The First Guide to What Really Matters in Life* (London)

Beales, H. L. and Lambert, R. S. (1934) *Memoirs of the Unemployed* (London)

Beard, Madeleine (1989) *English Landed Society in the Twentieth Century* (London)

Beaverbrook, Lord (1963) *The Decline and Fall of Lloyd George* (London)

Bechhofer, Frank *et al.* (1974) 'The Petits Bourgeois in the Class Structure: The Case of the Small Shopkeepers', in Frank Parkin, ed., *The Social Analysis of Class Structure* (London)

Beer, Samuel H. (1965) *Modern British Politics: A Study of Parties and Pressure Groups* (London)

(1982) *Britain Against Itself* (London)

Bell, Lady (1907) *At the Works* (London)

Beloff, Max and Peele, Gillian (1980) *The Government of the United Kingdom: Political Authority in a Changing Society* (London)

Benney, Mark (1936) *Low Company: Describing the Evolution of a Burglar* (London)

Benney, Mark *et al.* (1956) *How People Vote* (London)

Benson, John (1983) *The Penny Capitalists: A Study of Nineteenth-Century Working-Class Entrepreneurs* (Dublin)

(1989) *The Working Class in Britain 1850–1939* (London)

Best, Geoffrey (1971) *Mid-Victorian Britain 1851–1875* (London)

Bevan, Aneurin (1952) *In Place of Fear* (London)

Beveridge, William (1932) *Changes in Family Life* (London)

Birkenhead, Earl of (1965) *Halifax: The Life of Lord Halifax* (London)

Birnbaum, Norman (1955) 'Monarchs and Sociologists: A Reply to Professor Shils and Mr. Young', *Sociological Review* 3

Bishop, T. S. H. (1967) *Winchester and the Public School Elite* (London)

Black, Margaret (1994) 'Clerical Workers in the 1950s and 1960s: the Use of Oral Evidence', *Oral History* 22

Blackburn, R. M. and Mann, Michael (1979) *The Working Class in the Labour Market* (London)

Blake, Robert (1985) *The Conservative Party from Peel to Thatcher* (London)

Blatchford, Robert (1893) *Merrie England* (London)

(1937) *My Early Years* (London)

Bonham, John (1954) *The Middle Class Vote* (London)

Booker, John (1991) 'Historically Speaking', *The Stable Companion: The Newsletter for Lloyds Bank Pensioners* 7

Booth, Alan (1982) 'Corporatism, Capitalism and Depression in Twentieth-Century Britain', *British Journal of Sociology* 33

(1987) 'Britain in the 1930s: A Managed Economy?', *Economic History Review* 40

Booth, General (William) (1890) *Darkest England and The Way Out* (London)

Bottomore, Thomas (1954) 'Social Stratification in Voluntary Organizations', in D. V. Glass, ed., *Social Mobility in Britain* (London)

Bowley, A. L. (1920) *The Change in the Distribution of the National Income* (Oxford)

(1921) *Prices and Wages in the United Kingdom, 1914–1920* (Oxford)

(1931) *Some Economic Consequences of the Great War* (London)

Bowley, A L. and Hogg, M. H. (1925) *Has Poverty Diminished?* (London)

Bowley, Marian (1945) *Housing and the State* (London)

Boyd, Robert and Richerson, Peter J. (1985) *Culture and the Evolutionary Process* (Chicago)

Braddock, Jack and Braddock, Bessie (1963) *The Braddocks* (London)

Bradley, Ian (1982) *The English Middle Classes are Alive and Kicking* (London)

Brenan, Gerald (1957) *South From Granada* (London)

Briggs, Asa (1961) *A Study of the Work of Seebohm Rowntree 1871–1954* (London)

(1964) 'The Political Scene', in Simon Nowell-Smith, ed., *Edwardian England 1901–1914* (London)

Broady, Maurice (1956) 'The Organisation of Coronation Street Parties', *Sociological Review* 4

Brogden, Mike (1991) *On the Mersey Beat: Policing Liverpool between the Wars* (Oxford)

Brooke, Stephen (1991) 'Problems of "Socialist Planning": Evan Durbin and the Labour Government of 1945', *Historical Journal* 34

(1992) *Labour's War. The Labour Party during the Second World War* (Oxford)

Brown, Colin (1984) *Black and White Britain: The Third PSI Survey* (London)

Brown, Kenneth D. (1982) 'Trade Unions and the Law', in Chris Wrigley, ed., *A History of British Industrial Relations 1975–1914* (Amherst, Mass.)

(1985) 'The Edwardian Labour Party', in Kenneth D. Brown, ed., *The First Labour Party 1906–1914* (London)

Brown, R. K. *et al.* (1972) 'The Contours of Solidarity: Social Stratification and Industrial Relations in Shipbuilding', *British Journal of Industrial Relations* 10

Brown, Richard (1982) 'Work Histories, Career Strategies and the Class Structure', in Anthony Giddens and Gavin Mackenzie, eds., *Social Class and the Division of Labour* (Cambridge)

Buchan, William (1982) *John Buchan: A Memoir* (London)

Buck, Nick (1992) 'Labour Market Inactivity and Polarisation: A Household Perspective on the Idea of the Underclass', in David J. Smith, ed., *Understanding the Underclass* (London)

Buck, Nick *et al.* (1994) *Changing Households. The British Household Panel Survey 1990–1992* (London, ESRC)

Bullock, Alan (1960) *The Life and Times of Ernest Bevin I* (London)

(1967) *The Life and Times of Ernest Bevin II* (London)

Burgess, Keith (1980) *The Challenge of Labour: Shaping British Society 1850–1930* (London)

Burke, Joanna (1994) 'Housewifery in Working-Class England 1860–1914', *Past & Present* 143

Burn, W. L. (1964) *The Age of Equipoise: A Study of the Mid-Victorian Generation* (London)

Burnett, John *et al.* (1987) *The Autobiography of the Working Class. An Annotated Critical Bibliography II: 1900–1945* (Brighton)

Bushell, S. M. (1921) 'The Relative Importance of Cooperative, Multiple and Other Retail Traders', *Economica* 1

Butler, D. E. (1953) *The Electoral System in Britain 1918–1951* (Oxford)

Butler, D. E. and Kavanagh, Dennis (1992) *The British General Election of 1992* (London)

Butler, D. E. and Stokes, Donald (1969) *Political Change in Britain: Forces Shaping Electoral Choice* (London)

Buxton, N. K. (1970) 'Entrepreneurial Efficiency in the British Coal Industry Between the Wars', *Economic History Review* 23

Cain, P. J. and Hopkins, A. G. (1993) *British Imperialism: Crisis and Deconstruction 1914–1990* (London)

Cairncross, Alex (1985) *Years of Recovery: British Economic Policy 1945–51* (London)

Campbell, Beatrix (1993) *Goliath: Britain's Dangerous Places* (London)

Campbell, John (1987) *Nye Bevan and the Mirage of British Socialism* (London)

Cannadine, David (1990) *The Decline and Fall of the British Aristocracy* (London)

Capie, Forrest (1987) 'Unemployment and Real Wages', in Sean Glynn and Alan Booth, eds., *The Road to Full Employment* (London)

Cardiff, David (1983) 'Time, Money and Culture: BBC Programme Finances, 1927–1939', *Media, Culture and Society* 5

Carnegie Trust (1945) *Disinherited Youth* (Edinburgh)

Carpenter, L. P. (1973) *G. D. H. Cole: An Intellectual Biography* (Cambridge)

Carr, E. H. (1961) *What is History?* (London)

Carr, Gordon (1975) *The Angry Brigade* (London)

Carr-Saunders, A. M. and Jones, D. Caradog (1927) *A Survey of the Social Structure of England and Wales* (1st edn, Oxford)

(1937) *A Survey of the Social Structure of England and Wales* (2nd edn)

Cavalli-Sforza, L. L. and Feldman, M. W. (1981) *Cultural Transmission and Evolution: A Quantitative Approach* (Princeton)

Cecil, David (1964) *Max* (London)

Chandler, J. A. (1991) *Local Government Today* (Manchester)

Chesterton, G. K. (n.d.) *Autobiography* (London)

Chinn, Carl (1988) *They Worked All Their Lives: Women of the Urban Poor in England, 1880–1939* (Manchester)

Citrine, Lord (1964) *Men and Work: An Autobiography* (London)

Clark, Colin (1937) *National Income and Outlay* (London)

Clarke, Peter (1978) *Liberals and Social Democrats* (Cambridge)

(1990) 'The Treasury's Analytical Model of the British Economy between the Wars', in Mary O. Furner and Barry Supple, eds., *The State and Economic Knowledge: The American and British Experiences* (Cambridge)

Clegg, H. A. (1979) *The Changing System of Industrial Relations in Great Britain* (Oxford)

(1985) *A History of British Trade Unions since 1889 II: 1911–1933* (Oxford)

Close, David H. (1977) 'The Collapse of Resistance to Democracy: Conservatives, Adult Suffrage, and Second Chamber Reform, 1911–1928', *Historical Journal* 20

Coates, R. D. (1972) *Teachers' Unions and Interest Group Politics: A Study of the Behaviour of Organized Teachers in England and Wales* (Cambridge)

Cobb, Richard (1983) *Still Life* (London)

Cockburn, Cynthia (1986) 'Opportunity is Not Enough', in Kate Purcell *et al.*, eds., *The Changing Experience of Employment: Restructuring and Recession* (Basingstoke)

(1987) *Women, Trade Unions and Political Parties* (London)

Cohen, Ruth *et al.* (1992) *Hardship Britain. Being Poor in the 1990s* (London)

Cole, G. D. H. (1927) *A Short History of the British Working-Class Movement 1789–1927* (London)

(1956) *The Post-War Condition of Britain* (London)

Cole, Margaret I. ed., (1952) *Beatrice Webb's Diaries 1912–1924* (London)

ed., (1956) *Beatrice Webb's Diaries 1924–1932* (London)

Coleman, D. C. (1973) 'Gentlemen and Players', *Economic History Review* 26

Collison, Peter (1960) 'Occupation, Education and Housing in an English City', *American Journal of Sociology* 65

Common, Jack (1951) *Kiddar's Luck* (London)

Cook, Chris (1975) 'Liberals, Labour and Local Elections', in Gillian Peele and Chris Cook, eds., *The Politics of Reappraisal 1918–1939* (London)

Cook, Dee (1989) *Rich Law, Poor Law: Differential Response to Tax and Supplementary Benefit Fraud* (Milton Keynes)

Cooper, Duff (1953) *Old Men Forget* (London)

Cordery, Simon (1995) 'Friendly Societies and the Discourse of Respectability in Britain, 1825–1875', *Journal of British Studies* 34

Cowling, Maurice (1971) *The Impact of Labour 1920–1924* (Cambridge)

Crompton, Rosemary and Jones, Gareth (1984) *White Collar Proletariat: Deskilling and Gender in the Clerical Labour Process* (London)

Crompton, Rosemary and Sanderson, Kay (1990) 'Credentials and Careers', in Geoff Payne and Pamela Abbott, eds., *The Social Mobility of Women: Beyond Male Mobility Models* (London)

Cronin, James E. (1984) *Labour and Society in Britain 1918–1979* (London)

Crosland, Anthony (1956) *The Future of Socialism* (London)

(1960) *Can Labour Win?* (Fabian Society)

Crouch, Colin and Dore, Ronald (1990) 'Whatever Happened to Corporatism?', in Colin Crouch and Ronald Dore, eds., *Corporatism and Accountability: Organized Interests in British Public Life* (Oxford)

Crowther, M. A. (1981) *The Workhouse System, 1834–1929. The History of an English Social Institution* (London)

Currie, Robert (1979) *Industrial Politics* (Oxford)

D'Aeth, F. G. (1910) 'Present Tendencies of Class Differentiation', *Sociological Review* 3

Daniel, W. W. (1987) *Workplace Industrial Relations and Technical Change* (London)

(1990) 'Needed: A Policy for Industrial Relations', *Policy Studies* 11

Darwin, John (1980) 'Imperialism in Decline? Tendencies in British Imperial Policy Between the Wars', *Historical Journal* 23

Daunton, M. J. (1996) 'Payment and Participation: Welfare and State-Formation in Britain 1900–1951', *Past & Present* 150

Davidson, Roger (1978) 'The Board of Trade and Industrial Relations 1896–1914', *Historical Journal* 21

Davies, Andrew (1991) 'The Police and the People: Gambling in Salford, 1900–1939', *Historical Journal* 34

Davison, R. C. (1938) *British Unemployment Policy since 1930* (London)

Dayus, Kathleen (1985) *Where There's Life* (London)

Deacon, Alan (1977) 'Concession and Coercion: the Politics of Unemployment Insurance in the Twenties', in Asa Briggs and John Saville, eds., *Essays in Labour History 1918–1939* (London)

(1982) 'An End to the Means Test?', *Journal of Social Policy* 11

Deacon, Alan and Briggs, Eric (1974) 'Local Democracy and Central Policy: The Issue of Pauper Votes in the 1920s', *Policy and Politics* 2

Dearlove, John and Saunders, Peter (1984) *Introduction to British Politics. Analyzing a Capitalist Democracy* (Cambridge)

Delafield, E. M. (1951) 'Introduction' to 'Pont', *The British Character Studied and Revealed* (London)

Delamont, S. (1989) *Knowledgeable Women: Structuralism and the Reproduction of Elites* (London)

Demant, V. A. (1931) *Unemployment: Disaster or Opportunity* (London)

Dench, Geoff (1985) *Minorities in the Open Society: Prisoners of Ambivalence* (London)

Dennett, Daniel C. (1995) *Darwin's Dangerous Idea: Evolution and the Meanings of Life* (London)

Dennis, Norman *et al.* (1956) *Coal is Our Life* (London)

Descamps, P. (1914) *La formation sociale de l'anglais moderne* (Paris)

Devine, Fiona (1992) 'Social Identities, Class Identity, and Political Perspectives', *Sociological Review* 40

Dex, Shirley (1987) *Women's Occupational Mobility* (London)

Ditton, Jason (1977) *Part-time Crime: An Ethnography of Fiddling and Pilferage* (London)

(1979) 'Baking Time', *Sociological Review* 27

Donnison, David (1982) *The Politics of Poverty* (Oxford)

Dore, R. P. (1973) *British Factory-Japanese Factory. The Origins of National Diversity in Industrial Relations* (London)

Douglas-Home, Charles (1978) *Evelyn Baring. The Last Proconsul* (London)

Duckers, Nigel and Davies, Huw (1990) *A Place in the Country: Social Change in Rural England* (London)

Dunleavy, P. (1980) *Urban Political Analysis* (London)

Durant, Ruth (1939) *Watling: A Social Survey* (London)

The Economist

Elias, N. and Scotson, J. L. (1965) *The Established and the Outsiders: A Sociological Enquiry into Community Problems* (London)

Elliott, Brian *et al.* (1983) 'Bourgeois Social Movements in Britain: Repertories and Responses', in Roger King, ed., *Capital and Politics* (London)

Emy, H. V. (1972) 'The Impact of Financial Policy on English Party Politics before 1914', *Historical Journal* 15

Ensor, R. C. K. (1936) *England 1870–1914* (Oxford)

Evans, Geoffrey (1993) 'The Decline of Class Divisions in Britain? Class and Ideological Preferences in the 1960s and the 1980s', *British Journal of Sociology* 44

Exell, Arthur (1980) 'Morris Motors in the 1940s', *History Workshop* 9

Field, Frank (1995) *Making Welfare Work: Reconstructing Welfare for the Millennium* (London)

Financial Times

Finlayson, Geoffrey (1994) *Citizen, State and Social Welfare in Britain 1830–1990* (Oxford)

Fitzgerald, Marion (1992) *Ethnic Minorities and the Criminal Justice System* (Research Study 20, Royal Commission on Criminal Justice. London, HMSO)

Flanders, Allan (1964) *Trade Unions* (London)

Forrester, Helen (1981) *By the Waters of Liverpool* (London)

Forster, Margaret (1995) *Hidden Lives: A Family Memoir* (London)

Fowler, David (1992) 'Teenage Consumers? Young Wage-earners and Leisure in Manchester, 1919–1939', in Andrew Davies and Steven Fielding, eds., *Workers' Worlds: Cultures and Communities in Manchester and Salford 1880–1939* (Manchester)

Fox, Alan (1985) *History and Heritage* (London)

Freud, Sigmund (1955) *Moses and Monotheism* (2nd edn, London)

Fulcher, James (1995) 'British Capitalism in the 1980s: Old Times or New Times?', *British Journal of Sociology* 46

Fuller, Ken (1985) *Radical Aristocrats: London Busworkers from the 1880s to the 1980s* (London)

Fussell, Paul (1975) *The Great War and Modern Memory* (London)

Gallagher, John (1982) *The Decline, Revival and Fall of the British Empire* (Cambridge)

Gallie, Duncan and Marsh, Catherine (1993) 'The Experience of Unemployment', in Duncan Gallie *et al.*, eds., *Social Change and the Experience of Unemployment* (Oxford)

Gallie, Duncan and Vogler, Carolyn (1994) 'Unemployment and Attitudes to Work', in Duncan Gallie *et al.*, eds., *Social Change and the Experience of Unemployment* (Oxford)

Garrett, Eilidh and Reid, Alice (1994) 'Satanic Mills, Pleasant Lands: Spatial Variation in Women's Work, Fertility and Infant Mortality as seen from the 1911 Census', *Historical Research* 67

Garrett, Geoff (1994) 'Popular Capitalism: The Electoral Legacy of Thatcherism', in Anthony Heath *et al.*, eds., *Labour's Last Chance? The 1992 Election and Beyond* (Aldershot)

Garside, W. R. and Gospel, H. F. (1982) 'Employers and Managers: their Organisational Structure and Changing Industrial Strategies' in C. J. Wrigley, ed., *A History of British Industrial Relations 1875–1914* (Amherst, Mass.)

Gattrell, V. A. C. (1990) 'Crime, Authority and the Policeman-State', in F. M. L. Thompson, ed., *The Cambridge Social History of Britain 1750–1950 III: Social Agencies and Institutions* (Cambridge)

Gavron, Hannah (1966) *The Captive Wife: Conflict of Housebound Mothers* (London)

Geary, Roger (1985) *Policing Industrial Dispute: 1893 to 1985* (Cambridge)

Geertz, Clifford (1988) *Works and Lives: The Anthropologist as Author* (Cambridge)

Gerstl, J. E. and Hutton, S. P. (1966) *Engineers: The Anatomy of a Profession* (London)

Gilbert, C. Nigel (1986) 'Occupational Classes and Inter-class Mobility', *British Journal of Sociology* 37

Gilbert, Martin (1988) *Never Despair. Winston S. Churchill 1945–1965* (London)

Gilmour, Ian (1992) *Dancing with Dogma. Britain under Thatcherism* (London)

Gilroy, Paul (1987) *'There Ain't No Black in the Union Jack'. The Cultural Politics of Race and Nation* (London)

Glass, D. V. ed., (1954) *Social Mobility in Britain* (London)

Gleason, A. L. (1920) *What the Workers Want* (London)

Gloversmith, Frank (1980) 'Changing Things: Orwell and Auden', in Frank Gloversmith, ed., *Class, Culture and Social Change: A New View of the 1930s* (Brighton)

Glucksmann, Miriam (1986) 'In a Class of their Own? Women in the New Industries in Inter-War Britain', *Feminist Review* 24

Goldthorpe, John H. (1980) *Social Mobility and Class Structure in Modern Britain* (Oxford)

(1984) 'Women and Class Analysis: A Reply to the Replies', *Sociology* 18

Goldthorpe, John H. *et al.* (1968) *The Affluent Worker: Industrial Attitudes and Behaviour* (Cambridge)

(1969) *The Affluent Worker in the Class Structure* (Cambridge)

Gorman, John (1993) 'Another East End: A Remembrance', in Geoffrey Alderman and Colin Holmes, eds., *Outsiders and Outcasts* (London)

Gospel, Howard F. (1987) 'Employers and Managers: Organisation and Strategy, 1914–39', in Chris Wrigley, ed., *A History of British Industrial Relations II. 1914–1939* (Brighton)

Graves, Pamela M. (1994) *Labour Women: Women in British Working-Class Politics 1918–1939* (Cambridge)

Graves, Robert (1957) *Goodbye to All That* (2nd edn, New York)

Graves, Robert and Hodge, Alan (1940) *The Long Week-End: A Social History of Great Britain 1918–1939* (London)

Green, David G. (1994) 'Liberty, Poverty and the Underclass: A Classical-liberal Approach to Public Policy', in David J. Smith, ed., *Understanding the Underclass* (London)

Griffiths, R. (1980) *Fellow Travellers of the Right. British Enthusiasts for Nazi Germany 1933–39* (London)

Grigg, John (1988) 'Making Government Responsible to Parliament', in Richard Holme and Michael Elliot, eds., *1688–1988. Time for a New Constitution* (London)

Gyford, John (1985) *The Politics of Local Socialism* (London)

Halévy, Elie (1961) *A History of the English People in the Nineteenth Century V: Imperialism and the Rise of Labour (1895–1905)* (London)

Hallpike, C. R. (1988) *The Principles of Social Evolution* (Oxford)

Halsey, A. H. (1981) *Changes in British Society* (2nd edn, Oxford)

Halsey, A. H. *et al.* (1980) *Origins and Destinations: Family, Class and Education in Modern Britain* (Oxford)

Halsey, Margaret (1938) *With Malice Towards Some* (New York)

Hamnett, Chris and Randolph, Bill (1988) *Cities, Housing and Profits* (London)

Hannah, Leslie (1983) *The Rise of the Corporate Economy* (2nd edn, London)

Hannington, Wal (1936) *Unemployed Struggles 1919–1936* (London)

Hargreaves, D. H. (1967) *Social Relations in a Secondary School* (London)

(1982) *The Challenge for the Comprehensive School: Culture, Curriculum and Community* (London)

Harris, José (1977) *William Beveridge. A Biography* (Oxford)

(1986) 'Political Ideas and the Debate on State Welfare 1940–45', in Harold L. Smith, ed., *War and Social Change: British Society in the Second World War* (Manchester)

(1990) 'Society and the State in Twentieth-Century Britain', in F. M. L. Thompson, ed., *The Cambridge Social History of Britain 1750–1950 III: Social Agencies and Institutions* (Cambridge)

(1993) *Private Lives, Public Spirit. A Social History of Britain 1870–1914* (Oxford)

Harris, Kenneth (1982) *Attlee* (London)

Harrison, Brian (1978) *Separate Spheres: The Opposition to Women's Suffrage in Britain* (London)

(1989) 'Class and Gender in Modern British Labour History', *Past & Present* 124

Harrison, J. F. C. (1971) *The Early Victorians 1832–51* (London)

Harrison, Paul (1983) *Inside the Inner City: Life under the Cutting Edge* (Harmondsworth)

Harrison, Royden and Zeitlin, Jonathan, eds. (1985) *Divisions of Labour: Skilled Workers and Technological Change in Nineteenth Century Britain* (Brighton)

Hart-Davis, Rupert ed., (1985) *The Lyttleton Hart-Davis Letters I & II. 1955–1957* (London)

Healey, Denis (1989) *The Time of My Life* (London)

Heath, Anthony (1981) *Social Mobility* (London)

(1992) 'The Attitudes of the Underclass', in David J. Smith, ed., *Understanding the Underclass* (London)

Heath, Anthony *et al.* (1985) *How Britain Votes* (Oxford)

Heath, Anthony and Britten, Nicky (1984) 'Women's Jobs Do Make a Difference: A Reply to Goldthorpe', *Sociology* 18

Heath, Anthony and MacDonald, Sarah K. (1987) 'Social Change and the Future of the Left', *Political Quarterly* 58

Heath, Anthony and Savage, Mike (1994) 'Middle-class Politics', in Roger Jowell *et al.* *British Social Attitudes: the 11th Report* (Aldershot)

Hennessey, Peter (1992) *Never Again. Britain 1945–51* (London)

Hennock, E. P. (1976) 'Poverty and Social Theory in England: the Experience of the Eighteen-eighties', *Social History* 1

(1991) 'Concepts of Poverty in the British Social Surveys from Charles Booth to Arthur Bowley', in Martin Bulmer *et al.*, eds., *The Social Survey in Historical Perspective* (Cambridge)

Henry, Stuart (1982) 'The Working Unemployed: Perspectives on the Informal Economy and Unemployment', *Sociological Review* 30

Herring, E. Pendleton (1930) 'Great Britain has Lobbies Too', *Virginia Quarterly Review* 6

Hill, T. P. (1955) 'Incomes, Savings and Net Worth: The 1953 Savings Survey', *Bulletin of the Oxford University Institute of Statistics* 17

Hiller, Peter (1975) 'Continuities and Variations in Everyday Conceptual Components of Social Class', *Sociology* 9

Hillyard, Paddy and Percy-Smith, Janie (1988) *The Coercive State: The Decline of Democracy in Britain* (London)

Hilton, John (1944) *Rich Man, Poor Man* (London)

Hilton, John *et al.*, eds. (1935) *Are Trade Unions Obstructive?* (London)

Himmelfarb, Gertrude (1984) *The Idea of Poverty: England in the Early Industrial Age* (London)

Himmelweit, H. T. (1954) 'Social Status and Secondary Education since the 1944 Act: Some data for London', in D. V. Glass, ed., *Social Mobility in Britain* (London)

Hindess, Barry (1971) *The Decline of Working-Class Politics* (London)

Hobbs, Dick (1991) 'A Piece of Business: The Moral Economy of Detective Work in the East End of London', *British Journal of Sociology* 42

Hobsbawm, Eric (1964) *Labouring Men: Studies in the History of Labour* (London)

Hobsbawm, Eric and Ranger, Terence, eds. (1983) *The Invention of Tradition* (London)

Hoggart, Richard (1957) *The Uses of Literacy* (London)

(1990) *A Sort of Clowning: Life and Times 1940–1959* (London)

(1994) *Townscape with Figures* (London)

Hollins, T. J. (1981) 'The Conservative Party and Film Propaganda between the Wars', *English Historical Review* 96

Hollis, Patricia (1987) *Ladies Elect. Women in English Local Government, 1865–1914* (Oxford)

Holt, Catherine (n.d.) *Letters from Newnham 1889–1892* (mimeo)

Holton, Sandra Stanley (1986) *Feminism and Democracy. Women's Suffrage and Reform Politics in Britain 1900–1918* (Cambridge)

Hope, Francis (1971) 'Schooldays', in Miriam Gross, ed., *The World of George Orwell* (London)

Hopkins, Deian (1985) 'The Labour Party Press', in Kenneth D. Brown, ed., *The First Labour Party 1906–1914* (London)

Hoskins, W. G. (1955) *The Making of the English Landscape* (London)

Howard, Anthony (1963) ' "We are the Masters Now" ', in Michael Sissons and Philip French, eds., *Age of Austerity 1945–1951* (Harmondsworth)

Howarth, T. S. B. (1978) *Cambridge Between Two Wars* (London)

Howell, Sara *et al.* (1990) 'Gender and Skills', *Work, Employment and Society* 4

Hudson, Mark (1994) *Coming Back Brockens: A Year in a Mining Village* (London)

Hughes, Ann and Hunt, Karen (1992) 'A Culture Transformed? Women's Lives in Wythenshawe in the 1930s', in Andrew Davies and Steven Fielding, eds., *Workers' Worlds: Cultures and Communities in Manchester and Salford 1880–1919* (Manchester)

Humphries, Stephen (1981) *Hooligans or Rebels? An Oral History of Working-Class Childhood and Youth 1889–1939* (Oxford)

Humphries, Steve and Gordon, Pamela (1994) *Forbidden Britain. Our Secret Past 1900–1960* (London, BBC)

Hunt, Agnes (1935) *Reminiscences* (Shrewsbury)

Husband, Charles, ed. (1987) *'Race' in Britain: Continuity and Change* (2nd edn, London)

Hutber, Patrick (1976) *The Decline and Fall of the Middle Class – and How it can Fight Back* (London)

Hyman, Richard (1972) *Strikes* (London)

Jackson, Alan A. (1991) *The Middle Classes 1900–1950* (Nairn)

Jackson, R. V. (1994) 'Inequality of Incomes and Lifespans in England since 1688', *Economic History Review* 47

Jackson, Brian and Marsden, Dennis (1962) *Education and the Working Class* (London)

Jacobs, Eric and Worcester, Robert (1990) *We British, Britain under the Moriscope* (London)

Jalland, Pat (1988) *Women, Marriage and Politics 1860–1914* (Oxford)

James, Winston (1989) 'The Making of Black Identities', in Ralph Samuel, ed., *Patriotism II: Minorities and Outsiders* (London)

Jarvis, David (1996) 'British Conservatism and Class Politics in the 1920s', *English Historical Review* 111

Jay, Douglas (1937) *The Socialist Case* (London)

Jeffery, Keith (1981) 'The British Army and Internal Security 1919–1939', *Historical Journal* 24

Jeffery, Keith and Hennessy, Peter (1983) *States of Emergency: British Governments and Strikebreaking since 1919* (London)

Jefferys, James B. (1946) *The Story of the Engineers 1800–1945* (London)

Jenkins, Peter (1987) *Mrs Thatcher's Revolution: The Ending of the Socialist Era* (London)

Jenkins, Roy (1993) *Portraits and Miniatures* (London)

Jennings, Hilda (1934) *Bryn Mawr* (London)

Johnson, Paul (1983a) *Saving and Spending: the Working-Class Economy in Britain 1870–1939* (Oxford)

(1983b) 'Credit and Thrift in the British Working Class, 1870–1939', in Jay Winter, ed., *The Modern Working Class in British History* (Cambridge)

(1988) 'Conspicuous Consumption and Working-Class Culture in Late-Victorian and Edwardian Britain', *Transactions of the Royal Historical Society* 5th Series 38

(1994) 'The Employment and Retirement of Older Men in England and Wales, 1881–1981', *Economic History Review* 47

Jones, Gill (1990) 'Marriage Partners and their Class Trajectories', in Geoff Payne and Pamela Abbott, eds., *The Social Mobility of Women: Beyond Male Mobility Models* (London)

Jones, Helen (1987) 'State Intervention in Sport and Leisure in Britain between the Wars', *Journal of Contemporary History* 20

Jones, Trevor *et al.* (1994) *Democracy and Policing* (London)

Joseph Rowntree Foundation (1995) *Inquiry into Income and Wealth* (York)

Kahan, M. *et al.*, (1966) 'On the Analytical Division of Social Class', *British Journal of Sociology* 17

Kahn-Freund, Otto (1977) *Labour and the Law* (2nd edn, London)

Kavanagh, Dennis and Morris, Peter (1989) *Consensus Politics: From Attlee to Thatcher* (Oxford)

Kee, Robert (1984) *The World We Left Behind. A Chronicle of the Year 1939* (London)

Kelsall, R. K. (1974) 'Recruitment to the Higher Civil Service: how has the Pattern Changed?', in Philip Stanworth and Anthony Giddens, eds., *Elites and Power in British Society* (Cambridge)

Kent, Susan Kingsley (1988) 'The Politics of Sexual Difference: World War I and the Demise of British Feminism', *Journal of British Studies* 27

Kiddle, Margaret (1950) *Caroline Chisholm* (Melbourne)

King, Anthony (1991) 'The British Prime Minister', in G. W. Jones, ed., *West European Prime Ministers* (London)

King, Desmond S. (1989) 'The New Right, the New Left and Local Government', in John Stewart and Gerry Stoker, eds., *The Future of Local Government* (London)

Kirby, M. W. (1987) 'Industrial Policy', in Sean Glynn and Alan Booth, eds., *The Road to Full Employment* (London)

Klein, Josephine (1965) *Samples from English Cultures I* (London)

Klingender, F. D. (1935) *The Condition of Clerical Labour in Britain* (London)

Kohn, Marek (1992) *Dope Girls. The Birth of the British Drug Underground* (London)

Koss, Stephen (1975) *Nonconformity in British Politics* (London)

Krafchick, Max (1983) 'Unemployment and Vagrancy in the 1930s', *Journal of Social Policy* 12

Krausz, Ernest (1971) *Ethnic Minorities in Britain* (London)

Lambert, Angela (1989) *1939: The Last Season of Peace* (London)

Lane, Christel (1988) 'New Technology and Clerical Work', in Duncan Gallie, ed., *Employment in Britain* (Oxford)

Larkin, Philip (1983) *Required Writing* (London)

Layard, Richard *et al.* (1969) *The Impact of Robbins* (Harmondsworth)

Layton-Henry, Zig (1984) *The Politics of Race in Britain* (London)

Lee, John (1921) *Management* (London)

Lees-Milne, James (1975) *Ancestral Voices* (London)

(1985) *Midway on the Waves* (London)

(1994) *A Mingled Measure* (London)

Legge, Karen (1987) 'Women in Personnel Management: Uphill Climb or Downhill Slide', in Anne Spencer and David Podmore, eds., *In a Man's World: Essays on Women in Male-Dominated Professions* (London)

LeMahieu, D. L. (1988) *A Culture for Democracy. Mass Communication and the Cultivated Mind in Britain between the Wars* (Oxford)

Leventhal, F. M. (1989) *Arthur Henderson* (Manchester)

Lewis, Jane (1980) 'Women Between the Wars', in Frank Gloversmith, ed., *Class, Culture and Social Change: A New View of the 1930s* (Brighton)

Lewis, Roy and Maude, Angus (1949) *The English Middle Classes* (London)

Lipset, S. M. (1963) *The First New Nation: The United States in Historical and Comparative Perspective* (New York)

Loane, Margaret E. (1908) *From Their Point of View* (London)

(1911) *The Common Growth* (London)

Lockwood, David (1966) 'Sources of Variation in Working Class Images of Society', *Sociological Review* 14

(1987) 'Schichtung in der Staatsburgergesellschaft', in B. Giesen and H. Haferkamp, eds., *Theorien der Ungleichheit* (Giessen)

(1989) *The Blackcoated Worker: A Study in Class Consciousness* (2nd edn, Oxford)

(1992) *Solidarity and Schism* (Oxford)

Lomas, Janis (1994) ' "So I married again": Letters from British Widows of the First and Second World Wars', *History Workshop* 38

Londonderry, Marchioness of (1938) *Retrospect* (London)

Lowe, Rodney (1986) *Adjusting to Democracy: The Role of the Ministry of Labour in British Politics 1916–1939* (Oxford)

(1990) 'The Second World War, Consensus and the Foundation of the Welfare State', *20th Century British History* 1

Lowerson, John (1980) 'Battles for the Countryside', in Frank Gloversmith, ed., *Class, Culture and Social Change: A New View of the 1930s* (Brighton)

Lowndes, G. A. N. (1937) *The Silent Social Revolution: An Account of the Expansion of Public Education in England and Wales, 1895–1935* (London)

Lunn, Kenneth (1985) 'Race Relations or Industrial Relations? Race and Labour in Britain, 1880–1950', in Kenneth Lunn, ed., *Race and Labour in Twentieth-Century Britain* (London)

Lyman, R. W. (1958) *The First Labour Government, 1924* (London)

Macintyre, Stuart (1980) *Little Moscows* (London)

Mackenzie, John M. (1984) *Propaganda and Empire: The Manipulation of British Public Opinion 1880–1960* (Manchester)

Mackenzie, R. F. (1963) *A Question of Living: What Do they Miss at School?* (London)

Mackenzie, W. J. M. and Grove, J. W. (1957) *Central Administration in Britain* (London)

Macnicol, John (1986) 'The Effect of the Evacuation of Schoolchildren on Official Attitudes to State Intervention', in Harold L. Smith, ed., *War and Social Change: British Society in the Second World War* (Manchester)

Macqueen-Pope, W. (1948) *Twenty Shillings in the Pound* (London)

Madge, Charles (1943) *War-time Pattern of Saving and Spending* (Cambridge)

Mars, Gerald (1982) *Cheats at Work. An Anthology of Workplace Crime* (London)

Marsh, David C. (1958) *The Changing Social Structure of England and Wales 1871–1951* (London)

Marshall, Gordon *et al.* (1988) *Social Class in Modern Britain* (London)

Marshall, T. H. (1950) *Citizenship and Social Class* (Cambridge)

(1965) *Social Policy* (London)

Marsland, David (1988) *Seeds of Bankruptcy* (London)

Martin, Bernice (1985) *A Sociology of Contemporary Cultural Change* (London)

Martin, J. P. (1987) 'The Police', in Gordon A. Causer, ed., *Inside British Society: Continuity, Challenge and Change* (Brighton)

Martin, Jean and Roberts, Geridwen (1984) *Women and Employment: A Lifetime Perspective* (London, HMSO)

Martin, Ross M. (1980) *TUC: The Growth of a Pressure Group 1868–1976* (Oxford)

Marwick, Arthur (1964) ' "Middle Opinion" in the Thirties: Planning, Progress and Political "Agreement" ', *English Historical Review* 79

(1982) *British Society since 1945* (Harmondsworth)

Mason, Philip (1982) *The English Gentleman: The Rise and Fall of an Ideal* (London)

Masterman, C. F. G. (1909) *The Condition of England* (London)

(1922) *England After War* (London)

Matthew, H. C. G. (1987) 'Rhetoric and Politics in Britain, 1860–1950', in P. J. Waller, ed., *Politics and Social Change in Modern Britain* (Brighton)

Matthews, Derek (1988) 'Profit-sharing in the Gas Industry', *Business History* 30

McAllister, G. (1935) *James Maxton* (London)

McCallum, R. B. and Readman, Alison (1947) *The British General Election of 1945* (Oxford)

McConville, Mike *et al.* (1991) *The Case for the Prosecution: Police Suspects and the Construction of Criminality* (London)

McGeown, Patrick (1967) *Heat the Furnace Seven Times More* (London)

McKenna, F. (1976) 'Victorian Railway Workers', *History Workshop* 1

McKenna, Madeline (1991) 'The Suburbanization of the Working-class Population of Liverpool between the Wars', *Social History* 16

McKenzie, Robert and Silver, Allan (1968) *Angels in Marble: Working-Class Conservatives in Urban England* (London)

McKenzie, R. T. (1955) *British Political Parties* (London)

McKibbin, Ross (1974) *The Evolution of the Labour Party 1910–1924* (Oxford)

(1990) *The Ideologies of Class. Social Relations in Britain 1880–1950* (Oxford)

McLean, Iain (1974) 'Popular Protest and Public Order; Red Clydeside, 1915–1919', in J. Stevenson and R. Quinault, eds., *Popular Protest and Public Order* (London)

Meacham, Standish (1977) *A Life Apart: The English Working Class 1890–1914* (London)

Mendl, R. W. S. (1927) *The Appeal of Jazz* (London)

Mercer, D. E. and Weir, D. J. H. (1972) 'Attitudes to Work and Trade Unionism among White-Collar Workers', *Industrial Relations Journal* 3

Middlemas, R. K. (1965) *The Clydesiders* (London)

(1979) *Politics in Industrial Society* (London)

(1991) *Power, Competition and the State III: The End of the Postwar Era: Britain since 1974* (London)

Middlemas, R. K., ed. (1969) *Thomas Jones, Whitehall Diary* (London)

Middleton, Sue and Thomas, Michelle (1994) 'The "Bare Essentials": Parents' Minimum Budget for Children', in Sue Middleton *et al.*, eds., *Family Fortunes* (London)

Miller, Frederic M. (1979) 'The British Unemployment Assistance Crisis of 1935', *Journal of Contemporary History* 14

Millerson, Geoffrey (1964) *The Qualifying Associations: A Study in Professionalization* (London)

Modood, Tariq (1994) 'Political Blackness and British Asians', *Sociology* 28

Moore, Barrington (1966) *Social Origins of Dictatorship and Democracy: Lord and Peasant in the Making of the Modern World* (London)

Moorhouse, H. F. (1976) 'Attitudes to Class and Class Relationships in Britain', *Sociology* 10

Morgan, Jane (1987) *Conflict and Order: The Police and Labour Disputes in England and Wales, 1900–1939* (Oxford)

Morgan, Kenneth O. (1979) *Consensus and Disunity. The Lloyd George Coalition Government 1918–1922* (Oxford)

(1984) *Labour in Power 1945–1951* (Oxford)

Motion, Andrew (1993) *Philip Larkin: A Writer's Life* (London)

Mottram, R. H. (1969) *The Twentieth Century. A Personal Record* (London)

Mullard, Chris (1973) *Black Britain* (London)

Muggeridge, Malcolm (1981) *Like It Was* (London)

Muir, Ramsay (1933) *How Britain is Governed* (3rd edn, London)

Murray, Charles (1995) 'The Next British Revolution', *The Public Interest* 118

New Survey of London Life and Labour (London, 1934)

Newby, Howard (1977) *The Deferential Worker. A Study of Farm Workers in East Anglia* (London)

(1979) *Green and Pleasant Land? Social Change in Rural England* (London)

Newsam, Sir Frank (1954) *The Home Office* (London)

Newton, Scott and Porter, Dilwyn (1988) *Modernization Frustrated. The Politics of Industrial Decline in Britain since 1900* (London)

Nichols, Theo and Beynon, Huw (1977) *Living with Capitalism: Class Relations and the Modern Factory* (London)

Nicolson, Nigel (1966) *Harold Nicolson. Diaries and Letters 1930–1939* (London)

(1967) *Harold Nicolson. Diaries and Letters 1939–1945* (London)

Niven, M. M. (1967) *Personnel Management 1913–1963* (London)

Noble, Trevor (1985) 'Inflation and Earnings Relativities in Britain after 1970', *British Journal of Sociology* 26

Nordlinger, Eric A. (1967) *The Working-Class Tories: Authority, Deference, and Stable Democracy* (London)

Nugent, Neill (1979) 'The National Association for Freedom', in Roger King and

Neill Nugent, eds., *Respectable Rebels: Middle Class Campaigners in the 1970s* (London)

Oakeshott, Robert (1978) *The Case for Workers' Co-ops* (London)

O'Brien, Patrick K. (1988) 'The Costs and Benefits of British Imperialism 1846–1914', *Past & Present* 102

O'Connell Davidson, Julia (1993) *Privatization and Employment Relations. The Case of the Water Industry* (London)

Ommanney, F. D. (1966) *The River Bank* (London)

Oram, R. B. (1970) *The Dockers' Tragedy* (London)

Orwell, George (1933) *Down and Out in Paris and London* (London)

(1941) *The Lion and the Unicorn* (London)

Osborne, John (1981) *A Better Class of Person* (London)

Page, Robin (1973) *Down among the Dossers* (London)

Pahl, R. A. (1984) *Divisions of Labour* (Oxford)

Panitch, Leo (1980) 'Recent Theorizations of Corporatism: Reflections on a Growth Industry', *British Journal of Sociology* 31

Parker, Tony (1983) *The People of Providence. A Housing Estate and Some of Its Inhabitants* (London)

Parkin, Frank (1968) *Middle Class Radicalism. The Social Bases of the British Campaign for Nuclear Disarmament* (Manchester)

(1971) *Class Inequality and Political Order* (London)

Partridge, John (1966) *Middle School* (London)

Paterson, Alexander (1911) *Across the Bridges, or Life by the South London Riverside* (London)

Pawley, Martin (1978) *Home Ownership* (London)

Payne, Geoff and Abbott, Pamela (1990) 'Beyond Male Mobility Models', in Geoff Payne and Pamela Abbott, eds., *The Social Mobility of Women: Beyond Male Mobility Models* (London)

Peden, G. C. (1983) 'The Treasury as the Central Department of Government, 1919–1939', *Public Administration* 61

Pelling, Henry (1958) *The British Communist Party* (London)

(1968) *Popular Politics and Society in Late Victorian Britain* (London)

Pember Reeves, Maud (1913) *Round About a Pound a Week* (London)

Penn, Roger (1984) *Skilled Workers in the Class Structure* (Cambridge)

PEP (1952) 'Poverty: Ten Years after Beveridge', *Planning* 19

Perkin, Harold (1989) *The Rise of Professional Society: England since 1880* (London)

Perks, Robert B. (1982) 'Real Profit-Sharing: William Thomson and Sons of Huddersfield, 1886–1925', *Business History* 24

Petter, Martin (1994) ' "Temporary Gentlemen" in the Aftermath of the Great War: Rank, Status and the Ex-officer Problem', *Historical Journal* 37

Phelps Brown, E. H. (1959) *The Growth of British Industrial Relations* (London)

Phillimore, Peter (1979) 'Dossers and Jake Drinkers: The View from One End of Skid Row', in Tim Cook, ed., *Vagrancy: Some New Perspectives* (London)

Phillips, G. A. (1971) 'The Triple Industrial Alliance in 1914', *Economic History Review* 24

(1987) 'Trade Unions and Corporatist Politics: the Response of the TUC to Industrial Rationalization', in P. J. Waller, ed., *Politics and Social Change in Modern Britain* (Brighton)

Pigou, A. C., ed. (1925) *Memorials of Alfred Marshall* (London)

Pike, E. Royston (1972) *Human Documents of the Lloyd George Era* (London)

Pilgrim Trust (1938) *Men Without Work* (Cambridge)

Plumb, J. H. (1967) *The Growth of Political Stability in England 1675–1725* (London)

Ponsonby, Arthur (1912) *The Decline of Aristocracy* (London)

Porter, Roy, ed. (1992) *Myths of the English* (Cambridge)

Potter, Allen (1960) *Organized Groups in British National Politics* (London)

Powell, David (1986) 'The New Liberalism and the Rise of Labour, 1886–1906', *Historical Journal* 29

Prandy, K. *et al.* (1983) *While-Collar Unionism* (London)

Price, Robert (1983) 'White-Collar Unions: Growth, Character and Attitudes in the 1970s', in Richard Hyman and Robert Price, eds., *The New Working Class? White-Collar Workers and their Organizations* (London)

Price, Robert and Bain, G. S. (1983) 'Union Growth in Britain: Retrospect and Prospect', *British Journal of Industrial Relations* 21

Priestley, J. B. (1934) *English Journey* (London)

Pugh, Martin (1982) *The Making of British Politics 1867–1939* (Oxford)

Pumphrey, Ralph E. (1959) 'The Introduction of Industrialists into the British Peerage: A Study in Adaptation of a Social Institution', *American Historical Review* 65

Purcell, Kate (1988) 'Gender and the Experience of Employment', in Duncan Gallie, ed., *Employment in Britain* (Oxford)

Ramdin, Ron (1987) *The Making of the Black Working Class in Britain* (Aldershot)

Redcliffe-Maud, John (1981) *Experiences of an Optimist* (London)

Reid, Alastair (1985) 'Dilution, Trade Unionism and the State in Britain during the First World War', in Steven Tolliday and Jonathan Zeitlin, eds., *Shop Floor Bargaining and the State: Historical and Comparative Perspectives* (Cambridge)

(1987) 'Class and Organization', *Historical Journal* 30

Reid, Ivan (1981) *Social Class Differences in Britain* (2nd edn, London)

Reiner, Robert (1985) *The Politics of the Police* (Brighton)

Reith, J. C. W. (1949) *Into the Wind* (London)

Reynolds, Stephen (1911) *Seems So! A Working-Class View of Politics* (London)

Rhodes R. A. W. (1988) *Beyond Westminster and Whitehall: The Sub-Central Governments of Britain* (London)

Rhodes James, Robert, ed. (1967) *Chips: The Diaries of Sir Henry Channon* (London)

Richardson, C. J. (1977) *Contemporary Social Mobility* (London)

Roberts, Elizabeth (1984) *A Woman's Place: An Oral History of Working-Class Women 1890–1940* (Oxford)

(1993) 'Neighbours: North West England 1940–70', *Oral History* 21

Roberts, K. *et al.* (1977) *The Fragmentary Class Structure* (London)

Roberts, Richard (1984) 'The Administrative Origins of Industrial Diplomacy: An Aspect of Government-Industry Relations, 1929–1935', in John Turner, ed., *Businessmen and Politics: Studies of Business Activity in British Politics, 1900–1945* (London)

Roberts, Robert (1971) *The Classic Slum: Salford Life in the First Quarter of the Century* (Manchester)

Roberts, Stephen and Marshall, Gordon (1995) 'Intergenerational Class Processes and the Asymmetry Hypothesis', *Sociology* 29

Rodgers, Terence (1986) 'Sir Allan Smith, the Industrial Group and the Politics of Unemployment', *Business History* 28

Roper Power, E. R. (1937) 'The Social Structure of an English County Town', *Sociological Review* 29

Rose, E. J. B. and Deakin, Nicholas (1969) *Colour and Citizenship. A Report on British Race Relations* (London)

Rose, Kenneth (1975) *The Later Cecils* (London)

(1979) *Curzon: A Most Superior Person* (London)

Rose, Lionel (1988) *Rogues and Vagabonds: Vagrant Underworld in Britain 1815–1985* (London)

Roseveare, Henry (1969) *The Treasury: The Evolution of a British Institution* (London)

Ross, Ellen (1983) 'Survival Networks: Women's Neighbourhood Sharing in London before World War I', *History Workshop* 15

Routh, Guy (1965) *Occupation and Pay in Great Britain 1906–60* (Cambridge)

Rowntree, B. Seebohm (1901) *Poverty, A Study of Town Life* (London)

(1922) *Poverty* rev. edn (London)

(1941) *Poverty and Progress* (London)

and Kendall, May (1913) *How the Labourer Lives* (London)

and Lavers, G. F. (1951) *Poverty and the Welfare State* (London)

Royal Commission on Trade Unions and Employers Associations (1968) *Report* (London, HMSO)

Rubery, Jill (1988) 'Employers and the Labour Market', in Duncan Gallie, ed., *Employment in Britain* (Oxford)

Rubinstein, W. D. (1974) 'Men of Property: Some Aspects of Occupation, Inheritance and Power among Top British Wealthholders', in Philip Stanworth and Anthony Giddens, eds., *Elites and Power in British Society* (Cambridge)

(1981) *Men of Property: The Very Wealthy in Britain since the Industrial Revolution* (London)

(1986) 'Education and the Social Origins of British Elites, 1880–1970', *Past & Present* 112

Runciman, W. G. (1966) *Relative Deprivation and Social Justice* (London)

(1970) 'Misdescribing Misdescriptions', in *Sociology in its Place and Other Essays* (Cambridge)

(1989) *Confessions of a Reluctant Theorist* (Hemel Hempstead)

(1990) 'How Many Classes are there in Contemporary British Society?', *Sociology* 24

(1991) 'Explaining Union Density in Twentieth-Century Britain', *Sociology* 25

(1993) 'Competition for What?' (London, ESRC)

(1995a) 'The "Triumph" of Capitalism as a Topic in the Theory of Social Selection', *New Left Review* 210

(1995b) 'New Times or Old? A Reply to Fulcher', *British Journal of Sociology* 46

(1996a) 'Why Social Inequalities are Generated by Social Rights', in Martin Bulmer and Anthony M. Rees, eds., *Citizenship Today: The Contemporary Relevance of T. H. Marshall* (London)

(1996b) 'Introduction', in W. G. Runciman, J. Maynard Smith, and R. I. M. Dunbar, eds., *The Evolution of Social Behaviour Patterns in Primates and Man* (Oxford)

Rutter, Michael and Madge, Nicola (1976) *Cycles of Disadvantage* (London)

Saifullah Khan, Wendy (1987) 'The Role of the Culture of Dominance in Structuring the Experience of Ethnic Minorities', in Charles Husband, ed., *'Race' in Britain: Continuity and Change* (2nd edn, London)

Samuel, Raphael (1981) *East End Underworld* (London)

Saunders, Peter (1990) *A Nation of Home Owners* (London)

(1995) 'Might Britain be a Meritocracy?', *Sociology* 29

Savage, Mike (1988) 'Trade Unionism, Sex Segregation and the State: Women's Employment in the "New Industries" in Inter-war Britain', *Social History* 13

Scase, Richard and Goffee, Robert (1980) *The Real World of the Small Business Owner* (London)

(1982) *The Entrepreneurial Middle Class* (London)

Schneer, Jonathan (1982) *Ben Tillett: Portrait of a Labour Leader* (London)

Scott, John (1988) 'Ownership and Employer Control', in Duncan Gallie, ed., *Employment in Britain* (Oxford)

Searle, G. R. (1983) 'The Edwardian Liberal Party and Business', *English Historical Review* 98

Semmel, Bernard (1960) *Imperialism and Social Reform* (London)

Shaw, Bernard (1962) 'The Basis of Socialism: Economics', in *Fabian Essays* (6th edn, London)

Sherard, R. H. (1898) *The White Slaves of England* (London)

Shils, Edward (1968) 'Deference', in J. A. Jackson, ed., *Social Stratification* (Cambridge)

Simnett, W. E. (1923) *Railway Amalgamation in Great Britain* (London)

Sinfield, Adrian (1981) *What Unemployment Means* (Oxford)

Sked, Alan and Cook, Chris (1984) *Post-War Britain: A Political History* (2nd edn, Harmondsworth)

Skidelsky, Robert (1983) *John Maynard Keynes: Hopes Betrayed 1883–1920* (London)

Smith, David (1992) 'Defining the Underclass', in David J. Smith, ed., *Understanding the Underclass* (London)

Smith, Elaine R. (1989) 'Jewish Responses to Political Antisemitism and Fascism in the East End of London, 1920–1939', in Tony Kushner and Kenneth Lunn, eds., *Traditions of Intolerance: Historical Perspectives on Fascism and Race Discourse in Britain* (Manchester)

Smith, Harold (1981) 'The Problem of "Equal Pay for Equal Work" in Great Britain during World War II', *Journal of Modern History* 53

Social Trends (London, HMSO)

Spencer, John (1964) *Stress and Release in an Urban Estate* (London)

Springhall, J. O. (1971) 'Boy Scouts, Class and Militarism', *International Review of Social History* 16

Spurling, Hilary (1984) *Secrets of a Woman's Heart. The Later Life of Ivy Compton-Burnett 1920–69* (London)

Stacey, Margaret (1960) *Tradition and Change: A Study of Banbury* (Oxford)

et al. (1975) *Power, Persistence and Change: A Second Study of Banbury* (London)

Stansky, Peter and Abrahams, William (1966) *Journey to the Frontier* (London)

Stedman Jones, Gareth (1983) *Languages of Class* (Cambridge)

Stevenson, John (1975) 'The Politics of Violence', in Gillian Peele and Chris Cook, eds., *The Politics of Reappraisal 1918–1939* (London)

(1984) *British Society 1914–1945* (Harmondsworth)

Stewart, A. et al. (1980) *Social Stratification and Occupations* (London)

Sulter, Maud (1988) in Lauretta Ngcolo, ed., *Let it be Told. Essays by Black Women in Britain* (London)

Summers, Anne (1976) 'Militarism in Britain before the Great War', *History Workshop* 2

Sunday Telegraph

Supple, Barry (1977) 'A Framework for British Business History', in Barry Supple, ed., *Essays in British Business History* (Oxford)

Sutherland, Gillian (1990) 'Education', in F. M. L. Thompson, ed., *The Cambridge Social History of Britain III: Social Agencies and Institutions* (Cambridge)

Svalastoga, Kaare (1964) *Social Differentiation* (New York)

Swenarton, Mark and Taylor, Sandra (1983) 'The Scale and Nature of the Growth of Owner-Occupation in Britain between the Wars', *Economic History Review* 28

Sykes, A. J. M. (1969) 'Navvies: Their Work Attitudes', *Sociology* 3

Tawney, R. H. (1943) 'The Abolition of Economic Controls, 1918–1921', *Economic History Review* 13

(1952) *Equality* (4th edn, London)

Taylor, A. J. P. (1965) *English History 1914–1945* (Oxford)

Taylor, John (1977) *From Self-Help to Glamour: The Working Man's Club, 1860–1972* (Oxford)

Taylor, L. and Walton, P. (1971) 'Industrial Sabotage: Motives and Meanings', in S. Cohen, ed., *Images of Deviance* (Harmondsworth)

Taylor, Pam (1979) 'Daughters and Mothers – Maids and Mistresses: Domestic Service between the Wars', in John Clarke *et al.*, eds., *Working-class Culture: Studies in History and Theory* (London)

Thane, Pat (1984) 'The Working Class and State "Welfare" in Britain, 1880–1914', *Historical Journal* 27

(1986) 'Financiers and the British State: The Case of Sir Ernest Cassel', *Business History* 28

(1988) 'Late Victorian Women', in T. R. Gourvish and A. O'Day, eds., *Later Victorian Britain* (London)

(1991a) 'Visions of Gender in the Making of the British Welfare State: The Case of Women in the British Labour Party and Social Policy, 1906–1945', in Gisela Bock and Pat Thane, eds., *Maternity and Gender Policies. Women and the Rise of the European Welfare State, 1880s–1950s* (London)

(1991b) 'Towards Equal Opportunities? Women since 1945', in T. R. Gourvish and A. O'Day, eds., *Britain since 1945* (London)

Third Winter of Unemployment (London, 1923)

Thom, Deborah (1986) 'The 1944 Education Act: The "Art of the Possible"?', in Harold L. Smith, ed., *War and Social Change: British Society in the Second World War* (Manchester)

Thomas, Hugh (1959) 'The Establishment and Society', in Hugh Thomas, ed., *The Establishment* (London)

Thompson, Flora (1939) *Lark Rise to Candleford* (London)

Thompson, F. M. L. (1963) *English Landed Society in the Nineteenth Century* (London)

(1988) *The Rise of Respectable Society. A Social History of Victorian Britain, 1930–1900* (London)

(1991) 'English Landed Society in the Twentieth Century: II, New Poor and New Rich', *Transactions of the Royal Historical Society* 6th ser. 1

(1993) 'English Landed Society in the Twentieth Century: IV, Prestige without Power?', *Transactions of the Royal Historical Society* 6th ser. 3

Thompson, Paul (1988) 'Playing at Being Skilled Men: Factory Culture and Pride in Work Skills among Coventry Car Workers', *Social History* 13

(1992) *The Edwardians: The Remaking of British Society* (2nd edn, London)

Thompson, Thea ed., (1981) *Edwardian Childhoods* (London)

Thomson, David (1950) *England in the Nineteenth Century* (Harmondsworth)

Thornhill, W. (1971) *The Growth and Reform of English Local Government* (London)

Thwaite, Ann (1990) *A. A. Milne: His Life* (London)

The Times

Timmins, Nicholas (1995) *The Five Giants: A Biography of the Welfare State* (London)

Titmuss, Richard M. (1950) *Problems of Social Policy* (London, HMSO)

 (1958) *Essays on 'The Welfare State'* (London)

 (1962) *Income Distribution and Social Change* (London)

Tomlinson, J. D. (1995) 'The Iron Quadrilateral: Political Obstacles to Economic Reform under the Attlee Government', *Journal of British Studies* 34

Tooby, John and Cosmides, Leda (1992) 'Psychological Foundations of Culture', in J. H. Barkow, Leda Cosmides, and John Tooby, eds., *The Adapted Mind: Evolutionary Psychology and the Generation of Culture* (New York)

Tout, H. (1938) *The Standard of Living in Bristol* (Bristol)

Townsend, Peter (1979) *Poverty in the United Kingdom* (London)

Townshend, Charles (1993) *Making the Peace. Public Order and Public Security in Modern Britain* (Oxford)

Trades Union Congress *Annual Reports*

 (1979) *Equality for Women within Trades Unions* (London)

Turnbull, Peter (1992) 'Dock Strikes and the Demise of the Dockers' "Occupational Culture"', *Sociological Review* 40

Turnbull, Peter and Sapsford, David (1992) 'A Sea of Discontent: The Tides of Organised and "Unorganised" Conflict on the Docks', *Sociology* 26

Turner, Graham (1963) *The Car Makers* (London)

Turner, H. A. (1962) *Trade Union Growth, Structure and Policy* (London)

Turner, John (1984) 'The Politics of Business', in John Turner, ed., *Businessmen and Politics: Studies of Business Activity in British Politics 1900–1945* (London)

 (1992) *British Politics and the Great War: Coalition and Conflict 1915–1918* (London)

University of Liverpool (1954) *The Dockworker* (Liverpool)

Vaizey, John (1962) *Education for Tomorrow* (Harmondsworth)

Veit Wilson, John (1986) 'Paradigms of Policy: A Rehabilitation of B. S. Rowntree', *Journal of Social Policy* 15

Waites, Bernard (1987) *A Class Society at War: England 1914–1918* (Leamington Spa)

Wallace, Claire (1987) *For Richer for Poorer. Growing up in and out of Work* (London)

Wallas, Graham (1908) *Human Nature in Politics* (London)

Waller, P. J. (1981) *Democracy and Sectarianism. A Political and Social History of Liverpool 1868–1939* (Liverpool)

 (1987) 'Democracy and Dialect, Speech and Class', in P. J. Waller, ed., *Politics and Social Change in Modern Britain* (Brighton)

Warr, Peter (1978) 'A Study of Psychological Well-being', *British Journal of Psychology* 23

Webb, Beatrice (1942) *My Apprenticeship* (2nd edn, London)

Webb, Beatrice and Webb, Sidney (1919) *Industrial Democracy* (2nd edn, London)

 (1920) *A Constitution for the Socialist Commonwealth of Great Britain* (London)

Webb, Sidney (1962) 'Historic', in *Fabian Essays* (6th edn, London)

Webber, G. C. (1986) *The Ideology of the British Right 1918–1939* (London)

Webster, Charles (1985) 'Health, Welfare and Unemployment during the Depression', *Past & Present* 109

(1990) 'Conflict and Consensus: Explaining the British Health Service' *20th Century British History* 1

Wedderburn, Dorothy Cole (1962) 'Poverty in Britain Today – the Evidence', *Sociological Review* 10

Weekes, Brian *et al.* (1975) *Industrial Relations and the Limits of Law* (Oxford)

Wertheimer, E. (1930) *Portrait of the Labour Party* (2nd edn, London)

Westergaard, John (1995) *Who Gets What? The Hardening of Class Inequality in the Late Twentieth Century* (Cambridge)

Western, Bruce (1995) 'A Comparative Study of Working-Class Disorganization: Union Decline in Eighteen Advanced Capitalist Countries', *American Sociological Review* 60

White, Jerry (1986) *The Worst Street in North London: Campbell Bunk, Islington, between the Wars* (London)

Whiteley, Paul F. and Winyard, Stephen (1987) *Pressure of the Poor: The Poverty Lobby and Policy Making* (London)

Whiteside, Noelle (1979) 'Welfare Insurance and Casual Labour: A Study of Administrative Intervention in Industrial Employment, 1906–26', *Economic History Review* 32

Whiting, R. C. (1983) *The View from Cowley: The Impact of Industrialization upon Oxford 1918–1939* (Oxford)

Wickham, Chris (1991) 'Systactic Structures: Social Theory for Historians', *Past & Present* 132

Wight, Bakke, E. (1933) *The Unemployed Man* (London)

Wilkinson, Frank (1977) 'Collective Bargaining in the Steel Industry in the 1920s', in Asa Briggs and John Saville, eds., *Essays in Labour History 1918–1939* (London)

Williams, Raymond (1958) *Culture and Society 1780–1950* (London)

Willis, Paul E. (1977) *Learning to Labour: How Working-Class Kids Get Working-Class Jobs* (Farnborough)

Willmott, Peter (1966) *Adolescent Boys of East London* (London)

Willmott, Peter and Young, Michael (1960) *Family and Class in a London Suburb* (London)

Willmott, Phyllis (1979) *Growing Up in a London Village. Family Life Between the Wars* (London)

Wilson, H. H. (1961) *Pressure Group: The Campaign for Commercial Television* (London)

Wilson, Trevor (1968) *The Downfall of the Liberal Party 1914–1935* (London)

Winter, J. M. (1976) 'Some Aspect of the Demographic Consequences of the First World War in Britain', *Population Studies* 30

Woolf, Leonard (1965) *Beginning Again* (London)

Wrigley, Chris (1987a) 'The First World War and State Intervention in Industrial Relations', in Chris Wrigley, ed., *A History of British Industrial Relations II: 1914–1939* (Brighton)

(1987b) 'The Trade Unions Between the Wars', *ibid.*

Wynn, Margaret (1970) *Family Policy* (London)

Young, G. M. (1953) *Portrait of an Age* (2nd edn, Oxford)

Young, Michael and Willmott, Peter (1956) 'Social Grading by Manual Workers', *British Journal of Sociology* 7

(1957) *Family and Kinship in East London* (London)

(1973) *The Symmetrical Family. A Study of Work and Leisure in the London Region* (London)

Zimmeck, Meta (1986) 'Jobs for the Girls: The Expansion of Clerical Work for Women, *1850–1914*', in Angela John, ed., *Unequal Opportunities* (London)

Zweig, Ferdynand (1948) *Labour, Life and Poverty* (London)

(1961) *The Worker in an Affluent Society* (London)

Index